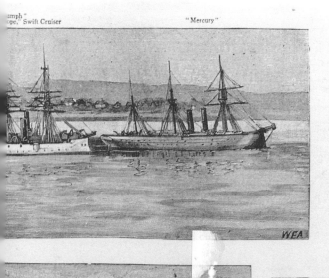

"iumph"
ope," Swift Cruiser
"Mercury"

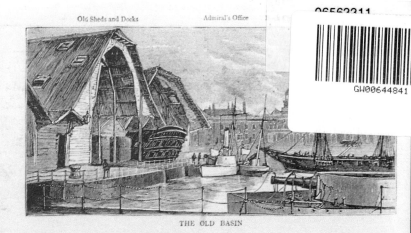

Old Sheds and Docks
Admiral's Office

THE OLD BASIN

TORPEDO LAUNCHES IN OBSOLETE

THE "MEDINA," A LARGE MODERN GUNBOAT IN OLD DOCK

"Devastation"
"Active

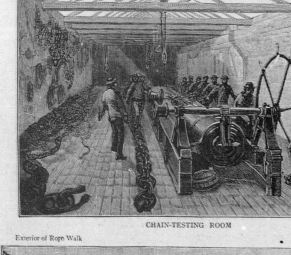

CHAIN-TESTING ROOM

Exterior of Rope Walk
Furniture Store

KING'S ROAD

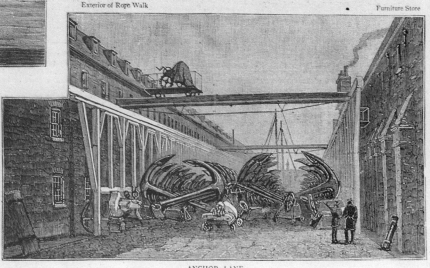

ANCHOR LANE

Building the Steam Navy

Building the Steam Navy

Dockyards, Technology and the
Creation of the Victorian Battle Fleet

1830 — m — 1906

David Evans

CONWAY MARITIME PRESS

ENGLISH HERITAGE

(Previous pages) The covered slips at Chatham. In the foreground is the gunboat HMS *Gannet* (1878) undergoing restoration. *(Mike Williams/English Heritage)*

(Endpapers) Engraving of Portsmouth Dockyard *(Portsmouth Museums and Records Service)*

First published in Great Britain in 2004 by Conway Maritime Press

An imprint of **Chrysalis** Books Group plc

The Chrysalis Building
Bramley Road
London W10 6SP
www.conwaymaritime.com

Distributed in North America by
Naval Institute Press, 291 Wood Road,
Annapolis, MD 21402-5034, USA

British Library Cataloguing in Publication Data
A record of this title is available on request from the British Library.

ISBN 0 85177 959 X

Design and layout by Stephen Dent

Printed in China by CT Printing Limited.

Contents

Foreword

IN THE EIGHTEENTH and nineteenth centuries the Royal naval dockyards were amongst the largest manufacturing complexes in Europe, a direct consequence of the Royal Navy's role not only as Britain's first line of defence but as the means of protecting and promoting her worldwide imperial power and influence.

Separated from the outside world by walls and gates, the secrets of the dockyards have been slow to reveal themselves to the wider public. A systematic programme of research was first undertaken by Jonathan Coad of the then Ancient Monuments and Historic Buildings Inspectorate from the late 1960s, aimed at securing the protection of many of the most important elements of both the naval yards and their associated ordnance and victualling depots.[1] English Heritage, in close liaison with the Ministry of Defence, embarked on a fresh evaluation of the standing structures and below-ground archaeology of these remarkable sites in the mid-1990s. The aim was to ensure up-to-date and appropriate levels of protection, and to inform the continuing use and management of fabric that still serves the modern navy at Portsmouth and Plymouth, and which has been put to new civilian uses at Chatham, Portland and Sheerness.

It became apparent that little was known about the workshops and massive extensions undertaken for the Steam Navy, whose engineers drew upon a rich fund of private expertise for the supply of new machine tools and the development of innovative types of workshops and pioneering constructional systems. The research commissioned by English Heritage from Dr David Evans made some significant new discoveries and, when placed in the broader context of the Industrial Revolution, and other comparable military sites, has contributed to our understanding of the national and international significance of what has survived. Much of this infrastructure had been put in place by the the time the first ironclad warships were launched in the 1860s: a remarkable achievement, but one not immediately apparent to the students of the ships that, superficially at least, experienced little fundamental change in terms of their armament, design and construction until after this period.

This book now forms part of a rich body of research on military and naval sites, published by English Heritage, extending from coastal fortifications and barracks to the archaeology of the Cold War. The research has primarily been based on the examination of original documents, its aim being to provide the foundations for the understanding, further recording and ongoing use of a hitherto uncharted aspect of our remarkable naval and industrial past.

The project was managed by Jeremy Lake, Inspector of Historic Buildings with English Heritage. In particular, we acknowledge the contribution that the staff of Defence Estates, the Royal Navy, Unicorn Consultancy at Portsmouth and Devonport Management Limited in Plymouth have made towards this programme of research. I would like to thank Tony Whitehead who, in his position as Principal Conservation Architect, liaised with the many individuals responsible for the management of the yards at Portsmouth and Plymouth, and who secured a generous contribution towards the cost of editing the text of this book.

Sir Neil Cossons
Chairman
English Heritage
February 2004

---

[1] The results were published in J. Coad, *The Royal Dockyards, 1690-1850* (Aldershot, 1989)

ACKNOWLEDGEMENTS

Author's Acknowledgements

This book could not have been written without the aid of a large number of people, far too many to be all named individually. Foremost among these is Jeremy Lake, whose persistence and labours far exceeded the call of duty; other staff of English Heritage whose contributions were essential included Jonathan Coad, Keith Falconer and Martin Cherry. Lionel Browne's text editing, in partnership with Jeremy Lake's restructuring and enhancement of the text, certainly made the end product more readable. The staff of all the archives repositories and libraries mentioned in the Bibliography could not have been more helpful. The greatest part of the workload was laid on the staffs of the Public Record Office (now The National Archives) and the National Maritime Museum, and special mention must be made of Alan Giddings, late of the National Maritime Museum, who magnificently managed to supply a continuous flow of documents. The Reprographics staff of the National Archives made a large part of the illustrations possible. Commander Crichton and Gerry Rendle of Plymouth Naval Base Museum, Brian Patterson of Portsmouth Naval Base Property Trust and Roger Lyndon of the Devonport Naval Base Services Department gave invaluable access to the buildings and records in their charge. Mike Hesketh Roberts of English Heritage and Mike Williams provided additional photography. Others whose help was invaluable include Robin Taylor and Neil Collins at English Heritage and John Steadman at Portsmouth City Museum. Thanks are also due to John Lee and Stuart Robertson of Conway Maritime Press, to Martin Robson for his copy editing of the text and especially to Stephen Dent for his excellent layout and design work.

Finally, I cannot overestimate the help given, in a thousand ways, by my wife Valerie during what at times must have seemed the endless gestation of this book.

Picture Acknowledgements

The sources of all illustrations used in this book are provided in the captions; some exist in abbreviated form, and require fuller explanation as follows:

English Heritage Plans Room .... National Monuments Record, English Heritage, Swindon
TNA . The National Archives (formerly The Public Record Office, Kew)
NMR .... National Monuments Record, English Heritage, Swindon
NMM .... National Maritime Museum, Greenwich

Abbreviations used for archive sources

Public Records Office, Kew ..... ADM, WORK, WO, MFQ, MPH, MR
National Maritime Museum .... NMR, POR, CHA
British Library .... BL
Keysign House (KH) .... English Heritage Plans Room, now archived in the National Monuments Record, Swindon
Unicorn Consultancy, Devonport .... UD
Unicorn Consultancy, Portsmouth .... UP
Devonport Dockyard Museum .... DDM (uncatalogued drawings)
Devonshire Record Office, Plymouth .... DRO (P)
Portsmouth Local Studies Collection, Portsmouth Library .... PLSC
Portsmouth City Archives .... PCA
Boulton and Watt Archives, Birmingham Reference Library .... BW

Primary sources

British Library
Martin, Halifax and Gladstone manuscripts and papers, all Additional Ms.

The National Archives, Kew

ADM 1	Correspondence with all departments of the Admiralty
ADM 2	Admiralty out-letters, including those of the Steam Department
ADM 3	Admiralty Minutes
ADM 7	Admiralty Miscellanea
ADM 12	Index and Digest of Admiralty In-letters
ADM 13	Includes Secret and Confidential Documents, 1844-1856
ADM 50	Admiral's Journals
ADM 53	Ships' Logs
ADM 83	Surveyor of Navy In-letters
ADM 84	Steam Department In-letters
ADM 85	Steam Department In-letters
ADM 86	Steam Department Register of In-letters
ADM 87	In-letters relating to Ships
ADM 89	In-letters relating to Yards
ADM 92	Surveyor of Navy's Submission Letter Books
ADM 93	Steam Department Letter Books
ADM 95	Controller of Navy Papers, including Steam Department
ADM 106	Navy Board records
ADM 110	Victualling Office Out-letters
ADM 111	Victualling Office Minutes
ADM 116	Cases (bound files of documents dealing with specific topics)
ADM 135	Ships' Books
ADM 140	Maps and Plans
ADM 195	Photographs
ADM 214	Civil Engineer-in-Chief's Department papers
ADM 222	Surveyor of Navy's submissions to Admiralty Board
ADM 224	Victualling Yard Records
WO 44	Board of Ordnance correspondence
WO 55	Board of Ordnance miscellanea
WORK 41	Maps and plans
MFQ, MPH, MR	Maps and plans
T	Treasury

National Maritime Museum, Greenwich

ELL	Minto Papers
WWL	Baldwin Walker Papers
MLN	Milne Papers
CHA	Chatham Dockyard Records
POR	Portsmouth Dockyard Records
PLY	Plymouth Dockyard Records

Institution of Mechanical Engineers
MS/233   Nasmyth's Sketchbook

Institution of Civil Engineers Archives
Rennie's Reports

Birmingham Public Library
BW   Boulton & Watt Collection

Science Museum Library

GOOD	Goodrich Collection
MS 446	James' Notebook
Nasmyth Order Books	

UD	Unicorn Consultancy, Devonport

(Microfiches now held by Devonport Management Limited)

UP	Unicorn Consultancy, Portsmouth
PLSC	Portsmouth Local Studies Collection
MOD	(Admiralty) Library
DOC 19	Chatham Historic Dockyard Library

Plymouth Naval Base Museum
Uncatalogued drawings

Bolton Archives
ZHH   Papers of Hick & Son

Royal Engineers Library, Brompton Barracks, Chatham

Coode Blizard archives

DRO(P)   Devonshire Record Office (Plymouth)

Tyne & Wear Archives

Introduction

THIS STUDY aims to give an account of the evolution of the built environment of the home bases of the Royal Navy between 1830, when the first purpose-built workshop for the maintenance and repair of steam engines was finished at Portsmouth, and 1906, which marked the completion of HMS *Dreadnought*.

By the end of the Napoleonic Wars the two South Coast yards of Devonport (Plymouth) and Portsmouth had become the two most strategically vital of the bases that, besides their ship-building roles, docked and refitted the ships of the Royal Navy. It was here that land was acquired in the 1840s for two massive steam-engine-powered engineering factories (Figure 2), although other yards will also feature in this story. Prior to this, for a brief period from 1831, the Navy's steam facility was concentrated at Woolwich, close to the commercial yards of the Thames, which comprised the national centre of marine steam engineering. Pembroke had opened as a building yard in 1815, and this function underpinned the continued importance of the old yard at Chatham on the Medway. In contrast Sheerness, though rebuilt in the 1830s and reworked in the 1850s, remained stunted through the restrictions of its peninsular site. A further consequence of the transition to a steam-driven fleet was the need for coaling stations around the coast, strategic concerns contributing to the establishment in the same decade of the secure anchorage and coaling facility at Portland, facing the large French naval dockyard at Cherbourg.

It will be seen that building programmes, and the degree of technological innovation and upgrading, were strongly affected by the degree of political support afforded to this new technology and events on the world stage, in particular the response to the real or perceived threat posed by the French navy that characterised the period either side of the Crimean War of 1854-6. The Royal Navy's first steam ship, the *Comet*, was launched in 1822, and the *Alban* class ordered in 1824, established the paddle warship as a new class of ship. The celebrated *Rattler* versus *Alecto* trials of 1843 had demonstrated the superiority of screw propulsion over paddles, which were also more vulnerable to enemy fire, and the navy's first screw frigate, *Dauntless*, was built in the following year. Britain's first screw-propelled battleship, *Agamemnon*, was designed in 1848 and launched in 1852, and over the same period the *Duke of Wellington* class of battleships were converted to auxiliary screw propulsion (Figure 1).

These line-of-battle ships, at a superficial glance, looked little different from their predecessors that had fought at Trafalgar half a century earlier. But the test of battle was to soon demonstrate that steam-powered boats, which could operate regardless of the limitations of wind and tide, were a vital logistical arm of war. Thus the Crimean War had provided the inspiration for Captain Cowper Coles's development of the rotating gun turret, but its efficacy was proven during the American Civil War. A further turning point in battleship design was marked by the construction of the first screw-propelled ship-of-the-line, *Napoleon*, in 1850 and then the world's first ironclad battleship, *Gloire*, in 1858. In Britain, the foundation of the Institute of

Naval Architects in 1860 provided the technological platform for the reaction to this threat, from the turret ships of the 1860s to the centre-battery ships of the 1870s designed by Edward Reed, Chief Constructor between 1863 and 1870. Reed's *Devastation* of 1869 (Figure 4) was the first of the mastless turret ships that marked the end of the traditional full-rig and broadside design. The *Royal Sovereign* class of battleships designed by Sir William White, Director of Naval Construction (DNC) between 1886 and 1902 (Figure 227), comprised the most revolutionary breakthrough in ship design of the nineteenth century. Powered by triple-expansion engines, armoured with steel and armed with hydraulically loaded breech guns, they looked forward to the *Dreadnought* class designed by his successor, Philip Watts, and the next 70 years (Figures 4, 239, 240).

Until the advent of the ironclad all capital ships had been built in the Royal Yards. However, private yards had proven expertise in the construction of seagoing iron-framed ships since the late 1830s, much of this being concentrated in the yards of the Thames. The 1850s witnessed the zenith of Britain's leadership of this industry on the world stage, the Thames yards at the Millwall Iron Works and the Thames Iron Works & Ship Building Company having, in the opinion of one contemporary observer, a production capacity greater than that

1 The *Duke of Wellington*, a 114 gun 1st Rate built at Pembroke and launched in 1852. One of the last pre-ironclad battleships, she was ordered as a sailing ship but converted to screw propulsion while under construction. Reduced to harbour service in 1863, a dramatic indication of her near instant obsolescence once *Warrior* had entered service, she wasn't sold for scrapping until 1904, after spending her last years mastless and roofed over as a depot ship in Portsmouth. *(Chrysalis Picture Library)*

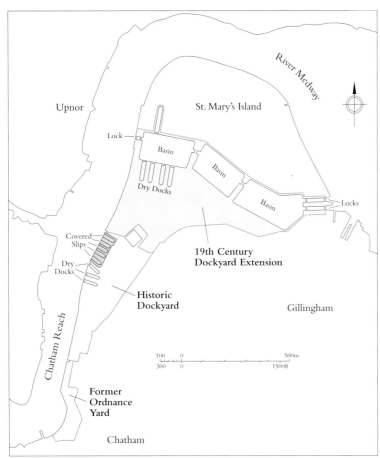

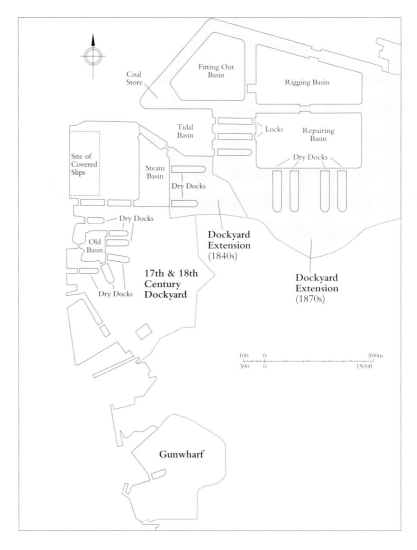

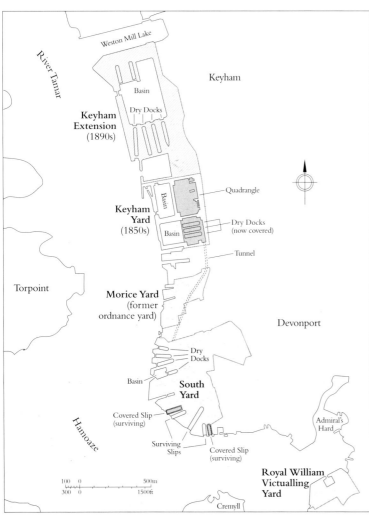

2 The expansion of the yards at (top left) Chatham, (top right) Portsmouth and (left) Plymouth, showing the steam facilities developed from the 1840s in relationship to their earlier boundaries. Steam basins and associated dry docks at Portsmouth and Devonport, developed in the 1840s and 1850s, were followed by the great extensions commencing in the 1870s and 1890s. At Devonport, the old South Yard had to be connected by a tunnel to the steam yard at Keyham. At Chatham, the old yard accommodated the construction of new generations of steam ships and associated buildings, most dramatically the covered slips that still survive, until the development of a new steam factory on St Mary's Island to the north from the 1860s.

Shown on the plans are the older Ordnance Depots at Chatham and Devonport (Morice Yard). By the end of the Napoleonic Wars, new sites had been added to the depots at Plymouth, Portsmouth and Chatham, all catering for the storage and later the manipulation of guns, their ammunition and propellants. These were subject to further development and expansion throughout the period of this book. *(Maps by Stephen Dent)*

3 (Right) These two photographs taken in Portsmouth Harbour dramatically illustrate the total transformation in warship design that took place during the period covered in this book.

The main picture, showing from left to right HM ships *Vernon*, *Rattler* and *Renown*, was probably taken during the years immediately prior to the First World War. The Torpedo School *Vernon* consisted of the hulks of the wooden ships of the line *Donegal* (1858) and *Marlborough* (1855), and of the ironclad *Warrior* (1860). *Rattler* was a composite screw gunboat from 1886, and *Renown* a battleship of 1895; both had been reduced to harbour service by 1910. All were rendered obsolete by the rapid pace of techological change, culminating in the *Dreadnought* of 1905. Beyond lies Portsdown Hill, crowned by the forts of the 1860s which, like the ships, became outdated within years of their construction.

The smaller photograph, taken from Gosport between 1895 and 1897, shows HMS *Victory*, built at Chatham in 1759-65, and beyond her the battleship *Inflexible* of 1874. Despite their vastly different ages, both were only good for harbour service by the time this picture was taken, *Victory* serving as Flagship of the Commander in Chief Naval Home Command and *Inflexible* as Portsmouth Guardship.

Of the vessels pictured, *Victory* and *Warrior* are still at Portsmouth, the others had all been scrapped by the mid 1920s. *(Chrysalis Picture Library)*

of their French competitors combined. At the former, developed from 1835 by William Fairbairn, Isambard Kingdom Brunel had joined forces with the shipbuilder John Scott Russell to build the world's largest and most powerful ship, the *Great Eastern*, and the contract for the construction of HMS *Warrior*, the Royal Navy's answer to *Gloire*, was awarded in 1859 to the latter.[1] The *Achilles*, laid down in 1861 at Chatham, was the first iron ship to be built in a naval yard, but private yards, notably William Beardmore and Company and Vickers at Barrow, continued to be responsible for building a good deal of the iron navy.

The Steam Factories and their associated structures cannot, moreover, be fully understood without an understanding of the new types of industrial plant that they were designed to accommodate, or indeed of their associated workforces. These machines, supplied by famous names in the history of engineering, such as Henry Maudslay, his pupil James Nasmyth, Joseph Whitworth and William Fairbairn, were operated by workmen with a whole new range of skills. By the 1840s and

early 1850s they effectively formed a separate workforce, hired and fired on terms that had little relationship to the traditional conditions of employment within the Yards. These matters have also been examined in this study in an attempt to put the buildings into context.

The background of these buildings' designers changed significantly during this period. Building design work had traditionally been the responsibility of Shipwright officers, showing what could be done in a well-established and amenable tradition without either formal architectural training or guidance by aristocratic *cognoscenti*. This succession of men produced a sequence of dignified and functional buildings: storehouses, roperies, smitheries, mould lofts, and, moving into polite architecture with its vocabulary of ornament and layout, chapels, terraces of officers' houses, and, grandest of all, commissioner's houses.

Not until 1796 was a formally trained architect, Samuel Bunce, appointed by the Navy Board, a venerable organisation responsible for the provision of ships, and hence dockyards, for

4 Two revolutionary
battleships, each in
their time the most
powerful warship
afloat. The upper
picture shows HMS
Devastation, built
between 1869 and
1873 at Portsmouth.
The lower one
depicts HMS
Dreadnought of
1906, heading a line
of pre-Dreadnought
battleships, with
cruisers beyond, at a
fleet review shortly
after her completion.
*(Chrysalis Picture
Library)*

the Admiralty. He was followed by Edward Holl and then George Taylor, both of whom displayed through their designs a strong awareness of the latest developments in structural ironwork. Taylor resigned in 1837, five years after the abolition of the Navy Board, which, with the acquisition of its first steamships, had developed its own in-house expertise to evaluate and advise on the purchase of the rapidly increasing flow of mechanical contrivances. From this date administration of the dockyards was taken over by Royal Engineer officers working at the Admiralty Works Department. The new system ensured the maintenance of a Supervising Engineer in each of the dockyards, and names such as Scamp, Greene, Beatson and Murray will figure prominently in this study. These 'army architects' were at this time the only people with a systematic training in building. Today their contribution to a wide range of improvements in both civil and military construction is increasingly well recognised.

Their impact on the dockyards was both rapid and profound. It can be summarised in two parts. First, their own buildings: these included the massive new steam basins and associated workshops at Woolwich, Portsmouth and Plymouth, the workshops and stores which pioneered the development of metal dock and slip covers, which presaged the railway sheds of the 1840s and 1850s, and rigid portal framing, the system adopted for the world's first skyscrapers in Chicago. The second influential aspect of the working habits of the Royal Engineers was in their cooperation with the private sector. Many of the projects referred to above were worked out in detail with iron founders and engineers such as Fox Henderson, Henry Grissell and George Baker. This cooperative practice, building as we shall see on firm foundations laid by the Navy Board in the early nineteenth century, was at the heart of the rebuilding of the dockyards as multi-functional centres of expertise under the Admiralty between 1840 and 1860.

This close working relationship between the Royal Yards and civilian manufacturers and engineers comprises a major theme of this book. It underpinned Britain's lead in so many aspects of industrial technology, and the effectiveness of the British battle fleet as a deterrent. Although the fleet was mobilised in answer to the Bosnian crises of 1878 and 1885 it only went into action once between 1856 and 1914, at Alexandria in 1882, and not in opposition to a major power. From the 1900s, renewed naval rivalry with Germany and Russia, as well as the French, forced continued renewal of the fleet with improved vessels, and huge investment, under a series of Naval Loans, in the dockyards. Lord Fisher took over the Admiralty in 1904, and the construction of HMS *Dreadnought* commenced in the following year. Her size set a new threshold for British naval docks, and her oil-powered turbine engines spelt the end of coaling stations and their replacement by oiling depots, as at the Navy's principal new base at Rosyth in Scotland, strategically sited in opposition to the German fleet. In terms of the dockyard workshops and docks, however, the late Victorian and Edwardian navy continued to be largely serviced by the built infrastructure that was in put place by the 1860s, when the first ironclads moved off the slipways.

In pressing ahead with the construction of buildings and the provision of modern machinery for servicing steamships, the Admiralty had thus established a secure technological base considerably in advance of that possessed by any other navy. This runs counter to popular historical mythology, which has visualised early Victorian Boards of Admiralty as populated by fabulous animals, the very stuff of anecdote, whose ignorance of technology was exceeded only by their dogged opposition to its introduction. But, as we shall see, the Steam Factories in the 1850s were well-equipped multifunctional centres of expertise. Many of the buildings themselves demonstrated the engineering lead of Great Britain. The designing of a factory so that it is ergonomically efficient, ordering the optimum mix of machine tools for a workshop, can be far more significant than decisions, supposed by their authors to be of the greatest import, made at the highest level. The architects and clerks of works, the chief engineers and their subordinates, the machine tool designers, the steam engine manufacturers, did all these things in a great collaborative enterprise, one of the successes of the first great capitalist country. But all the bricks were laid, the iron cast, and the rivets driven home by the English, Scottish, Welsh and Irish labourers, craftsmen and mechanics whose works have outlasted the transitory achievements of First Lords of the Admiralty.[2]

Closure and adaptation

The buildings erected in the Royal Dockyards for the sailing navy from the late seventeenth century, and the organisation and performance of the labour force, have thus been the subject of several studies. The pioneering research undertaken from the late 1960s by Jonathan Coad[3] has underpinned the protection of key buildings and dry docks, which were managed under the regime of restricted access necessary to active defence sites. From the 1980s, however, Government policy toward the naval dockyards changed, and as part of the Options for Change review of the country's defence establishment, a programme of closure and privatisation was undertaken. This has had profound consequences, as for the first time the Chatham Yard and parts of Portsmouth became much more widely accessible to the public, and their buildings receptive to a new diversity of civilian uses. The Ministry of Defence and other owners, in addition to those responsible for making decisions about the conservation management of these sites, also needed a fresh evaluation of their built fabric and related archaeology. The result was a review of the protection through listing of the dockyards at Portsmouth, Plymouth, Portland, Sheerness and Chatham, completed in 1999, as part of a continuing exploration of their layered archaeology. These exercises, and the future management of these sites, needed to be informed by an overview of the development of the Steam Factories and their associated structures, about which very little was known. This research, and the contextual overview of the significance of what survives within its full national and international context, has served to underpin the protection, often through listing at a high grade, of many buildings which feature prominently in this book. Thus the importance of the Sheerness Boatstore (1858-60), designed by Colonel G T Greene and his assistant William Scamp with the iron founder Henry Grissell, has long been recognised. Now listed at grade I, it is celebrated for its pioneering use of the portal-braced frame, subsequently adopted by the skyscraper pioneers in Chicago. Also listed grade I are the metal slip covers at Chatham, which as a group exemplify the development from braced construction to portal framing. Research for this book has also highlighted the engineering importance of many lesser-known buildings and features, such as Bentham's North Smithery at Devonport (now listed at grade II★), and the development of the remarkably advanced materials handling system used at the Sheerness Boatstore, and in No 7 Slip at Chatham, which culminated in the vast Quadrangle workshop at Devonport (now listed at grade I). As completed by around 1864 it represents a revolutionary concept in factory planning, whose inherent flexibility as a working space has enabled it to continue to play a key role in servicing the Royal Navy today.

The general effect of the Steam Factories as they survive today, however, is quite different from how they were envisaged, the disappearance of chimneys being the most visible reminder of the supersession of the power systems that made the whole

thing function: coal-fired, and later oil-fired, steam machinery. The pipes of the hydraulic systems remain buried underground for some archaeologist of future centuries to uncover and reconstruct; the accumulator towers hold nothing; the engine houses, with luck, retain some of the iron frames of their engines. Not part of the buildings, but contributing powerfully to the ambience, the arrays of cranes, visible from miles around, have shrunk to a fraction of their former number. The machinery that maintained and serviced the Steam Navy has long been scrapped, and the din of the smitheries has been replaced by the silence of the storehouse.

Disposal has also resulted in mixed fortunes, from wholesale demolition to sympathetic reuse. Only part of the Woolwich steam factory remains, surrounded by the infilled archaeology of its related docks and basins. Sheerness was always an awkward place for the Navy to operate, and to turn it into a viable commercial enterprise was clearly going to demand pretty drastic alterations. The polite buildings were, as to be expected, retained, but Rennie's Basins were filled in to make way for much-needed storage space. Holl's Great Storehouse and all the associated workshops adapted to service the Baltic Fleet in the Crimean War have gone, but the Boat Basin, with its associated dry docks and slip, remains, as do a range of technical and domestic buildings, including some of those which will feature prominently in this book: Holl's Working Masthouse, with a fine display of ironwork, Greene's Sawmills and most importantly Greene's Boat Store. Sadly, no significant reuse has been found for this latter building, unless the periodic descent of parties of architectural historians may be so termed.

The case of Chatham is different. The eighteenth and early nineteenth-century buildings formed a self-contained and reasonably compact site, geographically separate from the St Mary's Island extension. The latter was completely redeveloped for new housing and a commercial port, leaving the great Basins and associated docks, pumping engine house and one of the reused Woolwich covered slips. Chatham is best known as the most intact dockyard of the age of sail, and now serves as a 'living museum' in addition to a variety of commercial functions and housing. Despite the demolition of No2 Smithery in the late 1990s (including the Metal Mills described

6 The demolition of part of the Woolwich factory in the early 1980s proceeds. *(English Heritage)*

zenith of Britain's leadership of this industry on the world stage.[4] They thus form a material resource of great value, being potent relics of an age when Britain was on an industrial roll, before being overtaken by American and German technology and production.

—⚓—

in this book) it has retained some buildings created and adapted for the Steam Navy, notably the Smithery, covered slips and the workshops built for the construction in the 1860s of HMS *Achilles*, the first ironclad built in a Royal Yard.

Portsmouth presents a similar face to the public, though in this case for security reasons, as the post-1848 areas remain a working Yard. The eighteenth-century storehouses form a homogeneous group as background for the *Victory*, and with museums and displays concentrated in a small area there is much to see. The Block Mills remain just off public access, although much of their historic machinery is on display in the Science Museum. Devonport, as will be seen, is a split site. The South Yard, containing Bentham's North Smithery, Greene's South Smithery and Sawmills, with the surviving eighteenth-century buildings, is now relatively little used. An excellent in-house museum has been formed over the years, though public access is restricted. Because of the self-contained nature of this part of the Dockyard no inherent obstacles, other than the large spaces of the Smitheries, lie in the way of the future reuse and display of the whole area. The North Yard, centred around Keyham Factory (still adapting, but now with many areas distinctly underused) is tooled up for refitting frigates and nuclear submarines, and boasts, in the frigate repair hangars, noble successors to Greene's covered slip at Chatham. No public access is to be expected there.

Be all this as it may, more has survived than has been lost, and the adaptability of most buildings to new functions has ensured that the shells of the majority of those described in this book survive today. Demolition and redevelopment along the Thames and elsewhere has also resulted in their survival as an ensemble far in advance of anything in the civil field, representative the

Notes:

[1] D K Brown, *Paddle Warships*, (London, 1993). The Millwall site is described in P Barry, *Dockyard Economy and Naval Power*, (London, 1863), pp.223-31; notes and information from Tom Ridge of GLIAS; Edward Sargent, 'The Millwall Ironworks Site', in Stuart Rankin (ed) *Shipbuilding on the Thames and Thames-Built Ships*, (London, 2001), pp.95-102; Tony Arnold, 'The Failures of Millwall Ironworks and Overend Gurney', in Rankin, pp.87-93.

J Weiler 'Army Architects, the Royal Engineers and the development of building technology in the nineteenth century', unpublished PhD thesis, 1987, University of York. This carries a full discussion of the organisation of the Royal Engineers, and biographical details.

[2] The buildings of the Royal Navy in the period preceding that covered in this book are definitively described by J G Coad, in *The Royal Dockyards, 1690-1850*, (Aldershot, 1989); *Historic Architecture of the Royal Navy, an Introduction*, (London, 1983); and in 'Historic architecture of HM Naval Base, Portsmouth, 1700-1850', *Mariner's Mirror*, vol. 67, 1981, pp.3-59; 'Historic architecture of Chatham Dockyard, 1700-1850', *Mariner's Mirror*, vol. 68, 1982, pp.133-188; 'Historic architecture of HM Naval Base, Devonport, 1689-1850', *Mariner's Mirror*, vol. 69, 1983, pp.341-392.

The buildings and docks (a subject scarcely touched on in this book) of Portsmouth Yard during the nineteenth century have been surveyed in R C Riley, *The Evolution of the Docks and Industrial Buildings in Portsmouth Royal Dockyard 1698-1914*, (Portsmouth, 1985), and much pertinent material is in E A M Laing, *Steam Wooden Warship Building in Portsmouth Dockyard 1832-52*, (Portsmouth, 1985).

Bentham's achievements are assessed, as part of a comprehensive study of the Yards, in R Morriss, *The Royal Dockyards through the Revolutionary and Napoleonic Wars*, (Leicester, 1983).

The classic source of anecdotes about the Admiralty is Sir John Briggs, *Naval Administrations 1827-1892*, (London, 1897); a modern historian's view is N.A.M. Rodger, *The Admiralty*, (Lavenham, 1979).

The traditional view of the technical backwardness of the Navy has been shown to be untenable in recent years; the principal proponents of this dislodgement have been P W Brock and B Greenhill, in *Steam and Sail in Britain and North America*, (Newton Abbot, 1973); A Lambert, *Battleships in Transition: the Creation of the Steam Battle Fleet 1815-1850*, (London, 1984); 'The Royal Navy and the introduction of the screw propeller, 1837-1847', in *Innovation in Shipping and Trade* (ed. S Fisher), (Exeter, 1989); contributions in *Steam, Steel, and Shellfire* (also ed. Lambert), (London, 1992); D K Brown, *Before the Ironclad*, (London, 1990); contribution in *Steam, Steel, and Shellfire* (see above); *Warrior to Dreadnought*, (London, 1997); R Morriss, 'Sir George Cockburn and the Management of the Royal Navy, 1841-6', in *Parameters of British Naval Power 1650-1850* (ed. M Duffy), (Exeter, 1992); and B Greenhill and A Giffard, *Steam, Politics, and Patronage: The transformation of the Royal Navy 1815-54*, (London, 1994).

The political background for the earlier and most significant part of the period has been covered by C J Bartlett, *Great Britain and Sea Power 1815-1853*, (London, 1963), and, with more attention to the internal politics of the Navy, by A Lambert, *The Last Sailing Battle fleet: Maintaining Naval Mastery 1815-1850*, (London 1991), parts 1-3. C I Hamilton, Anglo-French Rivalry, 1840-1870, (Oxford, 1993), covers some of the ground of the present book, from a different perspective.

[3] Coad, (1989).

[4] The large Heavy Engineering Shop of Vickers in the centre of Barrow includes an erecting shop of the 1870s, the other principal survivors being on the Clyde, namely the Fairfield Works at Govan, designed in 1869, the Linthouse marine engine works at Glasgow of 1872 and the boiler shop of 1888. All these have been accorded protection through listing.

CHAPTER 1

The Birth of the Steam Navy

Forging the wooden navy

By the end of the eighteenth century the Dockyards of the Royal Navy were the largest industrial complexes in the land, both constructing and maintaining an enormous fleet, which at its peak in 1809 numbered 728 ships of all classes. The scale of the storehouses and roperies dwarfed that of private factories, as did the workforce. In March 1814, when swollen to its greatest extent, it comprised 15,598 men and boys. All the ships were wooden and propelled by the power of the wind. By the end of the next major war in 1856 the 240 ships inspected by Queen Victoria at Spithead were virtually all fitted with steam engines, all maintained in purpose-built dockyard facilities; and in a further five years the construction of iron ships in the Yards would begin, necessitating the provision of further specialised building types. The workforce of 1859, at 16,334, was much the same size as in 1814, but many hands were now employed at skills previously unknown.[1]

This massive nineteenth-century industrialisation of the Yards did not come out of the blue. It had a significant prehistory, and the importance of the Portsmouth Block Mills as one of the world's first steam-powered machine shops has long been recognised (Figures 7, 8).[2] The moving force behind the introduction of steam machinery in the Yards was Samuel

7 Built to house the most advanced industrial equipment in the world at the time, to serve the sailing Navy, the Block Mills remained at work till the middle of the twentieth century, steam ships requiring blocks for their tackle as well. Bentham's steam-driven saws were installed at Portsmouth in 1798, combined with a pump to empty the docks. The engine was placed within one of a pair of three-storey brick buildings, designed by Samuel Bunce. Two years after steam-powered sawing had begun, Marc Brunel offered his patented block-making machinery to the Admiralty. Supported by Bentham, the machines were made by Maudslay's, and installed in a single-storey shop fitted into the space between the two earlier ranges. They were in operation by 1803, powered by a larger engine bought from Boulton and Watt in 1800. Inside, power was transmitted by overhead shaft drives with belts connected to individual machines. *(Elaine A Wakefield © Wessex Archaeology)*

Bentham, brother of the Utilitarian philosopher Jeremy Bentham. Samuel was appointed Inspector-General of Naval Works in 1795, having worked in Russia for 15 years and acquired the rank of Brigadier-General. He advocated the use of machinery and steam power, and the appointment of qualified men to the posts of architect, engineer, mechanist and chemist (though the last post soon lapsed). This ensured that Portsmouth and Chatham could boast the most advanced facilities of any dockyard in the world prior to the advent of steam navigation. His poor relationship with the Navy Board, which as the organisation responsible for the provision of ships (and hence dockyards) for the Admiralty had resented the existence of Bentham's separate department, was a major factor in the abolition of his office in 1812. With the acquisition of its first steamships the Navy Board found the legacy of Bentham's small department invaluable: it provided the only in-house expertise to evaluate and advise on the purchase of the rapidly increasing flow of mechanical contrivances. Simon Goodrich, who had entered Bentham's Portsmouth office in 1799 as a draughtsman, functioned as Engineer and Machinist to the Navy Board from 1814 to 1831, and after Bentham's departure was the prime mover in the industrialisation of the Dockyards.

Goodrich was to draw on the expertise of an array of engineers who were at the forefront of innovation. One of the most notable was Henry Maudslay, who between 1801 and 1806 had constructed the blockmaking machinery designed by Marc Brunel at the Block Mills, and went on to establish his reputation as one of the principal machine tool manufacturers of his age. The workshops of Maudslay, Son and Field,[3] set up in 1810 in Lambeth, produced some of the world's first marine engines and fostered some of the most noted industrial designers: prime amongst these were Joseph Clement, who refined marine engine design and whose facing lathe of 1827 comprised a milestone in machine tool design, and James Nasmyth, who after Maudslay's death in 1831 went on to found his famous Patricroft Works, primarily for the supply of the early rail industry, and to design the steam hammer that revolutionised the production of heavy forgings. These were personalities whose skills and talents formed a vital component of the private expertise upon which the likes of Goodrich and later the chief engineers at the Steam Factories could draw.

Steam power was used in the Yards considerably before the advent of the marine steam engine, for pumping and to a lesser degree for driving machinery: Bentham had introduced a small pumping engine at Portsmouth in 1798. Boulton & Watt supplied their first dock engines to the West India Docks in 1800, and in March that year made a 30hp engine for Portsmouth, which after 1803 drove Marc Brunel's blockmaking machinery as well as pumping docks. It was not until 1813 that two more engines were supplied by that firm, this time to Sheerness, one of 49.1hp to work Rennie's dry docks (then in course of construction), and the other, less powerful, to drive the mortar mill and other machinery (Figure 9). A second 49.1hp engine was added in 1823. The next batch of Boulton & Watt engines were for Woolwich Smithery. In 1814 two engines were installed, one as a blowing engine for the forge and one to power a tilt hammer; a second forge engine was added the next year. At Chatham, other firms supplied engines to power the machinery for Marc Brunel's Sawmills and Edward Holl's Lead and Paint Shop, which were operational in 1814 and 1819 respectively. Table 1 lists the Boulton & Watt engines placed in the Yards during the first half of the nineteenth century. Comparable records do not survive for other manufacturers.

The relationships between private manufacturers and the Naval authorities now took on a new dimension. The pattern of future procurement policies when an entirely new article was adopted was established on the introduction of chain cables into the Service. These were invented by Captain Sir Samuel Brown RN in 1810, who offered both twisted and plain parallel-sided chains. The Navy Board, in a conservative first response, preferred the twisted version because of their resemblance to traditional rope, and introduced them experimentally that year. At that time no means had been devised for testing their strength; after two ships had parted their cables in a gale, Brown devised a compound lever machine for this purpose.

The first trial of cables took place at Shadwell in July 1810. The cables and the testing equipment were considered so important that the trials were attended by the First Lord of the Admiralty, the Comptroller of the Navy Board, and the Chancellor of the Exchequer.[4] These clearly demonstrated chain cabling's superiority to rope, and showed that the combination of a reliable method of testing with the improved construction of the chains was the key to the success of the innovation (Figure 10). The first parallel-sided cables, supplied to the frigate Crescent in 1812, came up to expectation. Brown and Goodrich were asked to draw up a schedule of dimensions of chain cables; with very slight modification this was still in force 50 years later.

The replacement of the traditional cables was necessarily slow, but by 1820 Brown had been joined by two other firms (Messrs Middleton & Brunton, and Messrs Hawkes) to supply

8 A poor quality but nonetheless interesting aerial view of the Old Basin area of Portsmouth dockyard, taken during the years immediately before the First World War. The dry docks to the left now contain HMS *Victory*, the *Mary Rose* and the monitor *M33*, while to the right can be seen Brunel's Block Mills. Also note the coaling float C1. *(Portsmouth Dockyard Historical Trust)*

9 Engine houses were capable of being treated with considerable architectural dignity. This is well demonstrated in the design of Edward Holl's surviving Engine and Boiler House at Chatham. This building, for which the first drawings had been submitted in March 1819, was approaching completion in March 1821 when Edward Holl forwarded drawings for the ironwork of the roofs and gutters. The ironwork was entrusted to the firm of Sturges & Company, at an estimated cost of £550 to £600: the original estimate for the whole building was £14,000. (English Heritage)

the Navy. In 1830 it was decided to accelerate their introduction. Several other firms had offered to manufacture the cables, and the Navy Board saw no reason why the three firms should have the field to themselves, so in the spring of 1830 Goodrich was sent to the North and the Midlands to inspect the likely competitors. He prepared an extensive report on chain cables and their manufacturers, which was completed by October. The suppliers were told that a cautiously competitive procurement policy was being initiated. By this time many private manufacturers had their own testing machinery: a Devonport ironmaster had got wind of the vast new market to be tapped, and informed the Board that in addition to 'as good Workmen as all England can produce' he possessed a machine capable of proving to 80 tons. Gordon & Co. made significant improvements by introducing square links, to fit into the cogs of the capstan, which they were allowed to try out on HMS *Hebe*.[5] Nevertheless, the Navy Board considered as vital the retention of their own facility for checking on the proof of cables, a fact that several firms were not keen on.[6]

Contemporaries considered 1831 as the year in which chain cables were 'fairly established' in the Navy. In that year the Comptroller of the Navy, Admiral Sir Thomas Byam Martin, informed his First Lord, Sir James Graham, of the economies that had resulted. Between 1821 and 1825 the average number of ships in commission was 157, with an annual average expenditure of 3,050 tons of cordage. Between 1826 and 1830 the average number of ships had risen to 180, but the cordage used had fallen to 2,500 tons. Some chains lasted a whole commission, three or four years, while hempen cables needed to be replaced two or three times a year. The saving was some £30,000 a year, in addition to which it was politically

Table 1 Boulton & Watt steam engines placed in the Yards during the first half of the nineteenth century

Location	Date	No.	Horsepower	Purpose[a]
Portsmouth	March 1800	1	30	
Sheerness	1813	2	28 and 49.1	
Woolwich	June 1814	1	20 or 24	Forge engine for Smithery
Woolwich	1814	1	28	For tilt hammer
Woolwich	1815	1	20	For forge
Chatham	1815	1	49.1	
Woolwich	1819	1	10	
Sheerness	1823	1	49.1	
Deptford	August 1826	2	40	For corn mill
Chatham	1828	1	10	
Weevil	March 1829	1	40	For corn mill
Royal William Yard	1829	1	20	
Royal William Yard	September 1830	2	45	
Deptford	November 1833	1	30	For oat and chocolate mill
Devonport	1834	1	15.1	
Devonport	1835	1	20	
Chatham	1836	1	14	
Portsmouth	February 1837	1	30	For rolling mill
Woolwich	1840	1	27.6	
Chatham	1841	1	16	
Portsmouth	December 1842	1	80	For rolling mill
Portsmouth	1843	1	80	For rolling mills
Chatham	1843	1	80	For rolling mills
Keyham	1847	1	98.2	
Devonport	1850	1	98.2	
Portsmouth	1855	1	80	

[a] Purpose shown when recorded by the firm

important that the Navy was not dependent on Russia for hemp. The chain cable was to remain in service with the Navy, and cable testing houses (see Chapter 5, p.51) were to be continually added to and updated during the twentieth century.[7]

The first steam ships and warships

Steam machinery went afloat in 1802, again at Bentham's suggestion, in a dredger built for Portsmouth harbour. Only the dredging machinery was powered, by a 12hp engine constructed by John Lloyd of Westminster. Lloyd was also entrusted with the machinery of a second dredger, which began work at Woolwich in October 1807. Goodrich was almost certainly the designer of this successful equipment. Relatively few specialised personnel were required to run these engines, but with the introduction of steam machinery into ships it was clear that a continuously expanding number of engineers and mechanics would have to be supplied.[8]

The development of the marine steam engine during the first two decades of the nineteenth century was entirely the work of private manufacturers, largely in the United States and Great Britain, with France trailing behind. However, the industrial revolution had an impact upon naval technology long before any steamship came into service with the Royal Navy.

The application of steam machinery to drive industrial equipment was well established. Its use to propel ships was of much more recent date. The first steam ship to operate commercially in Europe, Henry Bell's *Comet*, was not launched until July 1812; in the United States William Fulton's *Clermont* had initiated steam navigation as a practicable means of transport in 1807. By 1819 some 100 steam ships had been built in the United States and by 1820 British industry had built 43. However, geography determined that many British ships were conceived for more ambitious ends than their transatlantic

counterparts. American engineers and shipbuilders found that the great rivers of their country provided an ample market for several decades following Fulton's pioneering enterprise, while British constructors were forced to tackle the problem of commercially viable ocean-going vessels. However, for many years the functions of these ships were restricted by the limitations of the machinery, and until the general adoption of the compound engine during the 1870s steamships were unable to challenge sailing vessels as bulk carriers. The first steamships to be purchased for the Royal Navy were mainly used for towing purposes.

At first the Navy relied heavily on the firms that manufactured marine engines to supply not only the men to operate them at sea, but also those to fit them out and maintain them in the dockyards. In January 1827 *Echo* and *Confiance* were being fitted out at Woolwich by men from Maudslay, Son & Field, and *Alban* and *Carron* at Devonport by Boulton & Watt. However, Goodrich was slowly building up an industrial base at Portsmouth, where there were few civilian engineers available with skills capable of being tapped. He had a talented subordinate in John Kingston, who was probably related to William Kingston, the Master of Millwrights, whose hoop-bending machine had been installed at Portsmouth in 1818. Kingston's principal invention, the Kingston valve, will be dealt with later on (see p.36).

The first measures to ensure an in-house training programme for engineers had been initiated by George Smith, the Secretary of the Navy Board, in three papers written in the autumn of 1825. First he suggested the recruitment of apprentices to train on steamships, to be bound to Simon Goodrich for five years, with the obligation afterwards to serve as Master Engineers (the style Chief Engineer had not yet been adopted) for five more years. This proposal was adopted by the Board. Maintaining a dockyard tradition, sons of Yard staff, such as the son of the Cabin Keeper of Shipwrights and Joiners at Plymouth, saw this as a career opportunity.

Next, writing on 'The 20th Anniversary of the Glorious Battle of Trafalgar', Smith foresaw the need for a more fundamental change than apprenticeship schemes:

> The introduction (of late years) of the practice of Steam Boat Navigation has made so wonderful a change…that I cannot contemplate the subject without feeling the Conviction…that still more extraordinary changes will take place…and as it is a generally received opinion that the system of war will also be changed by it, in a great measure, it appears to me that some changes should be introduced without delay, in the plan of education in the Navy…

Nothing was to come of this for some time.

George Smith's final suggestion was the creation of a steam-engine-making establishment in the Yards, to ensure supply in the event of sudden rearmament, a likely occurrence as

> …we cannot be at peace with the whole World much longer. We have already enjoyed that Blessing during a period to an extent unknown as a state of profound peace in the annals of History…

This was not to happen. The Navy relied until much later in the century on private manufacturers to provide the motive power

10 Admiral Sir Thomas Hardy was particularly interested in the development of chain cables, patenting a mooring swivel. Here is a drawing showing proposed alterations to the end link. *(TNA ADM 106/1913)*

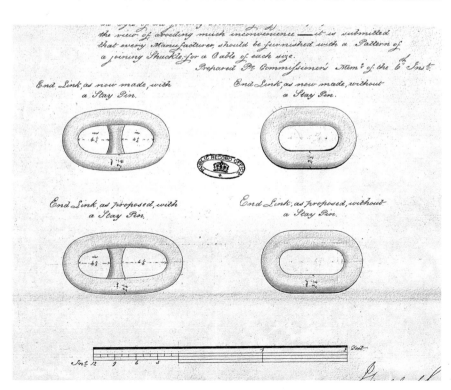

for its ships, but at the instigation of Admiral Byam Martin, abetted by Goodrich, the Navy Board was shortly to take the first steps towards providing a properly equipped facility for the maintenance and repair of engines.[9]

—w—

Notes:

[1] Morriss, (1983), pp.108-9; D K Brown, (1990), p.168.

[2] The Portsmouth Block Mills and its machinery has a small literature of its own: K R Gilbert, *The Portsmouth Blockmaking Machinery*, (London, 1965), C C Cooper, 'The production line at Portsmouth Block Mill', *Industrial History Review*, 1982, pp.28-44, and the same author's 'The Portsmouth system of manufacture', in *Technology and Culture*, vol. 25, 1984, pp.182-225, will orient the reader. A particularly valuable account, drawing on first-hand experience, is A Barlow, 'The Blockmills at Portsmouth Dockyard in the eighteenth to twentieth century', *Mariner's Mirror*, vol. 88, no.1, February 2002, pp.81-9.

[3] This firm changed its title several times; this version has been settled on throughout.

[4] A twisted iron cable 2⅛ inches in diameter was tested against a piece of new 24in hempen cable, the largest size made. When wrought iron pins were inserted in the middle of the chain links the hempen cable broke at 84 tons; the iron cable had not fractured, and the reinforced links had kept their shape.

[5] *Catalogue of the International Exhibition of 1862. Building Contrivances*, 334; GOOD A/1495, ADM 106/1529, ADM 106/1475, ADM 106/1554.

[6] The Board insisted that no scrap iron be used in the manufacture, causing one concern to pull out, while John Abbot of Gateshead, whose tender had been accepted with the proviso that the cables would be tested at the Yards, wished to know if the retesting would

> '...exonerate me from all further risk when approved previous to my entering into the contract as I have always found that the retesting chain deteriorates the quality and...renders the risk much greater.'

Goodrich replied implacably:

> 'If the Chain Cable be well made and well Tested and all defective links renewed I am of opinion that they will stand retesting...Messrs Gordons do not object to retesting'.

Following Goodrich, the Board took a hard line on the matter, deciding that instant notice of discontinuance of contract would be given on the first instance of discovery of defective workmanship: this would apply to the first discovery made after 12 months. This severity was slightly mitigated a week later, allowing the contractors' liability to cease after retesting at Deptford Yard.

[7] In 1845 the Master Attendant at Woolwich Yard published comparative data for chain and hempen cables tested there 'where the only testing machine of any magnitude belonging to Government has long been in use.' Nicholas Tinmouth, *An Inquiry relative to various important points of Seamanship, considered as a branch of practical science*, (London, 1845).

[8] BW Arch/05/1, Catalogue of Old Engines; ADM 106/3183, NMM P/76. A W Skempton, 'A history of the steam dredger, 1797-1830', in *Transactions of the Newcomen Society*, vol. 47, 1977, pp.97-116.

[9] ADM 106/1638. GOOD B/56, ADM 92/2, GOOD B/57, ADM 106/1638, *Minutes of Evidence before Committee of Inquiry on the Economy of Her Majesty's Dockyards*, 1858, pp.213-214.

CHAPTER 2

Building Foundations

Using Metal

The use of metal on a significant scale in the Royal Dockyards began long before the advent of the marine steam engine, as copper and iron components and accessories gradually played an increasingly important part in the construction and operation of sailing ships. Small iron articles had always been forged in the Yards, and a smithery had always been an essential building, but buildings for processing copper had been a relatively recent introduction.

Copper sheeting was introduced as a measure to check the depredations of maritime worms on the hulls of wooden ships, and involved a considerable expenditure, amounting to £2,272 for the largest type of warship.[1] The copper was partly supplied by private firms, and partly remanufactured in-house at the now-demolished Portsmouth Metal Mills.

The Metal Mills, probably designed by Holl,[2] were constructed in 1805 on the north side of the Smithery of the 1790s, and powered by a 56hp beam engine supplied by Whitmore of Birmingham. By 1813 these mills were rolling 6,700 sheets of copper a week. This facility had been part of Samuel Bentham's programme of introducing steam-powered machinery and other innovations, both procedural and mechanical, into the Yards. Simon Goodrich paid occasional visits to the principal copper-smelting works at Swansea, as part of a programme of keeping in touch with current industrial technology and checking on the quality of the products of the Mills. He saw to it that the relations between private industry and the Yards were to the benefit of the Admiralty. In the case of chain cables it had been they who set the standards; here, the firms provided the check on the Yards. In 1827 he concluded that the copper remanufactured in the Yard was in no way inferior to the new copper supplied by private concerns, no one firm among whom appeared to have the edge.[3]

The growth in the size of ships and the increasing difficulty of procuring seasoned timber for curved pieces necessitated the use of wrought iron. Roberts, the Master Shipwright at Pembroke, was responsible for the introduction of iron knees, generally adopted about 1808. As a result of this increased pressure on the Smitheries, in 1807-8 Bentham designed a new North Smithery for Devonport, which survives in a clearly recognisable form today (Figures 13 and 107). A first version of the design supported the roof on masonry pillars, but these were revised as double iron columns. The roof trusses remained

wooden, but the traveller crane supported by the columns is one of the earliest examples known.[5] The smithery operations were all to be done by manual work, Bentham considering that, whatever mechanisation might be decided upon in the future, there would always be a requirement for this number of hand forges, and forging by hand was indeed to remain as a traditional unmechanised skill. The beer cellar was an integral part of the building, a necessity where heavy manual work was conducted in high temperatures. The old South Smithery, dating from the 1770s, was presumably where the heavy forging was to be concentrated. Heavy forging work, such as the manufacture of anchors, and later chain cables, was done at this time by means of tilt hammers, powered by steam, by water (not used in the Yards), or by hand. These were large and cumbersome machines, which had the fundamental flaw, inherent in the design, that the larger the workpiece the feebler the blow that could be dealt upon it (Figure 11). Bentham's smithery was in place to cope with the great increase in the number of large iron components of sailing ships, necessitated by the new structural techniques introduced by Sir Robert Seppings (Surveyor of the Navy 1813-1832), though these had been anticipated both at home and abroad.

The first workshops

The major component of a steam engine, marine or stationary, that needed most frequent renewal was the boiler (Figure 12). They had been constructed in Portsmouth Yard on an

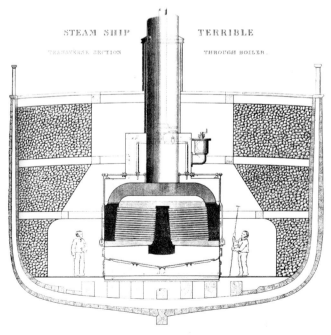

12 Section through the boiler of *Terrible*, which was one of the last generation of paddle frigates. *(Tredgold on the Steam Engine, Marine Engines and Boilers, vol.1, new edn. (n.d.), London & New York, plate 3)*

11 James Nasmyth's drawing of a tilt hammer. The amount of floor space taken up by the device is apparent, as is the small distance the hammer has to fall. *(Papers on subjects connected with the duties of the Corps of Royal Engineers, Vol. VIII, 1845)*

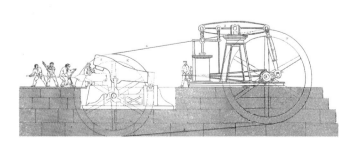

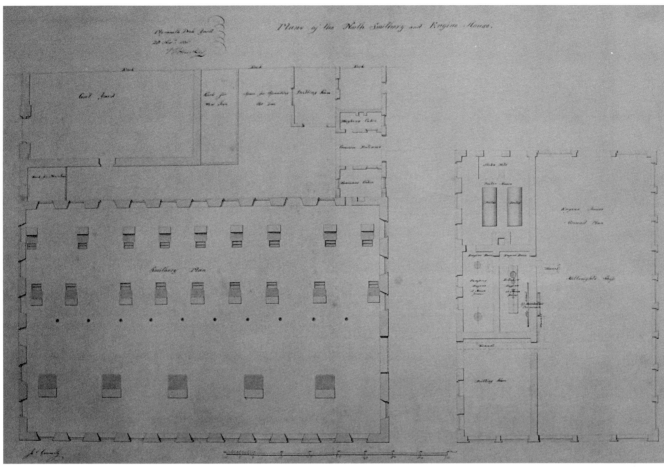

13 The North Smithery (to left) drawn in 1836. Apart from the use of metal columns, it is a typical smithery of the period. The traveller road, supported by an additional row of columns, is a later addition.

The eastern half of the building held 18 small forges, the western half five large ones. The establishment was relatively small: by comparison in 1829 the Portsmouth Smithery housed 50 single and nine double forge fires. (TNA ADM 140/244). (Internal picture English Heritage)

occasional basis for replacement purposes, certainly since 1817 when orders were given to make one (which would not have been for a steamship, but for one of the Yard engines). By the summer of 1827 precisely 237 tons of copper had been used for this purpose, with a roughly similar amount being used for fireproofing timber roofs. This architectural use of copper plates had not been allowed for, and the stock was running down. A properly planned facility for making boilers and other repairs to steam engines, both marine and stationary, was necessary.

The next year Rear-Admiral Sir Thomas Byam Martin, after consulting with Goodrich, who had prepared a report on the possible manufacture of engines in the Yards, wrote to the engineering firm of Maudslay, Son & Field for information about the types of building required for these purposes. The manufacture of complete engines was not ruled out as an eventual possibility. Byam Martin was well aware that a firm that was a front runner in the field of marine engineering might not wish to help in setting up a workshop that would effectively act as a competitor, but the firm was happy to collaborate, no doubt calculating (rightly) that it would then supply the heavy plant required.

Field travelled down to Portsmouth for a site meeting with the Comptroller, Goodrich, Nolloth (the Master Shipwright) and George Taylor, the Architect to the Navy Board. Goodrich's report was discussed, and a site near the Smithery, then occupied by a Russia deal store, was selected. Discussions continued for several days: some involved the Master Millwright, William Kingston. By June 1829 Taylor's drawings for the Boiler House, as it was to be generally known during its short active life, had been received, and work had begun on clearing the ground and amassing materials.[6]

14 The price list sent by Fox to Goodrich. See Figure 71 for a planing machine. (*Goodrich Collection, Science Museum*)

There was, however, a lack of clear support at a crucial level for investing in the infrastructure demanded by steam power. Goodrich's and Byam Martin's plans for Portsmouth received a setback in November 1829 when, following the submission of a report by the Comptroller, the Treasury approved the work on consideration that only repair work to engines and boilers would be carried out in the buildings. However, the same machinery to bend plates to shape and punch them for riveting was required to mend a boiler as to make it, and badly worn boilers had to be replaced rather than repaired, so the Treasury's ruling was to be tacitly ignored in practice. By Christmas 1829 the sum of £4,068 had been spent on the buildings, and it was estimated that a further £5,082 would be needed in 1830 to complete the project.

With the prospect of the imminent Boiler House, Goodrich toured Cornish steam engine factories and mines with a view to considering the possible application of Cornish boilers to

maritime use, but with no positive outcome. During his tour of chain cable manufacturers he also visited many ironworks and factories of all kinds, including, with the imminent transformation of the Navy's manufacturing resources in mind, machine tool makers.

The celebrated engineer, James Fox, who had produced his first planing machines and lathes before 1820 (tools originally designed for the manufacture and maintenance of textile machinery, see Chapter 7), had clearly been seeking to break into a new growth area in May 1829 when he sent Goodrich a list of his products, of interest as showing the range of sizes on offer at such an early date (Figure 14). Goodrich now visited Fox's Derby works and inspected the machines, noting in particular one destined for a Berlin firm. On his return he drew up, in collaboration with Maudslay, Son & Field a set of rules for the care of boilers, which were printed and distributed by the Admiralty.

By October 1830 the Portsmouth Boiler House was now at the stage where the skylights were ready for glazing, and the procurement of the machinery and fittings was imminent. Shearing, bending and punching machines were the essential tools for boiler-making, also forges and furnaces (Figure 15). New lathes were required for the Millwrights' Shop, and Goodrich thought that those made for Devonport (see p.29) might be diverted to Portsmouth. The types of furnaces required were one of the areas where Goodrich was to rely on the advice and experience of Maudslay's.[7]

Goodrich was obviously a mechanical man, but Byam Martin was also clearly seen at the time as a man sympathetic to new technology. For instance the Cornish inventor, Richard Trevithick, now completely strapped for money, wrote to the Comptroller recommending the adoption of his type of engine, and asking for the loan of a vessel to be fitted with his machinery. The Admiral judged that private firms would have taken it up had it been promising, and passed the matter to Goodrich for his opinion, who was unenthusiastic, both about the design of the engine and its tubular boilers and surface condensers.

Towing was the principal naval use for steamers at this date, and Goodrich investigated the performance of the Clyde tugs: these boats could make 5 knots against a moderate tide and breeze hauling a 500 or 600 ton ship, 4½ knots with one of 1200 tons. A glimpse of how these first steamers were maintained by the Yards when the manufacturers' mechanics were not in attendance is given by a letter of September 1830 from Hearle & More's Devonport Foundry. This firm were the contractors for iron and metal castings for the Yard, and complained about the extra trouble and expense they had been put to by work for steam vessels, which had not been originally contemplated:

> Such is the necessity of the work, that patterns are frequently sent us from the Dock Yard at night, when the people leave work, our men are employed the whole of the night at extra wages in order to get the articles in on the following morning.

The wooden patterns, replicas of the components around which moulds of sand were formed to cast them in metal, would have been produced by the millwrights of the Yard. Millwrighting at the time was the leading-edge job, equivalent to information technology today: many of the great nineteenth-

15 A machine for punching boiler plates by Maudslay, Son and Field, illustrated in *Buchanan's Machinery*, edited by George Rennie and published in 1841.

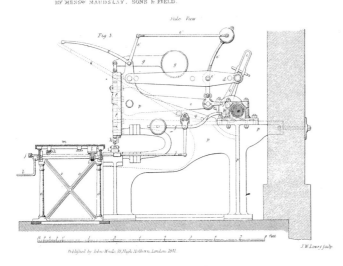

century engineers, such as Fairbairn, began their careers as millwrights. Fairbairn's classic exposition of millwrighting covers, among much else, wheels and pullies, the geometry of gear wheels, calculations of strain and torsion in shafting, and the mechanism of couplings and clutches, as well as the theory and operation of the steam engine and the construction and machinery of all types of mill building. Here was the knowledge required to successfully oversee the introduction of steam power into the Navy and maintain its operational efficiency.[8]

The logic of the situation meant that the creation of a new Department solely concerned with steam machinery and all its ramifications, under the charge of a suitably qualified man, clearly could not long be delayed, and in November 1830 George Smith took the opportunity to resurrect his papers of 1825 and send them to Byam Martin with a covering letter:

> I am unwilling to delay doing this any longer as I find that our Steam Vessels are likely to involve the Board in great trouble and responsibility....Steam Navigation is becoming every day more an object of attention with the Public...practice has proved what was before only theoretically demonstrable, and men of scientific acquirements and mechanical information are now able to speak decidedly on points which were before left in doubt...the Reports which have (particularly of late after long voyages) been made of the state of the Engines and defects in their Boilers, are circumstances which lead me to suggest the idea, of having at this office a Surveyor or Superintendent of Steam Engines...quite distinct from and totally unconnected with the department of the Surveyor of the Navy...

He suggested Goodrich, naturally enough, as the man for the job, bringing him from Portsmouth to London. However, such a position would definitely not carry with it a seat on the Navy Board. The mechanicals would have to be kept in a properly subordinate position, for if they were allowed a position of equality their monopoly of technical expertise would lead to their 'gaining overwhelming influence, and obviating all the good that their confined and subordinate situation is likely to produce': the rank should be equivalent to that of a Surveyor of Buildings, an attitude that would be familiar to Engineer Officers a century later.

The Comptroller agreed with all this, while being much concerned at the lack of in-depth knowledge of machinery at present current in the Service. The engineers were for the most part mere engine-minders, with little grasp of the construction of the machinery, which was naturally enough badly kept. His answer to this, however, was the authoritarian one of issuing improved regulations (as the instructions regarding the care of boilers drawn up by Goodrich and Maudslay's) rather than instituting a proper educational regime for technical workers. He could consequently see no merit in appointing another highly qualified engineer at Portsmouth in the event of Goodrich being removed to London.

The Admiral had other, perhaps more powerful, motives for keeping mechanics subordinate and in carefully controlled quantities:

> Let us be very careful how we multiply manufactures in our Dock Yards — Such an arrangement may at critical moments be subversive of all order & the ruin of the country —

Manufacturers (Mechanics) are remarkable for their extortionate demand for wages and for discontented & disloyal feelings — let us take heed how we introduce any such large establishments in the yards.

Byam Martin, a true representative of the interests of his class, had loaned workers from the Royal Yards to help break the 1825 strike of the Shipwrights Union. During the Napoleonic Wars the Yard workforce had steadily consolidated its position, but in time of peace the Navy Board naturally had an advantage, and coping with the demands of the artificers, who had shown themselves capable of considerable militancy in the past, was nothing new. The irruption of the industrial proletariat, whose 'vile' and 'insolent' disposition was described by the Admiral to his old friend and shipmate King William IV, would pose another set of problems entirely, which the administrators had not the slightest desire to get to grips with.[9]

The self-evident necessities of the Service, however, enabled Byam Martin to play a decidedly progressive role in the industrialisation of the Yards: in his comments on Smith's papers he stated that:

> I am much inclined to question the policy, or economy, of being our own manufactories, but if there is any exception to this rule it must be with regard to Steam Vessels and it was under this impression that I proposed a Boiler house at Portsmouth now finished, and at the same time suggested having similar Buildings at Plymouth and Woolwich.

The structure of the Portsmouth Boiler House was completed by November 1830, when Goodrich visited Maudslay's factory to inspect their boilermaking equipment, with the intent of ordering similar installations. He sketched two types of plate-heating furnace, one for heating the edges of plates prior to bending them (Figure 16).

Also required would be a large fly press for bending and stamping copper, and a smaller one for punching. The actual shaping of the plates was done on bending frames supplied with a variety of formers for different contours. There was still a place for unskilled labour in Maudslay's establishment; the actual cutting of the plates was done with a hammer and chisel 'by Irish Labourers – any Labourer when the Plate is properly marked can do this'.

At the end of the year Goodrich informed Martin that Maudslay, Son & Field's estimates had arrived. The innovative nature of this machinery may be judged by Goodrich's comment that it was very difficult to estimate accurately for

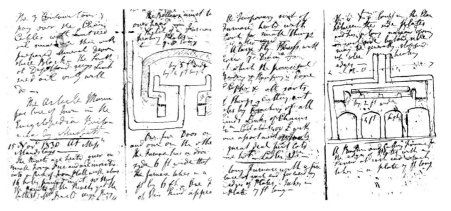

16 These sketches, made by Goodrich in Maudslay's factory, are the only visual record of the fittings intended for the Boiler House. *(Goodrich Collection, Science Museum, GOOD/B/70)*

17 The north elevation of the Millwright's and Engine Maker's Shop (1 on plan, below), now offices. The workshops, including the Smithery of the 1790s, to the west of the Camber leading to Bentham's North Basin have been demolished. (© Crown Copyright. NMR AA045913)

18 Portsmouth Metal Workshops in 1831. (Re-drawn from TNA ADM 140/335/19)

Key
1   Millwright's Shop
2   Boiler Shop
3   Smith's Shop
4   Metal Stores
5   Iron Store
6   Coal Cellar
7   Firehearth Shop
8   Smith's Shop
9   Iron Store
10 Coal Yard

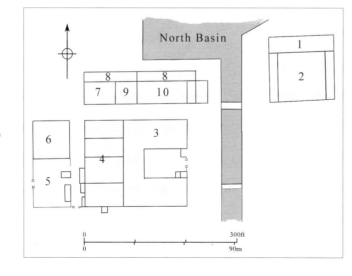

'new work and Inventions of this kind' and that Maudslay's should not be held to the exact figures. The whole order was a sizeable one,[10] and, apart from the immediate financial reward, the firm had benefited from becoming closely associated with the Navy Board in the most significant development of the early 1830s.

The shearing and punching machines were driven by a 6hp steam engine in the adjacent Millwrights' and Engine Makers' Shop. It was originally proposed that duplicate boiler plates ready punched be made and stored, but Goodrich thought this inadvisable given the constantly changing nature of boiler designs. The building was not apparently completely finished till 1832, when a chimney was ordered to be built for it. This was designed by George Taylor, who probably had been responsible for the whole building.

Unlike the Block Mills, this pioneering building was soon made obsolete by the development of the Steam Basin in the next decade which substantially redeveloped Bentham's North Basin and led to the infilling of the Camber that separated this building from the now demolished and forgotten Smithery and Metal Mills. A plan of January 1831 shows it as an oblong Millwrights' Shop with two projecting wings enclosing a yard designated as the Boiler Shop, the standard design for an eighteenth-century smithery (Figure 18). By 1849 the whole block was infilled and described as a Smithery (see Figure 59); by 1858 the Millwrights' Shop had become the Engineer's Office, and the rest of the building a Gally Shop, for the manufacture and maintenance of ships' hearths. By 1878 the whole building was set aside as offices, a function it still performs (Figure 17).[11] As it was the first purpose-built workshop connected with steam engines to be built in a Naval Yard, its historic importance, in spite of all subsequent alterations, can hardly be exaggerated.

—∿—

Notes:

[1] In 1761 the bottom of the frigate HMS *Alarm* was experimentally sheathed with copper, secured by iron bolts, with a certain degree of success, limited by the rapid oxidisation of the fastenings, and by 1783 a satisfactory material for the bolt had been devised. R J B Knight, 'The Introduction of Copper Sheathing into the Royal Navy, 1779-1786', *Mariner's Mirror*, 1973, pp.299-309

[2] This complex was demolished following the redevelopment of the north end of the Yard in the late 1840's, and the relocation of the Mills at Chatham.

[3] Coad, (1989), p.234. The introduction of iron ships, which could not be sheathed with copper because of the electrolytic action set up, drastically reduced the need for copper sheeting, and the Chatham Mills were adapted and enlarged as a Smithery, which was demolished in 1984 after the closure of the Yard.

[5] W L Clowes, *The Royal Navy*, (London, 1900), vol.5, p.13. R S Fitzgerald, 'The anatomy of a Victorian crane: the Coburg Boiler Shop and its technological context', *Industrial Archaeology Review*, XII, 2, Spring 1990, pp.185-204.

[6] ADM 92/2, ADM 106/3239, BL Add. 41397, ff. 307v,308r; GOOD B/59, ADM 106/1907.

[7] ADM 106/3239, GOOD B/65, GOOD B/75, ADM 106/1907, ADM 92/4, ADM 106/1908, ADM 106/1529, GOOD B/66, ADM 106/1910, GOOD B/67, GOOD A/1432, GOOD B/70.

[8] ADM 106/1649, ADM 106/1667, ADM 106/1545; W Fairbairn, *Treatise on Mills and Millwork*, 2 vols., (London, 1863).

[9] ADM 106/1638, GOOD A/1575, Lambert, (1991), p.167; *Journals and Letters of Sir T. Byam Martin*, vol. 3, (London), p.117.

[10]

	£
1) Large fly press for bending Chimneys, and the corners of Boilers as well as for bending Heavy Work Generally	300
2) A smaller fly press for punching holes in Boiler Plates where the Machine Press cannot be brought to bear	110
3) Machinery complete for punching Boiler Plates similar to that used at Lambeth	500
4) A machine for shearing the edges of Plates after Punching	400
5) A middle sized cutting and bending machine	85
6) The Iron work for a large Furnace for heating Boiler plates	78
7) The Iron Work for a Furnace for heating the Edges and Middle of Plates	56
8) 2 Drilling machines	160
Total	1,689

[11] ADM 106/1638, GOOD B/70, ADM 12/262, ADM 140/555/19, GOOD A/1621, ADM 1/3501.

CHAPTER 3

Retrenchment in the Name of Reform

Cutbacks

Despite the encouraging start the whole project for creating facilities for the Steam Navy was about to be seriously affected. On 25 November 1830, following the fall of the Tory administration, Sir James Graham had become First Lord of the Admiralty. Devoted to suppressing, in the name of economy, real or imagined extravagances in the public sector, he proposed to act with speed. What was a more natural target than a new and rapidly expanding dockyard facility, demanding experienced technical personnel? The Navy Board, aware that their bureaucratic organisation was at the head of Graham's hit list, could see what was immediately proposed, and, in an attempt to consolidate Goodrich's position, asked him if he had any objection to moving to London, possibly at an increased salary. Once ensconced in their offices at Somerset House Goodrich would probably have been safe until Graham's efforts to abolish the Navy Board had been successful.

Goodrich's journal shows that he was apparently unaware of the threat to his position and all that was implied in the way of undermining the progress that had been started by Bentham, who had been himself, ironically, a stern advocate of efficiency. However, he knew about engineering and steam; there is no reason to suppose Graham knew anything about these things.

The first inkling Goodrich seems to have had that a sea change was going to occur was at the end of the year, when he received a minute not approving the purchases for the Portsmouth Boiler House, and asking for a report on the size of Maudslay's estimate. He reported that the estimates were reasonable, and had the *chutzpah* to ask for an additional drilling machine as well. He was also asked whether there was a necessity for the size of the present staff at the Wood Mills, Metal Mills, and the Millwrights' Shop, and to select men from among their number as staff for the Boiler House. Fifty-one men were currently employed at the Metal Mills, the lowest number practicable to carry out the work; there were 49 men in the Millwrights' Shop, comprising 18 millwrights, 16 engine makers, 8 smiths and hammermen, and 7 engine keepers. Two of the smiths and three hammermen had been much occupied in boilermaking, and would be suitable for the new building, but they would need to be replaced. In short, the establishment needed to grow rather than shrink.

The Admiral Superintendent of the Yard supported Goodrich, adding for good measure that contract buying rather than in-house work was frequently a false economy. There had recently been an example of this; the lack of facilities had meant that work could not be done on the engine and boilers of *Hermes*. It was suggested that she be sent to Woolwich, but this was countermanded, and workmen from Maudslay's were sent down from London. They found the boilers to be in such a state as to be unrepairable and the ship had to be sent to Woolwich after all.[1]

The first blow fell on 21 January 1831. An Admiralty letter announced that

> His Majesty's Government are determined that all the Public Departments shall be reduced to as small a scale of salaried officers as can be consistent with the nature and quantity of business to be performed…without regard to the increasing amount of superannuations that may in consequence be entailed…

Posts were permanent, but pensions ceased with the death of the recipient.

The course of events was, of course, to impose its own logic of development, posts in engineering had to be established and pensions still had to be paid. To expedite this decision many Masters of Trades were to be dispensed with. Portsmouth was the only yard to have Masters of mechanical trades, all to go: those of the Wood Mills (there was, however, a change of mind about this post), the Metal Mills, and Millwrights. Goodrich was informed that the Navy Board had told Graham, off the record, that they considered him indispensable and would like him at Somerset House, but, seeing the way the wind was blowing, he hinted that as he was now 58 retirement on a satisfactory pension might be the best solution.

Byam Martin (himself a marked man, a Tory under a Whig administration, among other things) protested to no effect at this initial measure of Graham's. He wrote to him that the branches of the Engineers and Mechanists Department required very able and efficient superintendence, particularly with the new facilities about to come on-line at Portsmouth. The next day Byam Martin saw Goodrich, who naturally urged the necessity of retaining these key personnel. Goodrich recorded the ensuing conversation:

> …the Admiralty…had determined on the dismissal of these Persons…without consulting him [i.e. Byam Martin]…he had urged all he could about retaining me, but it was not listened to. I explained that I hoped for his good offices in respect to myself he told me not to depend the least upon him he had no weight he could do nothing not for want of will but want of power — Afterwards saw Mr Smith who told me the matter had been urged last night when the Estimates were out, about retaining me, but my name was left out, they could not prevail…The Comptroller saw me by chance and…told me I had better see Sir James Graham myself and tell him that I had spent all my Life in the Service and…I expected they would make some provision

for me. I replied that I expected provision of course. My good Sir said he dont depend upon any thing of course, there is no telling what they may do…

Goodrich could not get to see Graham, but was told that his pension would be £400. Graham's secretary did not think the decision would be altered, nor was it. A week later Goodrich went to the Navy Board and found his name was down in the list of approved pensioners at £400, two-thirds of his salary. He had been appointed Engineer & Mechanist on 3 May 1814, and his pay was the equivalent of the Captain of a third rate. His draughtsman, William Head, had been appointed on 10 May 1814, on £250. The other heads of departments at Portsmouth were superannuated: Peter Holmes (Master of Wood Mills, appointed 1 August 1828) got £166, two-thirds salary; Hamlet Vernon (Master of Metal Mills, appointed 28 May 1814) £125, half salary; William Kingston (Master of Millwrights, appointed 28 May 1814) £104, five-twelfths salary.

Goodrich's future still hung in the balance. Byam Martin wrote to Graham that if Goodrich were removed an advisor on steam machinery would have to be appointed in his place:

> …a person of the highest integrity intelligence & general information, not only to advise us upon matters involving such enormous expenditure, & of such growing interest & importance, but to visit the different establishments for manufacturing Steam Engines, Chain Cables &c &c — by which a person holding such a situation is brought into direct contact with those whose employment or otherwise must depend upon the immovable integrity of the servant of the Crown entrusted with such a duty — upon his fidelity and judgment the efficiency of our Steam fleet (if I may use the expression) will depend — as well as the judicious or injudicious expenditure of thousands & thousands of pounds.

Kingston, the late Master Millwright, had been suggested for this job, but Byam Martin thought him unsuitable. Reading between the lines, Kingston was too much a man of the workshops.

On a further visit to Somerset House Goodrich was told that the Admiralty now wished to keep him on, but the Comptroller thought he should take the money and go. He had advised the Surveyor, Sir Robert Seppings, to do the same thing. (Seppings was to be dismissed in March 1832.) Goodrich wrote a final letter of protest against suppressing the Master Millwright and the Master of the Metal Mills, which the Navy Board entirely agreed with and sent to the Admiralty, but it was to no effect.

Things were still uncertain at the beginning of March when Goodrich wrote 'I cannot learn any thing positive about myself'. But on 12 March an Admiralty Order reduced the number of artificers and labourers in the Yards to 6,000 (a figure that the previous administration had hoped to achieve), and abolished the Masters of Trades, with the exceptions of the Master Smiths at each Yard and the Master Sailmakers at Deptford, Chatham, Portsmouth and Plymouth. They were replaced by foremen on day pay, in no case to exceed 12s 6d a day. At Portsmouth the establishments were reduced to 20 at the Wood Mills, 40 at the Metal Mills, and 40 millwrights. Three engine repairers (who repaired Yard fire engines) were allotted to Woolwich, and two founders to Portsmouth. Goodrich was

still at Portsmouth, looking over the new Boiler House, but at the end of the month he cleared his office and sent his papers out of the Yard ahead of him in a cart. In future he would work as a consultant, the next month Byam Martin wanted him to inspect steam engine factories, anticipating the career style of 160 years on.[2]

At the end of April 1831 the final costs of the building and equipping of the Boiler House (save the chimney, not yet built) were calculated as £13,990, though Maudslay's machinery had still not been authorised. That would not happen until July, doubtless reflecting Byam Martin's struggle to realise his programme in the face of Graham's resistance.

In June Goodrich was asked to advise on the supervisory appointments, and on his recommendations George Hackney, the superintendent of the Millwrights and Engine-makers was given the superintendency of the Boiler House on 12s 6d a day, with Robert Taplin, a first-class millwright, as his assistant on 7s a day. Another millwright was required for preparing working drawings, keeping accounts and stores, for 6s a day. A leading man of boilermakers, experienced in the trade, would also be required, with two boilermakers, four assistant boilermakers, and four engine makers. Additional men would need to be taken on in busy times. In spite of Graham's fixing the size of the mechanical establishments at Portsmouth in March, by September the necessities of the service had increased their number to 24 at the Wood Mills, 51 at the Metal Mills, 51 millwrights, and no less than 14 engine repairers with a junior officer over them.

Graham was soon to succeed in removing Byam Martin from the Comptrollership of the Navy, and then in abolishing the Navy Board, a measure for which he has usually been praised. The rights and wrongs of this decision form no part of this study, but the lack of forward planning seen in his treatment of the key growth point of the Navy's technical back-up is self-evident. Not surprisingly, Goodrich was not inclined to put himself out as a consultant for Graham's Board of Admiralty, and 1834 found him moved to Portugal, where his knowledge of the latest technology must have made him a very big frog in a small pond. He remained there till his death in 1847.[3]

The final word on Graham's dealing with the skilled personnel of the Yards can be left to Byam Martin. A clear-sighted old Tory, he recognised the realities of the class struggle and could see that when a national emergency arose then payback time would come (a fact he would never express publicly lest it put ideas into the heads of any imperceptive labourers):

> …having destroyed the machinery by which the civil branch of the service was worked, the next effort of Sir James Graham was, with the same indiscriminate hand, to sweep away many of the most valuable of our artificers, and to disgust all who remained in the Dockyards….The Government may grind the men down in peace, but when war comes…I venture to predict that the injured shipwrights will paralize the country until they obtain redress, and security against the ungenerous & fickle treatment of every new Board of Admiralty…three hundred of our best shipwrights & Anchor Smiths lately discharged are employed in Toulon and Brest Yard, and probably many more at the other French ports. Our friend Nicholas of Russia has also gladly availed himself of the services of active intelligent men who,

scorning to become inmates of our poor Houses in England, find a protecting encouraging liberal welcome into the service of foreign princes.[4]

Graham's achievements in downsizing his workforce make him appear a curiously modern figure, the only note that now rings untrue is that far from inflating his own salary as a reward, he actually slightly reduced it. *Autres temps…*

Operating on a shoestring: Portsmouth and Devonport

Graham's attacks had one obvious consequence, in that the limited facilities at Portsmouth and Plymouth struggled to function as the twin foci of the nascent steam navy's industrial infrastructure, sustained by the expertise of the private yards.

Goodrich's Boiler House at Portsmouth soon received its first orders, for both marine and dockyard use. By this time 14 steamships had been supplied to the Navy. Boilers for *Columbia* (which had been built at Woolwich in 1829) were to be assembled from plates supplied by a contractor (many proved to be defective or of inferior quality when they eventually arrived), and a new pair for the second 30hp engine in the Wood Mill were to be made on the pattern of those provided in 1825 for the other engine, at a total cost of £1,102. The labour costs were estimated at only £151, reflecting the small number of men employed. However, the established staff were too small in number to carry out the quantity of work visualised, and clearly needed the training afforded by working with experts. In December 1831 a student at the School of Naval Architecture, gaining work experience at Maudslay's, was authorised to engage eight boilermakers with eight assistants to go to Portsmouth to assist in the work for *Columbia*. In the end six, with two assistants, were sent in the following March.

By February 1834 the Foreman of Millwrights was greatly in need of clerical assistance, as his time was fully occupied in keeping accounts, writing notes for men to draw stores, making drawings of patterns and other essential activities.

The workload of the Boiler House may have been affected by the machinery procurement policies initiated by Goodrich. In October 1831 the firms of Boulton & Watt, Butterley Iron Company, Morgan, and Barnes & Miller had been asked to indicate on what terms they would supply new marine engines to the Admiralty provided they kept them in repair (this would include the boilers); an annual payment for the use of the engines and boilers was suggested. The firms could nominate their own engineer to look after the engine, who would be paid directly by the Government.

Boulton & Watt declined directly. Barnes & Miller responded by offering to keep the engines in perfect repair for a lump sum, in preference to an annual payment, though a second engineer would need to be provided, and extensive repairs must be done by the firm 'as we would not wish our engines to fall into the hands of strangers' and the replacement of the boilers after fair wear and tear was to be at the cost of the Admiralty. The offer would run for a sufficient number of years to give the system a fair trial. Sir Robert Seppings' successor as Surveyor of the Navy, Sir William Symonds, wished this policy to be pursued, following the examples of private companies, who considered maintenance by contract to be the most economical plan.

After some negotiations in January 1835 Seaward's finally agreed to supply a pair of engines with copper boilers for £6,000, to be maintained at an annual rate of £4 10s per hp, the lowest rate any manufacturer had offered. The rate would be increased to £5 were the boilers to be of iron, which had a shorter life. Symonds was all in favour of the adoption of copper boilers, noting that the boilers (which had been made from copper at Portsmouth) of *Confiance* and *African*, completed at Woolwich in 1827 and 1825 respectively, had lasted till 1834 without needing any repair. Iron ones only lasted three or four years.

The maintenance arrangement for new engines and boilers lasted until February 1837, when Symonds compiled the costs of construction and wear and tear of steamers to date. The first three classes had not been in existence long enough for any accurate maintenance figures to be prepared, but the fifth class of eight vessels had been in service for nearly 10 years. Their machinery had cost £9 16s per hp per year; the contractors who had recently supplied copper boilers to *Volcano* engaged to keep them in complete repair for nine years at £4 10s per hp, while the cost for *Megaera* with iron boilers was £5 10s per hp. No such requirement had been stipulated for the new tenders for the machinery of *Cyclops*, a change in policy that Symonds found regrettable.

Apart from the Boiler House and the Metal Mills, Portsmouth's resources were still very restricted. In November 1835 the Admiral Superintendent reported that the Foundry was on so limited a scale that they could not cast a spare spur wheel for the pumping machinery, and the usual standby of the Yard, Mr Rennie (no relation to *the* Rennies) of Portsea, did the job. On the recommendation of the Shipwrights a new furnace was installed in the Metal Mills to cope with future eventualities. The Boiler House itself had limitations. Perhaps with the departure of Maudslay's hired men some vital expertise had been lost. In December 1836 the defects of *Pluto's* boilers could not be properly made good there.

Another consequence of Graham's cutbacks was the inevitable pressure that bore down on those responsible for nurturing this new technology. By 1838 Robert Taplin, who had apparently succeeded George Hackney as Superintendent of the Boiler House after a short time, was carrying an enormous load of responsibility. Trained as an engineer by Goodrich, he had spent much time recently in drawing up plans and directing the execution of the various works connected with engineering and machinery. He supervised all Yard machinery, including the 50hp engine at the Metal Mills, the machinery for copper and iron milling, the 2 x 30hp engines at the Wood Mills, the blockmaking machinery, turnery and sawmills, the pumps, the 6hp ropery engine with tarring machinery and cordage machinery, a 2hp engine at the Smithery, with drilling and blowing machinery, and a 6hp engine at the Millwrights' Shop, with lathes and boring mills. As well as all this, he was frequently called on to repair the machinery of steam vessels.

All this in Goodrich's day had been supervised by Goodrich on £600, a draughtsman on £250, a clerk on £150, the Master of the Wood Mills on £250, the Master of the Millwrights on £250, and 2 foremen on £160 each. Taplin, now in Goodrich's old position of Engineer & Mechanist, was on £200; following representations his salary was raised to £250. Rarely can a man in such a responsible job have been so overworked and underpaid.

The Foreman in Charge of the Metal Mills, John Newey, on £200, was similarly burdened. He was in charge of over 60 men employed in melting, refining and rolling copper, and manufacturing various kinds of wrought iron for smiths' work, as well as cast iron articles for winches, steering gear and Yard machinery. There had been a great increase in the demand for metal castings,[5] and in order to meet this the men had worked an extra three hours daily from April to November 1838, from 4 a.m. to 6 p.m. Only 30 tons of metalwork had been made in 1834 and 1836, while in 1839 it was to be over 100 tons, exclusive of the sheathing nail department, which produced 50 tons annually.[6]

The Admiralty were still concerned about maintaining unnecessary staff, and enquired about the numbers of millwrights employed. The Portsmouth officers responded by stating that the establishment, far from being excessive, needed to be built up:

> …from the great increase of Millwrights Labor in general, and Steam Engine Work not only in this Yard, but in the Victualling Department and Steam Vessels…we beg to state that one apprentice to six men can be employed with advantage.

The Plymouth officers agreed: 'millwrights are a difficult class of workman to obtain, and Machinery is about to be increased'.[7] In 1834 George Taylor had built there a remarkably advanced form of Millwrights' Shop. This had been part of the modernisation of the Yard. In 1828 the docks there were still being pumped by horse teams, and it was suggested that a steam engine installed for this purpose might also serve to power machinery. The Millwright, Mr Neil, was the only man on the spot who could give an opinion on the matter: he estimated the probable cost as £3,500 for two engines and pumps, and £2,992 for the Engine House. One of the engines could pull carts of waste timber up the inclined plane by the North Smithery to the Chip Yard, blow the forges in the North Smithery, and power drilling machines, lathes, a boring machine and grindstones. However, the Commissioner at Devonport did not have great confidence in Neil's ability to make such important decisions, and Goodrich was accordingly sent to attend to the business. The upshot at Devonport was the decision to build a two-storey millwrights' shop next to the North Smithery. Taylor designed a two-storey building with the steam engines and boilers, together with the heavier plant, on the ground floor, and light turning and pattern-making, models and plans on the first floor (Figure 19). Patterns had previously been made in house for casting by a contractor, the rough cast components being returned to the Yard for finishing and fitting. The design was remarkably advanced, comparable with the 1840 engine factory of the Birmingham and Gloucester Railway, located at Bromsgrove (Figure 20).

Meanwhile, an important new player now entered the stage. This was Thomas Lloyd, born in 1803, who had studied at the School of Naval Architecture at Portsmouth between 1819 and 1826. He was recommended in April 1831 by Professor Inman (of *Nautical Tables* fame) to be Superintendent of Portsmouth Block Mills, an ideal appointment for familiarising himself with

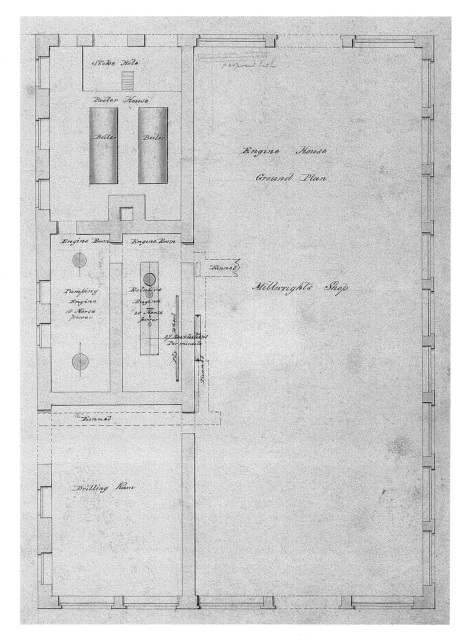

19 This 1836 drawing of the Millwrights' Shop is the earliest to be located showing the layout of an engineering shop in the Yards. The plan of the first floor of the building, which held the drawing offices, models and lathes, has not survived. *(TNA ADM 140/244). (External picture English Heritage)*

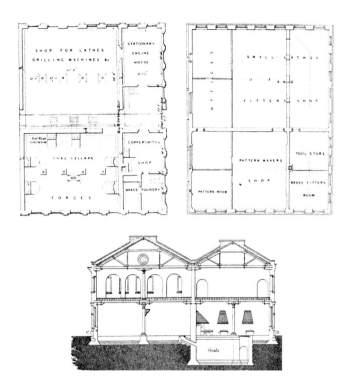

20 The Bromsgrove Workshops of the Bristol and Gloucester Railway were comparable with Taylor's Workshop at Devonport. (From W Moorson – G B W Jackson Drawings, Specifications, Qualities &c of the Bromsgrove Engine Factory, London 1840)

mechanical processes. At the same time Inman recommended Lloyd's fellow-student Jeremiah Owen for the charge of the Metal Mills, and plainly thought that highly qualified men should be masters of mechanical trades. In January 1833 Lloyd was promoted to be Inspector of Machinery at Woolwich. With two years' experience there under his belt, he was earmarked to get this second mechanical workshop off the ground. The local expertise was not up to the job; a representative of the Butterley Iron Company had complained that unnecessary and useless float gauges had been fitted to the boilers of Spitfire by the Yard men. By October 1834 granite was being delivered on the site, the contractors being Pilditch and Murch.

Another Scottish engineer, George Bathgate, had got wind of this new development. He realised that an experienced man would soon be required, and was told that in April 1835 there might be a slot for him. He duly presented himself, but no orders had been made for the Superintendent to take him on; however, he was hired, but on day pay rather than the salaried post he expected.

In July Lloyd reported on the Boulton & Watt machinery, which was ready to be forwarded, as the buildings were almost ready to receive them. The progress of the new Millwrights' Shop was slow. By December 1835 estimates were forwarded for setting boilers, and making tunnels, penstocks, engine foundations, and foundations for lathes and other machinery. Lloyd considered that the machinery on order was adequate to effect almost any repairs to steam engines, though tunnels should be provided for shafting between the rotative engine and Bentham's Smithery in case this was brought into use as part of the steam workshop, with punching and shearing machinery for boiler manufacture (though no boilermaking equipment, or practised boilermakers, had arrived by the end of 1837).

The Boulton & Watt machinery did not arrive until the end of January 1836; other equipment was on its way from Rennie's. The latter, two wall cranes and poppet heads for turning wood, was for the pattern shop on the first floor. A Hercules, a heavy hammer operated like a piledriver, in the

North Smithery was to be supplied by Rennie's with a power assist, but Lloyd thought this would be both expensive and difficult to fix. Nasmyth's eventually contracted for this job.

Staffing these two specialist workshops continued to present difficulties. Before Lloyd's arrival at Devonport, engineers from private firms working on ships' machinery had been reporting directly to Symonds. At that time there was no millwright on the books at Devonport. William Neil, who had prepared the original estimates for the building, had been Millwright and Engine Keeper, but had been promoted in 1833 to be an inferior officer as Engineer and Millwright at £160 a year and was in a supervisory job. He and Bathgate superintended the repair of Yard machinery and marine engines, with a staff of 18 smiths, three joiners and a turner working in the Millwrights' Shop (Figure 21). As Lloyd oversaw the slow kitting-out of the building he was also occupied, as he had been at Woolwich, in writing many reports on ships' machinery and, a new task, examining candidates for engineers afloat. A large proportion failed to pass his interrogations. There was no formal system of education in engineering in existence. Men were expected to pick up what they could, according to their abilities, in the workshops where they were employed. In some enterprises, such as Maudslay's, gifted men did indeed get a head start, but this was not the general case. This lack of technical education meant that many men, accustomed to work by rule of thumb and perfectly competent within a limited sphere, could not satisfy Lloyd's more rigorous demands. It will be seen that the provision of suitable personnel for this job was to cause difficulties for many years to come.

Finally, in April 1837, an engineer arrived to take charge of the steam engines, and in July the millwrights were made a separate establishment at Devonport, on Lloyd's recommendation. This had not taken place without opposition from the shipwright officers. Neil had asked to be appointed instructor to two millwright apprentices, but they opposed this, holding that they should be bound to the Master Shipwright, though instructed by Lloyd. Questions of both prestige and money were involved here: the shipwrights were defending their status in the Yards against the interloper, and the instructor received additional pay according to the number of apprentices set under him. The establishment was settled at:

Lloyd	Assistant Inspector of Machinery	£300
Neil	Engineer and Millwright	£160
Bathgate	Assistant Engineer	6s a day
1	Lathe Keeper	5s
1	First-Class Millwright	5s
2 (shortly raised to 4)	Second-Class Millwrights	4s 6d
2	Apprentices	

The management structure does not reflect the minuscule staff, but rather the number of contractors' men working on ships in the Yard who had to be supervised. Even this small number of established staff could not be found at Devonport, despite the proximity of the Cornish engine industry. Out of the four millwrights on the establishment at 4s 6d a day, only one had been procured by the end of the year.

Londoners who wished to come were to be interviewed at Woolwich. The demands imposed by the early railway industry undoubtedly contributed to the fact that skilled men were found to be just as scarce in 1839, when they were needed to cope with an increase in machinery. In January three engineers were hired to work on *Megaera*, whose condenser had become defective. One was a local man, having started as a turner at Devonport, then going to London to work for Seaward; one had been an engine maker at Patterson's, Glasgow; and the third had worked for Mr Green, Engineer and Mechanist, at Mansfield.

Lloyd next recommended the establishment of a power sawmill at Devonport, as the new engine house provided ample power to drive three circular saws and at least two frame saws, and as many grindstones as necessary. This would need to be placed close to the Millwrights' Shop, and he recommended blasting away 14 yards of rock behind the engine house. As all the machinery would be underground, the building would not need to be more than 10ft high. In January 1838 Captain Brandreth RE (the newly appointed Architect to the Admiralty), Lloyd and Admiral Warren (Admiral Superintendent at Plymouth), with the shipwright officers, viewed the site, and shortly after an estimate of £1,224 for the excavation and building works was prepared. Additional equipment was installed in the Millwrights' Shop.

It was still very difficult to attract key personnel. By July nobody had been appointed to work the large lathe in the Millwrights' Shop, and Lloyd considered that there was nobody in the Yard who could be trusted to work that valuable equipment, though the screw-cutting machine was now making nearly all the screws in the Yard, with a good operator doing work normally performed by a mechanic. He suggested that Boulton & Watt be asked to supply a qualified man, which they did: the value placed on this machine was such that he was paid 6s a day, the same rate as Bathgate.

An anonymous letter had fingered Bathgate for idleness, and Lloyd defended him, stating that he had not been hired to perform manual labour, though with the current level of work there was little for him to do. His value would be realised if Lloyd were away and Neil indisposed when steamers were under repair. Lloyd's report on this was minuted 'He will probably be removed to Woolwich when the establishment there is formed', and in fact his pay was increased the next year to 8s a day. Indeed, the falling off in work at Devonport that led to Bathgate's apparent idleness was probably due to a decision to switch scarce resources from Devonport and Portsmouth to the Thames, leading to the eclipse of the two pioneering workshops.[8]

—⁂—

Notes:
1. GOOD B/70, ADM 106/1911, ADM 106/1910.
2. ADM 1/3473, GOOD B/70, BL Add. 41399, f30r; BL Add. 41404, BL Add. 41399, ff. 34r,34v; GOOD B/71, BL Add. 41368, f. 332r.
3. ADM 106/1911, BL Add. 41368, f. 319.
4. ELL/239, ADM 1/3497; *Mechanics' Magazine*, vol. 32, 1840, p.176; ADM 1/3435; BL Add. 41375, ff. 95r,96r.
5. One borne chiefly by Portsmouth.
6. The relative importance of the Portsmouth industrial base can be seen by the fact that in the summer of 1839 the numbers of millwrights in service were as follows:

Woolwich	3
Chatham	5
Sheerness	6
Devonport	6
Portsmouth	45
Pembroke	0

7. ADM 106/1912, ADM 106/1913, ADM 1/4390, ADM 222/1, ADM 1/3475, ADM 1/3435, Institute of Mechanical Engineers, MS/233, ff. 1r-4r., ADM 222/5, ADM 222/6, ADM 1/3436, ADM 222/7, ADM 222/10, ADM 1/3409, ADM 1/3415, ADM 222/15, ADM 1/3412.
8. ADM 1/3412; Memoir of Thomas Lloyd in *Proceedings of the Institution of Civil Engineers*, 1875, pp.217-220, ADM 1/3519, ADM 222/2, ADM 222/3, ADM 1/3408, W Moorsom & G B W Jackson, *Drawings, Specification, Quantities &c of the Bromsgrove Engine Factory — Erected for the Birmingham and Gloster Railway Company*, (London, 1840); UD 012582, UD 012585, ADM 1/3418, ADM 1/3419, ADM 1/3420, ADM 1/3421, ADM 1/3424, ADM 1/3425, ADM 1/3426, ADM 1/3427, ADM 1/3412, ADM 140/244, ADM 1/3428, ADM 1/3429, ADM 1/3430.

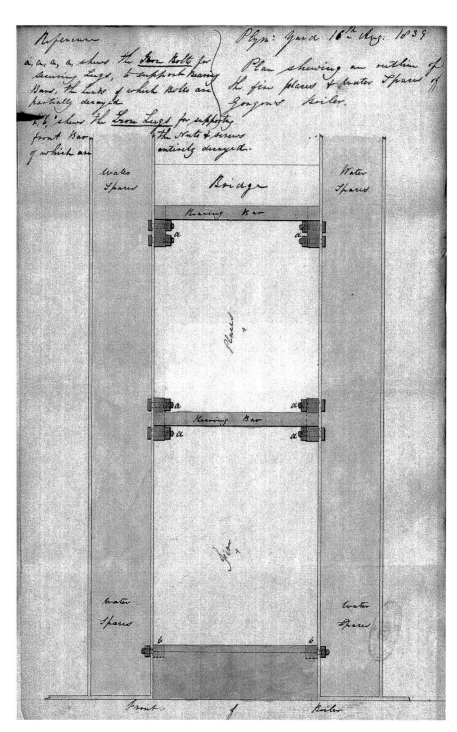

21 The relatively limited jobs that could be performed at Devonport are shown by the case of *Gorgon's* copper boiler, which had erroneously been fitted with iron bolts that had corroded. Ewart took the blame on himself, and Neil made replacement copper bolts. This drawing, probably made by Bathgate, shows the defective boiler. *(TNA ADM 1/3433)*

CHAPTER 4

Woolwich and the First Steam Factory

The Thames: a major centre of mechanical expertise

Despite the establishment of the Boiler Shop and the Millwrights' Shop at Portsmouth and Devonport, Woolwich was to become the most important Yard for the development of the Steam Navy. This was by virtue of its proximity to London rather than anything else, as its scope for expansion was limited, and silting was to plague it until its closure.

During the first half of the nineteenth century the bulk of steam engine makers and steam shipbuilders were concentrated in London and along the banks of the River Thames. The foremost shipbuilders included the firms of Ditchburn & Mare, Millwall Ironworks, John Scott Russell, the Thames Ironworks and Samuda Bros. The names associated with engine manufacture were even more prestigious: Maudslay Sons & Field, John Penn & Sons, Humphrys & Tennant, J & G Rennie. After the crash of the 1870s, a few of these firms struggled into the twentieth century before the total collapse of the shipbuilding industries on the River. Deptford Yard was already too small to have any future, so Woolwich was the obvious choice for development of the new technology, as it was close to the principal pool of skilled labour, management and design. We have already seen the difficulty that Lloyd experienced in procuring suitable staff outside London. The engineering firms could easily send their own mechanics to Woolwich (in December 1834 six Boulton & Watt employees worked for periods between 3 and 38 days on the *Carron*), or if necessary ships could be sent to their quays or hulks to be worked on. This kind of arrangement, less costly than dispatching men to Portsmouth or Devonport, was practicable only as long as the number of steamers remained very limited, and that situation was changing fast.

The rapidly increasing importance of steam power was acknowledged by an Admiralty Circular of 27 March 1835, which required captains to familiarise themselves with the engines, boilers and paddle wheels of the vessels under their command, so that with the assistance of the ship's engineers defects could be identified and rectified as soon as they occurred. Reports on the condition and use of the engines were to be sent in at the beginning of each month. On 19 May 1835 a decisive step was taken with the appointment of Peter Ewart as Chief Engineer and Inspector of Machinery at Woolwich Yard. Ewart, slightly older than Simon Goodrich, had spent a distinguished career in engineering. Born in 1767, he had been John Rennie's first apprentice, working as a millwright, then working as an engine erector for Boulton & Watt and becoming the friend of the great engineer. In 1795-6 he assisted James Watt junior in planning the Soho Foundry. This was one of the key sites of the Industrial Revolution, where complete steam engines were constructed for the first time; previously, key components had been bought in. The self-contained establishment was lit by gas before 1800, and in 1802, when its façade was illuminated to celebrate the Peace of Amiens, its gas lamps were the first to be seen in public. The manufacture of gas lighting equipment became a significant sideline, and after the Foundry completed its first marine engine in 1804, for Robert Fulton, their construction became increasingly important. After working at Soho, Ewart then abandoned engineering to run his own cotton mill in Manchester until he was recommended by the same James Watt for the post at Woolwich.

A man of nearly 70 was perhaps not the obvious choice for such a job. His obituarist noted that:

> His admiration of Watt, and his practice at Soho, inclined him to view with some degree of scepticism any innovation in the Engine, which he considered to have been almost perfected by his great master…

And added what was probably a powerful reason for his being preferred: 'for the war steamers in active service are not those in which new schemes should first be tried'. Ewart, however, was fortunate in his assistants. In January 1833 Lloyd had been promoted to Woolwich as Inspector of Steam Machinery; John Kingston came with him as Assistant Inspector. Lloyd worked closely with Symonds, whose hostility to steam power may well have been exaggerated by later commentators. He suggested that Lloyd keep a journal showing every work performed on a steamer, and on the departure of each vessel compiling a table of information, with comments on its performance.[1]

Lloyd set about accumulating information about his new province. Contractors were to send him the costs of different parts of engines and boilers for him to collate, and the logs of all steamers were to be sent to Woolwich for the extraction of information on the times the engines were run. Together with Kingston, he reported to Symonds on new types of engine, various mechanical failures, and other innovations such as Grant's condenser. After Lloyd's departure for Devonport, Kingston remained behind as his assistant.[2]

Ewart, like Goodrich, was entrusted with a brief to keep in touch with the latest developments by personal visits to manufacturers. Correspondence from the first year of his appointment shows how dependent Woolwich was on Boulton & Watt and Maudslay, Son & Field to function at all. Maudslay's took the engines and boilers out of *Blazer* and fixed them in *Echo*, and repaired the engines of *Firebrand* and adjusted them to take the new boilers that had been built at Portsmouth.

It will be no surprise, therefore, to learn that Ewart's old firm, Boulton & Watt, had a considerable hand in getting Woolwich off the ground as the first substantial home of the Steam Navy. This would have been inevitable anyway at this stage, as (counting the packet boats, shortly to be added to the Admiralty's responsibilities) they had already supplied the majority of the engines operated by the Navy.[3] But Ewart was not in the pocket of his old employers: he wrote reprovingly to James Brown, who ran the London end of the business, that he had been told that a boiler was ready at Soho for the *Carron*, but that Watt was now fobbing him off, promising him one in an advanced state of construction.[4]

At first Ewart acted, apparently, as little more than a coordinator of the requirements of the Navy and outside suppliers. Until suitable premises were supplied and tooled up he could do little more, though there was a very limited repair capacity, and a stock of spare parts was maintained. For instance, when *Comet* required new paddle wheels and engine parts, some were supplied by Boulton & Watt and others were put together from parts in store at the Yard. Ewart's initial staff was minute: one first-class millwright on 5s a day, and two second-class millwrights on 4s 6d a day. The first-class millwright was continuously employed in attending to the steam engines and boilers in the Smithery, whilst the second-class men attended to more routine tasks such as the repair of cranes, weighbridges and smithery machinery, and the adjustment of saws for cutting copper, machinery for rabbeting deals, and so on. Even commonplace tools, such as could be procured locally, were sent from Birmingham: chipping hammers, straight drill braces, taps and dies, screw bolts, screw rivets, pins and keys, calipers, and crank drill braces. Simple components that might have been fabricated in the yard, such as furnace bars and air pump rods, were also ordered. We have seen that some basic parts had been made there some 10 years earlier; presumably the increasing workload had now become too much for the existing facilities, whose expansion could not now long be delayed.[5]

The key to the development of Woolwich as the Navy's first steam factory was an increasing failure to deliver by the private firms, largely through very bad labour relations. In July 1836 Symonds visited the works of Miller, Ravenhill & Co. and Seawards. He found the men at the latter still on strike, and the former works disorganised as a result of a recent stoppage. As a consequence further time would be needed to complete the engines of *Blazer*. On October 1836 he wrote the following memorandum:

The endless delays to which His Majesty's Steam Vessels are subjected owing to a dependence upon private Individuals who have manufactured the Engines, Boilers and Wheels of those Vessels, which owing to the disputes that frequently occur between them and their Workmen, and also demands upon them which they cannot fulfil, has caused the greatest inconvenience and in fact embarrassment....The necessity for sending His Majesty's Steamers to those private Establishments and detaching Workmen from Woolwich Yard to assist in placing the Engines Boilers &c and the probability that the Post Office Steamers will shortly be made over to the Admiralty which I believe will nearly double the difficulty already experiencing. I am tempted to urge in the strongest terms the paramount necessity for forming a

Government Establishment in some convenient situation where Engines, Boilers, Wheels and every thing connected with Steam Navigation might be performed without interruption.[6]

He had inspected the Deptford yard of the General Steam Navigation Company, which, although on an inconvenient site and poorly arranged, maintained a fleet of 43 steamers. The workforce of 200 could shift a set of boilers in nine days, place engines and boilers in a ship in a month, ready for service, far quicker than had ever been done for the Royal Navy. Despite the exemplary performance of this firm, Symonds was increasingly dissatisfied with the dilatoriness of private manufacturers. Maudslay's had been working on *African* for more than six months, and when the ship had been sent to the City Canal at the request of the firm there was nobody there to take charge of her. He suggested Deptford as the location for a similar type of Yard reserved for the use of the Steam Navy; men might be drafted in from the other Yards to form the establishment. Ships should be classified according to their horsepower and standardised components held and ships of a similar class should be on the same station with commonality of spares.

The suggestion was rapidly acted on. Ewart wrote on 10 January 1837 that Taylor had prepared plans and estimates for 'erecting Buildings at Woolwich Yard for the purpose of making & repairing Engines Boilers &c for Steam Vessels and...altering certain buildings at Deptford for the same purpose'.[7] As the basin at Deptford, however, would not admit even the second class of steamers unless their paddles were removed, that Yard was clearly a non-starter.

The steam factory raised new problems of factory planning. Smitheries had traditionally been placed behind building slips, so that the components could be easily moved out to the ships lying in frame. A steam factory's function was to build and repair boilers, dismantle, repair, and reassemble engines, and make spare parts. However, boilers and engines were not placed in ships before they were launched, but as they lay alongside a sheer-hulk or, preferably, in a basin. It was the possession of basin accommodation, with the potential for its increase, as well as the location, that ensured Woolwich would be first off the ground (Figure 22).

A steam factory, then, had to lie alongside a basin, which itself would need to be equipped with sheers and cranes, and be deep

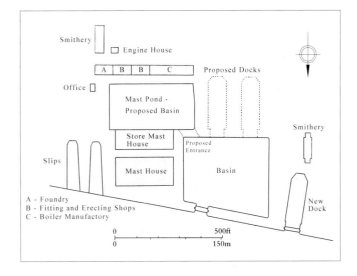

22 Note the Smithery behind the dock (the ill-fated concrete dock) for shipbuilding purposes. The suitability of the Mast Pond for conversion into a Basin beside the Factory is evident. *(Redrawn from TNA ADM 140/1153)*

enough to accommodate steamers of foreseeable draught. It had to be near enough to the basin to reduce transport of very heavy items, yet not so close as to provide inadequate working space. Perhaps even more important, it needed to be planned internally to allow easy movement of large pieces of machinery from one workshop to the other, to provide ample space for the machine tools that could be foreseen, and to allow for future contingencies.

Taylor, however, was not the man to produce a groundbreaking design. If his rambling quasi-autobiography is anything to go by, he had little interest in industrial planning. Though, as no plan survives of the original Soho Foundry, it is hard to determine what precedents there were for process-flow planning in a factory of this type, or if this was grasped as a concept. He was, however, one of the pioneers of iron construction. His mill and bakery at the Royal Clarence Yard at Gosport, dating from 1828-30, were successful and interesting buildings, combining cast-iron columns with timber joists and introducing as an arch a cast-iron curved beam, a device he was to use again at Devonport. However, these were well-established building types, and no new thinking about functional planning was required. The layout of his factory allowed for very limited communication between the various shops, expansion being allowed for, as noted above, only by constructing a duplicate building. The ergonomic potentialities offered by the space between the two buildings were not recognised, and it would be another decade before that principle was grasped. Though the drawbacks of the plan were soon recognised at Woolwich, the design was to persist and have unfortunate effects on the planning of the Yards for the next 20 years. With so many new problems having to be addressed simultaneously, probably the internal planning of factories seemed a secondary matter to everybody concerned.[8]

Taylor's design for the Factory was to be his last work for the Admiralty. He was censured for ordering extensive works at Woolwich river wall without sanction, and for submitting incorrect estimates. He resigned on 14 August 1837 in a huff:

> …my zeal to perform great additional Services not strictly within my Duty, for which I flattered myself I should derive Credit, & in which I have effected great Savings, appears, by a most extraordinary Perversion to lead to the loss of my Office…

Other factors were at work as well, as he complained. He was considered a Tory under a Whig Board, and Captain Brandreth of the Royal Engineers, appointed as his successor as Architect in November, with a salary made up to £600, was engaged to the niece of Lord Dalmeny, the Civil Lord, who was ultimately responsible for building works. But there was more to it than that. There was a growing dissatisfaction with the design and planning of dockyard works by people without the special qualifications required. Shipwrights had long had a hand in building design, though precise attributions have not yet been untangled.[9] The appointment of a Royal Engineer was clearly a rational decision to take: that it did not lead to the economies that had been expected was an inevitable consequence of the vast expansion of naval facilities over the next 50 years.

The Civil Lord, Dalmeny, at this time was the member of the Board of Admiralty responsible for everything to do with dockyards and buildings. A slightly later in-house account described his functions: he prepared the Naval Estimates and superintended all matters connected with finance and naval expenditure; directed all civil engineering works carried on in the Yards under the sanction of the Board; and ensured that all contracts were rigidly adhered to and all steam machinery delivered on time, and that the works in the Yards progressed in a satisfactory manner and in accordance with contract terms. He managed the Packet Service, and adjudicated all cases of pay in the Civil Department and the Yards. He also oversaw the Department of the Accountant General of the Navy, and that of the Director of Works. With such a vast range of notional responsibilities he could scarcely have an intimate knowledge of every aspect. The amount of work soon to be generated would mean that Brandreth would inevitably have largely a free hand, subject in effect only to financial constraints.[10]

Shortly before Taylor resigned, another appointment of importance was made: Captain Sir William Parry, the hydrographer and feted leader of the North-West Passage Expedition of 1819-20, became Controller of Steam Machinery and the Packet Service, a position under the immediate direction of the First Sea Lord. Although it was 'impossible to speak too highly' of Ewart's services, many matters had arisen that could be settled only by an experienced sea officer, and Ewart's steadily increasing workload had been further added to with the responsibility for the machinery of the packet boats, which had been transferred to the Admiralty, with a general renaming of all the ships. There would be plenty for an officer 'of skill & experience & with some scientific knowledge' to do. Though Parry's reputation rested on Polar exploration rather than mechanical engineering, it was doubtless thought (and, in those days when narrow specialisation was not highly esteemed, probably correctly) that a Fellow of the Royal Society would soon have a good grasp of the subject.

In the meantime, the number of firms producing engines for the Navy was increasing, and Boulton & Watt no longer predominated.[11] The same Admiralty memorandum that urged the appointment of a Controller of Steam Machinery also noted that the existing arrangements for the replacement of boilers, engines and spare parts for defective or worn-out machinery were now quite inadequate, particularly with the added responsibility for the mail packets, 'a service which brooks no delay'. Brandreth soon got into his stride, drawing up

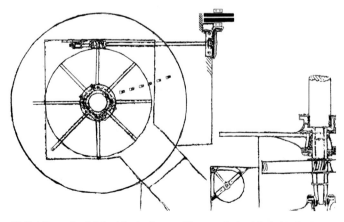

23 The Nasmyth sketch of the boring machine supplied to Woolwich Steam Factory. (*Adapted from Nasmyth's notebook, held by Institute of Mechanical Engineers*)

specimen report forms on buildings and works to be used in every yard, and taking that of Woolwich as a model.

Another Royal Engineer officer now came on the scene. Lieutenant William Denison was released by the Board of Ordnance to take charge of the new works at Woolwich in October 1837, but as the man charged with the responsibility of creating the first Steam Factory he had more on his plate than the simple mechanics of raising a structure, and Brandreth suggested his salary be raised accordingly. Denison had a previous, though slight, connection with the Admiralty. In 1834 he had been engaged in carrying out experiments on the strengths and qualities of different kinds of timber, and had been allowed specimens of foreign varieties from Chatham Yard. He was also a high-profile Royal Engineer officer, being the initial editor of the published papers of the Corps (printing the results of his experiments on wood in the fifth volume).[12]

The Steam Factory staffed and completed

The well-known London contractors Grissell & Peto, who had taken on the reconstruction of the dry dock at Woolwich following the fiasco of the experiment with concrete, gained the contract for the construction of the Factory on 9 April 1838.[13]

With the establishment of the Factory now in prospect, Ewart began to recruit a body of expertise for its management. Thomas Lloyd, earmarked in the summer of 1838 to come as his assistant, was anxious that his salary should reflect his duties, which were 'far more extensive and important' than they were when he was first sent to Devonport. Parry wondered whether the most valuable machinery at the Millwrights' Shop there, a large lathe, a planing machine and some drilling machines, might not be best moved with him to Woolwich. He left behind at Devonport six engineers, three of whom were Navy trained (and may have been former apprentices of Goodrich), two who had worked at Cornish engine factories, and one who had worked for an engineering firm in Devonport. Two additional millwrights had been examined at Woolwich and appointed at Devonport: their backgrounds were Napier's Lambeth Works and Eckford Mill, Kelso.

In November 1838 Mr Neil from Devonport Millwrights' Shop was considered by Ewart and Lloyd to be suitable for the position of superintendent of the Engineer Department at Woolwich, with Bathgate coming as his assistant. The entire original complement of senior engineers at Devonport was now proposed to be transferred to Woolwich, which indicates the great importance placed on the new establishment. In fact Neil and Bathgate remained at Devonport through 1839, superintending the erection of Rennie's sawmill machinery and the eventual installation of planing and punching machines, which gave a boilermaking capability to Devonport at last.

Also in November 1838 Lloyd recommended a batch of machinery for the Factory to be supplied by Maudslay's: punching, shearing, plate-cutting machines, a facing machine for angle iron, and two drilling machines, the same types of equipment they had supplied to the Portsmouth Boiler House. The firm had earlier been asked to supply a steam engine. James Nasmyth, after consultation with Lloyd, had sketched out a boring mill capable of dealing with cylinders up to 9ft in diameter (Figure 23).[14]

CONCRETE AT WOOLWICH

In 1834 Sir John Barrow, the Second Secretary of the Admiralty, and a supporter of Graham's measures, in listing his achievements singled out as an example of a technical advance sponsored by him the building of a concrete dock at Woolwich, which promised 'to be a most important plan, embracing both economy and despatch'. This proved to be an achievement on a par with removing the key technical personnel. The original contract with the patentee of the process, Mr Ranger, was for £4,367. By August 1835 George Taylor reported that the floor had not dried, and at a high tide the floor of the dock had been raised considerably. Granite inverts would have to be introduced at a cost of £8,603.

In December 1837 Ranger's contract was terminated and a new contract made with Grissell & Peto to complete the dock for £33,186. The costs then amounted to £51,549, and it was thought the final bill might prove to be greater than that. It was. By 1840 over £70,000 had been spent, but completion proved impossible because of strong springs, and the dock was filled up. A new one of conventional construction was begun on the south side of the basin. Ranger's contemporary use of mass concrete for the foundations for the masting sheers at Portsmouth Basin seems, however, to have been successful.

In March 1839 the site for the Foundry and Smithery was selected. The basin at that time abutted a mast pond and in April the Admiralty decided, probably on Brandreth's suggestion, to improve the layout of the Yard by turning this into an inner basin next to the Factory. The original basin was to have a dry dock constructed out of it.[15] In the same month the First Secretary to the Admiralty, Charles Wood, announced, when moving the Navy Estimates and having alluded to French dockyard expenditure, that at Woolwich 'this year we shall commence the construction of the docks, and we shall have completed, so as to be in operation before the end of the year, a large establishment for the construction & repair of boilers & steam machinery'.

By May the contractors, Grissell & Peto, were ready to complete the Smithery and the engine house. In August the work was sufficiently advanced for their tender for laying the wooden pavement in the punching and shearing shops to be accepted. In November it was decided that the machinery would be installed on Denison's plan, in preference to a scheme suggested by Ewart. Had the old millwright remained stuck in the practices of his younger days and had he any influence on Taylor's design? He would certainly have been consulted. By the end of the year blowing machines were needed and Dixon & Co. were asked the price of a portable punching machine.

In October the buildings were completed and machinery planned for. Denison had estimated the cost at £18,167. The actual cost was £16,964, largely because of the cheaper roofing material.[16] This was largely due to a suggestion made by Brandreth in January 1839 to roofing the Factory with zinc rather than lead as an economy measure. Zinc roofing had been used on the Continent for 40 years at least. Building slips at Amsterdam, Rotterdam and Flushing had been covered with it. Mosselman's zinc, from Liege, the most esteemed brand, had been imported since about 1829, and a roof of about 30,000 ft^2 had been covered at St Katherine's Docks. Zinc had also been employed at Liverpool Docks.

Nothing could be done, however, about Taylor's basic design, which had been decided on before Brandreth replaced him. But Denison improved it by lengthening it and raising the height of the roof to enable travelling cranes to be introduced (tenders for these were called for in April).[17]

It was already evident, indeed, that the facilities offered would be totally inadequate. The best that Denison could do (there being little spare land behind) was to build a parallel range, as suggested by Taylor, housing, from the east end, an engine smiths' shop 80ft long, a 30ft engine house, a punching and shearing shop of 160ft, a 45ft coppersmiths' shop, and a boilersmith's shop of 110ft. A tilt hammer was housed behind the last.

The only ergonomically efficient part of the layout was the connection between the fitting and erecting shops. The faults were clear, but, as Denison was to report in August 1841, nothing more could be done about enlarging the Factory until more land had been procured. He had suggested the previous year that it might be enlarged by appropriating part of the Mast House, but the Captain Superintendent ruled this out. The inner basin also needed to be deepened in order to get the most out of the Factory, but the extra depth would have entailed a disproportionate expense.[18]

Despite the flaws and still incomplete nature of the Factory, the complement of distinguished engineering staff had been increased by August 1840, when John Dinnen joined John Kingston (who had started as Lloyd's assistant) as Foreman of Engineers. The appointment was higher than the title suggests, they in fact joined Lloyd as assistants to Ewart. Kingston had by now made a name for himself, having been awarded a medal by the Royal Society of Arts in 1837 for the invention of the valve that bore his name, which enabled salt water to be blown down from the boilers into the sea in safety. Dinnen had been Kingston's apprentice at Portsmouth and as Chief Engineer to the *Lightning* and *African* had gained great practical experience on the management of boilers, on which he was a recognised authority. Their appointment indicates that the Factory was soon expected to get into its stride. More Royal Engineers had also been brought into Admiralty service; in 1839 Brandreth recommended Lieutenant George Burgmann for Plymouth and Captain Pooley for Portsmouth. Their services were expected to be needed for at least three years, probably five.[19]

The senior staff, as has been seen, were drawn largely from the small number of men who had been enticed into engineering for the Navy in the wake of Simon Goodrich,

THE KINGSTON VALVE

Boilers of steam vessels using sea water naturally soon accumulated a high concentration of salt. Every few hours, to get rid of this, the bulk of the water was blown out into the sea through a pipe leading to a cock near the keel of the ship. Goodrich stated in 1829 that such means had been used for several years in Government ships, but that he considered the regular changing of a fifth of the water by Maudslay & Field's Changing Pump, as used in *Lightning*, to be a safer method, as sometimes the stop-cock could not be closed, and then the fires had to be drawn to prevent serious accident. However, around 1832 John Kingston designed a valve that could be operated manually from within the ship (Figure 148). This had been fitted to 15 Navy steamers and two packet boats by 1836, with great success.

supplemented by a few trained in the School of Naval Architecture and some from private firms. Craftsmen and labourers now had to be recruited on a far larger scale than had sufficed for the two pioneering workshops, and they had to be offered a deal comparable with the other firms operating on the river. Captain Parry had concluded by October 1839 (by which time the repairing of boilers was about to commence) that though the market price would have to be paid, 'we ought…to get the same work out of them which is required in private manufactories, whereas I believe the Dockyard Hours and Regulations would not produce much above half, certainly not two thirds of the work'. The Captain Superintendent, Sir Phipps Hornby, agreed that the Factory would have to be run on lines dissimilar from the rest of the Yard:

> …a large body of men [will be] brought into the Yard wholly unaccustomed to all its existing Rules and Regulations, and which indeed, do not seem applicable to the peculiar situation in which the men will be placed…

He suggested that:

> …with the high Wages these men will require, the Hours of Work will not be confined to those of the other Artificers of the Yard; & under this impression, the Hours of attendance and conditions are assimilated (as nearly as possible as the differences between a Royal Dock Yard and Private Premises will admit), to those I find in practice at the Establishments of Messrs. Seaward & Co., Messrs. Maudslay & Co., & others in the vicinity of London, in the hope that good workmen will the more readily join the Service, & be more likely to remain, where most of their old customs and habits are respected.

He reckoned on a total establishment of 367, including 10 apprentices and 15 labourers to every 100 artificers. The Factory men were to be segregated from the Yard men as much as possible, being allowed in at the south-west gate only. The men were to be paid 'as is the practice in private Establishments' according to their skills; after a fortnight's trial Ewart and the Superintending Foreman (a Mr Hughes) would fix the man's rate of pay. Working hours of the Factory would be from 6.00 a.m. to 6.00 p.m., with breakfast from 8.00 to 8.30 a.m., dinner from 12 noon to 1 p.m., and an afternoon break from 4.00 to 4.30 p.m. If men were kept on from 6.00 p.m. to 8.00 p.m., after working a whole day, they would be paid time and a quarter; after 8.00 p.m., time and a half. Sundays and holidays would also qualify for time and a half. Boilermakers working in flues or on dirty work would get a shilling a day extra.

Ewart thought that it would be a mistake to enter a great number of men at the outset. Instead, a beginning should be made with 10 or 15 boilermakers, and having tried the regulations out, the other departments could then be gradually filled, as necessitated by the pressure of work. As the construction of boilers was expected to be the principal activity, a rough calculation could be made of the date when the Factory would need to be fully manned. The aggregate horsepower of boilers in service was 10,596, and as the average boiler life was three years, 3,532hp of boilers would need to be provided annually. As many boilers were nearly new, the full boiler establishment would not be needed till the end of 1841.

Table 2 **Ewart's estimates of the size of the Woolwich Steam Factory workforce, and the proposed pay scales**

Boilermaking and repairing establishment

Angle iron smiths	7	40s
Angle iron hammer men	7	26s
Builders-up	9	38s
Assistant builders -p	9	26s
Riveters	36	32s
Holders-up	18	22s
Rivet makers	2	32s
Caulkers	4	26s
Foremen	2	30s
Total 94		

Boys	20	6s
	5	8s
Labourers	5	16s
Total 30		

Engine-making and repairing establishment

Smiths	8	40s
Hammermen	8	26s
Founders	5	36s
Coppersmiths	2	36s
Engine fitters	60	34s
Engine fitters' assistants	18	26s
Vice men	20	34s
Turners and machine men	10	35s
Millwrights and patternmakers	5	38s
Labourers	12	15s
Boys	12	9s
Total 160		

Ewart estimated the size of the Factory workforce, and the proposed pay scales, to be as shown in Table 2.

Other matters related to the expense of running the Steam Factory required attention. In May 1841 Parry and Ewart made a tour of marine engine builders in the Midlands, Lancashire and Scotland, taking the opportunity to ask machine tool makers what orders they might have received from the French or any other foreign government. By October Ewart and Lloyd had gained enough experience to be able to estimate the likely future expenditure on repairs of boilers and engines, reckoning that the machinery should be taken out of the ship every three years. The cost averaged out at £8 per horsepower per annum. Next January they were sent to inspect a landmark building, which survives only as a footprint: the factory of the Great Western Steam Ship Company at Bristol, where the engines for the *Great Britain* were to be constructed, but which was now put up for sale because of chronic financial difficulties and dissension within the firm. However, nothing there was needed by the Admiralty.[20]

Denison was now at last in a position to put his mind to radically improving the physical layout of the Factory, helped by the imminent prospect of the purchase of land to enable the road to Greenwich to be diverted (Figure 24). However, immediate problems probably took up Brandreth and Denison's time to the exclusion of other matters. Foremost in their minds was the height of the chimney required to carry off the Smithery flues, which occasioned much debate. Denison

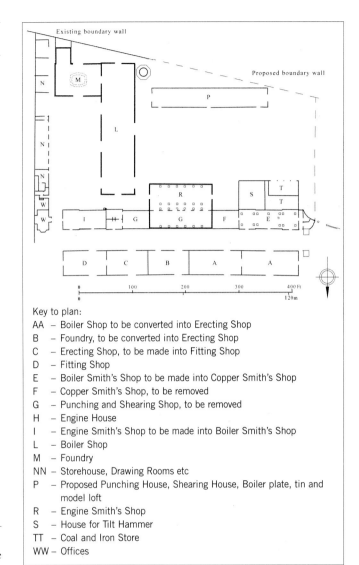

Key to plan:
AA – Boiler Shop to be converted into Erecting Shop
B – Foundry, to be converted into Erecting Shop
C – Erecting Shop, to be made into Fitting Shop
D – Fitting Shop
E – Boiler Smith's Shop to be made into Copper Smith's Shop
F – Copper Smith's Shop, to be removed
G – Punching and Shearing Shop, to be removed
H – Engine House
I – Engine Smith's Shop to be made into Boiler Smith's Shop
L – Boiler Shop
M – Foundry
NN – Storehouse, Drawing Rooms etc
P – Proposed Punching House, Shearing House, Boiler plate, tin and model loft
R – Engine Smith's Shop
S – House for Tilt Hammer
TT – Coal and Iron Store
WW – Offices

24 The Factory as improved and enlarged by Denison in his plan of September 1843. Even with the new ground purchased to the south of the original factory as shown in Figure 22, the site is still very constrained. Denison recast the original block (A-D) into just two units: an erecting shop covering some two-thirds of its length, and a fitting shop. The Boilersmiths' shop was to be turned into a Coppersmiths' shop, while behind the original ranges was a large Boiler Shop, with a new Smithery adjoining it at the far end. A punching and shearing shop parallel to the original buildings formed a rough quadrilateral. The estimate for all this was £27,036, with £2,000 for machinery and £1,268 for the cost of fixing it. *(Redrawn from TNA ADM 140/1153)*

originally proposed one 100ft high. However, Ewart favoured a plan submitted by Elsworth, a chimney engineer with 20 years' experience, which offered a chimney 208ft high and 25ft diameter at the base: this would cost some £3,300 as against £468 for Denison's. Ewart, drawing on his knowledge of the Lancashire industrial scene, maintained that anything less would not serve. Furthermore, Denison's chimney would draw on the smoke collected by hoods placed over the fires and then passing through main flues running over the windows of the building, while the design favoured by Ewart would draw it though underground smoke tunnels.

Experience had shown that smoke often failed to behave in the obvious way, and could be induced to perform the most unlikely convolutions. Notable examples were the hearths in the Anchorsmith's Shop at Chatham, where very large hoods placed over the fires had failed to prevent the smoke from filling the room. Mr Parkin, the Master Shipwright, abolished the hoods in 1823 and placed smaller flues behind the fires; the master smith and the oldest blacksmiths believed the scheme would fail, but the smoke then rushed 'apparently out of its natural direction' into the flues and an enormous improvement was effected.

Ewart's solution was favoured by the Yard Engineers, who were unanimous in their preference for the underground flue, and thought it desirable that its communication with the large chimney should be as low as possible in order to create the draught, which would be reinforced by the action of the drying stoves, which gave great heat and would, they thought, quickly draw the smoke of the Smithery fires. In addition, underground flues would not block the light within the workshop. They calculated that the chimney could be built for £2,703 (Figure 25).

The engineering firm of Fairbairn & Son testified to the efficiency of the chimney they had erected on this pattern. Brandreth decided in favour of Ewart after a visit to the Midlands and Lancashire, where he took the opportunity to investigate contemporary stacks, the average height of which proved to be between 150 and 200ft (Figure 26). There were thus ample precedents for the high chimney, which would also have the advantage of the capacity to take in additional flues when the probable expansion of the Factory occurred. By the early twentieth century the use of underground flues, for both blast and smoke extraction, had become the preferred technique (Figure 27).

The Chief Engineer did not live long to enjoy this minor triumph. Already 76 years old, on 15 September 1842 he was struck by a breaking chain in the Yard and was killed. Rolt's tender to heighten the chimney was accepted the next month.

The key post of Chief Engineer at Woolwich was now vacant. Lloyd was clearly worried by the presence of another young high-flyer in the Yard in the person of Dinnen, who could claim more practical experience with machinery, as well as unnamed civilians, possibly including Edward Humphrys. Lloyd wrote a letter to James Brown, now a partner with James Watt junior, which seems to show that the prejudice against graduates of the School of Naval Architecture that existed among Yard-trained Master Shipwrights also had a foothold in the growing engineering staff. Practical training was clearly preferred to a theoretical background.

I called at your Office yesterday, with a view of requesting a Testimonial, in the form of a letter…from your Firm. The Object of this I need not explain. It is, of course, to strengthen my claims to succeed the late Mr Ewart. I find several persons, not in HM service, are using their utmost efforts to obtain the situation, and, to prove their qualifications, will produce all the Testimonials they can obtain. Now, although I have some very strong ones from Scientific men, and from Superintendents of the Dock Yards and other official persons, I feel that it may be of essential service to obtain strong Testimonials from practical Engineers of high standing who have long known me, and who, from their own knowledge, can testify as to my knowledge and judgment, relating to matters purely professional. I had no idea until yesterday of taking this step, but, in justice to myself, I think I ought to take it, especially as the members of the Board of Admiralty have not been long in office, and I have lost the support of the late Mr Ewart, whose intention it was to use his utmost efforts to have me promoted his successor. It is somewhat repugnant to my feelings to have recourse to the aid of testimonials to obtain what I think is my right, but when I see a chance of some stranger being placed above me, it would be folly not to use every means in my power to prevent it…

25 The Woolwich chimney, showing the south gable of the demolished Boiler Shop to its right. *(English Heritage)*

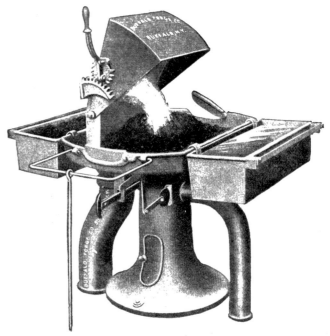

27 By the early twentieth century the use of underground flues both for blast and smoke extraction had become the preferred technique. Here is an American forge showing the smoke hood connected to the underground pipes. *(From H M Raymond (ed) Modern Shop Practice, (Chicago, 1917), vol.iv, p.211)*

He need not have worried. He was given the post and got firmly in the saddle as the Navy's leading engineer, remaining in charge at Woolwich for the next five years, during which period it was the sole steam factory serving the Royal Navy. That it would be unable to retain its pre-eminence was made clear in a memorandum from the Master Attendant, pointing out that when the basins were finished they would not hold more than 12 or 13 vessels with room to move, and as the average number refitting was 15 (19 at the time of writing) 'with the certain prospect of an increase in that number in proportion to the augmentation of the Steam Navy, it is evident that much more space will be required.'[21]

Ad hoc developments

In April 1842 it was decided to introduce steam machinery into the Smitheries at all the Yards:

> With the exception of Woolwich…the Yards have until a very recent period, been deficient in the Machinery, now ordinarily used, in private Establishments, of any magnitude, for Iron Work. Tilt Hammers, Hercules, and Fan bellows, are gradually being introduced, into all the Smitheries. The necessity of adding to the efficiency of the Smitheries, by every practicable means, may be inferred, 1st — from the extensive application of Iron work to Ships — 2nd to the demand for Anchors…

This heavy plant was quite different in scale from the lathes and planes that had equipped the Devonport Millwrights' Shop, and was the result of the application of steam power to drive adaptations of existing equipment, quite unlike the parallel development of machine tools, which was wholly innovative. The millwrights had the technological edge on the smiths. While Woolwich was developing, equipment and buildings for the metallurgical industries were introduced into the other yards, though these smitheries, millwrights' shops, drilling shops and foundries were, unlike Woolwich, all under the control of the Master Shipwrights, and the maintenance of steam machinery was no part of their original function. This was a transitional phase, when the use of steam-powered machinery and the production of metal components began to increase rapidly, particularly after the decision to introduce steam power into all the smitheries, necessitating the addition or enlargement of engine houses and modifying or adding to the buildings themselves. A set of ad hoc responses were made, for the decision implied that the introduction of power was a desirable addition to existing buildings rather than a factor with implications for overall yard planning and workshop arrangement, and financial constraints would have prevented any significant schemes of demolition and rebuilding.[22]

Pembroke Dock, established in October 1815 purely as a building yard, originally required only a smithery to manufacture structural components of ships.[23] However, when a station for the steam packet service to Waterford was established at Hobbs' Point, outside the Yard, a certain amount of mechanical work needed to be done, and some metalworking skills had to be provided by local staff in the Dockyard. Lloyd, reporting on the packet stations in 1838, noted that the Yard provided ample means for the efficient repair of boilers: brasses of moderate size and reasonable quality

could be cast, and common articles forged and turned. All this was performed by hand. Lloyd did not recommend any additional equipment until a steam engine had been installed, when boring and screw-cutting machines might be provided.

Serious engineering knowledge had not yet reached Pembroke Dock. Although the men could repair boilers, nobody there had the slightest knowledge of steam engines (they even polished parts of the machinery with brick dust), or was even accustomed to helping in their repair. All the work had to be done by the ship's engineer, who was sometimes so overburdened that repairs were neglected or, at best, inefficiently done. Lloyd recommended that two experienced engineers be appointed.

A 10hp engine not required at the brewery at the Royal William Victualling Yard at Devonport (the issue of beer to ships had been abolished in another of Sir James Graham's economies) was sent to the Yard, and erected in the pump house by the Butterley Iron Company, with shops erected next to it in 1838 for drilling machinery, lathes, and circular saws. This was the same pattern of development as at Sheerness, where the presence of an engine house dictated the close grouping of new facilities around it.[24] In 1841-2 a building was adapted as a sawmill, powered by steam, and the next year £5,000 was allowed for a steam engine, tilt hammer, fan bellows and alterations to the forges. Fox, Henderson were approached and asked to prepare plans and estimates for a smithery adequate to supply the requirements of an establishment of 300 shipwrights. The surviving drawings show that they had little scope for innovative ironwork here; the principal use of metal was an iron tank over the roof of part of the building. They were asked to send specifications for their ironwork in November 1844. Underground flues were not provided here; each furnace had its own chimney (Figure 28).[25]

At Chatham, Marc Brunel's sawmills, in operation since 1814, and a most original design in which the timber was transported by a combination of a canal, a counterpoise lift and an overhead railway, had always been steam powered. All the machinery was made by Maudslay's. However, the system gave a lot of trouble for many years before it was eventually sorted out. It was not until 1836 that the Roperies acquired an engine, made by Boulton & Watt, though designed by Ewart. The Smithery was upgraded in 1841,[26] and in the same year Devonport's North Smithery (see p.20) was greatly improved

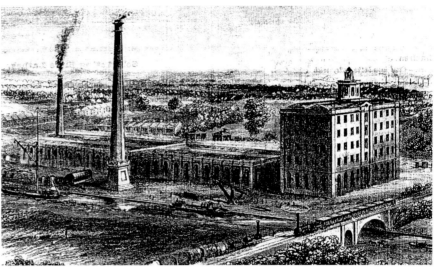

26 James Nasmyth's Patricroft Works, proudly displayed as his letterhead, demonstrates a chimney standing free from the buildings and fed by underground flues. A similar arrangement was installed in 1836-7 at William Fairbairn's shipbuilding yard at Millwall, just across the Thames from Woolwich. (TNA ADM 85/16)

28 The proposed additions to the Pembroke Smithery. *(TNA ADM 140/481/2)*

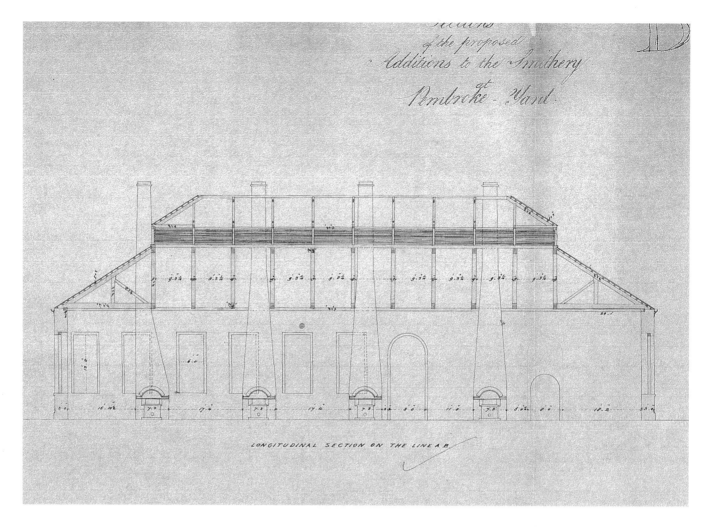

LONGITUDINAL SECTION ON THE LINE A B

by the replacement of the manually powered bellows by air blast supplied through blowing fans worked by the steam engine.[27] It is likely that the two Devonport smitheries had diverged in function by this time; the proximity of the Millwrights' Shop to the North Smithery, with the provision for power supply from the one to the other, had concentrated work on machinery in the North Smithery, leaving shipwright's work to be done in the South Smithery. An increase in the fabrication of heavy components at the North Smithery probably resulted in a design by Grissell for a travelling crane in November 1847, which was, however, turned down. The firm then offered to build one to the plans of Thomas Miller, the Chief Engineer, for £648.

The Portsmouth Metal Mills were also re-equipped with superior machinery: £3,000 was allowed, and Boulton & Watt were sent specifications for a 70hp engine (very soon altered to 80hp). This was to drive rolls both for copper sheeting and for copper and iron bolts or bars, and working drawings were produced during 1842. In March 1843 Brandreth complained about the delay in sending them to Portsmouth. The Smithery was now equipped with three Hercules hammers. A new batch of machine tools was supplied, presumably to update the equipment for Byam Martin's and Goodrich's Boiler Shop. Apart from the anchor fire cranes (the most expensive item by a long way), the tools were clearly for the fabrication of engine components.[28]

Notes:
1   Lambert, (1991), p.72. This chapter reinforces Lambert's view.
2   BW Box 11/25, ADM 1/3485, *Memoir* of Peter Ewart in *Proceedings of the Institution of Civil Engineers*, 1843, pp.25-28; H W Dickinson and R Jenkins, *James Watt and the Steam Engine,* 2nd edn, (Southampton, 1981), pp.288-289. No drawings of the original Soho Foundry survive.
3   Had Goodrich remained, it is possible that the close working relationship he had developed with Maudslay, Son & Field over the setting up of the Portsmouth Boiler House might have resulted in a slightly different procurement policy.
4   Ewart informed James Brown that the 20hp forge engine (now 22 years old and clearly in need of some maintenance) could not be stopped for three weeks because of pressure of work, and that he hoped Brown would be there in time for trying out *Comet*, bringing the specifications of what was to be done to *Carron*. At the end of the month *Carron* was ready to leave Woolwich Basin, being towed by *Lightning* to Boulton & Watt's hulk to place the new boilers in the ship, while in February Gilbert Hamilton, the manager at Soho, sent an estimate for the repair of *Alban's* machinery to Brown, all the articles required being put in hand at Soho within a fortnight. When it was discovered that *Pluto's* boilers could not be repaired, Ewart asked that the boilers taken out of *Carron* be repaired as soon as possible, and immediately applied to Birmingham for another 100hp boiler. £282 worth of articles were delivered to the Smithery, plus a cast iron crane, sent in dismantled condition for the Yard, as well as boiler plates and other components.
5   R A Buchanan and M W Doughty, 'The choice of steam engine manufacturers by the British Admiralty, 1822-1852', in *Mariner's Mirror*, vol. 64, 1978, pp.327-347; ADM 1/3408, ADM 222/7, BW Box 11/19, BW Box 11/22, BW Box 10/1, BW Box 11/25, BW Box 10/2.
6   ADM 222/9.
7   The works at Woolwich were estimated at £13,871 16s 9d, and at Deptford £17,414. The Woolwich building would have the dimensions 240ft x 40ft x 20ft high, divided into three 8 ft compartments. For a boiler manufactory another 200ft would be required:
    'If, at any time, it be deemed expedient to extend the Establishment, for manufacturing Engines as well as Boilers; an additional building of

similar dimensions & parallel to the first, would probably supply all that may be wanted.'

8 ADM 222/9, ADM 1/3410, ADM 1/3485, ADM 140/1153/1, ADM 1/3502, G L Taylor, *The Autobiography of an Octogenarian Architect*, (London (2 vols), 1870-2); J Cattell & K Falconer, *Swindon: the Legacy of a Railway Town*, (London, 1995), chapter 2; ADM 12/333.

9 Brandreth was to perpetuate this, he suggested next year that John Williams, a Shipwright Foreman, be appointed to take over the duties connected with the Civil Architects Department at Portsmouth, on £300 a year. Williams had been doing this job for three years.

10 ADM 1/3411, ADM 1/3493, Taylor, (1870-2), 1, p.179, ADM 1/3415, ADM 12/333, ADM 3/265, ADM 1/3491, ADM 1/5543.

11 Boulton & Watt were still expected to supply an engineer to adjust the slide valves of *Columbia*; blow-off pipes for *Arrow* were required from them urgently; and a lathe had been sent from Soho.

12 BW Box 8/17, ADM 1/3491, ADM 222/4.

13 ADM 1/3503.

14 ADM 1/3411, ADM 1/3433, ADM 1/3434, ADM 1/3503, ADM 222/4, ADM 1/3492, ADM 12/357, ADM 1/3428.

15 Brandreth produced a plan for this in April, and the contractor Peter Rolt secured the job for the dock, for £20,754; the connection between the basin and the mast pond was estimated at £14,000, with another £2,000 for an iron caisson.

16 Nasmyth's tender for a large drilling machine and Roberts' for punching and shearing machinery were accepted in April, and plans for the foundations of the latter were drawn up in August. Two pieces of heavy plant were ordered from Nasmyth: the vertical boring mill sketched two years previously, for £800, and a vertical planing machine for £650. Foundations for machinery for the Erecting Shop were estimated for in November.

17 Taylor's factory, as modified by Denison, came out as a long building some 430ft long by 40ft wide, partitioned from the east end as an 80ft fitting shop, a 75ft erecting shop, a 75ft foundry, and two 95ft boiler shops. Communication existed between the fitting and erecting shops and between the two boiler shops.

18 Rennie was consulted, and considered a depth of 24ft would be adequate; the Master Attendant of the Yard (responsible for moving, securing and refitting ships in dockyards) would have preferred 26ft.

19 *Mechanics' Magazine*, vol. 20, 1834, p.378, ADM 140/1147, ADM 1/3503, ADM 12/357, ADM 12/370, ADM 140/1153/2, ADM 1/5521, *Memoir* of John Dinnen in *Proceedings of the Institution of Civil Engineers*, 1867, pp.563-565.

20 ADM 92/4, ADM 1/3412, ADM 12/402. £6,802 had been spent on machinery for the Factory, and £15,000 on the Foundry, Boiler Sheds, and Smith's shop. The Estimates for 1842/3 now allowed £3,000 for factory machinery (the fall-off showing that the bulk had now been installed), £5,500 for cranes for the inner basin, and £16,770 for completing the inner basin.

21 ADM 1/5521, ADM 140/1153/2, Colonel C W Pasley, 'Captain Sandham's Mode of Curing or Improving Smoky Chimneys; with Remarks also on Count Rumford's System, &c.' in *Papers on Subjects connected with the Duties of the Corps of Royal Engineers*, ii, (1838), pp.251-262; *Mechanics' Magazine*, vol. 8, 1828, pp.242-3; [Anonymous] 'Description of the Large Chimney…in Woolwich Dockyard' in *Papers on Subjects connected with the Duties of the Corps of Royal Engineers*, ix, (1847), pp.70-76; ADM 12/397, BW Box 10/3.

22 ADM 1/3502, ADM 1/3503, ADM 140/927, ADM 1/5521, ADM 12/411.

23 A plan annotated by Taylor in November 1831 showed the only buildings then constructed to be the officers' houses, the guard house, chapel and suppling kilns (for preparing timbers for steaming).

24 At Sheerness, the Smithery was mechanised with the assistance of Ewart and the Master Shipwright at Chatham, John Fincham. By March 1836 the Cement Mill was about to be taken down and its engine placed in the Smithery Engine House, where a chimney had been built and nothing remained to be done but set the boilers in position. It was to power blowing machines, a Hercules, drilling machines and lathes in the Millwrights' Shop, plus circular and frame saws in the Boat House, while a set of millstones was to be set up in the new building. A tilt hammer was considered to be most desirable. This programme of works, however, seems not to have taken place as planned. Fincham proposed that the estimates for 1838-9 should leave out the blowing machines and the Hercules, which were much less important than the drilling machinery, as hand drilling was very labour intensive and often delayed the business of the Yard. A plan of 1841 shows the Smithery with an engine powering a tilt hammer and blowing fans for the forges.

By 1842 the old steam engine was still driving the Cement Mill and the Sawmills, but was now quite inadequate for all these purposes, and a new one of 25hp was planned, together with another Hercules; the old engine was to be sent to the Smithery to work as an auxiliary. In November 1843 tenders for the chimney, furnace and drying store of the Foundry were approved.

25 BL Add. 21/139, ADM 1/3428, BL Add. 41,398 f.147r, ADM 1/5521, ADM 140/481/1,2,3,4.

26 A Nasmyth planing machine was ordered, and Boulton & Watt sent a 16hp engine, while Portsmouth sent one of their tilt hammers. The 1842/3 estimates included £3,542 for a Hercules, cranes for the anchor fires, additional machinery, and another 8hp engine.

27 The blast was now continual instead of intermittent, producing savings all round: nearly double the work was reckoned to be performed in the same time. The air drains conveying the blast from the fans to the fires had to be channelled out from the solid rock, and to minimise the noise of the fans they were tightly enclosed within walls. In September 1844 Mr Murn was asked to provide an iron roof for the South Smithery for the same prices as his work at the Chain Cable Store.

28 BW Box 10/1, 10/2, 8/17, CHA/J/2, CHA/H/38, ADM 1/5521, POR/P/13, BW Box 10/8, BW Box 18/24, BW AV/70, *Mechanics' Magazine*, vol. 36, 1842, p.32, ADM 12/428, ADM 12/476, BW Box 10/9, POR/R/9, POR/P/15. The Boiler Shop equipment was:

		£
Whitworth:	Small planing machine	95
	Slotting machine	166
	crew bolt machine ¼ in to ¾ in	57
Nasmyth:	Shaping machine	150
	Screw bolt machine ½ in to 1½ in	90
	Surface plates	22
	Steel straight edges	11
	Cast iron straight edges	11
Gordon & Davis:	Four cranes for anchor fires	1,000

CHAPTER 5

Iron Construction

BETWEEN THE 1780s AND 1850s, constructional systems went through a revolution. Iron went from being a highly experimental material to a very widely employed and understood one. Its technical development was driven on by the needs of the railway industry for wide-span sheds and bridges. Originally associated with textile mill buildings, its use spread to politer building types such as greenhouses, exhibition buildings and market halls. Curiously, Samuel Bentham failed to make any extensive use of the material and although John Rennie, whose opinions the Navy Board valued highly, recommended in 1807 the adoption of an iron-framed construction 'upon the plan of the cotton and flax mills lately erected at Derby, Leeds, Manchester and Glasgow', nothing significant was done until 1812.

In that year Edward Holl designed a cast iron framing system to support two large water tanks at the Chatham Sawmill, and began to rebuild the fire-damaged Spinning House of 1763-72 at Devonport with a complete internal iron frame of similar design (Figure 29). The internal framework was completed in 1817, when work began on the potentially highly flammable Lead and Paint Mill at Chatham. In all, Holl was to be responsible for at least 14 dockyard buildings incorporating significant quantities of structural iron, then considered to play a key role in the creation of a fully fire-resistant structure. The two-storey frame in the Spinning House consists of a line of cast iron columns connected vertically through spigots, supporting T-section transverse beams with a lower flange and an elliptically-arched upper profile. The flanges extended into spanner-head ends, which met one another at the column, resting on a circular bolting plate 'capital' and clasping the spigot. Along the sides of the beams were cast square sockets, to carry secondary fishbelly joists spanning the gap between the beams. These gave simple support to a flagstone floor. This type of construction was used in 1810 at Armley Mill, Leeds, and by

29 The iron framework at the Spinning House. *(Ministry of Defence)*

the 1830s was one of two widely used types of iron frames in Yorkshire textile mills. (The alternative and more common system was for the floor to be formed by jack arches, springing from the bridging beams, as, for example, the earliest iron-framed mill, Ditherington in Shrewsbury, 1796–97, or Barracks Mill, Whitehaven, 1809.)

Holl's Working Masthouse at Sheerness was an early attempt to use cast iron for a different purpose, attaining an uninterrupted floor span by using cast iron columns with diagonal braces (Figure 30, 30A). However, it was not the first. The Skin Floor of the New Tobacco Warehouse, London, assembled between 1811 and 1813, used even more complex castings with both columns and diagonal braces that split into two, so that the roof was supported at six separate points. Holl may have been responsible for two more iron-framed buildings at Sheerness; these woodworking shops will be discussed in Chapter 10. After Holl's death the development of the Royal William and Royal Clarence Victualling Yards at Devonport and Gosport gave Rennie and Taylor respectively an opportunity to use iron. Rennie, in the Clarence Building at the Royal William Yard, carried the valley of the roof by cast iron arched longitudinal girders bolted to the central line of columns, so

30 The exposed ironwork in the Store Mast House at Sheerness. *(© Crown Copyright. NMR 3394/20779)*

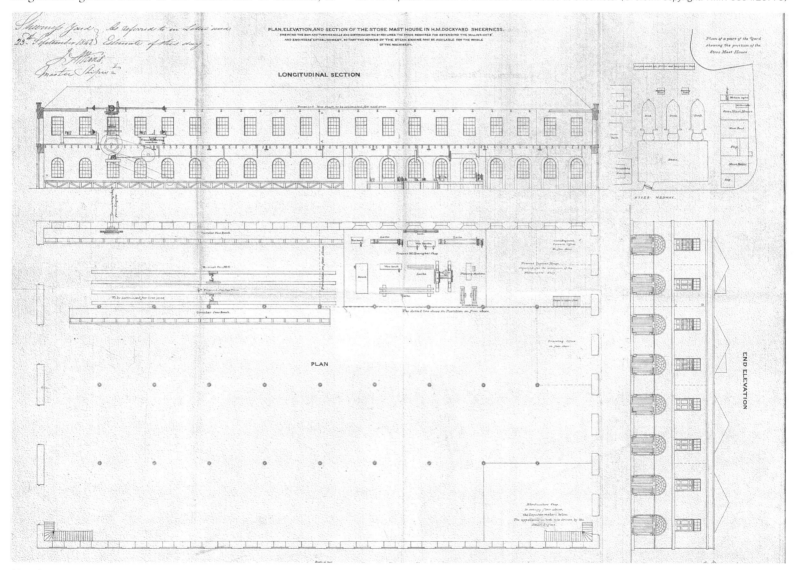

30A One quarter of the ground floor of the Store Mast House was adapted as a sawmill and millwrights' shop, with vertical and circular saws, five lathes and a planing machine. A trenail mooting machine (for making wooden dowels) was on the first floor, and it was proposed to extend the shafting there to run the whole length of the building. As this Mast House lay alongside the Engine House its adaptation was inevitable, as the shorter the length of shafting employed the better. *(TNA ADM 1/5518)*

forming a structurally static frame. He had previously used this device in 1813 at Stanley Mill, near Stroud. Another way of creating a rigid frame was developed by Charles Fowler in Hungerford Fish Market, where he employed spandrel brackets to form a rigid brace between beam and column.

The Fish Market had been built by one of the firms that specialised in the technique of iron construction. Henry Grissell, in partnership with Samuel Morton Peto, had been responsible for many important buildings, including the Hungerford Market, the Reform Club, Nelson's Column, and, more relevantly, Woolwich Steam Factory, where they also completed the graving dock after Ranger's abortive efforts. Grissell and Peto parted company in 1846, the former retaining the building contracts (which included the Houses of Parliament, another iron-roofed structure) while Peto took over the railway engineering work. By the time the Admiralty decided to adopt iron construction on a grand scale the most prominent practitioners were Thomas Grissell & Son, Fox, Henderson & Co., and George Baker & Son. Charles Fox had been appointed by Robert Stephenson to be assistant engineer on the London and Birmingham Railway when he was only 23, leaving this post in 1838 and forming a partnership with Francis Bramah. On Bramah's death in 1841 the firm became known as Fox, Henderson & Co. of the London Iron Works, Birmingham. On the evidence of their practice during the construction of their masterpiece, the Crystal Palace, Fox was the designer and Henderson the specialist in iron. Baker and Son were just beaten for the contract for the Houses of Parliament, and also for that of Nelson's Column, but offered successful tenders for Greenwich and Deptford railway stations. Far bigger jobs were the Fitzwilliam Museum at Cambridge and the dome of the British Museum Reading Room, but even these were eclipsed by their subsequent work for the Admiralty. Iron roofing was only part of this; the massive Keyham extension to the north of Devonport dockyard was one of the great civil engineering jobs of the century (see p.197).[1]

The first iron slip roofs

The impact of new technology was not confined to the design of workshops for the maintenance of steam engines. The most spectacular building type to be found in the Yards, the covered building slip, was to become an iron rather than a timber structure.

The provision of overall timber roofs for building slips, to protect the materials from the weather, had long been commonplace abroad, but it took the alarming prevalence of dry rot in many ships built during the Napoleonic War before they became an accepted feature of British shipbuilding practice. The first was constructed at Plymouth in 1814. Sir Robert Seppings quickly improved the design, and two roofs of his type survive, at Devonport and Chatham, the latter being designed in 1837. At Devonport in 1840 Nos. 1 and 3 were built, while at Chatham No. 2 slip was in need of repair, the latter providing a rare instance where timbers from an identifiable ship were reused in a building.[2] In April 1839 Brandreth instructed the officers at Pembroke Dock to forward a plan and section for two slip roofs; Burgmann was sent to frame the specifications and make drawings in February 1840. £12,000 had been allocated for this purpose, and in 1841 the

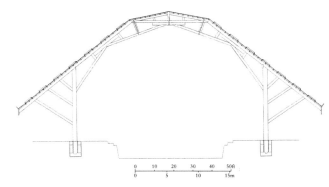

31 This roof at Pembroke Dock is a typical Seppings derivative. *(Adapted from Papers on subjects connected with the duties of the Corps of Royal Engineers, Vol. IX, 1847)*

last of the great wooden roofs there was constructed, at a cost of £7,500 (Figure 31).

In May 1842 the Admiralty decided that in future all slip roofs would be of iron construction. Brandreth was directed to find out the Master Shipwrights' opinions on their proposed standardised dimensions: the distance from centre to centre of standards across the slip being 82ft 6in, and the distance from centre to centre of standards along the sides of the slip being 13ft 4in (Figure 32). He was also required to enquire, in view of the fact that the slips were placed 70 to 80ft apart, whether it would be practicable to cover this intermediate space with a double roof supported by a row of columns along the centre. Abethell and Lang, respectively Master Shipwright and Assistant Master Shipwright at Woolwich, replied:

> 82 feet distance…is more than sufficient…the *Trafalgar* was built [at Woolwich] between standards, only 67ft 10in; and no difficulty was experienced, but a considerable advantage found in performing the works.

John Fincham replied from Chatham that there were no objections to the dimensions or the intermediate roofs. The Master Shipwrights at Sheerness and Portsmouth agreed, the latter writing:

> We take this opportunity to mention that the men working under the roof covering the Albion are suffering very much from the heat of the weather, and the additional heat created by the unavoidable use of candles in the lower part of the Ship, which together renders their situation very oppressive and scarcely supportable; we would therefore beg to suggest that in building new Roofs, it would be desirable to adopt some means for allowing the heated air to escape and to ensure a proper ventilation.[3]

Brandreth had clearly developed his own ideas on what these roofs should be like, and in September he sent tracings of plans and sections to Pembroke Dock. He proposed that the new roofs over slips 8 and 9, whose timber roofs were in total decay, be made of iron. The wooden roofs had been covered with a great variety of materials, sheet iron, sheet copper, zinc, slates, and tarred paper or canvas, but no covering could reduce the fire risk posed by these enormous structures.

Several designs were submitted, but the preferred solution was that of Fox, Henderson & Co. It is clear, though, that the placing of the standards and the dimensions were arrived at as a result of a consultation process with the potential users. The firm acted as their own contractors.

These slip roofs were buildings of enormous significance in the development of free-standing iron frames, and hence in architectural history. Historians of iron space frames have tended to concentrate on the development of greenhouses, leading to the inevitable climax of the Crystal Palace. However, many of the technical steps leading up to this were worked through in the dockyards, and the thinking of their designers can be traced like fossilised footprints.

The first independent iron-framed building was designed in 1803 by Humphrey Repton. This was the garden hall of Carlton House, and the form was developed for glasshouses both in England and in France. These structures, however, were significantly different from the modern space frame, depending for their stability on the arch and the shell effect of the glazing. The slip roofs were key steps in the evolution of the rigid iron-framed structure. No iron roof of such a size had ever been built before those at Pembroke Dock, and the general pattern of Seppings' design was followed, translated into the new medium, which enormously reduced the bulk of the trusses, which were composed of bar and angle iron. No single bar exceeded 4in x 4½in (Figure 34).

The two slip roofs cost £15,480, and are the only ones to

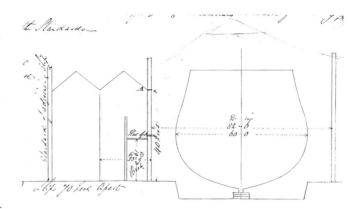

32 Sketch of slip roof and working shed produced by Brandreth in the discussion on the dimensions of slip roofs. *(TNA ADM 1/5521)*

which a designer, rather than a contractor, can be definitely attributed. They were constructed during 1843. In January 1846 Captain Montgomery Williams RE reported on the 'masterly manner' in which the roofs over slips 8 and 9 had been constructed by Fox, Henderson, though that did not prevent George Baker & Son getting the contract for slips 1 and 2 the next October. By 1848 there were five iron roofs at Pembroke. All have been destroyed.[4]

An interesting design, using Gothic detailing, and incorporating working sheds flanking the slip, though looking none too secure, was submitted at the end of 1842 by an engineer named G.M. Palmer (Figure 36). Brandreth, however,

33 Slips dominate this plan of Pembroke Dock, dating from the 1830s. It had been established in October 1815 purely as a building yard; the ships were taken to Plymouth for fitting out. *(TNA ADM 140/429)*

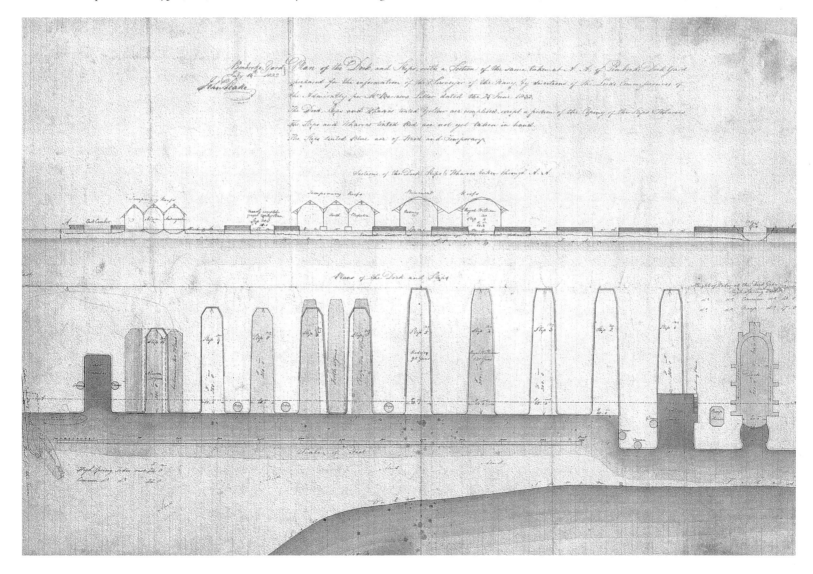

34 The contrast between the Seppings type roof and the Fox, Henderson roof at Pembroke Dock shown here is one of bulk and constructional detail: the design has not been thought out afresh. *(From* Papers on Subjects connected with the duties of Royal Engineers, *Vol. IX, 1847)*

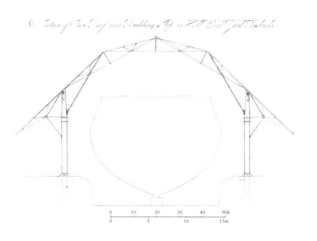

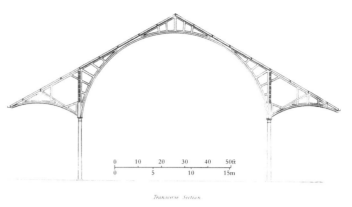

35 The drawings by Baker and Mould for the Chatham and Portsmouth roofs. *(From* Papers on Subjects connected with the duties of Royal Engineers, *Vol. IX, 1847)*

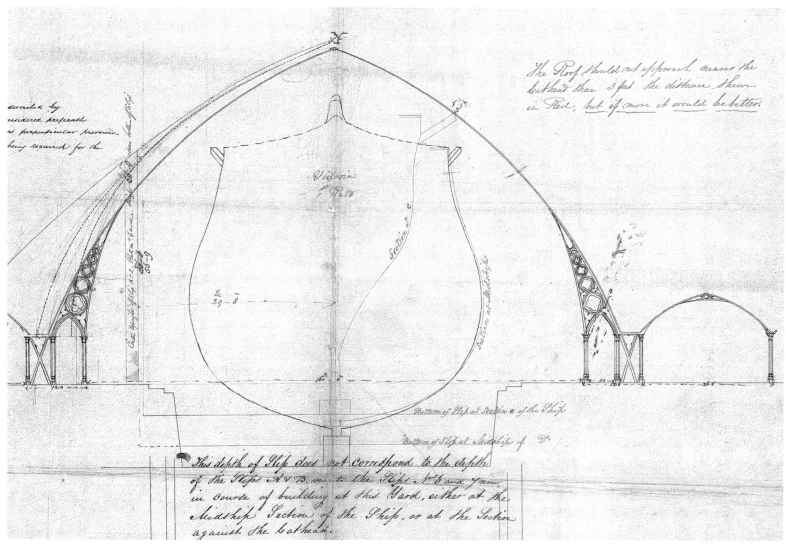

The Roof should not approach nearer the Cathead than 3 feet the distance shewn in Red, but if more it would be better.

This depth of Slip does not correspond to the depth of the Slips A & B. nor to the Slips No F and now in course of building at this Yard, either at the Midship Section of the Ship, or at the Section against the Cathead.

took it seriously, and noted that any quantity of light could be introduced into the roof, which was formed of plates of corrugated iron. That material, invented by a Mr Walker of Rotherhithe, had been used in the late 1820s as roofing material in the London Docks, and was enthused about in the technical press.[5] The proposal was circulated for comment, but the project was shelved on account of objections from some Master Shipwrights.[6] The slip roofs to be built at Portsmouth and Chatham were to be of a new type, owing nothing to wooden predecessors and without the charming eccentricity of Palmer's design.

The Chatham slip roofs

The set of three new slips with iron roofs mooted in 1843 for construction at Chatham formed part of a scheme for transforming that yard by the addition of a basin. Baker & Son undertook this contract, which comprised a cofferdam, reconstructing a portion of the river wall, constructing three building slips, and constructing a portion of the entrance to a basin, on 1 September 1844. The specification laid down that provision was to be made for the construction of the foundations of the pits in which the standards to support the roofs were to be fixed. Drawings for the slips themselves were soon produced by the firm.

Captain Thomas Mould RE, who had just been transferred from Pembroke Dock to Chatham, was of course familiar with the construction of the Fox, Henderson slips, and the evidence, such as it is, points to the design of the Chatham roofs being a collective Admiralty design. In June 1844 Denison met Mould in order to assist him in forming a specification for Rivers, the Clerk of Works, to complete the designs for the slips. Sectional drawings of the roofs exist signed both by Baker alone and by Baker and Mould jointly. These roofs were an advance over the Pembroke ones in abandoning the wooden model and greatly increasing the spacing of the frames.[7]

The contract for the roofs was signed by Baker's on 21 April 1847. The job was to be completed within 10 months for £32,590. The standards, arched ribs, posts and arches of side enclosures, framing of land end gables, longitudinal arched girders and posts in connection therewith were to be cast iron, but:

> The main arched ribs of the centre span, bounded by and riveted to the malleable iron T plates passing around the arched and raking line; the intersecting junction between the crown and spandrill pieces with its wedges…[were to be]…formed wholly of wrought iron.

Trussed purlins were to have malleable iron tension bars and pieces, with cast iron struts and sockets prepared for galvanised and corrugated iron of No. 18 Birmingham wire gauge, riveted

36 The Gothic Revival might have made its mark in the Royal Yards had this design by G.M. Palmer have found favour. *(TNA ADM 1/5521)*

37 (Opposite) The Baker roofs today. *(Mike Williams)*

38 Interior of the
Baker roofs today.
(Mike Williams)

to wrought iron trussed purlins. The use of cast iron with wrought iron tension pieces was common practice; the scale was not. Skylights were to be constructed with cast iron rims and wrought T bars and glazed with stout sheet glass. The land gables were to be enclosed with corrugated iron and glazed sashes down to the line of the caps of the main standards. The corrugated iron for the enclosure of the north and south sides was not included in this estimate. All cast and malleable iron except the galvanised covering was to be painted in three coats of good oil colour.

These roofs are closely related to those at Portsmouth. The Fox, Henderson model was not likely to be followed by Mould, for observation of the Pembroke roofs had not convinced him of their structural integrity. He felt that if one suffered a failure all would go, and apparently had worried about the Chatham roofs being a united structure, for, while they were under construction, he was informed:

> With reference to your letter of the 12th inst. relative to the Risk of the Iron Roofs of the Building Slips in Pembroke Dock Yard giving way, in consequence of these Roofs being united; I am commanded by my Lords to acquaint you, that notwithstanding the risk you have pointed out, the advantages of this mode of construction are such, as to counterbalance the Risk, and to justify the continuance of the present construction.

Events were to show he had a point.[8]

At the end of January 1850 what could have developed into a major disaster occurred: a partial failure of the foundations violently strained and damaged the roofs. Naturally, an inquiry followed, to see whether the responsibility could be pinned on Baker's, and Mould was ordered to forward all the instructions and working drawings in his possession to Somerset House. The design of the roofs was never called into question; the trouble lay in the foundations, and clearly with Baker & Son. A year after having signed the original contract, Baker's had proposed to adopt a quite different method of constructing the river wall and slips from that laid down; they were willing to incur all the risks and responsibilities attending their proposals, but after 'very full and careful deliberations' the suggestion was declined.[9]

After the incident it was found that all the side walls of the slips had more or less moved:

> ...having a tendency to separate from the bottom of the Slips and to turn over. The foundation of the North extension had sunk in some parts 5 inches, and it was evident that the sinking of the Standards, the Pits, and a continuous foundation of Concrete, weighing in all upwards of 200 Tons, and attached to the eaves of a Slight Iron Roof, could not but have tried the whole roof, severely.

An investigation revealed that the standard pits of the extension to the north and south did not rest on piles, and that the sheeting piles that ought to have been carried from the east end of the slips to the river wall, had been left out. It is not known how the blame was apportioned in the end;[10] Baker's were to get the contract for the next slip to be built at Chatham, but not for its roof. A critical feature, however, was the fact that the design for the roofs had not been decided upon when the contract was taken for the slips. However, as the pits for the standards were part of this contract a key decision governing the design of the roofs, the width between the standards, had already been taken: a decision, as noted previously, in which the demands of the shipwrights had played a significant part. The *ad hoc* elements in the whole project were quite understandable given its pioneering nature.[11]

Developments at Portsmouth

At Portsmouth, the existing covered slips were re-covered with fireproof materials, and a specification was sent to Captain Beatson for stripping the roofs of docks, slips and spaces between, and replacing the old material with slates, but this was altered to zinc, with galvanised iron eye bolts in the roofs.[12]

A sequence of newly constructed slips with roofs was projected, of which nos. 3 and 4 were shortly to be built. Beatson produced plans and sections of the masonry slips in November 1844, in which the positioning of the standards formed an integral part. The following month John Rigby of Hawarden Iron Works produced designs that were in effect a variant of the Fox, Henderson model, and which were not adopted (Figure 39A,

THE WATER TANK AT PORTSMOUTH

In April 1842 Beatson and Blake, the Master Shipwright, forwarded a plan to Brandreth showing their selected spot for an elevated iron water tank, part of a system of ring main fire precautions originally devised by Samuel Bentham. This structure was to be a typical example of the collaborative designing that was to characterise work in the Yards from then on.

It incorporated a feature derived from greenhouse design, the use of the hollow cast column as a water pipe. Water from the cistern was conveyed into the ring main through hollow columns placed on either side. Beatson and Brandreth thought the columns should be made thicker to allow for corrosion, with spare columns provided in case of mishap. The space beneath the tank could be usefully employed as a wood store, though only deals could be stowed there, as oak, especially, produced a chemical reaction with iron.

Bramah & Fox, of the London Works, Birmingham (shortly to become Fox, Henderson, and the constructors of the slip roofs and Smithery at Pembroke Dock), were the contractors for the metal components, and Brandreth consulted them 'as practical Engineers of experience in this particular work' over the best way of setting the columns on stone plinths, overruling Beatson's suggested method. Mr Bramble, a well-known local contractor, dealt with the foundations.

Before the tank was filled it was apparent that things were not quite as they should be, and Bramah & Fox were asked to provide four sets of wrought iron stays to reinforce the structure; perhaps they designed them as well. The resulting impressive array of iron looks good, though a consequence of faulty design. In November 1843 a tender was put out for piping to connect the tank with the salt water pump at the wood mills in order to bring it into operation, and in 1847 Messrs Baker & Son closed the open sides of the structure with corrugated iron to form a deal store (Figure 40 – overleaf).[13]

39A The Rigby
designs for the
Portsmouth roofs.
*(TNA ADM 140/625
Pt.2)*

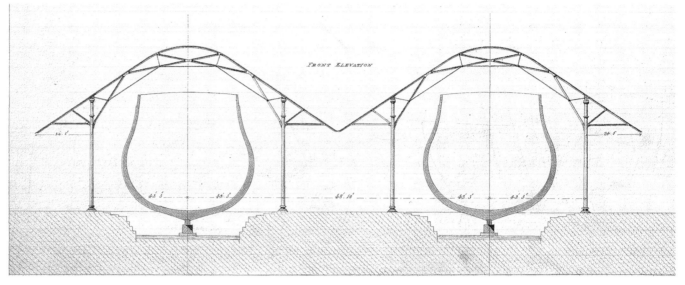

39B). Possibly at the same time Baker's produced a highly ornamental design, with massive castings in the spandrels as the principal structural elements: this also remained a paper project.

A design was under serious consideration in February 1845 when the Portsmouth officers were asked to report on drawing of the proposed roofs, and they asked to be provided with:

39B The Rigby
designs for the
Portsmouth roofs.
*(TNA ADM 140/625
Pt. 2)*

> …a Midship Section of the *Royal Albert*, and also a Section of the Bow shewing the height and spread of the Cathead of that Ship to enable us to test the framing of the Roof, with a view to

clearing the same when launching a Ship of the *Albert's* dimensions, which exceed those of the *Queen*, the only guide we have at present.

It was not until 25 September that Baker & Son got the contract for the roofs, and the next month the buildings at the head of the slips were to be cleared away so that work on the pits for the standards could begin. The distance between the standards was increased, perhaps because of a better grasp of what iron construction could achieve, or possibly as a result of user criticism of the Pembroke design. That, as has been seen, was a translation of a wooden original into metal. This idea was completely discarded, as was Baker's first concept. Whereas the Fox, Henderson roof had been put together from separate

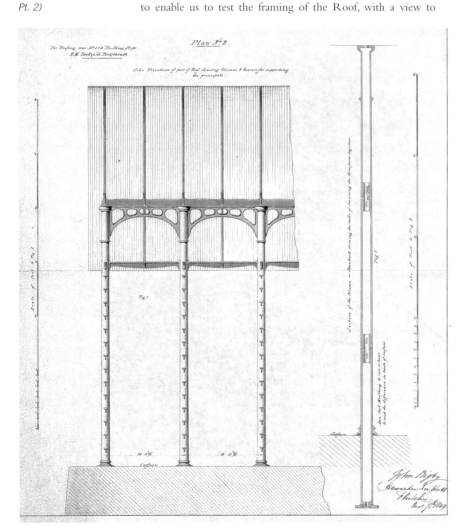

40 Beatson's iron frame for the water tank, now known as the Fire Station. *(Elaine A Wakefield © Wessex Archaeology)*

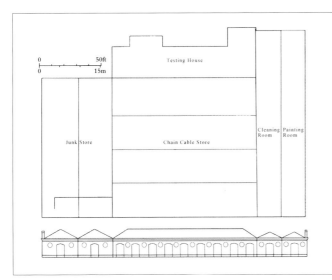

41A   Plan of the Chain Cable Store at Portsmouth. *(Redrawn from English Heritage A940956, English Heritage Plans Room)*

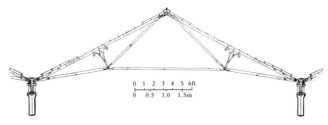

41B   The iron roof of the Chain Cable Store. *(Derived from English Heritage A940960, English Heritage Plans Room)*

components like a giant Meccano set, and erected at great risk by the workmen without the use of scaffolding, here each main truss was composed of six separate castings bolted together, with a much more user-friendly assembly technique involving permanent scaffolding.

Beatson was responsible for three more buildings at Portsmouth, comprising a water tank (Figure 40) and stores for chain cables and small boats. All these displayed a strong element of *ad hoc* thought in their design history. With the wholesale introduction of chain cables, testing machines had to be installed at the Yards. The first, probably designed by Goodrich, and built by the Bramah firm, was installed at Woolwich in 1832 (Figure 42). This hydraulic machine was the sole one in the Dockyards until 1842, when plans were drawn up for the foundations for a cable and anchor testing machine at Portsmouth.[14] Merely storing the cables posed problems that had not been encountered in storing rope cables. They

occupied considerably more space than rope, and were extremely heavy.[15]

Drawings of March 1843 show the testing machine in its house, and that month Bramble again got the contract to erect the building. However, these plans were clearly altered, for by June 1843 Beatson was asked to draw plans and estimates for the testing house and store (this is the second of the three notable buildings by Beatson referred to at the beginning of this chapter). Beatson's plans were prepared by November, though final decisions were to be deferred until after a site visit early the next year: the building was now to incorporate a junk store as well. In view of the weights and stresses to which the building would be subjected, a single-storey, iron-framed building covering quite a large area was an obvious solution (Figure 41A).

The foundations of a chain cable store were laid at the beginning of 1844 at Devonport, though this had three floors for multiple functions. It had an iron roof, by Murn, and was later adapted as a storehouse. The Portsmouth building was still not completed by December 1844, when Beatson drew up designs for cast iron circular windows and metal doors.[16] The contractor for the Woolwich Factory, Henry Grissell, won the tender to provide the extremely attractive and rather unmilitary-looking iron roof at the end of September 1845. This exploited the decorative potential of arched girders by bolting them, in an unhistorical mix of styles, to Tuscan columns. This combination of easily formed decoration in cast

42 A drawing of 1857 shows the Woolwich machine engaged in testing the strength of an anchor. *(TNA ADM 87/64)*

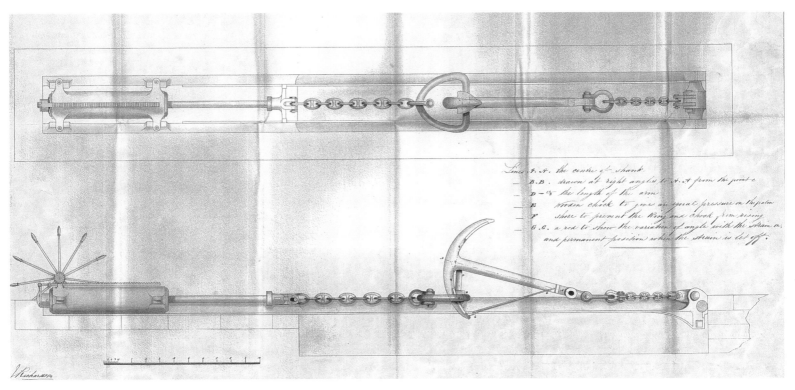

43A Beatson's drawing of the trussed beam.
(© Crown Copyright. NMR BB 96/10716)

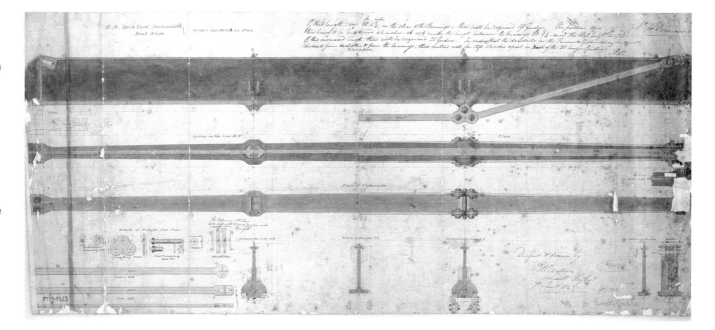

44 The interior of the Chain Cable Store. The cables were tensed in a central trough which has now been covered over.
(© Crown Copyright. NMR AA 045925)

iron with the arch was typical of the time. The construction dragged on, and it was left to Captain Henry James to complete the building in 1847. He hit on the perfect solution for flooring a building that was to have enormous weights dumped in it: the use of iron blocks of ship ballast (Figure 44).[17]

Beatson's best-known building at Portsmouth is the new Boat Store, the first surviving drawings of which date from the beginning of 1845. This was a massive, metal, three-storey structure within a conventional, and classically based, external cladding. Rigby's were the contractors. Internally, round cast iron columns supported the shorter spans with arched girders and the longer ones with trussed girders (Figure 43B). These were cast iron beams with wrought iron tie bars tensioned to resist bending, and were used in both buildings and railway bridges for about two decades. These trusses precede Sir William Fairbairn's experiments with trussed beams, which showed that the truss rod should never be carried to a height greater than the horizontal line passing through the centre of the beam, or structural failure is likely to result. The ends of Beatson's trusses do, but not to the extent of much contemporary practice, which led to the

45 The exterior of the Boat Store. *(Elaine A Wakefield © Wessex Archaeology)*

43B The Boatstore interior. *(© Crown Copyright. NMR BB/12875)*

disastrous collapse of the railway bridge over the Dee in 1847.

There is no reason to suppose that Beatson had calculated the safety of his structure, which had instructions cast on the beams that the maximum loading was to be 40 tons. Ships' boats weighed nothing like this (the 39ft launch, the largest boat in service in the 1830s, turned the scales at 96cwt), and the building was in fact massively over-engineered, which helped to produce an extremely expensive building. The extra third storey alone, added at Beatson's suggestion, was estimated at £6,000. It was also, like some other technology-led buildings since, a failure in practice, described as 'totally unsuited either for a Working Boat House, or a Boat Store', as it was too cramped, and it was awkward to shunt and rearrange boats within it. The building remains an interesting indicator of the state of structural understanding in the mid-1840s, and an example of a dead-end in constructional development. Lessons were learnt from its failure, and it was to be succeeded at Sheerness by a highly successful building at the leading edge of technology.[18] As will be seen, Beatson was shortly to be transferred to

Woolwich, where considerable structural ingenuity was displayed in the designs for slips 4, 5 and 6. There is no reason to suppose that he was not responsible for their design. Slip No. 4, made by Fox, Henderson and Co. and moved to Chatham in 1872 after the closure of Woolwich, survives as a very economical and practical design. According to Edward Cowper, the structural engineer who designed (and calculated) the Birmingham Central Railway Station roof for Fox, Henderson & Co., it was the first wide-span roof to be constructed with compound ribs rather than rolled iron ones (Figure 46).[19]

Testing and manipulating metals

The difficulties experienced by a skilled engineer such as Beatson provided a graphic illustration of the need to set iron construction on a more scientific footing. Correspondence dated September 1843 between two of the new partners of Boulton & Watt shows that they were to have a site meeting at Chatham with Brandreth and the Board of Admiralty, and that

46 The interior of Slip No 4, as resited at Chatham.
(© Crown Copyright. NMR BB 97/7703)

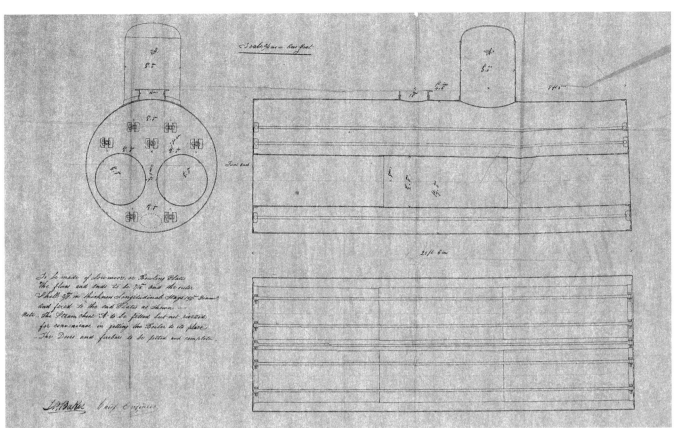

47A (left) and **47B** (below) Drawings of the Chatham Metal Mills. *(TNA ADM 140/109 (6, 5, 10))*

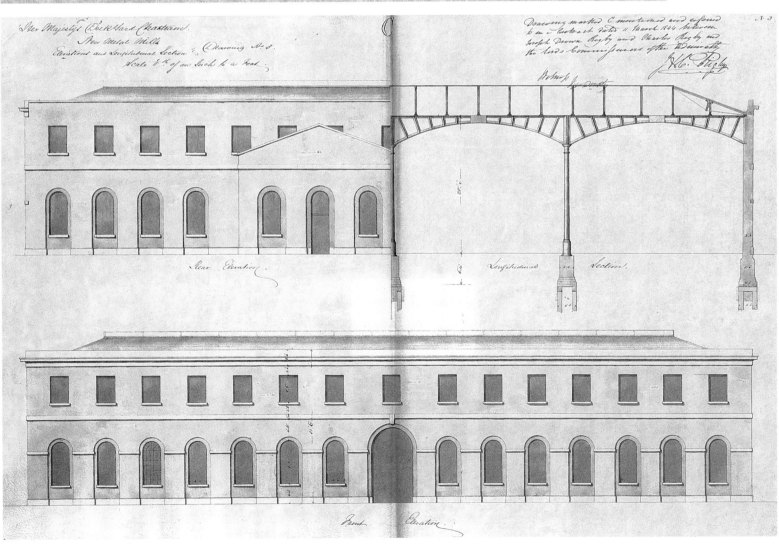

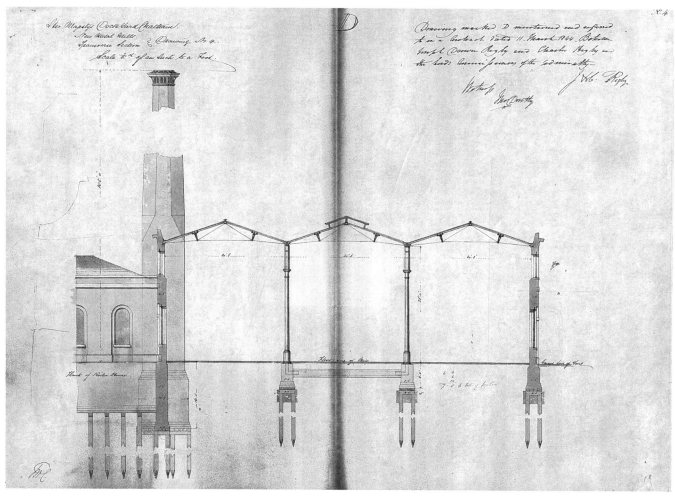

completed drawings of the machinery for the Metal Mills[20] were ready to be sent to John Fincham, the Master Shipwright, 'for [his] guidance in making the building', a very late instance of a shipwright being detected in the act of designing a dockyard facility. By the end of November Fincham had produced several sets of drawings, and further unsigned versions of the design of the metal roof date from January 1844. These last are complicated trusses, almost certainly not calculated, and possibly designs by Fincham (Figure 47A). In the event Rigby's built, and probably designed, the building (Figures 47B and C).

Iron was now seen as the preferred structural material by the Admiralty, an order being issued on 18 April 1845:

> With reference to their Lordship's direction that all buildings shall in future be of incombustible materials…My Lords positively desire that all permanent buildings shall be constructed of Iron where practicable, & that specific reasons be always assigned for any proposed deviation from this order, & that in erecting temporary buildings such as sheds, workshops etc combustible materials are as much as possible to be avoided — & you are to direct the Engineer Officers to pay the strictest regard to this instruction.

Shortly after this decision a Committee on Metals was set up, composed of Brandreth, Lloyd, James Nasmyth and Lloyd's old fellow-student Jeremiah Owen, now Supervisor of Metals to the Admiralty. It was to make an important contribution to the future construction of yard buildings. In what appears to have been a division of labour within the committee, Brandreth and Lloyd were to visit the yards to inspect the differing metallurgical techniques in use, while Owen concentrated on the structural uses of iron, now officially enjoined. The scientific testing of materials was not a new departure, Telford having conducted some experiments in 1814, followed by Captain Brown, whose chain cables have already been mentioned, in 1817. Marc Brunel tested Yorkshire iron, and in 1837 William Fairbairn read a paper on the subject to the Literary and Philosophical Society of Manchester, which drew on experiments performed by Lloyd at Woolwich Dockyard.[21] Owen had already published the results of tests on iron made at Messrs Walker's Works, Tipton, and further experiments for determining the strength of cast iron girders were performed and published in 1847. These tested ordinary cast iron girders against a compound of cast iron and scrap wrought iron, and it was found that the toughened cast iron girders broke at an average weight of 52.3 tons, as against 38.3 tons for the ordinary iron.[22]

The Committee on Metals produced two reports, in June 1846 and May 1847. The first included a string of decisions, some of which were to affect Yard buildings directly, others indirectly through their fittings, and matters of workshop practice. All new iron was to be kept under cover, which further increased the need to add metal roofs over previously open spaces. Scrap iron was to be cleaned in the chain cable cleaning machine recently devised by James Nasmyth. The rust had previously been removed from chain cables by beating the links with a small hammer: upwards of 1,000 blows were sometimes given to each link of the large sizes. Owen and Nasmyth condemned this practice, Nasmyth recommending mechanical cleaning of the cabling in revolving cylinders followed by annealing of the brittle iron.[23]

Accommodation had to be found for these cleaning machines; the first one was sent to Portsmouth in October 1845 and housed in an extension of the Chain Cable Store, which was just about to receive its elegant iron roof.[24] In August 1847 coking ovens at £50 each, for carbonising coal before use in the smith's forges, and annealing ovens at £180 were ordered to be supplied by Nasmyth's to all the yards. Design shortcomings of the old smitheries were indicated by the injunction that smitheries were to be well lit and kept as free from smoke as far as possible: the officers were to propose the best means of effecting this.[25]

New men and machines

The advent of new equipment (and consequently a new grade of skilled labour) was signalled by the intention to introduce a class of hammermen into the smitheries. Quality control and standardisation measures were initiated, with each article being marked with the initial of the smith, and threads and screws were to be made uniform. This last had long been necessary. Goodrich had confided to his journal 20 years before that 'Strodes Female Screw goes slackly upon my Male Screw — and his Male Screw scarcely goes upon my Female'. Finally, iron framing and corrugated iron were always to be kept in store for the temporary roofs that much of this programme envisaged.[26]

On 24 June 1846 Owen was appointed Supervisor of Metals in the Yards at £400 a year, borne on the books of Portsmouth Yard. He was in charge of smitheries and metal works of every description except those relating to steam engines and boilers. The machinery at the Metal Mills was still incomplete in July 1846, when a shearing machine and various rolls were still required. In November four key workmen were moved from Portsmouth to Chatham, together with their families, not to be returned to Portsmouth until new metal mills were built there. These mills, however, never were to be constructed, and soon another 17 'young, active and ablebodied labourers' in Chatham Yard were to be transferred to the establishment of the Metal Mills. 'The additional strength thus afforded will render the

48 The interior structure and a steam hammer are also exposed in this photograph, taken after the explosion of 1866. The Mills closed down in 1872. (Royal Engineers Library, Brompton)

THE NASMYTH HAMMER

James Nasmyth's patent had been enrolled on 9 December 1842, but the first model was not very satisfactory, and it was not until his works manager, Robert Wilson, had developed a gear to make the machine self-acting that the hammer was a commercial proposition. This mechanism was so crucial to its success that an early historian of the Steam Hammer stated, magnificently, 'For myself, I would be prouder to say that I was the inventor of that motion, than to say I had commanded a regiment at Waterloo…' (Figure 49).

The first hammer was delivered on 18 August 1843, to the Low Moor Works at Bradford, who had rejected the hammer in its unmodified form. Denison and Burgmann visited Nasmyth's factory at Patricroft to view the invention, and orders for the Dockyards followed next year. On 19 September 1844, 2½ ton and ½ ton hammers were ordered for Devonport, Portsmouth and Chatham, and a set of machinery for working the Hercules in Devonport North Smithery by steam was ordered the next month.

Next July further orders were placed for all the Yards:

Devonport, a 2½ ton hammer for the South Smithery and a 10 cwt one at the North Smithery;
Woolwich, a 2½ ton and a 15 cwt;
Chatham, a 10 cwt;
Sheerness a 2½ ton and a 10 cwt;
Portsmouth another 10 cwt;
Pembroke Dock ones of 2½ ton, 15 cwt and 10 cwt.

49 The height and scale of the Nasysmith Hammer is graphically displayed in this photograph of the interior of Captain James' Smithery at Portsmouth. *(Portsmouth City Library)*

In April 1846 2½ ton, 15 cwt and 10 cwt hammers were ordered for the new Factory Smithery at Woolwich and one of 25 cwt for Armand of Marseilles. (Nasmyth, on a fact-finding tour of the Continent in 1842, had seen many of his machines installed in shipyards.)

The hammers were not small pieces of equipment, and new buildings were required: the 1847/8 Estimates contained £12,675 for the extension of the North Smithery at Devonport, and the foundations were laid at the end of 1847. This extension was originally to have been furnished with a single large chimney, but this plan was soon abandoned, and six smaller ones designed by Nasmyth and built by Rigby's were substituted. Fox, Henderson were paid £500 on account for the structural ironwork in November 1848. It is possible that Nasmyth sold the Admiralty a pup in the form of at least some unmodified hammers, for in February 1848 Lawrie reported on the improvements of the Low

Moor machine, stating that Low Moor (which by now had a symbiotic relationship with Nasmyth's, who recommended Low Moor iron for their boilers) had offered to modify the Chatham hammer for £80, an offer that was accepted.

In June 1848 Nasmyth secured a further contract for hammers and ancillary equipment at Devonport:

	£
5 cwt Steam Hammer	320
10 cwt Steam Hammer	440
15 cwt Steam Hammer	450
New boiler for 2½ ton Steam Hammer	340
2 new cranes for Steam Hammers, with a 3 ton lift	460

though these machines were to prove the exception to the rule of the efficiency of the machinery. At that moment the provision of Nasmyth Hammers in the Yards was:

Deptford	2
Woolwich	5 at Dock Yard Smithery
	4 in Factory Smithery
Chatham	2
Sheerness	2
Portsmouth	2
Devonport	2 at work, 1 erecting,
	3 small just delivered
Pembroke Dock	2

The cost of the manufacture of iron blooms by the Nasmyths was lowest at Woolwich and highest at Pembroke Dock, with Devonport the next highest.[27]

power of the Chatham Mills available, not only in rolling sheets, and boltstaves, but also in attaining the long-desired objective of remanufacturing our own old iron', an affirmation of the critical and continuing importance of muscle power. All the ironworking tools still at Portsmouth Mills were to be packed up and forwarded to the new establishment.[28]

A Chief Engineer was now required at Chatham with the advent of all this machinery, and on 30 June 1846 Alexander Lawrie, another Scot, was appointed to the post at £400 a year. The offices of Master of Saw Mills and Conductor of Lead Mills were abolished; Lawrie had charge of all the machinery in the Yard. This now included that icon of the Smithery, a Nasmyth Hammer.

The second report of the Committee on Metals, in May 1847, proposed that the metallurgical capabilities of the Navy should be extended, and that means be afforded in the Dockyards for remanufacturing the whole of the scrap and old iron.[29] In some private establishments this was done with extraordinary care, the result being a very superior article. Portsmouth Metal Mills had done this to a very limited extent,

and all who used the iron agreed that it was the best they had ever met with for ordinary purposes. It was hoped that the work of the Chatham Mills and the use of rolls in conjunction with steam hammers would produce iron of similar quality.

The Committee were convinced that the quality of work done in the Yards was at least equal to that of private firms, and their dissatisfaction with the suppliers of chain cables led them to propose a completely new establishment specialising in heavy forgings.

Impressed by the results of the Woolwich smiths, who had made chain cabling superior to that supplied in the private yards,[30] the Committee recommended that an establishment be set up and equipped for the manufacture of anchors and other large iron articles. Not only anchors might be made, but also large wrought iron parts of steam engines, iron pillars and perhaps eventually chain cables. Such a factory would be an invaluable training ground for craftsmen:

The highest skill of the Smith is involved in the manufacturing of the largest articles of Iron Work, and it is therefore submitted that such an establishment might be made an excellent <u>Normal School</u> for the training of men to become Masters and Foremen of Smiths…

Uniformity of practice would also follow; this was a key theme in the industrialisation of the Navy, and in marked contrast to the multiplicity of practices that prevailed in private industry. Deptford was proposed as a suitable site, but nothing ever came of this far-sighted project for technical education. The office of Supervisor of Metals was abolished in August 1849, but Owen was retained on full salary to continue with his experiments on the strength of materials.[31]

—◊—

Notes:

[1] Johnson and Skempton, 'Willam Strutt's Cotton Mills', *Transactions of the Newcomen Society*, XXX, 1955-56, p.180. R Fitzgerald, 'The Development of the Cast Iron Frame for Textile Mills to 1850', *Industrial Archaeology Review*, X, 2, 1988; C Giles and I Goodall, *Yorkshire Textile Mills 1770-1930*, RCHME, (London, 1992), p.70. For detailed accounts of Holl's buildings see Coad, *passim*; J Barrett, 'On the construction of fire-proof buildings', *Proceedings of the Institution of Civil Engineers*, vol. XII, 1853, pp.244-271; W Fairbairn, *On the Application of Cast and Wrought Iron to Building Purposes*, (London, 1856); L Hurst, 'The age of fireproof flooring', in *The Iron Revolution… 1780-1880*, (London, 1990), pp.35-39. G Tucker, 'Warehousing' in R J M Carr (ed.) *Docklands*, 2nd.ed. (London, 1987). DNB, entry on Peto; speech by Fox quoted in C Tomlinson, *Cyclopaedia of Useful Arts & Manufactures*, (London, 1854), p.xxiii.

[2] The Shipwrights were asked which of *Black Prince*, *Defence*, *Devonshire*, and *Redoubtable* should be broken up to supply timber for its repair. The last vessel was selected, and the repairs were effected using inferior English oak and materials from *Redoubtable*.

[3] In a subsequent letter he added that where the slips were less than 80ft apart the central row of pillars in the intermediate building should be dispensed with. William Edye, the only dissentient, replied from Pembroke Dock: 'There are great objections to the distance of the standards across the slip being only 82ft 6ins, they should not be less than 100ft, but if 105ft could be obtained it would be much more convenient.' He also objected to columns in the intermediate space. He did not get his 100ft, which had been the width of the 1841 roof.

[4] Contemporary printed sources for slip roofs are Captain M Williams, RE, 'Description of Wrought Iron Roofs erected over two Building Slips in the Royal Dockyard at Pembroke…' in *Papers on Subjects connected with the Duties of the Corps of Royal Engineers*, vol. 9, 1847, pp.50-58, and in the same volume, pp.59-65, F W Cumberland, 'Iron Roofs erected over Building Slips, Nos.3 and 4, in Her Majesty's Dockyard, Portsmouth'. A modern examination of the subject is given by R J M Sutherland, 'Shipbuilding and the long span roof', in *Transactions of the Newcomen Society*, vol. 60, 1988-9, pp. 107-125; ADM 12/397, ADM 140/227-8, CHA/H/38, CHA/H/39, CHA/H/44, ADM 12/411, ADM 12/460, ADM 12/476, ADM 1/5521.

[5] Pembroke Dock — too low, and no means of securing staging. Chatham — light and elegant, but structurally weak, and liable to be objectionably hot in summer. Portsmouth suggested a small alteration. Brandreth considered it would not be judicious to adopt the roof, and Palmer was informed that his plan was not considered applicable to large slips, but that the experiment might be tried on a smaller scale. It never was, which seems a pity.

[6] *Mechanics' Magazine*, vol. 18, 1832, pp.113-115, ADM 1/5521.

[7] A drawing signed by Mould gives a section of one of the proposed slips 'shewing thereon sections of a First Rate and a First Class Steam Vessel, and the proposed positions of the Standards of the Iron Roofs. It will be observed by an inspection of this sketch that if the Roof were curtailed to 270 feet the Shipwrights would be much cramped in their operations'. Another plan 'of proposed iron Roof' over the three slips is signed by both Mould and Baker. It also shows the wooden roof over No. 3 'over *Mars*', and is annotated by Mould: 'The eaves of the wing of No. 4 Roof are not to extend beyond the dotted line from B2 to B, and there are not to be any side enclosures between those two points. The wooden Roof will be cut to suit the Iron Roof where the two come into contact'.

[8] CHA/H/78, ADM 12/428, ADM 140/60/1-3, NMM S/35, CHA/H/68.

[9] The difficulties of the site were caused by a stratum of silt from 5 to 7ft in thickness at an average depth of 3ft below low water. Firm gravelly soils were reached at 16ft below low water. As the original plan was to construct a deep basin at the back of the slips, it was expected that when that work was undertaken this bed of silt would flow into the foundations: pumping this away would cause a greater subsidence of the soil, and the slips would be wrecked. The preferred solution was to rest the slips on piles, so that the motion of the silt would not affect them, and to case each slip within an envelope of close-jointed sheeting piles. The Director of Works summed up Baker & Son's alternative suggestion:

> The Contractors on the contrary proposed to build on a bed of concrete resting on the natural soil. But as they intended to carry the Concrete foundations under the River Wall, down to the bed of Gravel, and in like manner to construct the foundations of the Side Walls of the entrance to the Basin, the effect would have been for that part of the work only which they proposed to carry down to the Gravel, to seal the bed of Silt within walls of Concrete, which so far as the Walls went, would have been an effectual protection to the foundations. But as the sides of the Slips for a length of 1800 feet would have been exposed to great risk, no provision having been made for all that length for retaining the Silt, the Contractors scheme was not entertained.

[10] By August Mr Rivers, the Clerk of Works, who must have had a lot of explaining to do, reported that the fractured standards and the coping of the extension of slip 6 had been effectually repaired. He was to report monthly on their condition, and on the surface level of the extension coping, to report on any deviation. He had presumably tried to suggest that the failure had been caused by the inadequacy of Baker's men, for

> Their Lordships differ from the conclusions at which he has arrived, and have no doubt that the irregularities in the surface line, were caused by the subsidence of the foundation, and by nothing else — If the irregularities in question could possibly be traced to careless workmanship, as stated by him, he would stand convicted of great negligence and inattention to his duty…

It is hard to see how failure to note the absence of the piles could be described as anything else.

[11] CHA/H/78, CHA/H/79.

[12] After the work was over, the Admiralty received an anonymous letter alleging that a fraud had been practised on the weight of the zinc roofing supplied, and the Admiral Superintendent was ordered to make the contractor (Messrs Walker) provide some explanations. It is not known how the matter was resolved.

[13] For iron construction and the contribution made by Royal Engineer officers, see J Weiler, 'The making of collaborative genius — Royal Engineers and structural iron 1820-1870', in *The Iron Revolution… 1780-1880*, (London, 1990); ADM 1/3503, ADM 1/5521, UP 333808, ADM 12/417, POR/P/13, ADM 12/411, POR/P/37.

[14] Earlier testing machines were operated by weights and lever systems; the Navy's were to be hydraulically operated. The equipment (originally for Deptford and Woolwich) was manufactured by Bramah, who had pioneered the construction of hydraulic presses. The design was probably drawn up in collaboration with Goodrich (who signed some of the surviving drawings). Trouble was experienced in manufacturing the Woolwich machine: the first Naval Lord, Admiral Sir Thomas Hardy, apparently instigated a demand that the machine be capable of exerting a force of 300 tons. Bramah's boggled at this, and replied that 180 tons was the limit of their warranty - and then the cylinder of the press turned out to be unsound. The demand was lowered to 250 tons, then to 200, and finally Bramah's were ordered to proceed with their original design. This is an early example of the Navy's expecting more from technology than contemporary practice could really offer. G W Lenox, 'On chain-cables', *Transactions of the Institution of Naval Architects*, vol. 1, 1860, pp.160-172, BL Add. 41399 ff. 8r, 9v, ADM 106/1668, ADM 106/1453, GOOD A/1675 1-4, GOOD A/1725; ADM 106/1913. I McNeil, 'Hydraulic power transmission - the first 350 years', *Transactions of the Newcomen Society*, vol. 47, 1977, pp.149-159, gives 1816 as the date for Bramah's first testing machine.

[15] GOOD A/1675 1-4; GOOD A/1725. A hundred fathoms of $3\frac{1}{2}$in cable weighed 588 cwt, and 100 fathoms of even $\frac{3}{4}$in cable weighed 27 cwt. (These figures are derived from a later period, but probably give a fair idea.) The space occupied was also considerable; closely stowed cable occupied $35d^2$ cubic feet per hundred fathoms, where d is the diameter of cable iron in inches.

[16] These components were supplied by Bailey, Pegg & Company: 24 cast and corrugated iron doors, and 37 cast iron windows and sashes. Two of the circular windows still survive within the building, as does the hole left by

the removal of another, enabling the original wall lines to be traced within the later additions.

[17] There was plenty of this to hand; in 1830 1,720 tons of it were in store at Portsmouth alone, 2,159 tons at Devonport, and 1,917 tons at Chatham. In October that year the smith in charge of the test house had his pay increased, a sure sign that the building was then functioning. UP 333643. N J McDermaid, *Shipyard Practice as applied to Warship Construction*, (London, 1911), p.279, ADM 140/517, POR/P/13, ADM 12/411, ADM 12/428, ADM 140/553, 554, POR/P/22, BL Add. 41,404, POR/P/39.

[18] R J M Sutherland, 'The right to survive' [on the Boat Store], in *New Builder*, May 17 1990, pp.28-29; PLSC, a large batch of drawings NMR PTM 1309-1342, BL Add. 41,404, Chatham Historic Dockyard Library DOC 19.

[19] Brandreth called on Fox, Henderson to tender for this roof; this was £12,000, but by the end of the year the firm had revised it upwards to £17,000. ADM 12/411, ADM 12/428, ADM 12/444, ADM 2/1387, *Minutes of Evidence before the Committee of Inquiry on the Economy of Her Majesty's Dockyards*, 1859, p.293; ADM 140/1153/3, ADM 1/6195. Sutherland (*op.cit.*) attributes the design of the Woolwich roofs to Fox, Henderson. E Cowper, 'Description of the wrought-iron roof over the Central Railway Station at Birmingham', in *Proceedings of the Institution of Mechanical Engineers*, 1854, pp.79-87; ADM 12/460. ADM 12/476, ADM 12/492.

[20] The modernisation of the Portsmouth Metal Mills, which were closed down in 1846, was suspended in September 1843, and the foreman was sent to Chatham to pass on his knowledge, as it was now proposed to construct metal mills there. On 11 March 1844 a contract was drawn up between Messrs Rigby and the Admiralty for the construction of the Mills, but the business proceeded very slowly. The buildings were of iron construction within brick walls.

[21] A summary of previous investigations, with the author's own exhaustive researches, is given by D Kirkcaldy, *Results of an experimental inquiry into the tensile strength and other properties of various kinds of wrought-iron and steel*, (Glasgow, 1862).

[22] POR/P/15, BW Box 11/23, ADM 140/109/1-10, CHA/H/58, ADM 1/5553, POR/P/20, POR/P/22, POR/P/30, CHA/H/61, ADM 1/5553.

[23] POR/P/20. Nasmyth stated:

> The most simple, expeditious & economical method of cleaning the chains would be to put them into a cylinder of wrought Iron, pierced full of holes, & cause the cylinder to revolve slowly, the result of this will be that by the mutual attrition of each link upon each, the entire chain will be in a very short time be rendered quite free from rust, and come out of its cage nearly bright. Several entire chains may be cleaned at once, in this manner, at a very small cost. These once thro' the annealing furnace, they are all ready for service.
>
> The operation of annealing toughens up brittle iron, and is accomplished by keeping the metal in ovens at about 1,600 °F for three to four days, after which the fire is allowed to slowly die down for another five days.

[24] The Devonport machine was not supplied until 1852, and then it was placed in the South Smithery rather than the Chain Cable Store, after some discussion. This was presumably to be on hand for the annealing furnace. Coals were to be slightly carbonised before use in smiths' forges, and it was immediately decided to introduce such an oven at Portsmouth. Internal changes in the foundries, affecting chimney arrangements, followed from the decision to substitute air furnaces for hollow fires as convenience might admit. Cold hammering was to be abolished unless the articles could be annealed afterwards: 'My Lords attach much importance to this point', from which the recommendation followed that annealing furnaces were to be introduced into the several yards.

[25] POR/P/28, POR/P/20, POR/P/23, ADM 85/5, Nasmyth Order Book no. 2, ADM 84/4, ADM 12/540.

[26] GOOD B/57.

[27] POR/P/28, CHA/H/63, T S Rowlandson, *Lecture on the History of the Steam Hammer*, (Eccles, 1864); the modern literature on the Nasmyth Hammer is J A Cantrell, 'James Nasmyth and the Bridgwater Foundry', (Manchester, 1984), and 'James Nasmyth and the Steam Hammer', in *Transactions of the Newcomen Society*, vol. 56, 1986, pp.133-138; J L Wood, 'The development of the Steam Hammer in Scotland', in *Transactions of the Newcomen Society*, vol. 56, 1986, pp.139-149; Nasmyth Order Book no. 2, Nasmyth's *Autobiography*, ADM 83/33, ADM 83/35, ADM 12/492, POR/P/18, POR/P/20, ADM 12/428, ADM 12/444, ADM 12/476, ADM 2/1389, ADM 2/1387, CHA/H/69, ADM 95/97, ADM 1/5590, GOOD B/57.

[28] It was almost certainly the Committee on Metals that made the decision in January 1846 to close down the Portsmouth operation and concentrate all the copper-processing operations at Chatham, as the space was needed for the new buildings in connection with the Steam Basin. The operations were maintained from November on a diminished scale, until the building was required for an extension of the Smithery facilities. Apart from the Boulton & Watt engines and rolling machinery, the new Chatham Mills were equipped with two 2 ton cranes by Messrs Gordon & Davis, and Rigby's paved them with iron ballast.

[29] Four kinds of wrought iron were in use in the Dockyards:
new iron manufactured from ore and supplied by contractors;
scrap iron sent from the Dockyards to be remanufactured by Johnson, Norton & Co.;
a small quantity of scrap remanufactured at the Metal Mills, Portsmouth;
scrap remanufactured in the Dockyards under steam and tilt hammers, and not afterwards rolled into flats, boltstaves, etc.
Portsmouth came out well from this scrutiny. The Committee found that of these kinds the best was that remanufactured at the Metal Mills, while the scrap remanufactured by Johnson & Co. was generally preferable to the new wrought iron.

[30] The materials were suspected of not always being up to specification, and no Government inspection of the processes took place. There was no incentive to provide cables stronger than required for proving, and smiths at Woolwich unaccustomed to the work had made links of superior strength to those supplied by private firms. Increasing the proof strain would not much mend matters, as the response would be to reach the target and no more, but an improvement could be enforced if the price of every cable were made dependent upon its absolute strength (ascertained by breaking a few of its links), and the scale of prices were so graduated that the contractors' profit should be little or nothing upon cables such as were currently supplied, but very liberal upon cables of the highest quality.

[31] ADM 1/5563, ADM 92/14.

CHAPTER 6

Gaining the Technological Edge

IN 1815 the Royal Navy was incontestably the most powerful force afloat. By 1840 there were concerns that the old adversary across the Channel was able to mount a serious challenge not just through the acquisition of steam warships, but by the provision of a supportive infrastructure on a scale not attempted in Britain. French technology lagged behind, but the purchase of large quantities of British machinery compensated for this deficiency in much the same way that the supply of American machine tools during the Second World War did for British backwardness in that department. By the early 1840s Cherbourg in particular was being developed on an incomparably grander scale than anything available for the Royal Navy's steamers.

Denison at Portsmouth

In 1839 the Admiral Superintendent at Portsmouth had proposed to convert the Inner Boat Pond, which gave access to the storehouses for ships' boats, into a basin for steamers. What was needed, however, was something to rival the massive constructional works that had been going on across the Channel. Many commentators had harped on the subject of English backwardness, a typical cry being 'If the English nation needed any stimulus to exertion, here it lies in the fiery bosom of these forges [of Cherbourg].'

Portsmouth was the obvious yard to take in hand, as it was strategically placed to counter Cherbourg. The Civil Lord of the Admiralty, Henry Lowry Corry, wrote in January 1843:

With regard to the proposed Steam Factory at Portsmouth, I am sure that I speak the universal sense of the Board when I say that it is their opinion, that this service, so far from admitting of further postponement, has been already too long delayed — The French have had the foresight to provide ample Basins for the equipment of their Steam Navy in all their Naval Arsenals — in the Channel, on the Atlantic, and in the Mediterranean — while the only Establishment in this country belonging to the Government for the repair of Steam Machinery (with the exception of a small one at Holyhead for the casual repairs required by the packets on the Irish Station) is at Woolwich, and we have not a single public (nor I believe private) Factory along the whole line of coast from Cape Clear to the Thames where any serious defects in a Steam Engine could be made good. Compare this with the State of preparation along the opposite Coast. We are informed by Mr Turnbull in his letter to the Foreign Office dated the 30th of last May 'that he observed at Cherbourg the same activity as last year in the Naval Dockyard, where the greatest attention is turned to hollowing out a Steam Basin, and constructing new buildings for making Steam Engines, and that they are most actively employed in every department connected with Steam Navigation'.

In his view the most striking feature of Cherbourg was the attention paid to machinery for the building and repair of marine engines. John Rennie had also recently reported that a 'magnificent' establishment was being created at Brest, equipped with 'a large collection of the best English tools and Machinery', and that similar establishments were in existence, or in course of erection, 'in all the Dockyards in France'. James Nasmyth, to name but one English manufacturer, had received orders in 1841 from the French Marine for a vertical boring mill for cylinders of a diameter of 18ft, drilling and planing machinery, and a slotting machine. Rennie also noted the factory dedicated to the construction of steam machinery lately established at Indret, and another alarming resource, the Basin at St Malo, 'within a few hours sail of the Channel Islands', which would be completed in the course of two years, and would accommodate 23 ships of the line, 58 frigates and steamers, and upwards of 100 sail of smaller vessels. These reports ensured that, although the Cabinet had insisted that the Naval Estimates be made as low as possible, and the vote for new works be reduced by postponing everything not absolutely essential, Portsmouth Steam Basin and its Steam Factory escaped the cuts.[1]

Two months later the Admiralty sent a plan of the Steam Basin to Portsmouth so that detailed drawings could be prepared and specifications drawn up. The nature and placing of the buildings was still to be determined, and £30,000 was allowed for work on it during that financial year. The Treasury's priorities were not those of the Admiralty; 'the general Restoration of Peace' was more obvious to them than the French threat, and they demanded that the Estimates for 1844/5 'be prepared on a scale suited to that change in the circumstances of the Country'.

Despite these demands for economy, Beatson's workload was now increasing rapidly, and he was allowed an additional draughtsman as a temporary arrangement, and a messenger. On 29 May 1840 Peter Rolt took up the contract for constructing the Basin, while an agreement was made with the Portsea Gas Light Company to bring that facility into the Yard. In September the demolition of the Smithery and other buildings near the Basin was about to take place in order to facilitate Rolt's operations; the machinery was relocated in any suitable buildings, such as the Boiler House and the Metal Mills, where Rennie re-erected the drilling machinery. The foundation stone of the Basin was laid on 13 January 1845.[2]

Beatson was now transferred. On 3 July 1845 Lowry Corry, now First Secretary at the Admiralty, wrote to the Admiral Superintendent at Portsmouth:

As the period approaches for entering upon the consideration of the arrangements for the Buildings and Machinery of the new Steam Factory at Portsmouth their Lordships are of opinion that it will greatly conduce to the successful execution of the work, that it should proceed under the superintendence of Captain Denison, so that the public may have the full benefit of the experience he has acquired in progress of the Factory at Woolwich.

Beatson was to replace him at Woolwich, so that he in turn could gain experience of the arrangement and workings of a steam factory. By rotation of the Royal Engineer officers the Admiralty intended to give 'the peculiar acquirements of each Officer…better scope for that exercise than at present'. Denison's experience was unique, and he was the obvious man to design a new factory, this time from scratch, there being no design for him to inherit. Beatson's peculiar experience was with iron construction; the Admiralty certainly did not want a repeat of the Portsmouth Boat Store at Woolwich, but they did require covered iron slips. The exchange made sense.[3]

The Boat Store was still unfinished, and Denison's first job was to design its roof. The slip roofs were now under construction, work having started in April, and some concern was expressed about the strength of the trussed purlins, which were of a different design from those employed at Pembroke Dock. Denison, who, as has been seen, had a track record of investigating the strength of materials, ordered two of the purlins to be tested, loading them with iron ballast. The breaking weight proved to be 7,410lb. As he calculated that a possible load of 7,980lb might, in extreme circumstances of weather, be placed on the purlin, he ordered the trusses to be strengthened.[4]

Another temporary draughtsman was added to Denison's staff to enable him to commence the designs for the Factory, and by March 1846 a general plan had been approved by the Admiralty. This plan, which provided for an initial building capable of future extensions, was drawn up in collaboration with Lloyd's new Assistant at Woolwich, Andrew Murray.

Murray was another of the young high-flyers attracted to Woolwich, which was now coming on stream as a centre for manufacture and repair as well as administration. The senior management there now had Kingston subordinate to Lloyd and Murray as Assistant Inspector of Steam Machinery, and Dinnen as Foreman of Engineers. Murray had originally intended to obtain a commission in the East India Company's Engineers, but was in the event apprenticed to William Fairbairn, and in 1836 at the age of 23 was appointed managing partner of Fairbairn's newly established Millwall branch. The experience of running a commercial enterprise was an invaluable qualification for Admiralty service.

On 20 June 1846 Murray was appointed acting Chief Engineer and Inspector of Machinery at Portsmouth, in charge of the Steam Factory, 'which with every thing connected with it will be under his special superintendence'. He was also to have charge of machinery of all steamers not in commission, and of all naval engineers borne on the books of the flagship,

and was to be available to visit other yards, and the private establishments where machinery was preparing for service. The chief engineers of all yards were to have similar duties. Murray was to have immediate superintendence of the steam engines and boilers of the Smithery, and to see the steam hammer, Hercules and cranes were efficient. He was to remain at Portsmouth for nearly 23 years, to supervise the establishment of the second Steam Factory and to play a notable part in the development of the industrial buildings and the engineering of the Navy.[5]

Portsmouth Factory, as planned by Denison and Murray, was to have been located on the east side of the Steam Basin between the two docks, where four ships could have been laid alongside it, and would have been a notable step forward in planning. This plan never materialised, as the ground had not been reclaimed, and the need for a new factory was pressing. An essential preliminary step did take place, however: Frederick's Battery, part of the Yard fortifications, had to be dismantled and rebuilt in advance of the new works, a task for which Denison's background made him particularly suited. Its new position, in fact, in the view of the Commanding Royal Engineer at Portsmouth (with whom Denison had naturally conferred) was a considerable improvement.

Denison had no hand in the new scheme, for he had designed his last building, being appointed Lieutenant-Governor of Van Diemen's Land in June 1846. The Admiralty had valued his services highly, and he was knighted on the recommendation of the First Lord, being also allowed as another, lesser, favour to use Naval packing cases for his furniture 'on understanding that he will return them to this country by one of the Convict Ships'. Captain Henry James RE was brought in to replace him, and the collection of building materials that Denison had formed for experimental purposes at Woolwich was forwarded to Portsmouth so that James could continue the work.[6]

Woolwich at work

In the meantime, events were proving that Woolwich was unable to keep up with the burgeoning demand for the service and repair of steam ships. The new Basin had been finished on 9 August 1843, and many leases were purchased during the summer and autumn of 1844 to enable the Yard to expand. The Smithery was already too small when Beatson replaced Denison at Woolwich,[7] and in 1847 he designed a new one specially to include accommodation for steam hammers, some two-thirds the length of the original range and twice as wide, conforming externally with Denison's buildings and probably incorporating the results of a visit that Denison made to Liverpool in 1845 to inspect fireproof storehouses there. It housed four Nasmyth hammers and 48 smiths' hearths, the smoke from which was led by underground tunnels to the great chimney.

Although the furnaces for the steam hammers soon gave trouble,[8] a report of February 1847 shows how things had changed since a decade past, when the bulk of the work was being done by private firms. The Factory was now considered to be almost complete, though because of the level of staffing (considerably below the maximum complement of 304) it was not working to full capacity (Figure 50). All substantial repairs to steam machinery were now done at the Factory, with a few exceptions, which included some of the mail packets and royal yachts. During the financial year 1846/7 £75,000 worth of work had been done, not all on marine engines, for machinery and engines for the use of the Factory itself had been made, as well as some machinery for other Yards. It was already obvious that Woolwich by itself would be put under severe pressure until steam factories were up and running elsewhere; 29 steamers had been under repair during the first nine months of the financial year, eight of which had received new boilers, and there were eight sets of boilers ready for fixing and an additional 15 in course of completion; these were for 23 vessels.

Sustaining this progress was the expertise of some new recruits. In June 1846 Charles Atherton became Lloyd's assistant, Dinnen was promoted to First Assistant Inspector of Steam Machinery to replace Kingston, and John Trickett joined as Second Assistant Inspector.

Atherton's CV began with an honours degree in mathematics at Queen's College, Cambridge (not dazzling: he was 33rd Wrangler in 1828), followed by a period of working under Telford and then becoming partner in Claude, Girdwood & Co., a Glasgow marine engineering firm, at the age of 29. After a strike terminated production there, he erected flax mills in Belgium and then went to Canada in charge of the St Lawrence navigation works. He returned to England in 1845 with the intention of practising as an engineer in Glasgow, but heard there was a vacancy at Woolwich and applied for the post. He succeeded Lloyd as Chief Engineer at Woolwich in the summer of 1847.

Trickett had a more conventional start in engineering, but he was also a fast mover: apprenticed at the Butterley Ironworks, he became assistant to the Managing Engineer of the General Steam Navigation Company at 20, moving to John Penn & Sons, who recommended him to the Admiralty. His principal achievements were to be made during the establishment of

50 The Woolwich factory in its final state. *(TNA ADM 140/1153/3)*

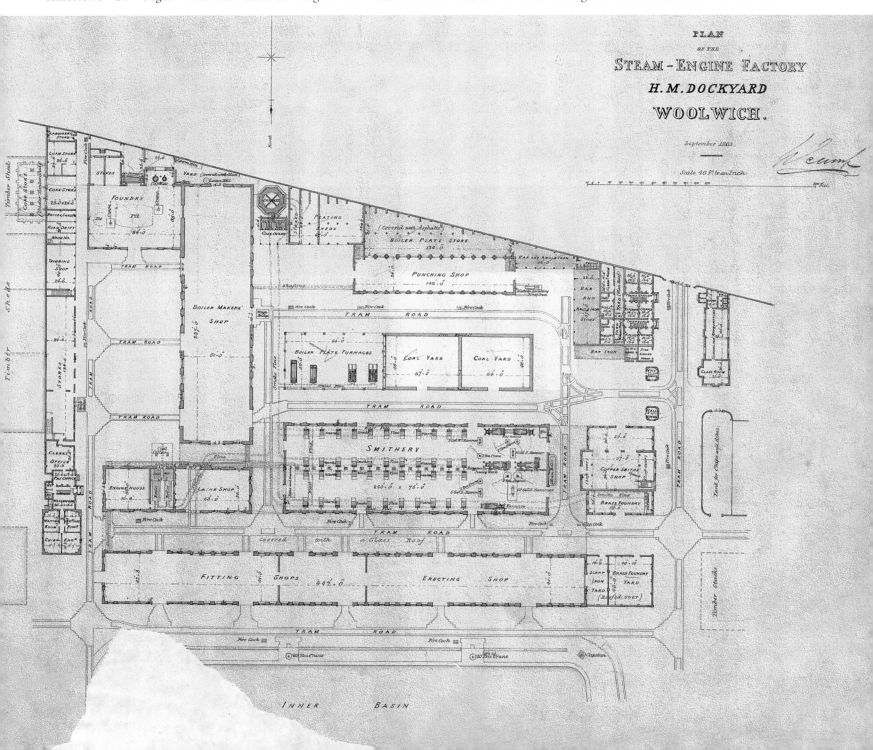

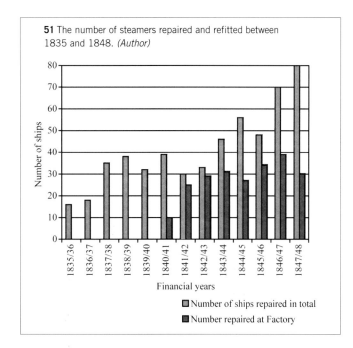

51 The number of steamers repaired and refitted between 1835 and 1848. *(Author)*

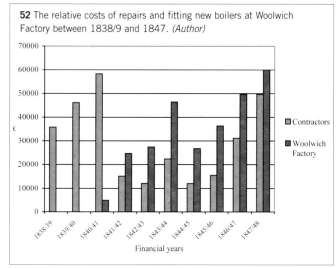

52 The relative costs of repairs and fitting new boilers at Woolwich Factory between 1838/9 and 1847. *(Author)*

workload for maintaining the Steam Navy, and the speed with which it became unable to cope on its own, is shown by the graph in Figure 51, which plots the number of steamers repaired and refitted between 1835 and 1848.

The extent to which the Navy was still dependent on contractors is shown by the figures for the relative costs of repairs and fitting new boilers between 1838/9 and 1847 (Figure 52). New factory capacity was clearly required. The efficiency of Woolwich may be seen by using the figures prepared by Ewart, Lloyd and Atherton, comparing the Factory wages with the value of works done. The performance was very consistent (Figure 53). The Factory's principal activity was the construction of boilers, and a sizeable proportion of the Steam Navy had its boilers replaced there during its first decade of activity. The extent to which this manufacture dominated the scene at Woolwich is seen by an order of 3 January 1848 to increase the strength of the Factory to the greatest possible extent, especially the Boiler Department. This was followed in May by Atherton's report that the Engine Department was short of work, a chance to get rid of the less efficient workmen. The graph in Figure 54 includes boilers that were made for Yard buildings and ones that had not been allocated to ships. The cost of a boiler was roughly proportional to its horsepower and so during 1847/8 and to a lesser extent 1848/9 a relatively large number of low-capacity

Keyham Factory. In December 1846 Captain Alexander Ellice RN succeeded Parry as Comptroller of Steam Machinery; he was to leave a much greater mark in the surviving correspondence of his department than his predecessor.[9]

Atherton was pleased with the performance of the Factory, and pressed for it to be used to its full capacity:

> To estimate fully the advantages of working the Factory to its full extent, it is necessary to enter into the details of the comparative cost of repairs and machinery when performed by Private Manufacturers & the Government…The expense of maintaining Engine & Boilers in efficient working condition, averages about £8 per horse power per year — When the repairs are performed in the private Factories — and about £6 — when executed at Woolwich…

As the total horsepower of the Navy amounted to 41,025, repairs by the Government would effect a saving of £32,000 a year, or 25 per cent. By maintaining an adequate workforce engaged in building new engines or boilers when repairs were not in hand, the machinery would not lie idle, a saving in cost would probably result and spares would be on hand to meet any emergency. The extent to which Woolwich took over the

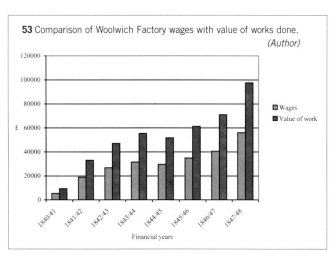

53 Comparison of Woolwich Factory wages with value of works done. *(Author)*

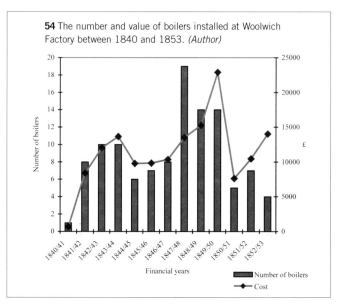

54 The number and value of boilers installed at Woolwich Factory between 1840 and 1853. *(Author)*

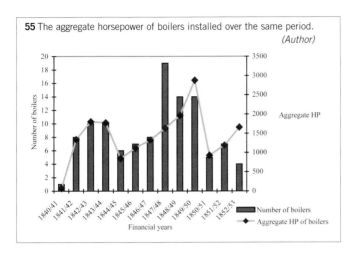

55 The aggregate horsepower of boilers installed over the same period.
(Author)

first operating year 4,000 aggregate horsepower of boilers would be constructed. The effective completion of Woolwich meant that in May 1848 Beatson's services were no longer required; meanwhile works were rapidly proceeding at the Hampshire Yard.[10]

Portsmouth established

The rapid creation of a second, larger base for the Steam Navy was necessitated not only by Woolwich's obvious inability to cope with a rapidly increasing demand, but also by continued apprehension about the intentions and resources of the modernised French fleet. The financial outlay was pretty evenly matched: in December 1847 the First Lord noted that the French vote for naval purposes was equal to £5,540,630, while the English gross estimate was £5,504,933 exclusive of half pay. In particular, the facilities being constructed at Cherbourg were on the grandest scale and looked good as well (Figure 56). A confidential report described the storehouses as a suite of magnificent buildings, combining stability of structure with:

> …fine proportions and beauty of look…All these undertakings as works of art, and works which are calculated to last, are greatly superior to any that I have ever seen, and I should say…as a

boilers were turned out, while at the end of this period a few large ones were made. Aggregate horsepower of boilers produced was one of the chief yardsticks by which the capacity of a steam factory was assessed. How did Woolwich stack up in this respect?

Figure 55 shows the close correlation between horsepower and cost, and also that Woolwich was going to be rapidly overtaken in the boilermaking department by the new Portsmouth Factory, where Murray predicted that during its

56 In this contemporary depiction of Cherbourg the dockyard and fortified anchorage are made to quite overwhelm the town itself. *(NMM, neg. no. PAH2276)*

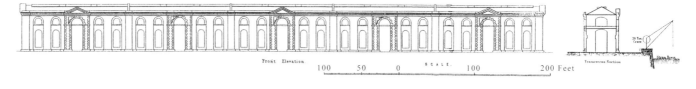

whole there is nothing in the world to equal them. When I remember that these works have been dug & cut out of the solid rock, on an exposed and open shore…I think the intelligence which first planned, or the enterprise that has carried it out, cannot be sufficiently admired.

However, the naval attaché who was so impressed also conceded that the utilitarian British Yards were probably more useful in practice.

Admiral Sir Baldwin Walker, who in 1848 had replaced Sir William Symonds as Surveyor of the Navy, wished the Navy to respond to the stylistic challenge as well as the naval and technological ones, and held that Brandreth and his staff were just the men to design for prestige as well as for practicality. The introduction of Royal Engineer officers to superintend all new works and repairs in the Yards had proved to be far superior to the old system, 'where the Master Shipwrights acted as Architects, Builders &c a system which will account for the incongruous and inconvenient Buildings to be found in most of the Yards'. To produce a superior effect, the elevations of new buildings should be made to correspond as closely as possible to the principal buildings already in place; this injunction was

ffollowed up most effectively at Portsmouth. Clearly, Walker wanted Captain James to come up with something more eye-catching than the Woolwich Factory.

Rarely can junior officers have been in charge of such important projects, disposing of enormous sums of public money. It is most unlikely that the training programmes of the Royal Engineers at Woolwich and the East India Company's military engineers at Addiscombe had given adequate preparation; they had to learn on the job. James's previous employment on the Ordnance Survey of Ireland would certainly have given him no practice in handling huge budgets, and it is scarcely surprising that at the beginning of his second year at Portsmouth he found that the excess expenditure during that financial year would be £25,000. Part of this was because of a determination to provide the Service with what it needed rather than what the financial constraints permitted, a justification that the Admiralty found intolerable, and slapped his wrists sharply:

My Lords…entirely disapprove of his Statements as to the causes of the excess…It has originated entirely in the non-observance of those rules as to timely communication with the Head of his Department…It is not for Capt James to decide whether the money voted by Parliament is, or is not, 'adequate to the wants of the Service'…though My Lords are willing to ascribe this error

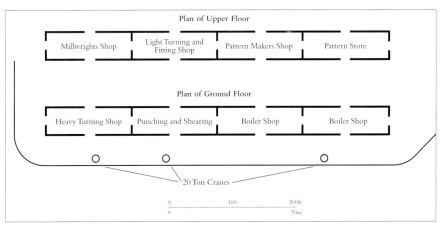

58A The layout of the Factory. *(Stephen Dent, based on* Papers on Subjects connected with the duties of the Corps of Royal Engineers, *vol.III, 1853)*

to an excess of Zeal, they feel it is their duty to acquaint Capt James that the practice of acting upon his own Judgment in these matters, is both inconvenient and objectionable, and cannot be repeated without drawing upon him the displeasure and censure of the Board.

There were to be continual complaints that James did not send his accounts in properly made up or on time.[11]

The technological edge held by Britain had of course been demonstrated in just those dockyard buildings that did not use conventional architectural rhetoric: the slip roofs, the Boat Store and associated structures demonstrated an across-the-board handling of current technology to which the granite-pillared slips of Lorient and elsewhere bore no relationship. James was to deliver a range of building types at Portsmouth that offered samples of all the building types currently on offer in the Yards: a straightforwardly constructed brass and iron foundry, an all-iron smithery and a monumental factory incorporating fireproof construction.

In terms of planning, no advance was made on Woolwich, though this was not all James's fault, as Denison's superior original scheme had been abandoned in 1847 because the ground was not ready, and there was a pressing need to get the Basin and its facilities open. James might have done better, though, than repeat the major fault of the earlier Factory, creating a building 687ft long by just under 39ft wide (slightly *narrower* than Woolwich), with a very high ground floor internally divided into five sections (a heavy turning shop, an erecting shop, a punching and shearing shop, and two boiler shops) albeit much more glorified architecturally than Woolwich (Figures 57, 57A, 58A). In the corner of each section was a cast iron winder stair.

The upper floor was very heavily built, with bridging girders almost 40ft in length, a remarkable span for a cast iron beam. Corbels along the sides supported intermediate joists, from which sprung jack arches, forming a solid horizontal mass. All the beams were I-section with parabolic bottom flanges widening to the middle, the form established by Eaton Hodgkinson in 1830, and widely propagated over the succeeding ten years by William Fairbairn, as giving the suitable distribution of metal in a cast beam to resist bending with only simple support at the ends. The jack-arched floor was a very widely used system of flooring fireproof mills, established at the end of the eighteenth century, and the common alternative to flagstone floors, but it seems not to have been employed in the dockyards before this point. (Figure 58B)

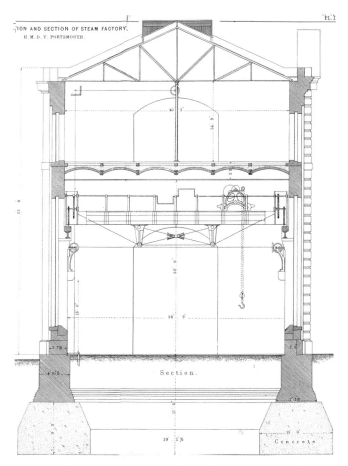

58B The section shows the jack-arched floor springing from I-section beams, a well-tried technique used since the 1830s, which was designed to take the vibrating machine tools on the first floor. The ground-floor workshop, with its overhead traveller crane, was designed to accommodate forging and forming machines. The roof trusses utilise rolled iron for the compression members and wrought-iron for the tensile ties. *(From* Papers on Subjects connected with the duties of the Corps of Royal Engineers, *vol.III, (New Series), 1853)*

59 The original
layout of the Steam
Establishment at
Portsmouth, showing
the Steam Basin at
the top.

Key to plan:
A – Saw Mills;
B – Engine and
     Boiler House;
C – Smithery;
D – Steam
     Hammers;
E – Master
     Blacksmith's
     Office;
F – Smithery;
G – Smithery;
O – Factory;
H – Smithery (former
     boiler house);
I – Stores;
J – Engine and
     Boiler House;
K – Saw Mills;
L – Block
     Machinery;
M – Engine and
     Boiler House;
N – Caulkers Cabin.
(TNA ADM 140/555)

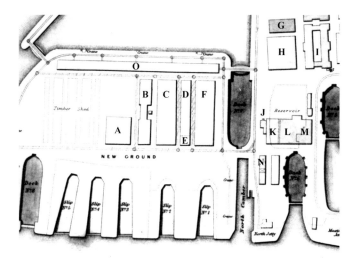

One side lay along the Basin, with a clear working space in between, but the other side of the building was crowded by an engine house for the 80hp machine that powered the whole undertaking, and a steam hammer shop flanked by two smitheries. As these presumably did not duplicate their functions, probably one was for the Yard and the other for Factory use (Figure 59). (These three buildings are shown as one on a later, though very small-scale, plan prepared by James: it is possible that they may have been projected as three functionally separate units within an overall building.) A sawmill of massive fireproof construction, with a water tank on the roof, also designed by James, was on the other side of the engine house, and driven from it (Figure 60). The maximum length of these units was determined by the necessary working distance behind the building slips. A grid of tramways ran between these shops, but there was no direct access from the rear of the Factory range. James claimed that these buildings prevented the Factory from being at least 45ft wide, but it is hard to see now why they could not have been slightly shortened.

These plans were submitted to Murray, and to Fincham, who was now transferred from Chatham as Master Shipwright, together with an alternative set drawn up by Lieut. Colonel Irvine, who had succeeded Brandreth in November 1846. Fincham preferred James's scheme, largely because of the superior facilities it offered for moving wood around the Yard.

The essential components of the scheme, the Factory, Engine House, and the Sawmills, were built first. The only working drawing for the Factory that apparently survives is a sketch by

Murray showing the position of the line of shafting required to drive the Sawmills, Pumps and the West Factory, dated 21 December 1847. Drawings for the foundations of the Sawmills and engine house date from the following spring.

The Factory was (and remains) a massive construction, built at great speed. Excavations of not less than 27ft 6in were necessary to reach the clay at the northern end, all being brought up to the level of the brickwork by a massive concrete infill. Although the placing of the brickwork followed as soon as the concrete was set, James recorded that no perceptible settlement had taken place. The main girders supporting the upper floors were 3ft deep, proved to carry 30 tons at the centre with an estimated breaking weight of 100 tons. These floors were for the Light Turning Shops, and were to carry a massive weight of machinery: mostly lathes, but also including screwing, slotting and shaping machines. Not only the weight but also the vibration of the machines had to be allowed for, hard to imagine in the relative silence of the building today. The original estimate was £50,500, but because of the enormous amount of labour involved in the foundations it in fact cost £60,347.

It needed little vision to see that this building, together with the seven acres of the Basin, would soon be much too small, and James suggested means and incorporated some ways to accomplish a future extension. This could only be done by accretion, given the unsatisfactory nature of the site: sheds for new boiler workshops were to be built along the rear of the building, behind the Sawmills, and the vacant shops occupied by other branches of the Factory. As it was assumed these did not need such high ceilings, James built in corbels in the walls and provided landings on the stairs to insert intermediate floors. Of course, all this tacking on of structures meant that the building as a prestige design would be hopelessly compromised, though, as will be seen, a grand design tricked out in the most elaborate fashion was slowly being concocted at Devonport.

A design decidedly not in the most approved fashion was undertaken by James, as his new Smitheries were set aside as an economy measure. Instead a temporary smithery was built on the adjacent side of the Basin, next to the Brass Foundry, completely constructed of iron, reusing, wherever possible, iron components from dismantled temporary buildings (Figure 61A).

Cast iron columns and semicircular girders, formerly parts of Taylor's cask sheds in Gosport's Royal Clarence Victualling Yard (built in 1830 and demolished in 1844),[12] formed the carcass of the building, which was 110ft long and 50ft wide. The cast iron window frames were of the pattern that James had designed for the Smitheries, and could be reused if those buildings ever materialised. Experience was also to be gained for these buildings by installing two types of forge, made by Nasmyth and Hick & Son of Bolton respectively, to determine which it would be preferable to standardise on. Hick's was chosen. The building was clad in corrugated iron, and remarkably well lit; when the time came that it was no longer required as a smithery, it could be simply adapted and reused as a timber shed (Figure 61B).

Because of the ample light and ventilation, the building was highly successful. James reported that 'it has been pronounced to be one of the best workshops that ever was'. It was a good deal for £2,127 (this included the forges). The smithery was eventually to go the way of all temporary buildings (though renewed in 1853), but was to be the forerunner of a far larger

60 Captain James's
Sawmill at
Portsmouth.
*(Redrawn from NMM
neg. D8872)*

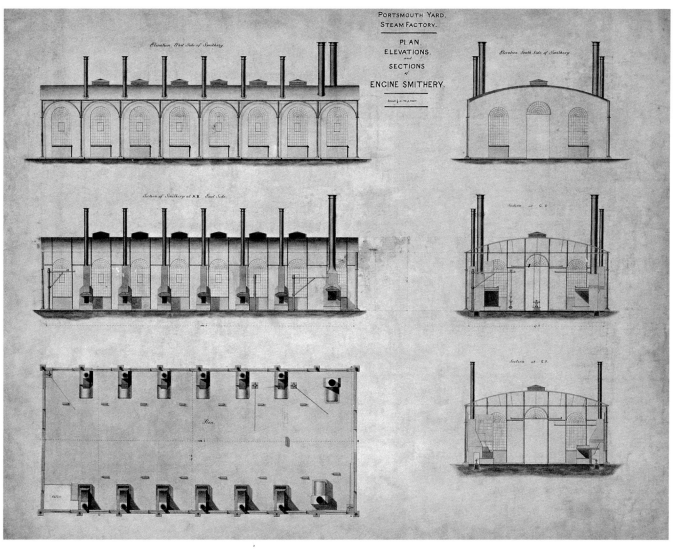

61A Highly successful, James' temporary Smithery disregarded contemporary architectural proprieties. *(NMM D8874)*

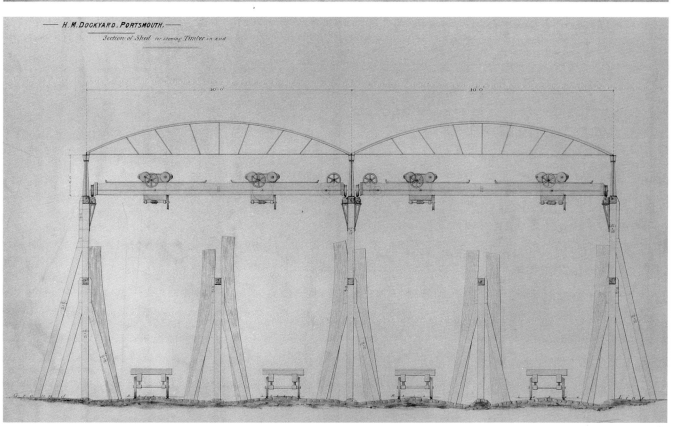

61B Some of the components may have been reused again after the Smithery's life; a timber shed of 1860 used a very similar roof truss. *(© Crown Copyright. NMR BB96/10714)*

62 James' drawing of his Iron and Brass Foundry shows the alternative smoke extraction techniques adopted by him. *(Papers on subjects connected with the duties of the Corps of Royal Engineers, Vol. III (New Series), 1853)*

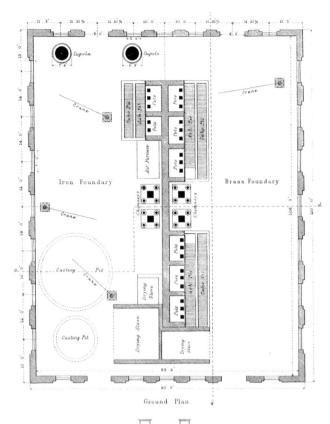

Ground Plan.

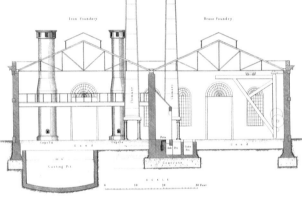

63 The construction of the seating of the boilers was no small part of the labour involved in factory building. Here is the boiler for Portsmouth Saw Mills, drawn in March 1848. *(© Crown Copyright. NMR BB96/10711)*

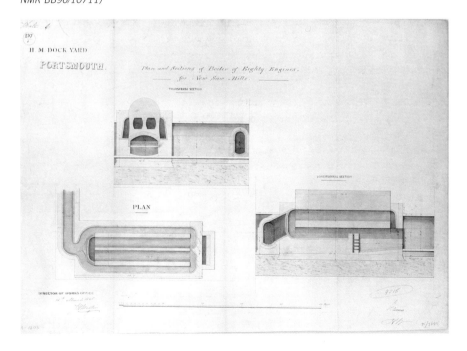

iron smithery, which survives in heavily disguised form to this day (see pp.115-117).

The Brass Foundry, which as built incorporated an iron foundry, was the first to be completed incorporating the decisions taken by the Committee on Metals, several drawings surviving from late 1846 (Figure 62). As such, it incorporated state-of-the-art equipment. An air furnace was accordingly provided for in the Iron Foundry with a capability of melting 5 tons, together with two cylindrical cupolas of 8 and 3½ tons' capacity. Cylindrical cupolas were now replacing the old oblong section ones (which were still to be found in use 30 years later), and these were an in-house design, by Murray. The tops of these wrought iron structures poking through the roof, with molten metal beneath and combustion products escaping, made metal-framed roofs covered with galvanised iron a necessity.

Cupolas (which looked like small blast furnaces) and air furnaces were both required for an efficient foundry. Cupolas afforded the most economical way of melting iron, but castings from air furnaces were of superior quality, which is why the Committee on Metals recommended them. Cupolas, furthermore, were only suited to iron founding, but air furnaces could handle either iron or brass, while melting in crucibles was the preferred means for brass or bronze. The air furnace, capable in the end of melting 9 tons of metal, was supplied by Maudslay's for £240. Three cranes transferred the molten metal, crane to crane, from the cupolas to the casting pits. In the Brass Foundry the metal was melted in 18 pot fires.

Unlike the arrangement at the Woolwich Smithery, at Portsmouth the flues did not lead to underground smoke tunnels; instead the smoke and fumes were drawn off above by iron hoods into four chimneys (Figure 62). As these were fed into the chimneys some 20ft above floor level, the chimneys could be free-standing; each was built on a cast iron frame supported by four cast iron columns with minimalist architectural detailing. Again, quite unlike the great chimney at Woolwich, the chimneys were square in plan, without and within, and were held together by angle irons at the corners. This design, together with the ease of access at ground level, made renewing the firebrick lining a relatively easy operation. James had reckoned the cost of this building at £7,800, the actual sum being less than the estimate by some £54.

While these buildings were being erected, the relentless increase in the number of steamers meant that work on boilers and machinery had to be carried out somewhere. Machinery had been crammed into the remaining parts of the old Smithery and Metal Mills, and there was the original Boiler House workshop, but the facilities for repairing boilers, in particular, were quite inadequate and could not cope. James and Murray prepared a plan for a temporary factory and sent it to Lloyd, who considered it would be unable to handle the work. Nonetheless by November 1847 construction of the temporary shops was under way, when Captain Ellice again pointed out their inadequacy. However, inadequate facilities were better than none, as the Steam Basin was to be officially opened in May 1848. The Factory building was finished in September, and by the spring of 1849 the greater part of the machinery had been installed.[13]

Captain James resigned from his post at Portsmouth in April 1850, to return to the service of the Ordnance Survey (where he was to have a most distinguished career, never returning to the practice of architectural design again). He was replaced by Mould, who left Chatham and was not replaced there. James had held a key position in the principal Yard during a period of considerable expenditure, and the general appearance of the area surrounding the Steam Basin today is still in large measure due to him.

The costs of the principal buildings were, as recorded by James in his notebook (figures in parenthesis as published by him after the event):

	£	
Chain Cable Store	9,282	
Tank	4,723	
Factory	60,000	(60,347)
Factory Machinery	25,000	
Iron Smithery	2,016	(2,128)
Brass Foundry	6,638	(7,746)

The creation of the Steam Basin was far more expensive than that of the buildings: it involved a large workforce to excavate and build the cofferdams, and extensive pumping operations. In the circumstances the original estimate, £240,000, was extraordinarily close to the final cost of £242,000.[14]

The beginnings of Keyham

With the renewed naval rivalry with France it was recognised that the facilities in the Plymouth area needed to be drastically upgraded, as Devonport was the naval base closest to Brest, Lorient and Rochefort. There was no room for expansion within the Dockyard and the area to the north contained the Board of Ordnance's Gunwharf, Morice Yard. Land to the north of this, at Keyham, was purchased on 3 February 1844, but in order to develop the facilities to the extent intended adjacent ground occupied by the Keyham Magazines would also be required. Captain Burgmann, the Royal Engineer in charge at Devonport (and recently promoted from Lieutenant), had surveyed the site for the future Steam Factory (Figure 64). A Clerk of Works was appointed in the same month. Two basins were at once projected with three docks leading off the southern one and a sketch for temporary buildings on the site was prepared by the end of the year, with work commencing on 19 November. Baker & Son were the contractors, initially for the South Basin and two docks, and they presented their bill for the site offices, workshops and ancillary structures in June 1845.

The site, like that of the rest of the naval facilities on the Hamoaze, was a rocky one, which needed to be levelled. This was the opposite of Portsmouth, where the land needed to be made good. The other difference between the two locations, which was to create considerable delays, was the presence of the Board of Ordnance's magazine on the site. The forward planning this entailed was accomplished in good time. In the autumn land at Bull Point was acquired for a new magazine and the first pile at Keyham was driven on 30 January 1846 by a Nasmyth steam-powered pile driver. Initial designs for the Factory were prepared by Captain Burgmann. In October 1847 Baker's were given the contract for building the Factory and the North Basin as well, at an initial estimate of £250,000.

Burgmann's plan differed in many respects from that eventually executed. It represents a type of factory plan that was

64 The land purchased for Keyham Steam Factory. Note the Magazines to top left. *(TNA ADM 116/463)*

clearly in the air at the time (Figure 65). James Nasmyth's sketchbook preserves the plan of an analogous design for Dixon & Co.'s Atlas Works, Amsterdam (Figure 66). This was a locomotive factory where a quadrangle, whose wings and rear range contained a foundry, trimming shop, erecting shop, smiths' shop and boiler shop, enclosed an engine house and a central chimney. Burgmann's principal block is similarly shaped, but the layout of the workshops is unknown.[15]

The principal feature to the eye would have been a single massive chimney, as at Woolwich, supplied with smoke from all the furnaces by underground flues. The theoretical performance of the chimney was, as at Woolwich, to collect the smoke from all the fires into one shaft, in order to discharge it at such a height as to clear neighbouring properties. The draught would be sufficient to down the smoke of the smiths' fires at once draw into the underground flue, which would carry it into the chimney. Internal stacks had often prevented cranes from being placed in their most advantageous positions, and their absence would be a great help.

Lloyd reported on these plans. From bitter experience at Woolwich he was strongly opposed to the idea of a single enormous chimney.[16] Such a construction was also expensive, and he recommended ordinary chimneys. He also disliked aspects of the layout. He considered the Boiler Shop to be too close to the Engine Shops, so that the inescapable noise of boilermaking would be a distraction from the more delicate operations of the Factory. He also, probably influenced by the cost-effectiveness of James's temporary smithery, thought it worth considering whether a large iron shed would be preferable to the more elaborate buildings contemplated.

With some degree of understatement, Lloyd continued: 'If

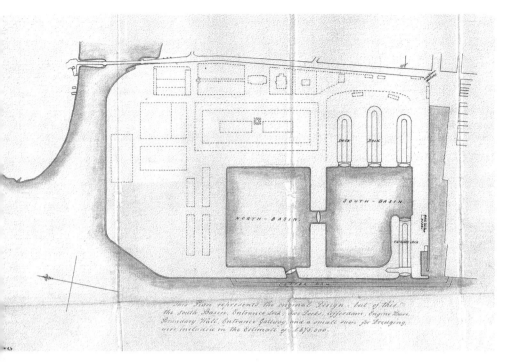

This Plan represents the original design - but of this
the South Basin, Entrance Lock, Dry Docks, Cofferdam, Engine House,
Boundary Wall, Entrance Gateway, and a small sum for dredging,
are included in the estimate of £875,000.

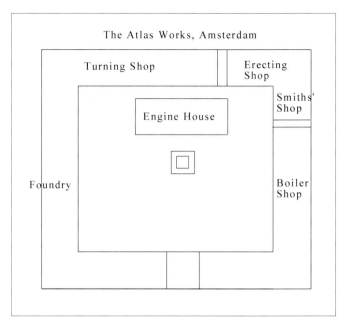

66 Nasmyth's sketch of the Atlas Works. *(Redrawn from Nasmyth's notebook, held by Institute of Mechanical Engineers)*

65 Captain Burgmann's plan for the Steam Factory. Note the similarity to Nasmyth's design for the Atlas Works. *(TNA ADM 1/5614)*

these suggestions…be approved, it will render necessary considerable alterations in the plans which have been placed in Mr Barry's hands'. The architect Charles Barry had clearly been supplied with Burgmann's plans with the intention of clothing them in some architectural finery. No correspondence has survived to cast any light on why Barry had been selected for

this job. Probably his experience of collaborative architecture (and use of iron roofs) in the building of the Houses of Parliament was the determining factor, together with the Admiralty's clear wish (at variance with the practicalities of their Engineer in Chief) for a prestige building to surpass the admired buildings across the Channel.

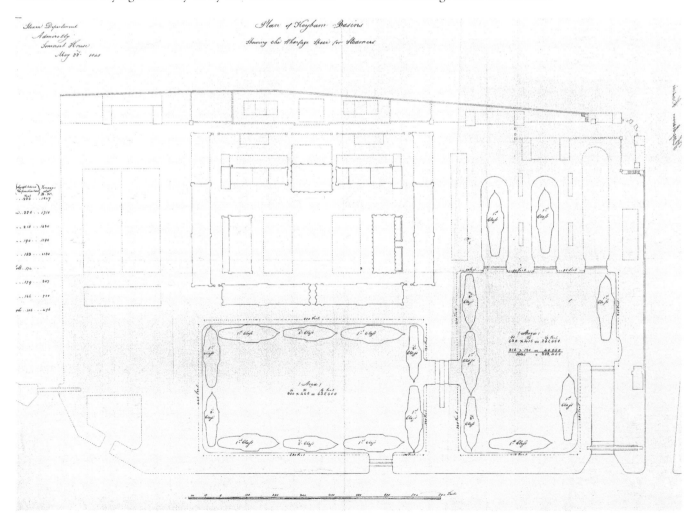

67 Keyham as visualised completely filled with paddle warships. *(TNA ADM 84/3)*

By 8 January 1848 Barry had produced a batch of drawings, to a plan quite different from Burgmann's original. This consisted of a quadrangle with open corners. Fireproof construction, as at Portsmouth Factory, was adopted. The dimensions of the docks and basins were calculated to accommodate paddle warships, as clearly shown by a Steam Department drawing (Figure 67). Barry's drawings set the style in which the masonry elements of the factory were to be constructed, though the final building was not exactly as he had visualised it (Figure 68). It is highly improbable that it was ever intended for Barry to carry out any detailed, or even semi-detailed drawings; his job was to provide a general outline. Indeed, his fellow architects thought so little of this activity as part of his *oeuvre* that it was not included in the list of his works appended to his obituary in the *RIBA Journal*. His son's biography probably states the case exactly as the Admiralty saw it, his designs 'were intended to give some more architectural character to the buildings, planned by the Government engineers',

The Factory was indeed to be extended, but not in the way visualised by Burgmann, Lloyd or Barry, the three men who had so far had a say in the design. At that stage the design was an improvement over Portsmouth and Woolwich to a certain degree, but only because the much greater space provided by a brand new site enabled the buildings to be placed further apart so that new elements could be added or inserted. In effect, the design was based on the two main blocks of Woolwich Factory, as amended by Denison and Beatson, placed much further apart and with the monumental appearance of Portsmouth, but the Factory was still conceived of as an assemblage of long, narrow building blocks (Figure 69).[17]

In July 1848 the Select Committee on Naval Estimates noted that the South Basin was already considerably advanced and in March 1849 tenders were called for four large and six smaller

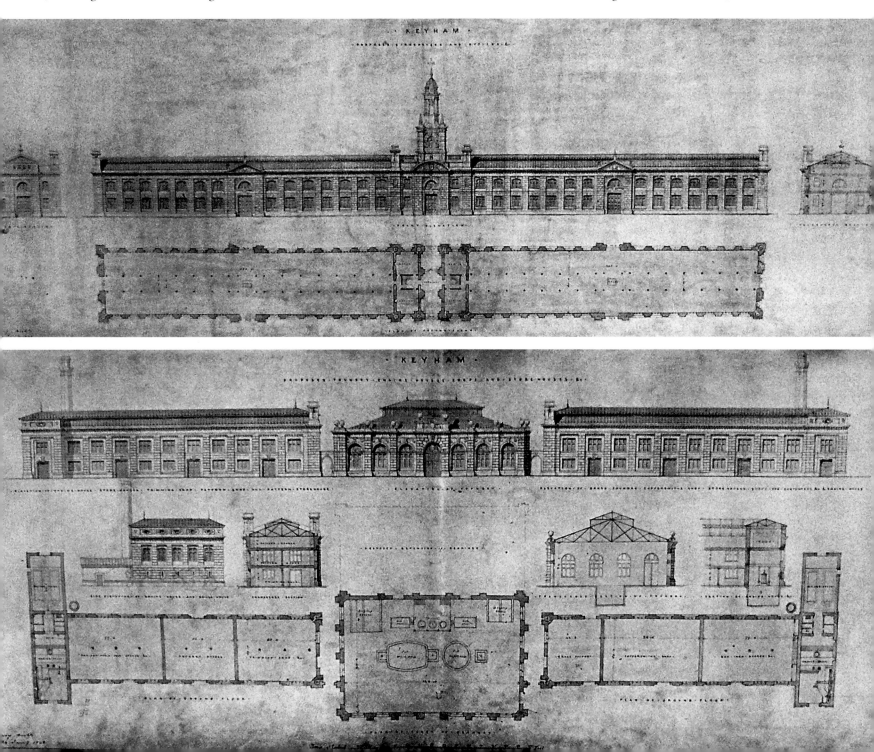

68 The fancy stuff as visualised by Barry. Something approximating to this was to be built, though designed *de novo*. (TNA ADM 140/363 pt.4 & pt.5)

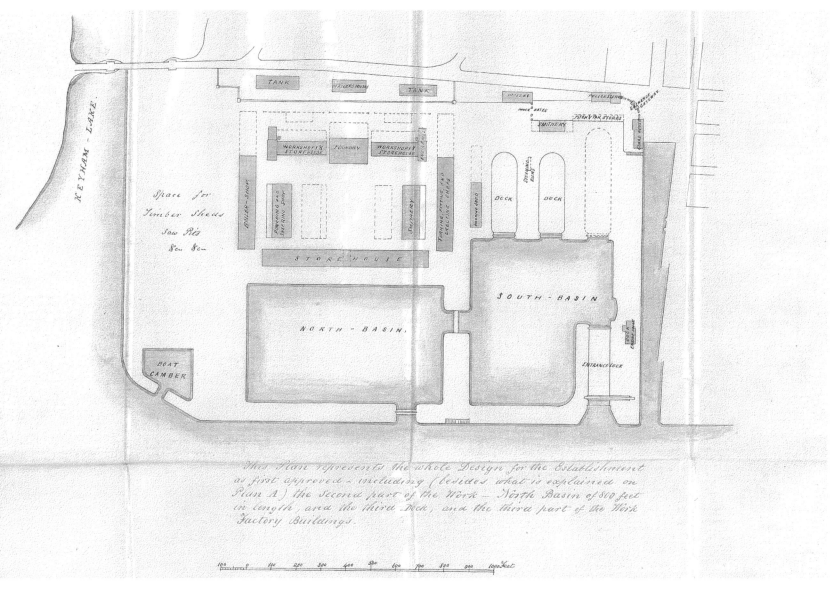

69 The Quadrangle as originally envisaged contained two sizeable free-standing buildings: a punching and shearing shop with the boiler plate furnaces, and a smithery. The four sides of the quadrangle, which had open corners for access, comprised a storehouse on the west side, a boiler shop on the north side, and a turning and erecting shop on the south. The eastern range was a free-standing iron foundry flanked by a brass foundry and coppersmiths' shop, stores and an engine house on one side, and a trimming shop, stores and a second engine house on the other. Room for extension was allowed for all the buildings save the storehouse and office block on the western side, and an additional smithery and erecting shop could be placed in the quadrangle, using up the bulk of its space. (TNA ADM 1/5614)

cranes, the larger ones to have jibs 40ft above ground level.[18] Cast iron was to be used very sparingly in the construction; the jibs were to be made of wrought iron. Table 3 lists the tenders as received. Again, the lowest tender was not accepted. Ellice recommended acceptance of Carmichael's tender for both the large cranes at Keyham. Grissells and Fox, Henderson put in lower tenders but Ellice could not recommend them: the Grissell type had been found not to answer well, and the Fox, Henderson design was inferior to those by firms 'who have had experience in works of this kind'. Fairbairn's tender was recommended for smaller cranes 'upon a principle similar to that of the Tubular Bridge recently constructed', one crane only to be made in the first instance and thoroughly tested at Fairbairn's expense. Fairbairn tubular cranes were to become a notable dockyard feature for another century; their removal has deprived the Yards of some distinctive sculptural shapes (Figure 70).[19]

Instructions were given for the work to proceed slowly,

undertaking nothing not already in progress. Burgmann left, and, in the circumstances, there was no need to replace him. Unless the basin could function, the enormous sums already spent (in the 1850/51 Navy Estimates it was stated that £592,337 had been spent on Keyham) would have gone for nothing, and so in August Watt & Co. were urged to complete their pumping engines there without fail. This took longer than hoped for, and it was not until the middle of January 1850 that they were ready for trials.

Table 3 **Tenders for the cranes for the South Basin, spring 1849**

	To lift 20 tons, proved to 40 tons	To lift 12 tons, proved to 24 tons
Carmichael	£1,500	
Fairbairn		£700
Grissell	£968	£568
Fox, Henderson	£630	£410

Table 4 **The first batch of machinery ordered for Keyham**

Machine	Cost (£)
26ft lathe	550
20ft lathe	350
15ft lathe	250
12ft lathe	180
12ft x 4ft x 4ft planing machine	332
Drilling machine	70
3 smaller	150
Screwing machine	120
Punching and shearing machine	110
above, portable	70
14 smith's hearths	278
2 rivet forges	16
2 grindstones with driving gear	40
20 vices, benches, braces, drills, hammers &c	140
2 blowing fans with driving gear	40
1 travelling crane for engine shop	250

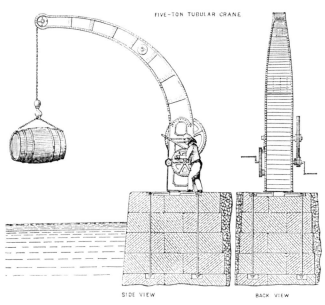

FIVE-TON TUBULAR CRANE

SIDE VIEW   BACK VIEW

70 The instantly recognisable shape of a Fairbairn crane was to be a familiar sight in dockyards until relatively recently. *(From Catalogue of the Great Exhibition of 1881)*

At the beginning of 1850 Burgmann was belatedly replaced by Captain Williams, but he was engaged only in furthering the basin and dock works, for in March the Admiralty decided not to start work on the Factory, but to concentrate on the completion of the works in hand. In the face of parliamentary concern over the expenditure, savings had been made,[20] enabling the construction of a third dock off the south basin.[21]

The first of the Fairbairn cranes was erected and proof-tested at Keyham at the beginning of October, and the first batch of machinery for the Factory was provided for in the next year's estimates (Table 4). Comparison with the equipment ordered for Portsmouth shows that, although small in quantity, it was a balanced selection of machinery, enough to equip small machine shops and a smithery in neat single-storey buildings beside and at the heads of the docks.

Several years were to pass before work on the main buildings got seriously under way, and it was to be these temporary workshops that sustained the workload at Keyham in the forthcoming war.[22]

Notes:

1. *The Ports, Arsenals and Dockyards of France. By A Traveller*, (London, 1841), p.40, ADM 3/256, Nasmyth Order Book 2.
2. POR/P/13, POR/P/17, WO 44/282, POR/R/9, POR/R/11.
3. POR/P/20.
4. Slips 3 and 4 were finished in March 1846, and on 25 November 1845 Baker's offered to roof No. 5 in the same manner, the work to be completed by the following March for £13,849. The structure was to contain 356 tons of cast iron and 190 tons of wrought iron. This offer was taken up, and next month the firm of Morewood & Rogers was asked to send 420 plates of corrugated galvanised iron, 20 gauge, 7ft 10?in by 6ft, riveted together, and galvanised angle iron. Galvanised iron was rapidly coming into use for factory buildings, and was an adaptable medium: Fincham had suggested using corrugated iron to roof over ships laid up in ordinary, and *Leander* was selected for the experiment; Fox, Henderson supplied the materials. *Britannia* was roofed over the next year. Cumberland, pp.62–64, POR/P/21, POR/P/23, POR/P/24, POR/P/31.
5. NMR PTM/1291-1308, POR/P/21, POR/P/22, *Memoir* of Andrew Murray in *Proceedings of the Institution of Civil Engineers*, 1873, pp.270-273, POR/P/28.
6. Captain Henry James, 'New works at Portsmouth', in *Professional Papers of the Corps of Royal Engineers*, n.s. vol. 3, 1853, pp.78, 88; POR/P/24; DNB, entry for Denison; POR/R/12A, POR/R/12B.
7. In December 1842 John Lloyd proposed that the new Smithery in progress at Woolwich be altered to a foundry, and this was agreed to in February 1843; Rolt's got the contract for the roof of the associated Boiler Shop in July. The central section of the rear block was greatly enlarged to become the new Smithery. Estimates for the new Punching and Shearing Shop were sent in October.
8. Brandreth's successor, Colonel Irvine, Nasmyth and the Supervisor of Metals reported in October 1847 on the poor draught, and recommended separate chimneys for each furnace. The air furnaces also did not draw properly into the high chimney; they were provided with four independent chimneys, and the smoke was only passably drawn from the fire hearths. The Yard Smithery (now destroyed) contained no less than five Nasmyths. It was built in 1846, and had probably been Beatson's first responsibility there; like its successor, it had brick walls, and an iron roof with skylights and louvres, covered with galvanised iron. It was paved with iron ballast.
9. *Memoir* of Charles Atherton, *Proceedings of the Institution of Civil Engineers*, 1875, pp.252-255; *Memoir* of John Trickett, *Proceedings of the Institution of Civil Engineers*, 1889, pp.393-3
10. ADM 95/20, ADM 83/48, ADM 93/2, ADM 2/1388, ADM 95/97/1, ADM 12/492.
11. ADM 13/185, ADM 1/5591, NMM Baldwin Walker Ms. WWL/5, POR/P/38.
12. ADM 1/3793, ADM 224/5, ADM 224/34, ADM 224/35.
13. Captain H. James, 'Description of the Steam Basin, Docks, and Factory, and other works recently executed in Portsmouth Dockyard', in *Professional Papers of the Corps of Royal Engineers*, 1853, pp.77-102, 33 plates, NMM ADM/Y/P/137, ADM 12/460, NMR PTM/1144/1146-7/1149/1151-9/1161-2/1190-8/1200/4204, ADM 93/1, ADM 2/1387, ADM 93/1, ADM 12/492, ADM 12/508, Science Museum Ms 446 (James's Notebook).
14. Science Museum Ms 446; James, *Description…* pp.92-93.
15. ADM/12/411, ADM 12/428, ADM 140/350, ADM 12/444, *The Builder*, 1846, p.449, ADM 1/5614, ADM 12/476. Institute of Mechanical Engineers, *James Nasmyth's Sketchbook*, f.32v.
16. Increased dimensions and altered proportions might make it function satisfactorily, but 'I venture to say, from the experience I have had with the Woolwich chimney…it is by no means certain that it would'.
17. ADM 2/1387, ADM 140/363/1-6.
18. The economies that uniformity of equipment promised led to the suggestion that these should all be of the same type, but, as with Atherton's attempt to introduce standardised patterns of boilers, this was premature. Lloyd considered that competitive tendering would, on the whole, produce better results as regards construction and price.
19. ADM 95/9, ADM 93/5, ADM 2/1391.
20. These were effected by:
    altering the method of executing the backing of the walls, basins, etc.;
    reducing the quantity of granite used in the walls;
    a great reduction in the prices of the excavation (it is not known how this was achieved);
    a speed-up in the rate of filling-in behind the walls.
21. ADM 12/508, ADM 95/9, ADM 1/5614.
22. ADM 84/3.

CHAPTER 7

Equipping and Running the Steam Factories

Tooling up

By the time the Portsmouth Factory was ready to be equipped, most of the varieties of machine tool that were to equip engineering shops at the end of the century had been developed; only the milling machine had to be introduced. Their inventors and developers were celebrated in the pantheon of Samuel Smiles, the popularising industrial biographer: first Joseph Bramah, the pioneer of machine tool manufacture and his sometime foreman, Henry Maudslay, who provided the precision skills to realise his master's concepts before setting up on his own and creating the modern lathe through the invention of the slide-rest, constructing Marc Brunel's block-making machinery and supplying the Navy with punching and shearing machinery for cutting boiler-plates, and pioneering screw-cutting machines. Joseph Clement, who set up on his own account after having been the chief draughtsman first for Bramah and then Maudslay, brought the lathe to such a state that Smiles could describe it as 'the most accurate and extensively applicable of all machine-tools.' He was one of the many pioneers of planing machinery, and through his reputation for extreme accuracy was selected by Charles Babbage to construct his Difference Engine (a mechanical computer). Other contenders for the invention of the planing machine were James Fox, Matthew Murray and Richard Roberts.

71 Nasmyth's planing machine, illustrated in *Buchanan's Machinery*, edited by George Rennie and published in 1841. *(From George Rennie (ed.) Illustrations of Mill Work. Atlas to the New Edition of Buchanan's Work, London, 1841)*

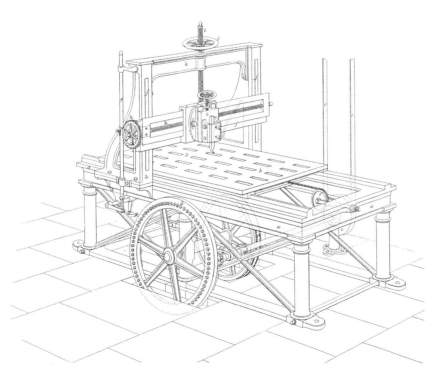

James Fletcher, an engineer who had grown up with the machinery, wrote towards the end of his career that the introduction of the planing machine had produced the greatest knock-on effect. The workpiece was drawn under a cutting tool, which moved sideways between every cut, giving a reasonably uniform surface, which could then be finished off by hand with a scraper (Figure 71). Previously the whole operation of levelling rough metal had to be done by hand, at great cost: levelling one square foot of iron by hand chipping and filing cost 12s in 1826, while 30 years later the cost had been reduced to under a penny. These machines were introduced rapidly: the range of planers that James Fox of Derby had on offer in 1829 has been given in an earlier chapter (p.22).

The ability to produce planed surfaces accurately and cheaply meant that other types of machine, such as the lathe, could be developed to new levels of accuracy and sophistication. Lathes and planes were made self-acting, so that the cutting tool was moved automatically. This was far from automation, but it was a vital step along the way.

Much was still being done by hand in workshops of the 1830s, but slotting and shaping machines were appearing at the start of the next decade and Portsmouth was supplied with these by 1843; if not in the lead, then still comfortably up with innovation. Grooved and slotted components played a large part in steam machinery: many components were fixed together by keys, precision-made metal plugs that fitted into slots. The slotter pared the metal away to the desired form, the cutting tool moved up and down, and the workpiece was placed on a circular table, which could produce self-acting transverse or circular movements if required. Nasmyth originally called his slotter a paring machine, so as not to confuse it with another machine he had developed to perform an analogous task, in which a modified drill bit produced a cutting motion when drawn sideways. This machine was also used to form keyways.

Shaping machines performed the same kind of function, but the cutting tool moved horizontally instead of vertically. Nasmyth's type, introduced in 1836, moved the cutting edge over the workpiece by a crankshaft and flywheel, but during the next decade an alternative design was introduced, in which the tool moved laterally across the workpiece. The later designs were largely adopted in the Factories as planing and shaping machines (Figure 72).

Each engineering shop, before Clement's time, had adopted its own screw-thread. He advocated, and created, a sequence of set pitches. One of his workmen, who became famous as Sir Joseph Whitworth, was to establish his own system as the universal practice. The Admiralty were keen to adopt uniform practices and were among the first to standardise on Whitworth's thread, ordering in July 1849 that all future steamships were to be supplied with taps and dies on that pattern. The general adoption of the system by industry had taken place by 1860. Screwing machines for cutting threads and tapping bolts were vital to produce the enormous number of nuts and bolts required. No great mechanical ingenuity was involved in shearing machines, but the application of steam power transformed their ability; they were usually combined with a punching machine. The combined machine was invented by Maudslay around 1812, for the purposes of manufacturing metal tanks to contain ships' drinking water. The equipment found a new use in perforating the holes in boiler plate. Holes produced by punching were weak around the edges, and needed to be reamed out to produce a sound surface; drilled holes were mechanically much sounder (see Figure 15).

In the 1840s everything was coming together:

> …by the gradual introduction and perfecting of the regulator screw, the wheel cutting engine, standard gauges, large surface plates, long straight edges, and scraped surfaces, combined with the improved tools, not only was the amount of manual labour considerably diminished, but the work was done more expeditiously, and a much greater degree of accuracy was attained…[1]

During 1848 the Portsmouth Factory, and to a lesser extent the Millwrights' Shop at Devonport (which, operating in conjunction with the North Smithery, acted in lieu of a Factory there), acquired suites of machine tools from the leading manufacturers. On 5 February 1848 a batch of tenders was accepted for the Factory. Some of the locations for the machinery can be identified and make it possible to reconstruct the original appearance of the Factory (Figure 73).

Many of the metal fittings for the shafting were built into the walls of the Portsmouth Factory building, and survive now as reminders of the days when it was the home of advanced technology. The boiler shops were supplied with two punching machines and two shearing machines by Maudslay & Co., and two patent riveting machines with their travelling cranes by Fairbairns (Figure 74). The heavy turnery was probably supplied with a slotting machine and two vertical drilling machines by Glasgow's, a planing and shaping machine and a large planing machine by Carmichael & Co., and a large boring and turning lathe by Messrs Hetherington (or possibly by Carmichael). The punching and shearing shop had two radial drilling machines by Lewis & Co.; the punching and shearing machines were possibly by Shanks, and ordered separately (Figure 75).

The light turning and fitting shops on the first floor were the destination for the rest of this batch of machinery, which included a screw-cutting lathe by Whitworth, three bolt and nut screwing machines by Glasgow's, a small bolt-cutting machine by Parr, Curtis & Co., 11 slide lathes by Glasgow and Lewis, two small slotting machines and a horizontal drilling machine by Hetherington, four small planing and shaping machines by Parr, Curtis & Co. and Shanks & Co. (Figure 76), five planing machines by Lewis and Shanks, and 10 vertical drilling machines by Parr, Curtis and Carmichael. Carmichael also supplied a large planing and boring machine and Shanks a horizontal boring machine, location uncertain. Other

72 Planing and shaping machines by Muirs of Manchester, illustrated in the International Exhibition catalogue of 1862. *(From* The Record of the International Exhibition, *1862, Glasgow, n.d.)*

73 The appearance of machine shops did not materially alter in the nineteenth century. Here is the impressive interior of the Vickers machine shop at Elswick seen in the 1890s. (*From The Navy & Army Illustrated, 16 April, 1898*)

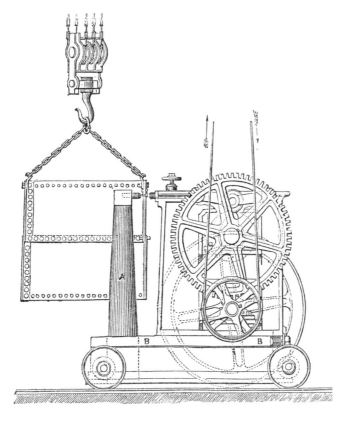

74 The Fairbairn riveting machine for the assembly of boiler plates, in a drawing taken from the Great Exhibition catalogue. (*From Catalogue of the Great Exhibition of 1851*)

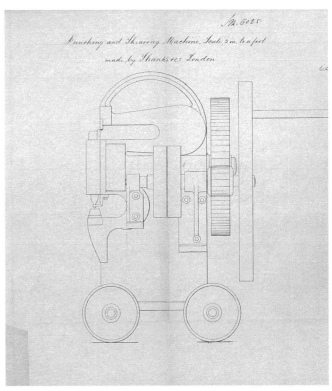

75 Shanks's portable punching & shearing machine. (*TNA ADM 85/14*)

equipment was also supplied; by autumn of 1850 there were 46 more lathes present, mostly in the light turning shops.

Ten wrought iron cranes were supplied by Fox, Henderson to the West Factory (presumably the temporary building on the Factory's west side), while the six travelling cranes to lift 20 tons each, for the heavy turnery, erecting shop and boiler shops, were made by Woolwich. All the metal parts were dispatched in April 1848.[2]

More is known about the system of procurement of the machinery ordered for Devonport Millwrights' Shop in June, since all the tenders, complete with drawings, have survived. Nasmyth undoubtedly supplied the classiest drawings (Figure 77), but this did not influence the selectors, and he failed to secure any orders at all. In fact Smith, Beacock & Tannett, a firm from Leeds, who had supplied no machinery to the Factory, scooped the pool this time, by undercutting everyone else, missing out only on the bolt-screwing machine, where the costlier machine by Whitworth was preferred because its construction was reckoned to be superior (Figure 78). Had Smith, Beacock & Tannett put in too high a tender for the Portsmouth machinery and revised their figures downwards this time? Other factors could be more important than price, as not only the Whitworth machine, but also Smith, Beacock and Tannett's drilling machine, were selected despite not being the lowest tender (see Table 5). These machines were built to last, and did. Probably some were working well into the twentieth century.[3]

In December 1848 there were changes in the top management. Ellice considered that the workload at Portsmouth, with 800 men proposed to be employed at the Factory during the next financial year, necessitated Murray's being provided with an assistant. Another man with a distinguished track record was just to hand: William Lambert, Chief Assistant to Messrs Maudslay, for whom he had worked for 15 years.

Table 5 Tenders for Machines for the Devonport Millwrights' Shop in June 1848

	Nasmyth	Whitworth	Hetherington	Smith, Beacock & Tannett
	£	£	£	£
15ft slide lathe	170	175	180	140
10ft slide lathe	110	120	105	77
Drilling machine	60	61	130	73
Slotting machine	220	196	220	155
Bolt-screwing machine	165	112	135	92
Nut-cutting machine	82		130	70

Service in the senior engineering posts in the Navy continued to attract men of outstanding ability (a sure sign that it was perceived to keep up with state-of-the-art engineering), and Edward Humphrys applied for a post. Humphrys had been born in 1808, and spent his career in a variety of engineering jobs, usually connected with marine engines. After an unsuccessful venture on his own he became manager of the Rennies' Blackfriars works, introducing improvements to slide and disc valves. Sir John Rennie made it clear in a personal interview with Ellice that he was willing to release him if he were allowed to stay to complete works in hand. The Comptroller of Steam Machinery decided that this was an opportunity to appoint an experienced engineer to Devonport, which had not had the benefit of one since Lloyd had been there, especially as it was now contemplated to maintain a reserve steam squadron at the base. Atherton was transferred from Woolwich to Devonport in December 1848, Humphrys succeeding him. E. A. Bernays, who was to play a prominent part later in the construction of Chatham Extension, had become acting Clerk of Works at Woolwich in August.[4]

This expertise was immediately put to good use. Humphrys, for example, went to Whitworth's factory in Manchester to

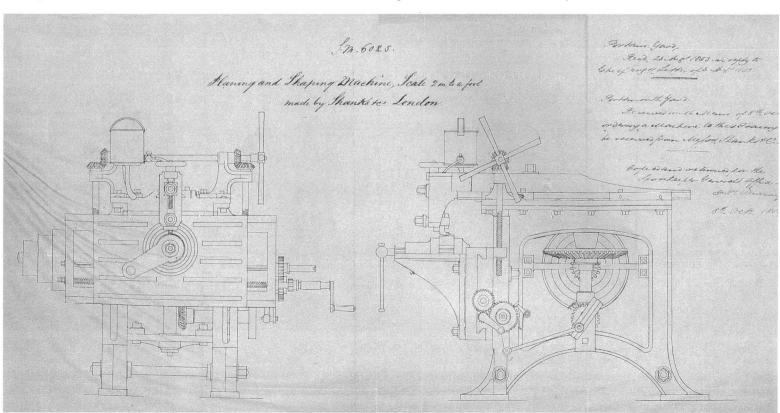

76 Shanks's planing and shaping machine. *(TNA ADM 85/14)*

inspect and report on the cost of making additions to a large surfacing lathe. The final bill was £2,091, excluding the face plate, which was to be made by the Factory. At the same time Ellice upgraded the capacity of Sheerness, to place it 'on a footing equal to meet the exigencies of the Service & render it efficient for the occasional repairs to Steam Vessels Machinery'.[5] Humphrys' inspection of a faulty large planing machine installed in the new millwright's shop, abutting the Chatham Metal Mills, resulted in a cut in price.[6]

As Portsmouth Factory was nearing completion, a list was compiled in which the Admiralty took stock of its industrial resources. It was an impressive catalogue. The manufacturing capacity in the Yards comprised:

Woolwich	Smithery, foundries, sawmill
Chatham	Lead mill, paint mill, sawmills,
	metal foundry, iron foundry,
	sheathing nail shops, metal mills, ropery
Sheerness	Sawmill, cement mill
Portsmouth	Sawmills, ropery, block mills,
	iron & brass foundry, steam factory
Devonport	Ropery, steam factory? [sic], sawmills
Pembroke Dock	None

The Yards were equipped with the steam engines as detailed in Table 6.[7]

Running and staffing the Steam Factories

By the end of the 1840s the steam factories were well established (Table 4). With the even more expensive establishment of Keyham clearly on the way, complaining voices in Parliament had to be persuaded that money was not being frittered away. The idea that the Yards and everything connected with them were inefficient and too large, through not being subject to market forces, inextricably mixed up with the largely

77 A paring machine by Nasmyth, Gaskell and Company, offered to the dockyards in 1847. *(TNA ADM 85/97 Pt.1)*

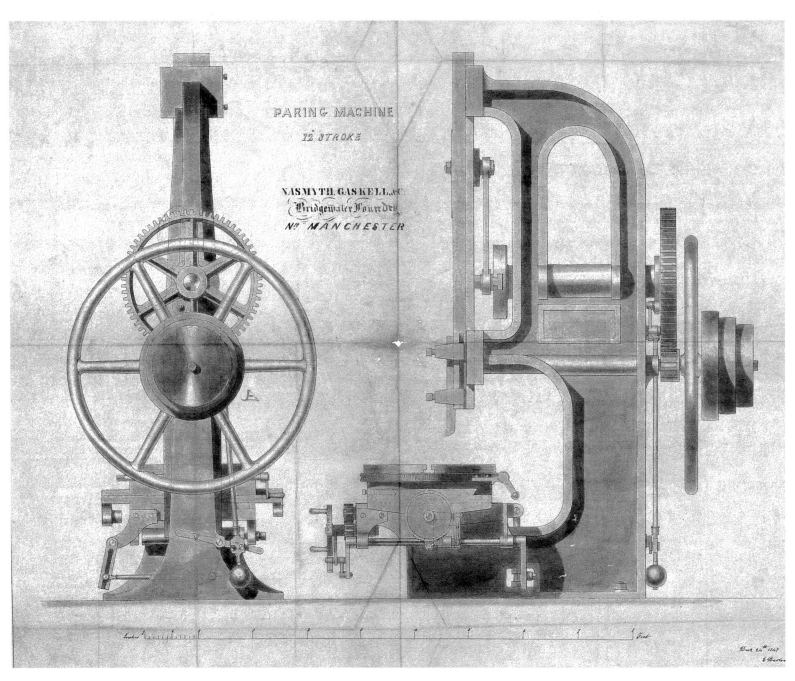

PARING MACHINE

12 STROKE

NASMYTH, GASKELL, &C
Bridgewater Foundry
N.º MANCHESTER

incompatible belief that the Admiralty discouraged all mechanical progress, was through constant reiteration to become one of the most deeply rooted of English myths. In order to mitigate these apprehensions a Committee of Revision of Dockyards was set up, which reported in December 1848. Its conclusion deserves to be read in its own words:

We have examined carefully the manufacturing Establishments of the Yards, to which our attention was more particularly called, both by the Board Minute, and by the Report of the Committee on Naval Estimates which expressed a not unnatural alarm at the rapid growth of these establishments, & some doubts as to their

Table 6 Steam engines in the Yards in 1848

Location	Number and hp	Purpose
Deptford	None	
Woolwich	2 x 40 hp	Factory
	2 x 30	Sawmills, Burnettizing apparatus[a]
	1 x 36	Pumping
	1 x 20	Tilt hammer in smithery
	2 x 14	Smithery
Chatham	1 x 20	Lead mill
	1 x 14	Ropery
	1 x 20	Pumping
	1 x 50	Pumping
	2 x 40	Metal mills
	1 x 16	Smithery
	1 x 8	Smithery
	1 x 36	Sawmill
	1 x 1½	Grindstone
	1 x 8	Auxiliary
Sheerness	2 x 50	Pumping
	2 x 14	Smithery
	1 x 25	Cement mill
	1 x 8	Well pump for watering vessels
	1 x 4	Millwrights
Portsmouth	1 x 16	Sawmills
	1 x 6	Tarring house
	2 x 30	Block mills (one duplicate)
	1 x 6	Illegible
	1 x 20	Smithery
	1 x 2	Drilling engine
	1 x 10	Burnettizing apparatus
	1 x 10	Rotatory pumping
	1 x 50	Metal mills (not at work)
	1 x 80	Smithery
Devonport	1 x 20	Sawmills & millwrights
	1 x 18	Pumping
	1 x 8	North Smithery and fan blowing
	1 x 6	North Smithery and fan blowing
	1 x 6	South Smithery and fan blowing
	1 x 10	South Smithery and drilling
	1 x 6	Burnettizing[a] apparatus
Pembroke Dock	1 x 10	Sawmills, dock pump
	2 x 12	Smithery (high pressure)[i]

[a] Burnettizing apparatus was a long tank filled with Sir William Burnett's patent compound, into which timbers were placed; hydraulic pressure on the liquid then forced the preservative chemicals into the wood. Opinions varied concerning the efficacy of the process, but at this time it was much in vogue.

utility. We admit that these doubts are warranted by the disadvantages, under which all manufacturing establishments must labor, which are not conducted under the eye of a Master and checked in their expenditure by the necessity of drawing upon Funds at his sole disposal. It is difficult to unite a rigid economy with that unlimited command of Capital, which Govt. Establishments possess; or to impress those, who administer them, by any written rules, with the same frugal ideas, which feelings of self interest naturally inculcate. The scale, too, of these manufactories is so vast, the number of hands employed in them so large, and the working machinery so complicated, that it will require the utmost vigilance to institute, and to preserve, a good system of management. But, on the other hand, Steam has rendered the most costly of these Establishments indispensable. The repairs of the Steam Navy, even in peace, would exceed the powers of all the private Factories now in existence; and, whatever difference of opinion may prevail as to the extent, to which Government ought to undertake new work, There can be no doubt that Repairs are the last thing, that should be contracted for. Besides, no contract could provide for the necessities of War, unless we can conceive a Capital fully equal to that already sunk by the Government at Woolwich, Portsmouth, & Devonport, employed by private Enterprise, upon the same spots, in preparations for such a contingency, with the certainty that, until it occurred, the outlay would produce little, or no,

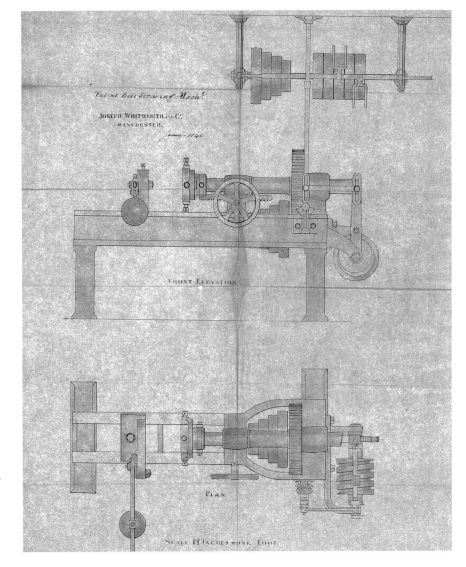

78 Drawings of a bolt screwing machine sent by Whitworth's to Devonport in 1848. *(TNA ADM 85/97 Pt.1)*

return, the great naval depôts of the country, not being the Ports, to which Commercial Steamers resort in time of Peace, for repairs, and the Commercial Ports being very difficult of access, in time of War, to Steamers crippled in a Channel action. These general considerations have determined the policy of this, and preceding Governments, to which Parliament has given its sanction. The outlay has been made; the new Steam Establishment has been created, — and the only practical course, is to take care that the Country derive the utmost possible benefit...[8]

In fact the Steam Factories were not operated on the same principles as the rest of the Yard. As has been seen, virtually all the Chief Engineers at the Yards had extensive experience in civilian factories before working for the Admiralty. From the first it was decided that Woolwich would be run on the same principles as a private factory: the men would be hired and fired as circumstances dictated, without any of the workmen having established status. This would go far to allay the terrors of those

---

DEFINING RESPONSIBILITIES

Together with Lloyd, Ellice had drawn up a set of regulations and instructions, to be applied at first only at Woolwich, to see how they worked in practice. These included the following:

The duties of the various officers were to be defined.

Existing orders relative to the Factory should be consolidated, omitting those that appeared to be questionable and supplying such as appeared to be required.

The principal charge and responsibility would be placed upon the First Assistant, under the Chief Engineer, in conducting the works of the Factory and on board steam vessels. His duties, previously unrestricted, had kept him busy with a multitude of activities and often taken away from the Yard, and the running of the Factory had often been left to the Chief Engineer, whose work in turn had been devolved to those below him, with the workmen consequently left without proper supervision.

The Chief Engineer, the First Assistant and the Chief Foreman should thereafter be relieved as much as possible from all duties that required their absence from the Yard, and the Chief Engineer or one of his assistants should be in attendance in the Factory the whole of the time the men were at work.

This measure would ensure proper vigilance on the part of the leading men, who were required to be at their post when any of their men were at work.

Periodical returns were to be made up showing the amount of work done, divided into various heads, and the cost of doing it. These returns would be a particularly useful management tool when the other two steam establishments were brought into operation, as they would provide a comparison of the expenses incurred at each of them in performing the same amount of work.

A similar costing of major works on steam vessels would also have this function.

It had apparently been the practice for the Commodore Superintendent at Woolwich to exceed his function and decide what engineering jobs were to be done. In future no work was to be undertaken without proper authority, and should anything be ordered to be done by the Superintendent that in the opinion of the Chief Engineer would interfere with more important matters, he was not to undertake it without expressing his views on the necessary priorities.

The Superintendent should make a quarterly report noting any deviation that may have been made from the Regulations: 'he will be directed to satisfy himself by personal observation that the Regulations are faithfully, & in their proper spirit, carried out.'

---

who, like Admiral Byam Martin, were uneasy at the prospect of a new type of class-conscious worker entering the Navy's service. There was of course a downside to adopting commercial practices: skilled workers, particularly in the London area, could obey market forces too, and be hard to find when the shipbuilding industry was on an upswing.

The records relating to the establishment of Woolwich are too few to give a fair picture of the recruitment there. For Portsmouth more has survived. The Factory there officially began work on 1 April 1847, the beginning of the financial year, when the men employed there were transferred from the books of the Storekeeper, and the Pay Clerk and Bookkeeper of the Factory began the full discharge of their duties. Murray was expected to see that the accounts were kept in such a way as to enable him to give an account of the work done and the vessels for which it had been performed. Woolwich was considerably under its maximum complement of 304, yet the Commodore Superintendent there was instructed to ask for volunteers to be transferred to Portsmouth, as 'no doubt… better Artificers in all respects are to be found in the river than at Portsmouth'. The men who had just been recruited locally could scarcely be turned away immediately work slackened off without giving an unfavourable impression at Portsmouth, and on 1 September instructions were issued that nobody was to be laid off through fluctuations of work. That could come later.

By 25 September no volunteers from Woolwich had come forward. Murray was later to state:

…we have always considered it to be our duty to engage Men fully competent to perform the work required, if we could obtain them at rates lower than the [Admiralty authorised rates] of 1847, especially as we knew that lower rates [are] being paid by the Steam Packet Companies at Southampton and other parties this side of London…these deviations are chiefly among the lower class of Men and we are not aware that any of these classes are discontented…

Atherton, back at Woolwich, was also to state his difficulties a few years later. Unlike Murray, he was competing in a high wage area:

…the present demand for skilled Labour is affecting the Factory at this Yard in a way that demands especial notice. Although but few of our hands have as yet left, the disposition to leave is general, the inconvenience of which to the Service will soon be felt if not anticipated and met. By the present regulation the Commodore of the Yard…is not authorised to enter workmen without authority previously obtained. The immediate consequence is that the Chief Engineer cannot avail himself of good hands that occasionally present themselves (for good hands if not put on at once never come back again) and unfortunate hands or such as are out of employment when workmen are wanted are seldom desirable…

He suggested that the Chief Engineer be allowed to hire, not exceeding the authorised appropriation, with the Commodore's approval, and that when men had to be laid off he should be able to dismiss the 'least eligible' workmen but not restrict the entries of desirable men.[9]

The demand for new labour was insatiable. In September

1847 only one of the four boilers of the *Scourge* could be taken in hand because there were so few boilermakers. He applied for six more, and was asked whether a larger number could be profitably employed. The next day the following artificers were approved for Portsmouth Factory: six engine fitters, two turners, three millwrights, two patternmakers, two assistant moulders, one coppersmith, six boilermakers, six assistant boilermakers, four hammermen, and ten engineer labourers. At the end of the month more hands were required: ten engine fitters, two turners, ten engineer labourers, five boilermakers, four assistant boilermakers, and two rivet boys.

At the end of 1847 Ellice, Lloyd, Murray and Atherton agreed on the rates of pay for the Factories (see Table 7). A comparison of these figures with men in private shipyards is given by some figures obtained by the Admiralty in 1835. Shipwrights on the Thames earned around 5s 6d a day on average, at Whitehaven about 3s 4d, on the Tyne between 3s 6d and 4s, at Liverpool 4s 6d, and at Plymouth between 3s 6d and 3s 9d.

With the rapid growth of factory capacity the position had to be regularised, and on 22 January 1848 Ellice wrote to the First Secretary that as Woolwich would soon be operating to the full extent that the buildings permitted, and shortly Portsmouth would be too, general principles for the running of the Steam Factories should be laid down. The running of Woolwich had in the past been left to Ewart and Lloyd, without any formal regulations laid down by the Steam Department.

He further strengthened his control during the next month, determining that in order to establish uniform practice through the establishments, and to ensure the equipment being 'of the most approved description', expenditure for new machinery was to be under his supervision.[10]

The Committee for the Revision of Dockyards was making its investigations, and a flurry of instructions attempted to tighten control over Yard manufactures.[11] Many works had apparently taken place without the sanction of the Board, unprovided for in the estimates, and Admiral Superintendents were to keep a careful check on this in future, while returns were to be prepared showing the work performed by each Nasmyth hammer, with expenses in wages, fuel and so on, explicitly to compare with the results obtained at Crewe Railway Works: 'A Private Establishment...ought not to be better conducted than a large Factory in one of Her Majesty's Dockyards & My Lords rely upon your exertions to bring matters to a similar issue.'[12]

The Committee's Report had nothing but praise for Murray and the arrangements at Portsmouth Factory, which with 678 workmen on its books was quantitatively of a different order from Woolwich:[13]

...the Committee has had for its object, the regulation of the Factories at Woolwich & Portsmouth, by the rules found to work best in private Establishments. We shall not pretend to anticipate results. We admit that, until a perfect system of Accounts, based upon taking Stock at the beginning of every year, has been in operation for at least a twelvemonth, no data can be obtained...that do not partake more of the character of an Estimate...we examined closely, the system of Factory Accounts, adopted both at Woolwich and Portsmouth. The last was in its infancy, the actual working of the Factory not having

Table 7 **Rates of pay in the steam factories at the end of 1847**

	Daily rate
Leading draughtsman	6s 8d to 8s 6d
Draughtsmen	5s to 6s 8d
Assistant timekeepers	4s to 5s
Messengers	2s 8d to 3s
Store porters	4s to 5s Not exceeding five
Engine keepers	4s to 4s 4d
Leading man	7s to 8s 6d Not exceeding 14
Engine fitters	6s to 7s Not exceeding 20
Engine Fitters	4s 6d to 6s
Assistant fitters	3s to 4s 4d
Boys	1s 4d to 2s 4d
Turners and machine men	6s to 7s Not exceeding two
Turners and machine men	3s 6d to 6s
Millwrights and patternmakers	6s to 7s Not exceeding two
Millwrights and patternmakers	4s 6d to 6s
Assistant millwrights and patternmakers wheelwrights	3s 8d to 4s 6d including
Engine smiths	5s to 7s
Hammermen	3s to 4s
Moulders	6s 4d to 7s Not exceeding three
Moulders	5s to 6s 4d
Assistant moulders	2s 8d to 5s
Coppersmiths	5s to 6s 4d
Assistant cvoppersmiths	3s to 4s 4d
Boilermakers	6s to 7s Not exceeding six
Boilermakers	5s to 6s Not exceeding 20
Boilermakers	4s to 5s
Assistant boilermakers	2s 8d to 4s
Painters	3s to 4s 6d

commenced at the time of our visit; but Mr Murray, the Chief Engineer, having had the benefit of long experience in Private Trade, as the working Partner in the House of Messrs Fairbairn of Manchester, had assimilated all his own Regulations to those in use in that Establishment. In justice to this gentleman, we must express our satisfaction at the method, and ability, displayed in these arrangements. The labor account appeared to us to be perfect. There was not a man, out of the 553 men employed, whose work upon any particular day, or half day, could not be at once ascertained and accounted for. Mr Murray also expressed his intention to take Stock at Xmas, and again on 1st April, as he had done, once a month, in the Brass Foundry, from the time that he took charge of it — the Metal Mills, when handed over to him by the Shipwrights Dept, shewing a Balance of 200 tons against them, for which he, naturally, declined to be responsible, the amount having been carried forward from year to year, and never checked by actual comparison...

Things were not so good on the river. Perhaps Ewart had been too old for the job:

At Woolwich, we cannot, conscientiously, say, that we were as well satisfied with the present state of the Factory, or with its future promise....It has grown up too fast, without good regulations at starting, and has been overloaded with work during the time that the whole of the Steam Repairs were concentrated there. The

Officers, too, have been, constantly, detached on other Services; and no general Factory Instructions having been issued by the Board, there has been a want, throughout, of proper method, and responsibility. Stock has never been taken…

It was noted, though, that Humphrys, the Chief Engineer, was fully alive to the defects of the system in his factory, and was anxious to change it for the arrangements he had been accustomed to in private trade. Ellice in response called a meeting at Somerset House with the two Chief Engineers, and the Committee of Revision, where the new Factory Instructions were read, and it was decided that the new system was to come into operation at both factories on 1 January 1849, stock having been taken previously. From 1 January 1849 the Metal Mills were taken away from the easy-going rule of the Shipwrights Department to work as a factory.

As the new regulations came into force the Admiralty reminded the Superintendents of the sensibilities of their paymasters:

> The only way to disarm the jealousy, with which the growing Expenditure of the Naval Yards is viewed, is to satisfy Parliament, and the Country, that these great National Establishments are conducted with the same strict regard to economy…that in all private Enterprises, have constituted the secret of success.[14]

The Factories as instructional resources

The Factories served other functions that were not so easily quantified. The manufacturers of marine engines provided engineers to operate them as part of the deal, though there were some men with in-house training who could be used as their skills allowed. For example in 1834 the Second Engineer of *Flamer* was ordered ashore at Woolwich in order to make dowelling machines.

Some of the men supplied proved unsatisfactory. In 1835 the First Engineer of *Meteor* was discharged for drunkenness; the First Engineer of *Pluto* went AWOL, and on his return said he did not care if he stayed in the Service or not. On *Messenger* an engineer apprentice discharged himself, while the Second Engineer of the ship was more enterprising. Not only was he detected selling spirits to the embarked troops, but he was surprised with two women he had secreted on board. Unlike the drink, these appear to have been reserved for himself, as when found he was in no fit state to do anything. Next year another engineer on *Meteor* maintained the tradition of the ship, being in a 'disgraceful state of intoxication' when the vessel left Jamaica.

Dockyard-trained men, such as the Woolwich millwright accepted for service as Third Engineer in 1836, and seconded to work at Rennie's until a post fell vacant, seemed a more reliable source. As a consequence, one of the most important secondary functions of the Steam Factories was to provide in-house training of engineers for the steamers of the Navy. In July 1837 Parry and Ewart had established a career structure for engineers, dependent upon Yard training. Fourth-class apprentices were entered at 14, and spent their first year at Woolwich. After their third year, if familiar with the names and uses of every part of the engine, they were transferred to the third class. After another year, being then aged 18, if thoroughly

79 Here (and opposite) are some student engineers engaged in practical training at Keyham Factory, at the end of the century.
(*From* The Navy & Army Illustrated, *20 August, 1898*)

conversant with the theory and practice of the engines and boilers, and able to take out and replace any of the working parts, pack the valves and so on, and become 'generally useful', they would go to the second class. Then they would be returned to a Yard to gain more practical experience, working at the forge, brazier's shop, lathe and foundry, and improving their mathematics, under the direction of the resident engineer. After this fifth year they were examined and if qualified to become third-class engineers, they ranked as first-class apprentices, and candidates for promotion. The posts of third-class engineers were filled both by these apprentices and by men appointed directly from a civilian factory. The three classes, First, Second, and Third, of Engineers were Warrant ranks, rated below Carpenters.

But by June 1839 the second secretary of the Admiralty, Sir John Barrow, complained, in a confidential letter to Dockyard Superintendents, of the difficulty in getting qualified men. This was partly due to the way they were sometimes treated. Most of the engineers serving afloat had not been brought up in the

Service and were unaccustomed to Naval discipline, and some officers gave orders to them in a manner guaranteed to give annoyance, though there had been instances where a proper attitude of the officers had maintained strict discipline while causing the Engineers to feel attached to the Service. Furthermore, the financial rewards were not such as to compensate for the lack of status.

New Regulations for Engineers were promulgated in June 1842. The *Mechanic's Magazine* considered that the financial rewards were perfectly reasonable, but was enraged that the Chief Engineer was still rated below the Ship's Carpenter: this would not encourage men of ability to join. Worse, it would produce some of the unfortunate results noted above:

...to give a man, pronounced by order of the Lords of Admiralty to be a fit companion for carpenters and caulkers only, the income of a first lieutenant, (much more, indeed, taking all the allowances into account,) must have an inevitable tendency to produce low, grovelling, perhaps dissolute and intemperate habits

— to break down and demoralise a class of men, whom it ought
to be our study, to elevate as much as possible in the scale of
intellectual vigour and moral worth.

The First Class Engineer's rate had risen to £13 12s by
November 1846, when Captain Lord John Hay again raised
within the Board of Admiralty the question of pay and
conditions of service for engineers. It was still proving very
difficult to recruit and retain good men. The comparable pay in
foreign service and the Merchant Marine for a First Class
Engineer was £18 to £25 per month, and the man ranked with
the Chief Officer, in foreign companies with the Captain. He
proposed a reclassification and an increase in pay. These
suggestions were adopted; it was hoped that they would:

induce…young men of education to enter the Factories of the
Engine Makers with a view to acquire the mechanical skill and
knowledge to render them eligible for entering Her Majesty's
Service, and…will prove efficacious in calling forth a large body
of very superior Class Engineers.

From 1 April 1847 engineers were classed in three divisions, the
first two being, for the first time, of commissioned rank, and to
mess with the officers: Inspectors of Machinery Afloat (John
Dinnen was the first), Chief Engineers (first, second, and third
classes), and Assistant Engineers (first, second, and third classes).
By 24 November the Engineers numbered 447 in all.

Though recruitment continued to be a problem, progress
was made in training. In February 1848 Ellice suggested that
engineers not currently serving on board ship be employed in
the Factories; the practical experience would be invaluable and
the cost trifling. While so employed they were to receive
harbour duty pay only, but on being certified by the Chief
Engineer that they had acquired a competent skill (and subject
to satisfactory conduct) Ellice proposed that half their time in
the Factory might be counted as sea time. A third-class
Assistant Engineer had to serve three years before he could
pass his examination in that grade. Ellice submitted that in
future the time that they were on harbour pay, or not
employed in the Factories, should not be allowed to count as
part of that period; and that in future, no officer should be
advanced to the rank of Chief Engineer unless he could show
'by his servitude in a Private Factory', or by a certificate from
one of the Chief Engineers of the Dockyards, that he had
acquired the necessary skills as a workman. As a consequence,
in June two shops were fitted up at Woolwich and Portsmouth
with lathes and tools for the employment and instruction of
engineers (Figure 79).

As well as providing in-service training for engineers in the
Service, the Factories also served as an original source for the
men themselves. In October 1851 there was a shortage, and the
Factories were asked to forward the names of men and boys
who were considered suitable. Atherton forwarded a list of
applicants for jobs at sea, with comments such as 'Well spoken,
but his appearance not very favourable', 'Personal appearance
much in his favour', 'A very fair workman, lost a thumb in the
Service — Not desirable as an officer'. The Board approved of
Baldwin Walker's suggestion to select a few of the best-qualified
individuals who could be obtained from private industry, and
from the boys in the Steam Factories, for entry as Junior

Engineers in the Service; but the number of 10 was not to be
exceeded for the time being.

There were three classes of boys working in the Factories, but
none were indentured apprentices. Rivet boys were selected by
the Chief Engineer from the sons of the most deserving
workmen; they would become boilermakers. Of superior status
were the boys learning the various factory trades, who were
selected by the Admiralty, usually on the Chief Engineer's
recommendation. At the top of the pile were the boys
nominated by the Admiralty to sit a competitive examination
set by the Chief Engineer; the successful candidates would be
trained in the Factory to be naval engineers. It was not easy for
the sons of factory men to attain this status, and not surprisingly
this caused some disgruntlement. In the spring of 1852 nine
Engineer Boys who had served five years in the Woolwich
Factory certified as third-class Assistant Engineers, and six from
Portsmouth; in October Walker approved 30 Junior Engineers
being recruited from factories of private establishments.

The better the elementary education the boys in the
Factories had received, the larger would be the pool of likely
candidates, and so by a decision of February 1853 the limited
facilities of the Dockyard schools were made available to them
after working hours. The numbers taking advantage of this were
to be reported. Some applicants were undesirable for reasons of
their physical condition: John Hopkinson, an engineer at
Holyhead harbour works, was sent to Woolwich for
examination and pronounced 'unfit for HM Service for want of
teeth and the formation of his Chest, predisposed to Chest
afflictions'. The engineers at Portsmouth had the advantage of
being allowed to use their free time to study at the Royal Naval
College, from March to June 1853. Fourteen attended, for
periods between 2 and 75 days, mostly studying algebra, four
trigonometry, and two arithmetic. Next spring the numbers
would be lower, but one of them, the Chief Engineer of HMS
Gladiator, was studying calculus. In August 1853 it was decided
that £1,406 would be spent in the next financial year on tools,
lathes and planing machinery for the Factory, for the use of
mechanics belonging to the Fleet.

Some unsuitable men slipped through. Daniel Bennet, third-
class engineer, was described by the Captain of HMS Ajax as:

…perfectly incompetent to perform the duties required of him,
from a total ignorance of all mechanical knowledge, from a
general ignorance of the practical working of Engines, in which
he is so deficient that the is not fit to be entrusted with the
charge of either Engines, or Boilers.

His conduct was unexceptionable, however, and he was a good
draughtsman. Atherton (who had passed him) stated that the
certificate was a very limited guarantee, no more than to say
that the man appeared to be eligible to be on a ship on
probation; the questions he had asked Bennet could not
possibly have been very searching. Perhaps it was just the
draughtsmanship that impressed.

Bennet was not alone, for an Admiralty Circular noted that
circumstances had forced the Navy to take on many engineers
who had not served at sea. The Senior Engineer of the vessel
was to make sure that inexperienced persons were not left in
charge, and to give them instruction. Two such men
volunteered from Devonport in response to an Admiralty order

asking for names of engineers in the Yard qualified and willing to serve as acting as first-class assistant Engineers. The Chief Engineer there commented on this that none of the engineers of the yard was competent for such service, as they had never been to sea. The two men in question had been instructed to work the two harbour tugs, but they had never been on the open sea, and could not be trusted with an engine outside the harbour. The Russian War was to lead to a sudden upsurge in the demand for sea-going engineers, and greatly increased the workload of the Factories.[15]

—ɯ—

Notes:

1. Samuel Smiles, *Lives of the Engineers*, (London, 1862), Vol. II, p.112; James Fletcher, 'On improvements in heavy tools for general engineering and iron shipbuilding work', in *Proceedings of the Institution of Mechanical Engineers*, 1864, pp.189-228; *Four Days at Portsmouth on the Eve of War*, anon., (London, n.d. [1854 — a reprint from *Rahper's Magazine*]); *Encyclopaedia Britannica*, 9th edn,1883, article 'Machine tools';W Steeds, *A History of Machine Tools 1700-1910*, (Oxford, 1969); I Bradley, *A History of Machine Tools*, (Hemel Hempstead, 1972); L T C Rolt, *Tools for the Job*, rev.ed. (London, 1986). The Admiralty's decision to standardise on Whitworth's thread is in ADM 2/1391. Whitworth had first proposed his system in a paper read to the Institute of Civil Engineers in 1841. Iron tanks were invented in 1809 by Trevithick and Dickenson. In 1813 Dickenson and Maudslay were given the Admiralty contract for their manufacture. ADM 110/59, ADM 111/247.

2. POR/P/39, James, *Description... .*, pp.89-91, ADM 2/1388, ADM 93/2.

3. ADM 95/97.

4. ADM 93/3, *Memoir* of Edward Humphrys in *Proceedings of the Institution of Civil Engineers*, 1868, pp.592-593, ADM 93/4, ADM 12/508.

5. This was done by by providing a screwing machine, a shaping machine, a strong punching and planing machine, two lathes (one of 24in headstock and 20ft bed, the other with 10in headstock and 18ft bed), a self-acting drilling machine, a portable punching and shearing machine, and 24 pairs of vices of the largest size. Tenders were to be asked from Whitworth, Glasgow and Collier. This time Whitworth's were the successful contender, getting all the orders except for the lathes; Glasgow's were the winners there.

6. Glasgow's supplied a large planing machine for it for £605. There was some trouble about this, and Lawrie complained about its performance. Glasgow's replied that it had been mishandled, with the casting being planed while raised up on blocks of timber, which would make it unsteady, and the part planed had a large and very uneven surface. Two or three light cuts were required, after the two first heavy cuts had been taken off, before a true surface could be attained. Humphrys was sent to Chatham to report on the machine. Not everything could be pinned on the workmen, who were not inexperienced, since Nasmyth had delivered a planing machine there in 1841. Baldwin Walker's response was that if no adequate reduction in the price was made the firm should never again be called on to tender. The workmanship and materials were inferior. Ten per cent off would be fair. Lawrie recommended a stiffer cut — £180 — as Collier's were able to supply one of similar dimensions for £425.

7. ADM 93/4, ADM 2/1390, ADM 93/5, ADM 93/7, ADM 93/3, ADM 85/1.

8. ADM 1/5591.

9. ADM 93/1, POR/P/33, ADM 2/1387, ADM 85/13, ADM 85/10, POR/P/39.

10. ADM 2/1389, ADM 2/1387, ADM 93/1, ADM 1/3485, ADM 93/2.

11. There were more practices going on for Ellice to worry about. It had been customary at Woolwich, and recently at Portsmouth, to make various articles not connected with repairs to steam machinery in the Factories for supply to the stores. An instruction was issued to stop this. Worse, it transpired in October that the Metal Mills and other manufacturing establishments at Chatham had not taken stock or kept books on the principles that applied in private factories. This was to be changed at once. Materials drawn were in future to be charged to the Chief Engineer at contract price; he was then to debit himself of this and add it to the cost of the whole process of manufacturing, with 10 per cent added for wear and tear of machinery and interest on the plant in cases where the building had been constructed within the last 10 years. The articles were then to be received by the Storekeeper at their increased value, and charged as such to the departments when reissued.

12. ADM 1/5590, ADM 2/1390, ADM 93/2, ADM 95/20, POR/P/47, POR/P/43.

13. By June 1848 there were at Portsmouth 678 workmen (including men at the block mills and sawmills) including 101 fitters, 13 engine keepers, 37 turners and machine men, 14 patternmakers, 21 engine smiths, 10 founders, 18 brass founders, 13 coppersmiths, 78 boilermakers, 27 hammer men, and 136 labourers. With this establishment, quantitatively of a different order from that at Woolwich, Murray felt confident enough to put himself on the line by stating that he hoped to complete vessels more quickly than ever before.

14. ADM 1/5591, POR/P/44.

15. ADM 85/6, ADM 84/4, ADM 84/5, ADM 84/7, ADM 84/17, ADM 85/13, ADM 85/16, ADM 84/9, ADM 93/14.

CHAPTER 8

Greene, Scamp and the Integrated Factory

IN 1847 the Navy disposed of 174 steam vessels of all descriptions with a total horsepower of 44,480, and the cost of the Comptroller's establishment had swollen from a staff of four in 1841 to thirteen.[1]

By 1850 it was clear that the Surveyor of the Navy was going to be primarily dealing with steam ships, their machinery and fittings, and on 11 February 1850 the Steam Department and the Surveyor's Department amalgamated and Ellice resigned. His name is not prominent in naval history, but during the few years of his Comptrollership he presided over an unparalleled rate of introduction of new technology. Sad to relate, when Goodrich's widow sent the Admiralty a catalogue of his drawings and models, Ellice considered that they were of no value and advised against purchase, an unfortunate tailpiece to his tenure of the post. The Surveyor, who since 1848 had been Captain Sir Baldwin Walker, was to prove equally supportive of mechanical innovation.[2]

Colonel Greene and Mr Scamp

By 1849 the two steam factory at Portsmouth had been built and equipped and some facilities were available at Keyham, but they were still inadequate to meet the imminent demands of the Navy. The next decade was to see this remedied, largely through the work of two remarkable men. They succeeded in creating a factory building adequate not only for current needs but also for future requirements, and still in use, though now too large for the current size of the Navy.

Captain Brandreth resigned as Director of Engineering and Architectural Works in 1846; he died of a stroke two years later. Shortly before his departure he had been provided with a job description. The scope of the position was formidable. He had

the general superintendence of all the works, buildings, repairs and steam and other machinery throughout the Dockyards, victualling yards, naval hospitals and infirmaries, Royal Marine barracks and other naval establishments both at home and on the foreign stations; also of the Admiralty buildings at Whitehall and Somerset House and the Royal Hospital and Schools at Greenwich. He was required to visit these establishments and check up on the officers in charge. The whole of the correspondence, plans, estimates, reports and accounts from these establishments were to be submitted by him for Admiralty approval, including the annual Estimates for the Works, Buildings and Steam and other machinery: at that time this was a sum of between £600,000 and £700,000.

Brandreth was replaced in November 1846 by Lieut. Colonel Irvine, who, like Brandreth, found that the enormous administrative load outlined above prevented him from taking an active part in design. He died in December 1849, after a severe fall in Portsmouth Dockyard. Captain James and a Colonel Lloyd applied for the post, but Colonel G. T. Greene, of the East India Company's Engineers, was appointed. Greene, in contrast to his predecessor, was deeply involved in original design work; much of the burden of administration was taken off his shoulders by his remarkable Chief Assistant, William Scamp.

Scamp was born at Georgeham in North Devon in 1801. His first work was the Assembly Rooms at Ilfracombe (now destroyed), after which he worked as a draughtsman for Wyattville during the restoration of Windsor Castle. He entered the service of the Admiralty in 1838, becoming Clerk of Works at Woolwich in July that year, and was transferred to Malta in 1841 in the same capacity, designing, with great success, new docks and shore establishments, including a bakery partly of

RESPONSIBILITIES

All artificers and labourers in the Dockyards except the shipwrights were under Brandreth's jurisdiction, and he was required to report by himself, or in conjunction with the heads of the departments, on their efficiency. As Chairman of the Committee on Metals he received the reports of the Supervisor of Metals, and in conjunction with that officer had charge of all matters connected with the Metal Mills and Smitheries, and metal manufactures throughout the Service. All inventions connected with engineering or architecture were referred to him. Finally, he also had the general superintendence of the construction schemes of harbours of refuge and the examination and approval of their accounts.

The duties of the office of Engineer at each of the several naval stations were also spelled out:

The superintendence of the Repairs to all the works and buildings throughout the Dock Yard, Victualling Yard, Hospital and Marine Barracks of his Station.

The repair of all the machinery of these establishments.

The repairs of all the works, buildings and machinery.

The alterations to and reconstruction of all works and buildings.

The providing and fixing of all new machinery for these establishments.

Direction of all new works and buildings in these establishments.

The general charge of all the works and buildings.

Each officer is occasionally called on to visit other establishments, both private and public, and to report on any inventions or improvements that might be applicable to the Service.[3]

NEW EQUIPMENT OF THE 1850's

The Great Exhibition of 1851 was a shop window for the British machine-tool industry, among many other things. Given inventors' and industrialists' tendencies to bombard the Admiralty with news of any invention that might conceivably be of service, and the close connections between the senior engineering officers in the Yards and private industry, it was unlikely that anything radically new would be on show that the Navy did not know about already, but just to be on the safe side a circular was issued requesting

> ...that upon the respective officers of the Dock & Victualling Yards visiting the Great Exhibition they will bring to the notice...for their Lordships information such inventions, new machinery, tools &c as they consider to be improvements upon articles now in use, and which might be introduced with advantage into the Naval Establishments.

The workers from Chatham (and probably Woolwich as well) were also encouraged to attend: they were given two days off with pay for this purpose, with a third day allowed for travelling. If this was abused 'the parties concerned [would] incur their Lordship's severe displeasure'. Nothing seems to have marred the improving occasion, and the men sent a letter of thanks to the Admiralty. In the event the Chief Engineers, notably Murray, were favourably impressed by quite a range of machines.[4]

Humphrys, Murray and Bennett (Timber Inspector at Portsmouth) recommended Fox, Henderson's crane. This was one of the stars of the Exhibition; it had been used to erect the building itself, and remained as an exhibit. These cranes were of very simple construction and were used by merchant shipbuilders. They needed no foundation of masonry and they could easily be moved; however, they were to prove far less successful in Admiralty service.

Bennett recommended an American oar-making machine. This recommendation was minuted 'Doubtful if it would be advantageous to the service to provide machinery for this purpose — but it may be an idea to buy oars made so cheaply.' Lawrie, the Chief Engineer at Chatham, noticed this machine, and decided to design one himself. He also recommended a patent steam travelling crane 'similar to the Timber Traveller at Portsmouth except worked by steam.'

Baldwin Walker noted, together with Lawrie and Bennett, Furness's mortising machine, and Barker's curvilinear sawing machine. Cotsell, the Master Smith at Chatham and Laire, the Master Shipwright, noted the Mersey Iron Company's rolled blanks, but this was minuted 'Such blanks

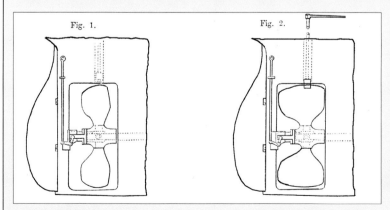

80 The Great Exhibition displayed many things of interest to the Admiralty's engineering staff; this is Maudslay's feathering propeller, designed to be rotated in order to minimise drag when the vessel was under sail. (*From* Catalogue of the Great Exhibition of 1851)

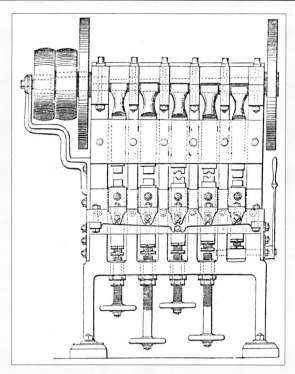

81 Mass-production of certain small parts entered the Yards with the acquisition of examples of Ryder's Forging Machine. (*From* Catalogue of the Great Exhibition of 1851)

are made with Nasmyth hammers...it does not seem advisable at present to incur the additional expense of providing new rolls or adopting existing ones.' Lawrie and Bennet reported Armstrong's hydraulic lift and crane; Lawrie and Laire, Hick & Sons' portable smith's hearth. Atherton recommended a marine steam engine designed by himself, which he had failed to get adopted by the Admiralty. Laire recommended Hick's punching machine.

Murray noted a string of equipment:

Maudslay's patent gun metal screw propeller ('The use of this Screw is increasing in the Merchant Service and there may arise particular cases in the Royal Navy where it may be applicable') (Figure 80);

Siemens' patent chronometric Governor ('The increased use of better Governors is much wanted for several Engines in the service');

Siemens' condenser and governor;

Tuck's pneumatic governor;

Galloway's patent lifting jacks;

Haley's lifting jacks;

Fairbairn's tubular crane;

Stanton's electro-magnetic engine ('one of the best proposals of the kind');

Whitworth's self-acting lathes ('Sets of standard gauges for long and circular measures if supplied and...strictly adhered to...in the Dockyards would be very beneficial to the Service');

Sharp's lathe slotting machine ('may hereafter be required in boiler department');

Ryder's forging machine (a means of mass-producing small components), which would be useful, especially at Portsmouth, for making block-pins (Figure 81).

Several of the machines noted at the Exhibition were to be ordered for Keyham and as additional plant for the other Yards. There was little new in the way of machine tools, with the exception of woodworking machinery, the development of which had lagged behind. Later in the decade new sawmills were to be built in the Yards, equipped with the new machinery.[5]

82A and **82B**
Scamp's Bakery in
the harbour at
Valetta, Malta.
(John Lake)

fireproof iron construction (Figure 82A and B). He also came to the rescue of the construction of the Anglican cathedral there, and received a decoration from Queen Adelaide in return. He returned to England as Chief Assistant to the Director of Works in 1845.

Greene was at first compared unfavourably with his predecessor by Captain Milne (later Admiral of the Fleet), the member of the Board of Admiralty at the time who appears to have taken the greatest interest in the Yards, no individual member being given this function. He seems to have had a good working relationship with Irvine, and considered that his untimely death had put a stop to the changes that they had jointly contemplated. These certainly included the mechanisation of the Sawmills. He considered that Greene was 'working in the dark', had no idea of the views and wishes of the Board, and should be superintended by a member with a practical knowledge of Naval affairs. In the meantime the Surveyor, the Director of Works and a Board member should visit the yards and investigate their inadequacies. In the light of Greene's subsequent attainments, it is difficult now to see what his supposed shortcomings could have been. Perhaps it was simply a matter of clashes of personality.[6]

Greene was to design several notable buildings, continuing the use of iron as a constructional medium, while Scamp's great achievement was in rational factory and yard planning. As a team they made the 1850s the most significant decade in creating buildings for the Steam Navy. They inherited a plan for Keyham, the greatest of the steam factories, which in its original state was another unfortunate design owing much to the Woolwich pattern, and effectively transformed the vast building into something so practical that it has served the needs of the Navy from that day to this without alteration.

Sheerness and the Russian War

All these preparations were made with a specific enemy in mind: France. However, when the fleets of the two countries met in 1854 it was as allies in war against Russia. The Navy operated in both the Black Sea and the Baltic. All the Yards played their part in the preparation and dispatch of the fleets, but one in particular was strategically far better placed than the others for the repair of battle-damaged ships from the Baltic.

There had been a resident engineer at Sheerness since July 1848, when George Blaxland (one of the many to have patented a type of screw propeller) was promoted from being foreman at Woolwich, and a basic set of machine tools was provided, but it had generally remained a technical backwater. In October 1851 the two 14hp engines for blowing the blast and driving machinery at the Smithery at Sheerness were very decayed and dilapidated. One had to be disconnected entirely and the majority of its components replaced: this left the Smithery wholly dependent upon one engine, which was in a very unsatisfactory state. It was necessary to take down a portion of the wheels and shafting to renew the working parts, and as these were in the vicinity of the flywheel it was impossible to do this while the engine was working. The shipwrights suggested that the work begin on Sunday morning so that the men might have the advantage of daylight in removing and lifting the 'heavy, cumbrous and greasy machinery, which appears unsafe to be performed by Candle light'.

War put an end to this situation. Chatham lacked a Basin, limiting its ability to repair damaged ships returning from the Baltic, so it was decided to prepare a factory equipped with the latest machine tools at Sheerness and Mr Scamp was entrusted with the job. A copy of the Factory instructions were forwarded on 23 May 1854, and in October £5,000 was appropriated for machinery, shafting, gearing and tools. In the event, no fleet actions occurred, but the wear and tear on the steam machinery ensured that in the winter, when large areas of the Baltic iced up and the ships had to return home, a great deal of heavy maintenance work needed to be done.[7]

On 13 October Scamp's plans were sent to Sheerness (Figure 83). There was a vacant space of about 110ft between Holl's great Storehouse Quadrangle and the Smithery, which Scamp divided into a central space 45ft wide with flanking aisles by iron standards set in concrete. Iron roofs completed a building that could be erected very rapidly: brick facades (there were still lingering inhibitions about appearances), tied it in visually with the flanking buildings, but were in no way essential, and it could be brought into operation while these were being built. The central space was appropriated for boiler work, and the aisle next to the Smithery for a punching and shearing shop and furnaces; the other aisle was left for general purposes and a thoroughfare, should one be required. The small dimensions of the standards meant that the maximum amount of floor space was made available for machinery, which could be disposed unhampered by dividing walls.

The iron roof truss, light, easily added and removed, and capable of being covered by glass, zinc or corrugated iron, had already proved to be an indispensable tool for enlarging and uniting existing factory buildings by infilling the spaces between them, providing multifunctional spaces at little cost. James Nasmyth claimed to have initiated the procedure at Woolwich Arsenal, where in 1847 he suggested roofing over the roadway spaces to provide additional working space; Fox, Henderson supplied the trusses. Railway works provide the closest parallel to the Steam Factories and comparable additions to them post-date Scamp's buildings. The usable space at Crewe Old Works, whose unsatisfactory layout has been noted, was increased between 1866 and 1874 by these means. Swindon Works had been far better arranged than Crewe from the outset, and its courtyards were gradually infilled, the first significant additions being the Steam Hammer Shop and the new Engine Shop of 1864. The latter was originally covered in

three spans of 45ft on cast-iron columns (it was later extended to occupy all available space), and so was larger than the Sheerness Factory.

Infilling by metal standards and iron roofs enabled construction to be very rapid, and speed was certainly achieved; by 29 December some machinery was ready to be erected. The nucleus of a factory was there, but a foundry was also required. In May 1855 it was decided that Blaxland was to visit the foundries at Portsmouth and Woolwich and a few private firms in London when he could be spared for a few days, presumably so that he could give an opinion on the internal arrangements. An engineer's foundry was eventually established on the site of, perhaps adapting, the Store Mast House, where the first modern machinery in the Yard had been installed in 1838 (Figure 30A).

Despite the factory's speed of completion, it was August before Whitworth and Collier were asked to tender for machinery, tools and shafting, and Nasmyth for a steam hammer, boiler and high-pressure engine. It was not until the end of September that the Boiler Shop machinery was being completed. Blaxland applied for more machinery at the beginning of November, by which time Sheerness was

84 A contemporary plan of the layout of the machinery at Sheerness Smithery extension. *(TNA ADM 85/41)*

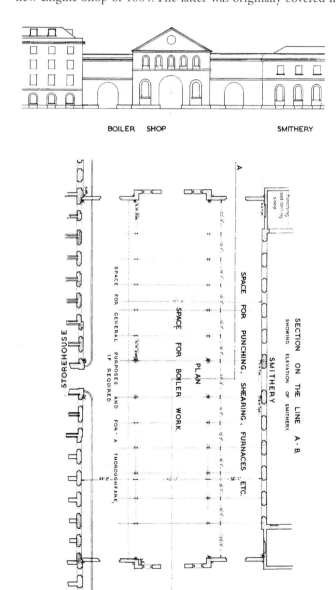

83 Mr Scamp's insertion of a Steam Factory between existing buildings at Sheerness. *(Adapted from TNA ADM 140/1951)*

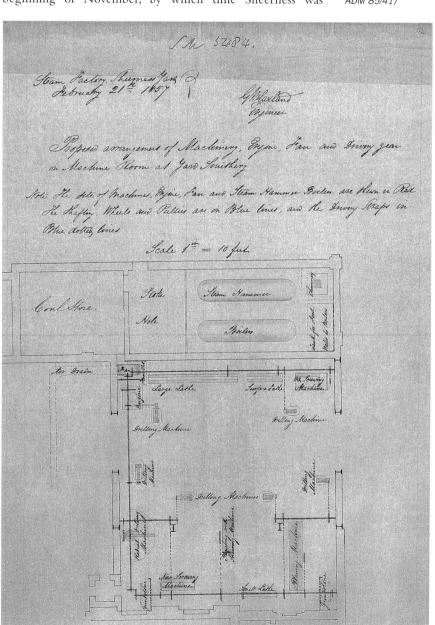

overwhelmed with repair work, the men working till 8 p.m. until the emergency was over. A temporary foundry was prepared in December and a new smithery extension was built on the disengaged side of the old one (Figure 84).[8]

These were of little importance, however, in the scheme of things. The structure of Scamp's infill Boiler Factory, on the other hand, contained design implications that were to be drawn out at Keyham, where another major project was under way.

Towards the integrated factory: Keyham gets under way

In July 1852 the long-postponed construction of Keyham Factory was advocated, and in August a report by Sir Baldwin Walker and Mr Scamp was delivered, setting out the order of proceedings. The Fitting, Turning and Erecting Shop, the Smithery, Foundry, Brass and Copper Shop and Storehouse, and the Engine House would all have to be completed and equipped before it could begin to function. The Boiler Shop would have to be built later, as its site was still occupied by the Powder Magazine. The site could not be cleared until the new Magazine at Bull Point was completed, and that work was not progressing very rapidly.

A plan and sections had been prepared and revised estimates laid before the House in 1849/50. Baldwin Walker and Scamp, in a draft letter to the Treasury, stressed the urgency of the work:

> The introduction of Steam Machinery into all classes of HM Ships, but more especially in those of the largest dimensions, has been found absolutely necessary for the public Service and to keep pace with the proceedings of neighbouring Powers…The number of ships that have been already fitted, is so far beyond what was contemplated when the Select Committee made their report that already the demands on the existing Factories of Woolwich and Portsmouth are more than can at times be met with convenience…it must be borne in mind that ships when so fitted cannot be repaired at one yard and their machinery at another; so that whilst the Navy is rendered more efficient in respect of steam power, the means of maintaining such efficiency are diminished, and the sphere of operations as regards Devonport, the most important of the Western Yards, is constantly contracting so long as the steam Works of Keyham remain in abeyance…[they reckoned it would take three years to bring the Factory into operation]…My Lords propose that the Engine House and Fitting and Erecting Shop should be commenced at once and kept in advance of the Smithery, Foundry and Coppersmiths' Shops, which must be proceeded with simultaneously in order to bring the Establishment into partial operation…The Boiler Establishment, Storehouses and Officers Houses cannot at present be taken in hand…

In fact, even with Keyham, the Navy would not be over-provided with resources. Three years earlier, Captain James had done a few sums. The total horsepower of the Steam Navy was reckoned as 48,000, with another 30,000hp available from merchant shipping in case of war (presumably for trooping, supply and miscellaneous duties). This was a total of 78,000hp, of which he reckoned a quarter, say 20,000hp, would be under repair at any time. Woolwich was supposed to be able to repair 5,000hp in a year, and Portsmouth 6,000hp, with Keyham having a capacity of 8,000hp. This was a total of 19,000hp, just about adequate for the demands of war.

Furthermore, the average size of the machinery was increasing, as line-of-battle ships were converted or purpose built to take engines driving screw propellers. These were now coming into service. Ellice had written in February 1849 that plans had been prepared showing the fitting of 780hp engines to the *Nile* and 700hp ones to *London*, both 90-gun ships: 'The Advantages to be derived from Steam Power in line of Battle Ships are now so fully understood and appreciated that it is unnecessary to make any observations on that subject'. Woolwich was suitable only for the repair of paddle steamers, because of its small basin capacity and shallow draught, so that Walker could pile on the arguments. Before the close of the next financial year there would be 24 line-of-battle ships fitted with screw propulsion (counting the four block ships, the first large warships to be so fitted). This number would be still further increased when the remainder of the screw ships now on the stocks and ordered were completed, and the maintenance problem would shortly become formidable.

Portsmouth was at that time the only suitable base with a steam factory, but this would be totally insufficient to meet the future requirements, even omitting a wartime scenario. Devonport would have to be made capable of repairing and refitting the screw battleships as soon as possible. It was unlikely that Keyham would be finished in time to meet the needs of the Navy when all the new ships were ready, but if the work was not pressed on with the consequences might be incalculable. Private trade could not be looked to for assistance: 'At the present moment they are so pressed with Engine Work that many of them are working night & day & there are scarcely any good workmen out of Employ'.[9]

Provisional dockside workshops, whose machinery, as has been seen, was already costed for, would be vital for several years, and tracings were forwarded for guidance in fixing their engines and machinery, which would follow at once; the fans and shafting would be made at Woolwich and sent on completion. Greene and Lloyd consulted together as to how best to spend £50,000 in providing a repair facility for steamers. The Admiralty were keen that no delay should take place in fitting out the screw liners ordered to be fitted out at Devonport and wanted a date from Greene when the basin and great crane necessary for fixing their machinery would be ready.[10]

However, a speedy way of bringing a large area into use as soon as possible was required, and in March 1853, the same month that Sir James Graham, First Lord of the Admiralty, made preparations for war, two solutions were laid before the Surveyor. One was devised by Sir Charles Fox, recently knighted for his work in the construction of the Crystal Palace, and the other came from Greene, though in fact it was the work of Scamp. Fox apparently offered a variant of the Crystal Palace, making a glass roof 'cover the entire space appropriated to Factory buildings & in fact to constitute the Factory Workshops', while Walker thought that 'the proposition of the Director of Works which is to cover over the central space with glass leaving surrounding buildings nearly as originally designed' would be preferable.

However, Walker thought that a number of problems would

arise in practice. The covered space would generate high temperatures; the light and ventilation of the surrounding buildings (if any were introduced) would be interfered with; it would be difficult and labour-consuming to keeping the glass clean and the roof watertight; and the 'almost unbearable noise of the Boiler making' would seriously interfere with the duties of the other branches of the Establishment. However, if these difficulties could be met, Walker could see no objection to the Quadrangle's being covered with a glass roof, with no deviation being made in the position, dimensions, or internal arrangements of the buildings originally determined. The next day Greene forwarded a detailed report (which has not survived) on Scamp's plan, and the matter was settled in principle. Many consequences were to follow from this decision.[11]

By 6 May the first two Carmichael cranes were tested and ready for use. A provisional source of power for the machinery was obtained by removing the 20hp engines from the *Rocket* (an iron ship of 70 tons) with boilers, pumps, fans and related machinery. By the middle of the month these were erected and complete at Keyham, and worked and tested as far as practicable, but the boilers still required felting, and the stone floor of the Engine House and stokehole and the pipes to lead the water from the pumps had not been commenced. By July Greene felt able to name 15 October as the date for bringing the docks into use, and in August a man was appointed to take charge of the caissons and sluices. The pumping engine broke a valve seat in September, but no delay was caused, and on 7 October HMS *Queen* entered No. 1 dock. The Admiralty sent a message to Greene and Walker: 'HM Ship *Queen* having this day been docked at Keyham in No 1 Dock & these great works being thus opened up for naval purposes, my Lords have been pleased to direct that the said dock be named after the above ship & be henceforth called the "Queen's Dock".' A note of disharmony was introduced when Fairbairn's 40 ton crane failed its proof test at 54 tons; 60 tons had been specified, and the firm now instructed their foreman to refuse any test over 50 tons.[12]

In August Greene sent Walker tracings of part of the Factory, stating that the Fitting and Erecting shops, engine house and so on were already in progress, and asking for the position of the engine and its shafting to be laid down on the plan, in order that the requisite preparations might be made in the engine house walls. Elevations and a plan of the Erecting and Turning block were produced, as well as details of girders and joists for the storehouses, and in October the specification was issued for tenders for a 50hp engine, with two boilers of 50hp each, with shafting and millwork.[13]

In December the tender of Hick & Son, £6,494, was accepted. This Bolton firm was to play an important part in the setting up of the Factory throughout the decade. In February 1854 Walker passed on to them tracings of the buildings in course of erection, and asked them to provide a drawing showing the proposed arrangement of the engine, boilers and shafting.

The works had now got to the point where a resident Chief Engineer and Inspector of Steam Machinery was required, and in April John Trickett was transferred from Woolwich. This was a notable appointment: in addition to supervising the establishment of the Factory he was to design several important items of machinery installed there. His first action was to go to

85 *Duke of Wellington* at Keyham, during March 1854, in the hands of Trickett's men, dealing with minor faults. *(NMM, neg. no. 4221)*

Bolton to liaise with Hick's, and by 10 May he had put the firm in possession of all the sketches required for the contract. In a month's time Hick's were making rapid progress with their plans and Trickett had approved of their plan for gearing, with a modification. Trickett's appointment was not the only event of the month to affect the progress of Keyham, for war against Russia was declared on 30 May, and things would have to move if the Factory was to play any part in it.[14]

Meanwhile, the Fairbairn crane was tested again, and the chain broke. The resulting jerk broke two teeth in the turning gear. This was the second time that this part of the machinery had failed: a similar accident had happened to one of Carmichael's 20 ton cranes. Fairbairn's claimed that the failure was the fault of the chain, which was Crown property, and they took the opportunity to state: 'No possible good can be attained by testing the crane with these extreme loads.' Nevertheless, the Admiralty pressed on with their researches, and on lifting 58 tons a serious fracture occurred in the top part of the jib. A rare photo opportunity came in March, when *Duke of Wellington* was docked for inspection of a Kingston injection valve (see p.36) reported to be detached from its spindle; the opportunity was taken to search for the cause of a leak in her bread room, which could not be traced from inside the ship (Figure 85).[15]

Keyham comes on line

In August 1854 Trickett wrote to Hick's that the buildings were in a very forward state, and that the foundations for the engine would soon be ready. Things were now in fact so advanced that the first batch of tenders for machine tools were accepted. This time Whitworth got the lion's share (Table 8). In addition Messrs Garforth were asked to supply a patent riveting machine.

Trickett was at the centre of all operations: checking tracings sent by Hick, which then had to be forwarded to Walker for his approval; writing to the contractors for the lathes to find out their various operating speeds, and then informing Hick of the sizes of driving pulleys that would be required; preparing the specification for the travelling cranes in the Erecting Shop; and progress-chasing generally. Drawings of the mill-gearing arrangements arrived, and Greene sent a general plan of the Foundry for guidance in preparing the ground. The Factory would soon be ready to operate in a limited way, and a timekeeper would be required. At the beginning of September a set of cast iron blocks for bending and flanging plates were required. Walker ordered these to be completed at Woolwich as soon as practicable, without giving them priority over more important work; there was a war on, and Keyham would not be able to make a significant contribution for some time.[16]

A temporary Boiler Shop was urgently required, and it was suggested that part of the Erecting Shop might be used for this purpose, but Walker considered this a most objectionable arrangement. He suggested instead that part of the proposed glazing of the quadrangle be carried out to form the workshop. The machine tool makers were holding things up. Most had not yet sent the necessary drawings and until these were received the foundations for the lathes could not be commenced, or the tools arranged in the shops, even on the drawings. However, by the beginning of October the matter was settled. Another aggravation was the discovery that the boilers supplied had been made too large, so that the Boiler House had to be extended by 10ft.

Table 8 **The first batch of machine tools for Keyham**

Whitworth	34 lathes
	10 nut shaping machine
	5 slotting machines
	5 radial drilling machines
	14 vertical drilling machines
	2 boring machines
	1 plate bending machine
	4 punching & shearing machines
	1 Ryders forge
	1 circular saw
	2 boring bars
Collier	4 sawing machines
	4 planing machines
	6 lathes
Nasmyth	2 planing machines
	1 vertical drilling machine
Glasgow	1 vertical drilling machine
Hetherington	1 horizontal drilling machine
	2 boring bars

Work was now being done of a different order from fiddling with Kingston valves and finding minor leaks. The profoundly unsatisfactory machinery of the *Algiers*, a 91-gun ship that had been launched at Devonport in January, was being repaired, as was that of the old steam packet *Avon*. Mechanics from Maudslay & Field were working on the 91-gun *Exmouth*, which

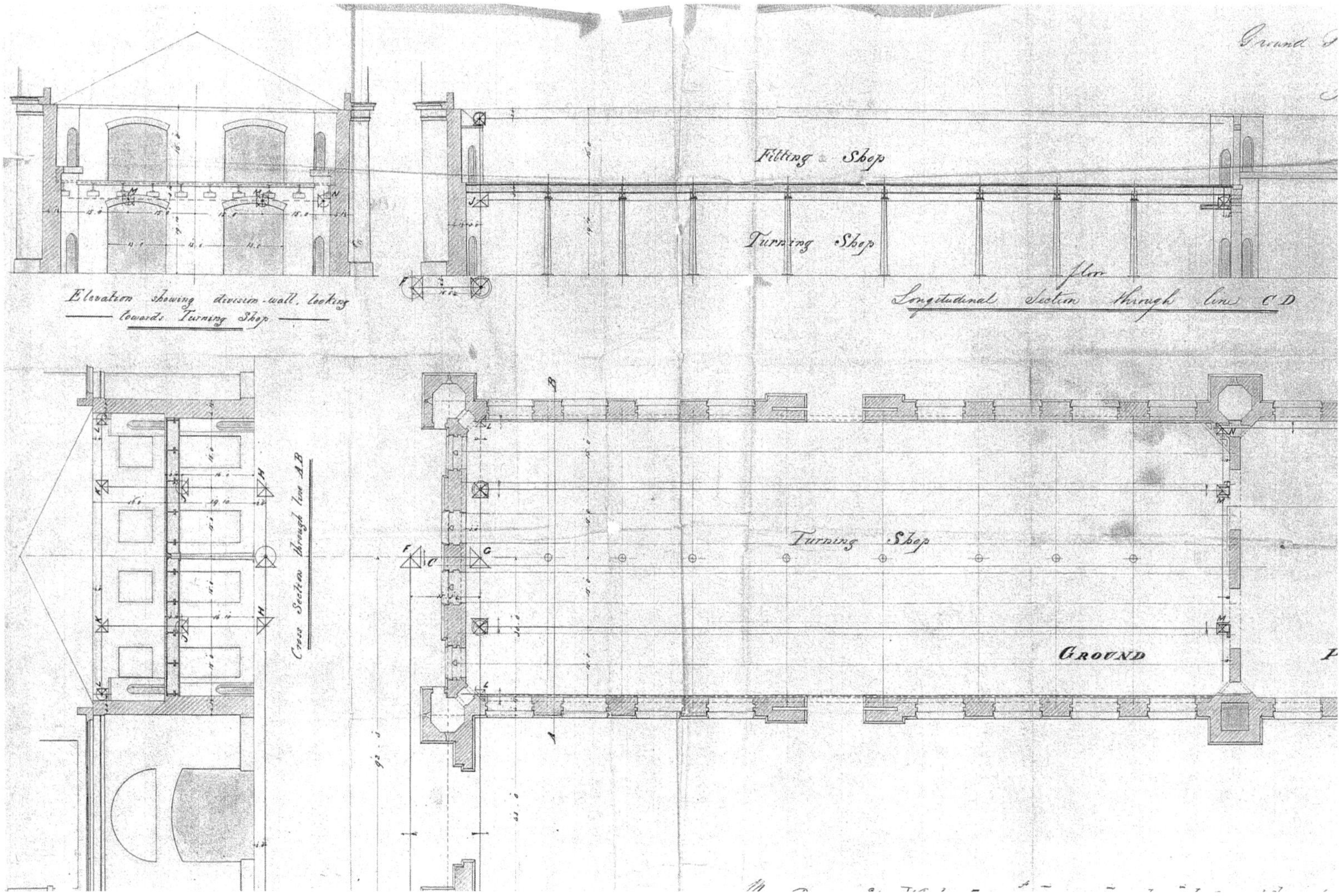
Fitting Shop
Turning Shop
Elevation showing division wall looking towards Turning Shop
Longitudinal Section through line C D
Cross Section through line A B
Turning Shop
GROUND

86 Messrs. Hick & Sons' drawing of the shafting arrangements for the Turning & Fitting Shops as sent to Trickett in 1854. *(TNA ADM 8518)*

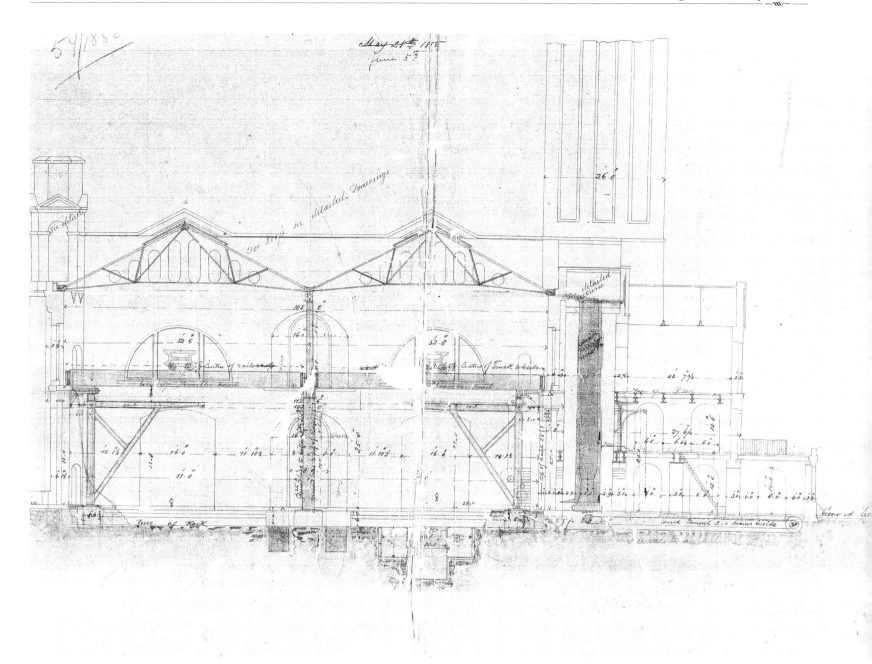

had just been converted to steam. At this time Trickett was writing every few days to Hick & Son, sometimes making last-minute alterations, as in asking whether the shafting round the Fitting Shop could be placed 9 inches higher:

> Be good enough to let me know by return of post as I am waiting for that point to be settled before I take final steps with Whitworth about his Hangers for the Countershafts of Lathes &c...

Sometimes keeping them informed of the progress of the work and their place in it:

> ...the Fitting & Turning Shops are now ready for you to commence fitting the shafting. The Foundations for the Engine & Boilers will be ready for you to commence erecting in about one month from this time, & the Foundations for the first line of underground Shafting form the engine into the Turning Shop will be ready in about two weeks...

Or sometimes engaging in a little mild scheming:

> Private...I shall be glad if you will be good enough to write a letter to the Surveyor of the Navy or to me stating that you are ready to commence erecting your work at Keyham and asking when the Buildings will be sufficiently advanced for you to begin. Your letter if sent to the Surveyor will no doubt be referred to me, or if sent to me by you I will submit it to the Surveyor. This will enable me to put the true state of the case before the Surveyor — I am most anxious that he should know that the delay does not rest with you, & I wish to keep him informed of the real progress without going out of the ordinary routine of duty...

This refers to delays in the progress of the Erecting Shop, again occasioned by the toolmakers' not having sent in drawings. By 18 December Hick & Son were ready to ship 100 tons of equipment; the temporary Boiler Shop, with a travelling crane, was ready; and one of the Whitworth punching and shearing machines ordered was now required.[17]

On 8 January 1855 Keyham was declared to be capable of performing extensive repairs to ships, and of functioning on a daily basis, and Treasury sanction was given for the appointment

87 Longitudinal elevation of the Foundry signed by Greene. Note the installation for travelling cranes and underground smoke tunnels. *(Plymouth Naval Base Museum)*

of Yard officers. The permanent buildings were far from finished and the Magazine of the Ordnance Board still blocked any progress of the Basin and the Factory to the north (though its demolition was imminent.)

An arrangement for the machinery in the Fitting, Turning and Erecting Shops that left space for more to be installed had been devised by Trickett, who together with Greene settled the position, number and description of cranes, position and size of foundry pits, and other matters for the Iron Foundry (Figures 86, 87 and 88). One of Trickett's modifications to Greene's original design was the deletion of the walls surrounding the spaces appropriated for air furnaces and cupolas, leaving them open, and supporting the charging platforms for the cupolas on iron pillars. He recommended that an excavation of not less than 3ft 6in should be made below the ground line for a bed of sand.

Trickett wanted everything connected with boilermaking as closely grouped as possible. The cranes for the Foundry Yards and Brass Foundry were now in course of construction, but that thorny problem, the position of the smoke tunnels, was not yet determined. Work, including cranes, was in hand for the Erecting, Turning and Fitting shops, as well as the Coppersmiths' Shop and the Brass Foundry; the three travellers for the Erecting shop were contracted for by Moore, North Foundry, Clarence Dock, Liverpool. They were to be proved to carry 30 tons, and to carry 20 tons in practice. The Iron

Store was complete and occupied.

While Trickett was orchestrating all this work, Greene was producing detail drawings for the storehouse and office wing and the gateway; this was another fireproof construction.[18] The Iron and Brass Foundries were badly needed, and Greene proposed a temporary foundry as a stopgap, but was overruled by Walker, who thought the facilities offered by such a building would be inferior to those of the local foundries, which for years had been performing contract work for Devonport.

An eight-day factory clock was requested on 13 July, a sure sign that Keyham was getting into its stride, and Trickett asked for the boilermakers' establishment to be increased because of the volume of work.[19]

A question of smoke

The perennial problem of smoke disposal reared its head again. Trickett had pointed out back in August 1853 that the bottom of the proposed officers' houses at Keyham would be about level with the roof of the Factory, and would get the full benefit of the smoke from the various fires and chimneys, the fumes from the Coppersmiths' Shop, the Brass Foundry, and the fire and products from the cupolas. This would make the situation untenable. How was the matter to be handled?

Trickett was not keen on the use of underground smoke

88 This sectional drawing of the Foundry, dated June 1855, shows the position of the traveller and crane. Note the iron-frame construction, the rigid bracing to the connections of the I-section beams being an advanced structural technique that Green developed at his ground-breaking Sheerness Boat Store (see Figures 126, 128). *(Plymouth Naval Base Museum)*

SCAMP'S PLANS QUESTIONED

Trickett gave an authoritative account as to how the Woolwich arrangements had worked out after over 10 years in operation:

> My opinion on this matter is strengthened by what has occurred at Woolwich Factory, where it has been found necessary to build separate chimneys for the Air Furnace in the Iron Foundry, as well as separate chimnies for each of the Air Furnaces, & for each Boiler for the Steam Hammers in the Smiths shop — one for the whole of the Boiler plate furnaces, one for the Pot furnaces in the Brass Foundry & Tin pit in the Coppersmiths shop & one for the boilers of the Factory Engine leaving the engine Smiths fires, 3 coke ovens & a small furnace for heating rivet iron, only, discharging into the tunnel connected with the large chimney, and although this is all the large chimney has now to do, yet a great quantity of smoke from the Smiths' fires does not go into the tunnel at all, but is discharged into the shop…Cupolas for

melting iron never answer better than when they discharge their products of combustion &c into the atmosphere, the top of the cupolas could be covered by a perforated hood as at the Woolwich Factory, which is found to check the issue of sparks without interfering with the perfect operation of the cupolas…

He also called into question the whole project of roofing in the Quadrangle, incidentally showing less foresight than Scamp about the future calls upon the capacity of the Factory:

> …the ventilation of the shops for the Engine & Boiler Smithy, and the shops for the Steam Hammer & for heating & bending boiler plate, is, in this…climate of such great importance, surrounded as they will be by the main Factory Buildings, that I would submit it is worthy of consideration whether it is desirable that the whole of the Quadrangle should be roofed over, as a greater amount of space will

be covered in than will be required for workshops…

Nor did he recognise the revolution in factory design implicit, though yet to be spelled out, in Scamp's design, suggesting that the extension of the turning shop planned by Barry be expedited:

> …as the Turning shop does not admit of a convenient purchase being used, capable of lifting the heaviest weights, that may be required to be placed in the largest lathes, I would submit…whether it would not be better to proceed with the extension of the Turning Shop, & to place the largest lathes (now being made for this Factory) in it. This shop if built without a floor over it, would admit of a Travelling Crane being used, & the large lathes could be placed more conveniently in it, & with less loss of room than if placed in the Turning shop already built…

tunnels in this case. The great length of tunnel required and the number of inlets to it would enfeeble the draught and render it insufficient to counteract the natural tendency of the smoke to ascend, so that a large portion of the smoke would remain and choke the shop. He considered that each of the air furnaces for melting brass, and for heating the iron for heavy forgings, should have its own chimney, so that the draught could be regulated with the greatest degree of control. Fine control was of less consequence for the furnaces used for making blooms and for heating boiler plate, and one chimney would serve for the whole of the furnaces for each of these classes of work. The smoke from the smiths' fires should be collected into a flue above the hearths and conveyed into one or more chimneys, where it could at once ascend (as in the smiths' shop already built by the docks at Keyham and in the Dock Yard Smithery at Woolwich), and no other flues should be in connection with them. The drawback to this system of lower multiple chimneys remained, however: the houses nearby would be uninhabitable.

Trickett clearly expected that the free-standing Smith's Shop and Boiler Shops of Barry's plan were still to be built, as he believed that provision should be made to admit more light into the covered quadrangle, and that a greater amount of ventilation be provided for the shops in the Quadrangle, and in the whole of the roofs over it.

Walker agreed in general with Trickett.[20] However, Greene was convinced his proposed arrangements would do the trick, and Walker did not press the point, though plainly unconvinced. In the event the draught for the air furnaces was so poor that only about half the work intended to be got through was performed.[21]

By July 1854, the matter of the proposed underground flues would have to be decided very soon. Nasmyth had got the contract for the machinery for the Smithery, which was placed in the south end of the Quadrangle, and Hick & Son the contract for the Foundry machinery. On 5 September Trickett

wrote that the underground flues had not worked well at Woolwich and Portsmouth, including reports on the working of the new Smithery at Portsmouth with a drawing of the section of the flue.[22] He had found an ally in Nasmyth, quoting from one of his letters:

> …not only will the adoption of the underground flue system for these eight Forge Furnaces involve vast additional outlay…[and] after all they will not be found in practice to be either so convenient or effective as that of giving to each Forge Furnace its own independent vertical Chimney.

89 One of the units formed within the grid of the Quadrangle was the Engine Smithery. Its layout, and the positions of the overhead flues which carried exhaust fumes into the twin stacks, can be seen in this plan of 1855. (*TNA ADM 140/366*)

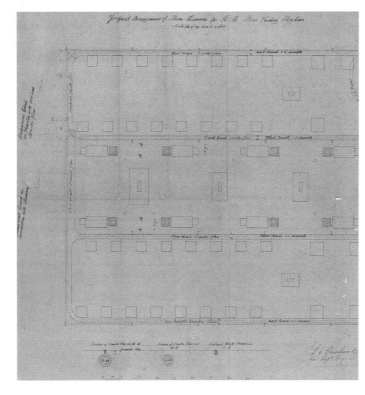

Table 9 Equipment present and wanting at Keyham, March 1857

Whitworth	Four lathes and related machinery
Hick & Son	Cupolas, cranes.
	Cranes for cupolas and furnaces, 20 ton traveller and parts of five 20 ton post cranes not delivered
Nasmyth	Hydraulic crane nearly complete
	Steam hammer nearly complete
	Portable engine not delivered
S. Moore	Travellers, greater part delivered
	Post cranes not delivered
J. Hulse	Drilling machine not delivered
Hick & Son	Engines, boilers, shafting partly erected
	Rails for foundry cranes and yard largely done
	Floor cupolas complete
S. Moore	Cranes for quadrangle mostly complete
	Cranes for foundry not delivered
	Rivet hearths and flues not delivered
Simpson & Barnes	Smiths' hearths partly delivered and erected
Fairbairn	Sea wall crane complete and tested
Glasgow	Machinery and tools mostly delivered
J. Hulse	Machinery and tools delivered

Many minutes went back and forth on this matter, but Lloyd decided that it should go ahead as planned, and that Nasmyth be sent the necessary drawings. A drawing of 28 September signed by Trickett probably shows the final arrangements: the furnace smoke went directly into the tunnels, while that of the forges went into an overhead flue, which was then directed underground (Figure 89). A large-scale drawing of the Portsmouth Smithery flues was sent to Trickett, with the comment that they had been reported to work exceedingly well.[23]

In September 1856 Hick & Son began to fix the moulding pits in the Foundry; 2,500 tons of sand were required. By the following March a lot of equipment had still to come, mostly for the Foundry and the Smithery (as the list of machinery present and wanting in Table 9 shows) and by May some additional equipment was asked for. At the end of November work outstanding at Keyham included items by the following firms:

Nasmyth — metalwork for crane, steam hammers, engine;
Hick & Co. — elevator, rails, etc.;
Easton & Amos — timber frames;
J. Glasgow — lathes;

90A The twin stacks to the Foundry still dominate views of the Quadrangle. The tops of the chimneys were removed c.1975. *(Plymouth Naval Base Museum)*

Simpson & Baines — smoke flue;
J. Hulse — drilling machines;
S. Moore — lathes, travelling cranes, cranes.

The Smithery had water laid on by the end of November and the steam hammers and their boiler could be tried. It was in full working order by 1 April 1858, when the Smithery building at the head of the docks was vacated, to be handed over to the smiths of the Master Shipwright's Department. Teething troubles were experienced, and the furnaces had to be removed and reconstructed on the model of those at Portsmouth. The following year the Committee on Marine Engines condemned the air furnaces at Keyham as inefficient, but Greene stoutly defended them:

> It is true that Mr Nasmyth was shewn at this office the arrangements proposed…for Keyham, and it is most probable he would have preferred each furnace having its own Chimney, but when acquainted with the reasons for adopting the underground Flues and tall Chimneys he certainly expressed his opinion that if ample space were provided in both there was no reason to doubt their success. I do not know what the Committee mean by the Plan adopted…'not being grounded upon ascertained laws'. The principle of construction adopted at Keyham is precisely the same as that most successfully carried out at Portsmouth, and if an equal measure of success has not attended the former it is owing to differences in the details which only

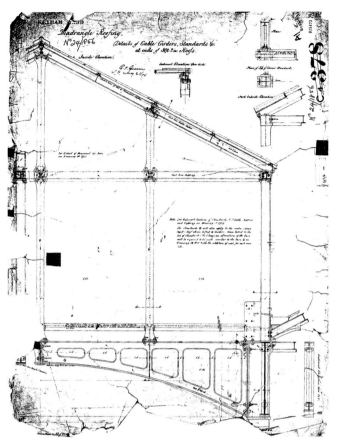

91 A drawing by Greene, dated May 1856, of the Quadrangle roof. *(Devonport Management Ltd, Fiche 15473)*

92 Scamp's plan of December 1857 shows both his projected Factory railways and the grid of standards within the Quadrangle. *(TNA ADM 1/5697)*

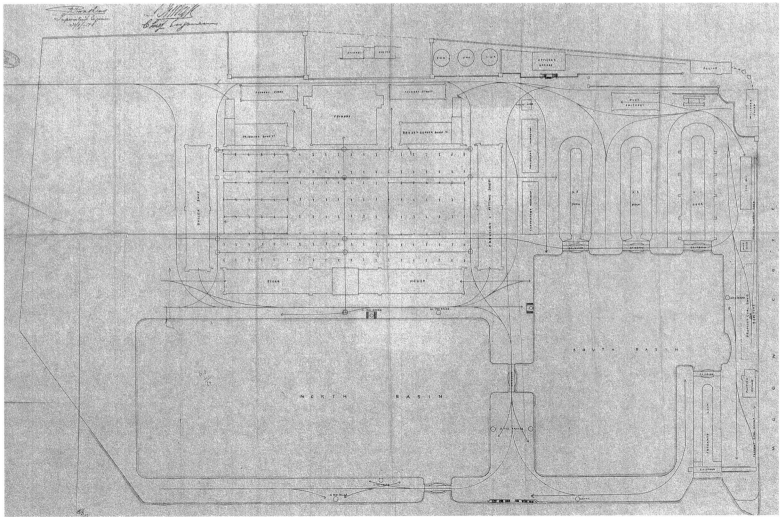

require to be rectified. Indeed had the arrangements been carried out at Keyham as originally intended, it is not probable that the Furnaces would have proved defective. Some of the suggestions for correcting the defects…have already been carried out with manifest advantage, and there is every probability that the Furnaces will ultimately be made wholly effective without resorting to the ordinary, but in this locality objectionable, plan of erecting a separate stack for each Furnace.

The smoke from the Smithery and Foundry was led by the underground flues, which were 5ft 3in in diameter (Figure 88), into two massive smoke towers, which must have been almost completed by the end of 1856, when a tender for their lightning conductors was accepted. Alterations were made to them in 1859, dividing the lower parts by boiler plates, presumably in connection with the furnace problems.[24] These smoke towers, like the central chimney at Greene's Smithery, were carefully designed monumental objects. As the most prominent elements of the Yard to be seen by outsiders they were required to make a public statement about the scale and importance of the operations within the walls, though the exotic appearance of some contemporary stacks, both projected and executed, was not aimed for (Figures 90A, 90B).

The Quadrangle: the integrated factory completed

In July 1855 Baker's had reported on the time taken for constructing the Quadrangle roof and the type of slates required (in the event, probably no slates were ever used). The grid of standards that Scamp had introduced at Sheerness was much more than a quick method of roofing over a large area without having to resort to wide-span roofs; it permitted the easy insertion of travelling cranes, and facilitated the transfer of heavy components from one part of the Factory to the other without hauling them from one building to the other on tramways. In March 1856 Walker approved Greene's and Scamp's plans that the cranes in the Quadrangle should communicate with those in the erecting and other shops. He suggested that as cranes would in all probability be required in the wider compartments of the Quadrangle, the standards should be constructed to allow girders for cranes to be placed there when the circumstances arose. The grid of standards was in place long before the roofing was finished, providing a matrix within which the workshops could be arranged.

Planning continued during the summer, with Trickett devising the best arrangements for erecting the roof while the costings were worked out. The main roof trusses were

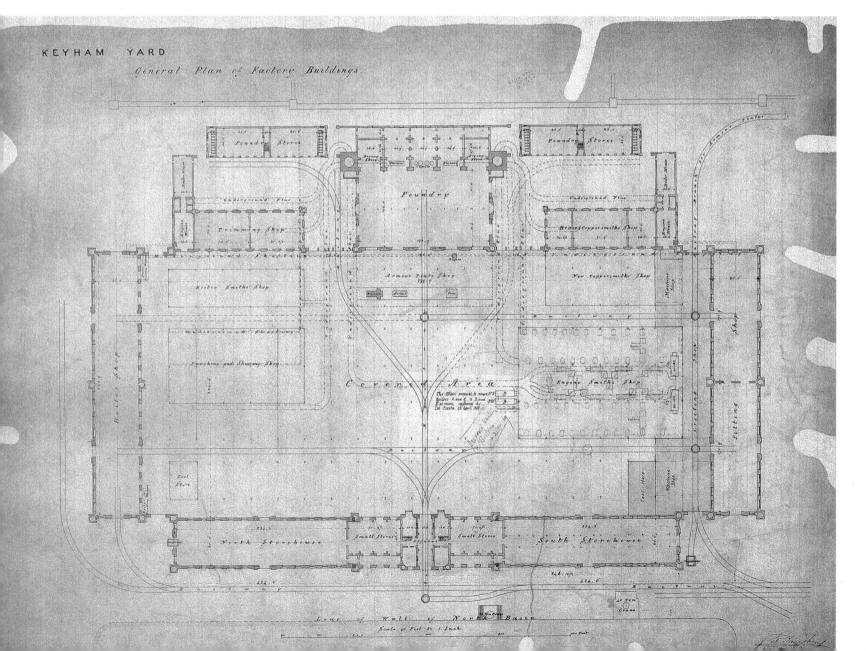

surprisingly complicated, considering the availability of well-tried simpler types, and incorporated compression struts made up of paired flat pieces held apart by short spacers. The lateral ties were in three sections with three compression struts all radiating from the mid-point connections to support the principal. The Quadrangle cranes were mostly completed by March 1857, but were not installed in a rush; it was evident that the hasty construction of the previous Factories had been paid for by inefficient arrangements, and this time Walker and Greene were determined to get it right for posterity. And so they did.

Scamp's design needs to be seen in the context of the increased importance being attached to efficient factory layout. The nature of the processes undertaken in cotton and wool mills had posed no particular problems for designers, who merely had to provide large spaces for storage and rows of duplicate machinery. The evolution of buildings for heavy engineering, where a multiplicity of processes were undertaken, each involving different and sometimes massive pieces of machinery, and with complex sequences of operations involved, was bound to proceed in fits and starts, sometimes taking place in existing buildings quite unsuited for the purpose, and being governed at all times by the continuing invention of new

industrial plant that needed to be fitted into what were often constrained sites. Farmhouse buildings may seem an unlikely model for industrial planning, but farms, like factories, were also places where bulky commodities needed to be transported from one location to another and where a congested layout and confused traffic flows could be very wasteful of time and money. Designers of model farms had, of course, the great advantage, not shared by all their industrial counterparts, of relatively limitless space to work in.

Scamp introduced an extra degree of flexibility by producing a plan for the insertion of railways within the Factory, working in conjunction with the travelling cranes, in a report of December 1857 (Figure 92). The tramroads laid down were composed only of granite chippings, except for a small portion where rails had been temporarily laid for removing machinery and boilers from the Basin cranes, and they were already in a bad state. The Yard was well adapted for a railway system, as it was perfectly level, and the roads could be formed so that the locomotive and trucks had access to the Great Storehouse, the Quadrangle, the Boiler Shop and the Erecting Shop. Great advantages would be gained by the use of railways rather than tramroads. The actual plan that Scamp produced was modified and simplified in practice: it depended on the use of an

93 (Below and opposite) Trickett's plan for the new erecting shop. New work, including the position of the travellers, the inserted roofs and the shafting to take power to the machine tools, is evident. *(TNA ADM 140/366)*

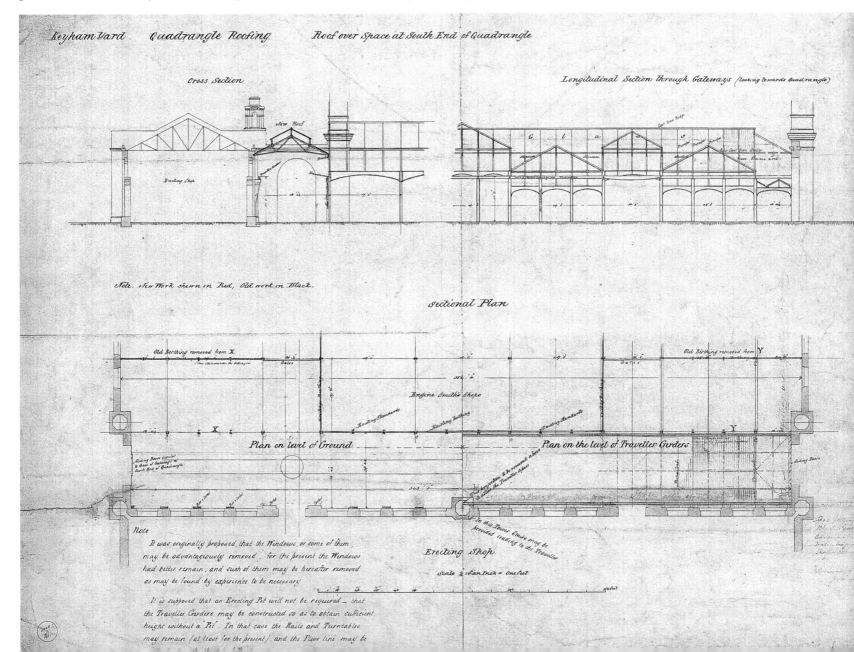

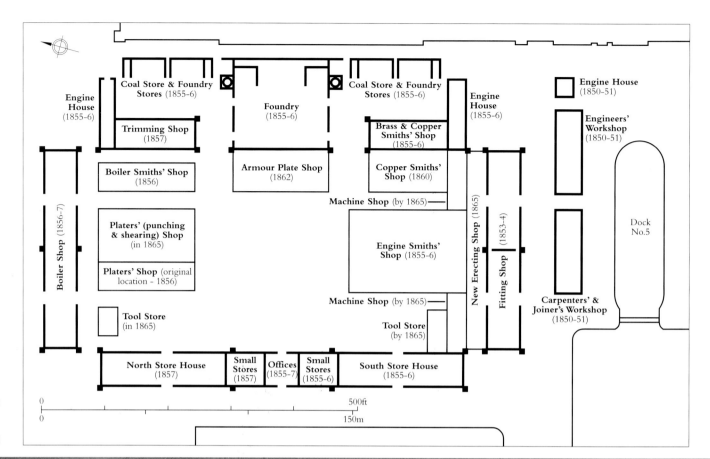

94 The Quadrangle in 1865. *(Stephen Dent, based on sketch by the Author)*

Engine House (1855-6)

Coal Store & Foundry Stores (1855-6)

Foundry (1855-6)

Coal Store & Foundry Stores (1855-6)

Engine House (1855-6)

Engine House (1850-51)

Trimming Shop (1857)

Brass & Copper Smiths' Shop (1855-6)

Engineers' Workshop (1850-51)

Boiler Smiths' Shop (1856)

Armour Plate Shop (1862)

Copper Smiths' Shop (1860)

Machine Shop (by 1865)

Boiler Shop (1856-7)

Platers' (punching & shearing) Shop (in 1865)

Engine Smiths' Shop (1855-6)

New Erecting Shop (1865)

Fitting Shop (1853-4)

Dock No.5

Platers' Shop (original location - 1856)

Machine Shop (by 1865)

Tool Store (in 1865)

Tool Store (by 1865)

Carpenters' & Joiner's Workshop (1850-51)

North Store House (1857)

Small Stores (1857)

Offices (1855-7)

Small Stores (1855-6)

South Store House (1855-6)

0   500ft
0   150m

95 Keyham Steam Factory as completed, the greatest achievement of Colonel Greene and Mr Scamp. *(Ministry of Defence)*

extremely short-wheelbase locomotive to negotiate the extreme curvatures. The locomotive would have its usefulness extended by the provision of lifting gear: this would give it a clear advantage over horses, which were the alternative motive power. The first step was taken in April 1858, when a railway truck was ordered to be made for the Factory for an estimated £30.[25]

A revised arrangement of the travellers must have been devised by May 1858, when Walker wrote: 'It is quite obvious that the importance of commanding by suitable travelling cranes every available space over which heavy weights have to be moved is of the highest importance.' It saved labour and time, and enabled a greater quantity of materials to be stored. He also stated: 'It is universally adopted by private manufacturers.' This was not true, some engineers preferred

swing cranes, particularly for foundry work, but it was a good policy statement.

Greene was to estimate the expense of the new arrangement, which involved the Quadrangle traversers carrying 20 to 25 tons instead of 40 tons. As originally devised the roof seems to have stood free in the Quadrangle, like that of a covered market, and the first suggestion to close up the gaps, that the roof should cover 'the North & South spaces', was made by Greene in January 1859. The 1860/61 Navy Estimates showed that £1,298,661 had been spent so far on Keyham. £2,000 was required for paving roads and tram roads (Scamp was going to get his railways), and £3,000 for standards and traveller ways for cranes in the Quadrangle. Hennet, Spink & Else were the only tenderers for the railways. New works and alterations allowed for in 1861-2 included constructing the railways throughout

95A Interior of the Quadrangle. (*English Heritage*)

96 The enormous scale of Keyham Factory can be seen by comparing it to a photograph of the 1860s showing the Maudslay factory at Lambeth and the Penn engine works at Greenwich. Note the timber travellers for the overhead cranes, a characteristic feature of civil yards well after they had been superseded in the Royal Yards. (*NMM, neg. no. 5275*)

the Quadrangle Factory and running to the cranes on the quays, completing the traveller ways in the Quadrangle, and making provision in its centre bay for a traveller way and travelling crane. The traveller arrangements, with hydraulic machinery for the storehouse cranes, came to £4,500.[26]

Scamp's grid was of 160 standards, disposed 20 by 8. The nine lengthways divisions were divided into five cells 50ft wide and traveller and circulation cells 35ft wide, with the travellers flanking three wide units in the centre. Another feature was the facility with which blocks within the whole could be set aside for different purposes. Should there be any need for a physical separation between areas so appropriated, corrugated iron or old boiler plates could be used for partitions, easily removable or alterable, at little cost. Some corrugated iron partitions of unknown date are present to this day.

The first shop to be so inserted was, as has been seen, the Engine Smithery, which occupied 24 rectangles of the grid (Figure 93). Drawings for this had been prepared by September 1855. £7,500 worth of steam hammers (five in all) and forge apparatus, including eight forge furnaces adapted for underground smoke flues, were delivered by Nasmyth by next March. Arrangements for the tools in the Punching and Shearing and Boilersmiths' shops, which occupied rectangles five standards long by one wide, were approved by June 1856.

The flexibility of the structure to accommodate new arrangements was soon demonstrated. By 1863 the Punching and Shearing shop had moved across a cell and doubled in size, losing its connection with a smoke tunnel in so doing, which is perhaps a comment on the use made of the tunnels by this date. A new Coppersmiths' shop was formed late in 1860, and on its completion the Brass Foundry took over the old Coppersmiths' shop in the Foundry wing.

The most significant insertion in the Quadrangle took place in 1863. The original Turning, Fitting and Erecting shop block, like every other design based on the Woolwich pattern, had rapidly proved to be too small, and the most pressing needs had

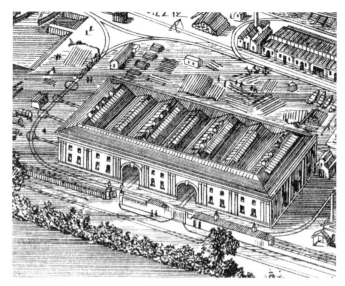

98 John Elder's works at Fairfield on the Clyde appears as a smaller echo of Keyham Factory. *(From Philip Hichborn,* Report on European Dockyards, Washington D.C. 1886)

resulted in its being used wholly as Turning and Machine shops. There were two alternative locations for a new Erecting shop: that originally planned by Barry, extending the existing block eastwards, and the Quadrangle. The first alternative was ruled out on the grounds of cost: the Admiralty was no longer prepared to pay for expensive masonry when a cheaper alternative existed.

Trickett produced a plan for the other solution, approved by Greene, fitting the Quadrangle bay between the Turning and Machine shops with a traveller, which necessitated corbelling out the inner walls of the shops and providing new standards on the other side of the bay to carry the rails, and inserting a new metal roof (Figure 93). Slightly later the portions of the next bay on either side of the Engine Smithery were taken in as Machine shops, enclosed by the corrugated iron berthing that had originally separated the new Erecting shop from the rest of the Quadrangle. £6,000 was made available for this work in October 1864; Scamp observed that bringing the Fitting and Erecting shops in parallel was an arrangement he had long favoured. The width of the Erecting shop formed in this way was perhaps insufficient, but it was the same as that of the Portsmouth Erecting shop, which had the disadvantage of being placed in series with the Fitting shop, not in parallel with it. Final drawings were produced in November, and at the end of the year a tender for the work was accepted, the Plymouth Iron Company supplying the cast iron girders.[27]

No significant additions were ever to be made to Keyham Factory, which stands today as the greatest single monument of the Steam Navy (Figure 94). Built on a scale beyond the reach of private manufacturers (Figure 95), it was never repeated by the Admiralty, though, had Scamp's designs for the Chatham Extension Works been fully realised, a variant would have been built there. The significance of the design did not go unnoticed by the private trade. John Elder & Co. acquired a greenfield site at Fairfield on the Clyde in 1860, and in 1868 began to construct an engine and boiler shop building there which bore more than a passing resemblance to Keyham, though of less than half the dimensions (Figure 98). But shipyards were far from being the chief users of the new factory layout; the real

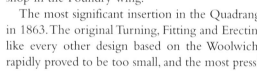

97 An aerial view of the Quadrangle, before the chimney tops were removed. *(Plymouth Naval Base Museum)*

beneficiaries of the innovations at Keyham were the tens of thousands of open-plan factories built, and still building, around the world. Scamp's Factory at Sheerness may have been an *ad hoc* solution to an urgent necessity, using constructional techniques which were to hand, but he saw that it contained the germ of a new concept of factory planning, and Keyham gave him the opportunity to realise this on a grand scale.[30]

—᠉᠉—

Notes:

[1]

From	£	to	£
Sir Edward Parry	700	Comptroller (Ellice)	700
House allowance	250	House allowance	250
Second-class clerk	350	Chief Engineer	700
Third-class clerk	130	House Allowance	200
Total	1,430	Assistant Engineer	500
		First draughtsman	250
		Second draughtsman	150
		First writer and calculator	150
		Second writer and calculator	80
		Writer	150
		Chief Clerk	600
		Third-class clerk	100
		One extra	100
		Total	3,930

[2] ADM 222/4, ADM 1/3408, ADM 1/3409, ADM 1/3437, ADM 1/3492, ADM 2/1695, ADM 1/5565, ADM 2/1387, ADM 93/6, ADM 89/4, 93/7.

[3] *Memoir* of Brandreth in *Proceedings of the Institution of Civil Engineers*, 1849, pp.42-43, ADM 1/5564.

[4] ADM 87/37, CHA/R/6, CHA/H/83.

[5] ADM 87/37.

[6] *Memoir* of Irvine in *Proceedings of the Institution of Civil Engineers*, 1851, pp.89-90, *Memoir* of Scamp in *Proceedings of the Institution of Civil Engineers*, 1873, pp.273-278, MLN/165/10.

[7] ADM 93/3, ADM 85/6, ADM 85/7, ADM 1/5888, ADM 93/11, ADM 12/588, ADM 85/21, ADM 85/22. Grissell's got the contract for cast and wrought ironwork, Rigby's for the boiler shop. Hick & Son were asked to tender for the shafting, and Fox, Henderson for travelling cranes. Whitworth got an order for a punching and shearing machine, two self-acting lathes 20ft long, one self-acting lathe 12ft long, two patent universal shaping machines, one patent setting and shaping machine, two self-acting overhead drilling machines, and a plate-bending machine to take up to 9ft width. Collier's of Salford supplied planing machines and bolt-screwing machines, a centring apparatus, and a cutter-making machine.

[8] By the beginning of 1856 the following machinery was either not yet delivered or in store waiting to be fixed:
one moulding machine,
one lathe for the boiler shop,
two punching and shearing machines,
one Nasmyth Hammer,
one radial drilling machine,
four self-acting double vertical drilling machines,
two self-acting single vertical drilling machines,
a self-acting slide lathe,
a screw-cutting lathe,
a surface lathe,
a planing machine,
a cutting machine.
One well-known firm did not come out of the Sheerness scheme at all well: by March 1855 Fox, Henderson could not produce a satisfactory explanation of their non-completion of the roofing over the Storehouse Yard, and in May the roof fell in.
ADM 140/1051-2; J Nasmyth, (ed.) Smiles, *Autobiography*, (London, 1883), pp.317-8; B Reed, *Crewe Locomotive Works and its Men*, (Newton Abbot, 1982), pp.66-67, 99; J Cattell and K Falconer, *Swindon, the Legacy of a Railway Town*, (London, 1995), pp.85-87, 92. ADM 93/11, ADM 93/13, ADM 93/14, ADM 85/29, ADM 85/30, ADM 85/33, ADM 12/604.

[9] ADM 12/556, ADM 1/5614, ADM 93/4, ADM 93/9.

[10] The caissons, which were being made by Grissell's, were expected to be ready by the middle of April 1853, but the machinery for the sliding caisson

(designed by Scamp and constructed by Fairbairn's) and the foundation for the 40 ton crane were not complete. The crane was to be made on the spot, and Fairbairn's engineer reckoned on finishing it by the end of May, though Colonel Williams, Burgmann's replacement, thought the end of June to be more probable. ADM 93/9, NMR PLM/24, ADM 12/572, ADM 85/13.

[11] ADM 93/9, ADM 12/572.

[12] ADM 85/12, ADM 89/1, ADM 85/14, ADM 87/46.

[13] Fairbairn, Watt, & Hick & Son were to be asked:
'It is intended at present to erect one Engine only, & the shafting is to be carried only to the extent shewn on the tracing with the exception of a short line from the main underground line of shafting to drive temporarily the punching & shearing machinery. The main underground line of shafting must be capable of transmitting the full power of the Engine so that either Engine may be used when the whole of the works are completed.'

[14] ADM 85/13, ADM 93/10, Bolton Archives ZHH/4/2, ADM 93/11, ADM 85/17.

[15] ADM 85/15, ADM 87/47, NMM/4221-2.

[16] Bolton Archives ZHH/4/2, ADM 93/11, ADM 85/18, ADM 85/19, ADM 140/365.

[17] ADM 85/18, ADM 85/19, ADM 12/588, Bolton Archives ZHH/4/2, ADM 85/20, ADM 84/13.

[18] ADM 1/5686, ADM 85/22, ADM 85/19, ADM 93/11, ADM 93/12, ADM 93/13, DDM, ADM 95/97, ADM 84/15, NMR PLM/10-11.

[19] Their temporary workshop was equipped with a Garforth's patent riveting machine worked from a portable high-pressure boiler designed by Trickett and built at the Factory. Hick's 50hp factory engine, together with all the shafting and gearing, was tried on 8 August and ran satisfactorily. However, it would be unsafe to work the machinery continuously until the trenches of the underground shaft (which ran at 90rpm) were covered over. The York paving for this was expected daily.

[20] In his view a tall chimney in a more central position, with the smoke from the smiths' fires carried into it by an overhead flue, would undoubtedly be successful. A separate part of this might be appropriated to the furnace and boilers in the smithery, and if it should be desirable to have separate chimneys for the air furnaces in the Foundry as suggested by Trickett, they might be easily led into another tall stack, the cost of which would be met by the great saving in the length of the underground flue.

[21] Nobody foresaw one drawback of the underground flues: in February 1868 they got so hot that they ignited the wooden sleepers of the internal railway system, and brick foundations for the track had to be provided. ADM 93/11, ADM 85/20, *Minutes of Evidence before the Committee of Inquiry on the Economy of Her Majesty's Dockyards*, 1859, p.128; ADM 12/812.

[22] He also stated that:
'Local circumstance of a peculiar kind appeared to demand that all the Smoke…should be taken away from the Factory Buildings at Keyham by lofty Smoke Towers, involving the necessity of taking the smoke from the Furnaces to the Smoke Towers by underground flues. The arrangement having received the concurrence of the Surveyor of the Navy…the details have been carried, or are being carried, into effect with more than usual care and at a considerable expense. With the proposed arrangements Mr Nasmyth was made acquainted…some months ago and with which he was understood to express satisfaction. To make any alteration in the arrangements for Keyham…I would submit that a plan of the Flues should be furnished to Mr Nasmyth and that he be directed to make his arrangements for his furnaces accordingly.

[23] ADM 12/604, ADM 85/27, ADM 84/12, ADM 85/25, ADM 85/27, ADM 85/28, ADM 93/14, ADM 95/97.

[24] ADM 12/624, ADM 93/16, ADM 85/41, ADM 85/43, ADM 85/45, ADM 1/5697, ADM 84/19, ADM 85/55, ADM 12/619, UD 002772/X, ADM 12/668; for some remarkable chimney designs see R Rawlinson, *Factory Furnace and other Tall Chimney Shafts*, (London, 1858).

[25] ADM 12/604, ADM 93/15, ADM 12/619, ADM 85/41; for model farms of the period, see Susanna Wade Martins, *The English Model Farm*, (Oxford, 2002), pp.112-169; ADM 1/5697, ADM 84/19.

[26] ADM 93/17, ADM 12/668, ADM 1/5752, ADM 87/76.

[27] ADM 1/5803, ADM 95/97, ADM 85/33, Nasmyth Order Book no. 1, ADM 93/15, ADM 1/5752, ADM 87/76, ADM 1/5830, ADM 140/367, ADM 1/5888, ADM 12/748, ADM 1/5929.

[30] H S Peebles, *Warshipbuilding on the Clyde*, (Edinburgh, 1987), pp.19, 27; the Elder factory is illustrated in P Hichborn, *Report on European Dockyards*, (Washington, D.C., 1886).

CHAPTER 9

HMS *Volcano* and the Development of Mobile Logistics

THE CRIMEAN WAR formed the background to another critical development in the servicing of the steam navy. In November 1894 an old paddle warship was finally towed away from Portsmouth to be broken up. Probably nobody remembered the small yet significant part she had played in the scheme of things some 40 years before, when HMS *Volcano* had provided the first example of mobile engineering back-up to an operational fleet. With hindsight, her importance is clear, as the forerunner of the repair and depot ships of the end of the nineteenth century and the great US Navy Fleet Train of the Second World War.

Possibly the first attempt at providing such a facility had been made in June 1837, when the Master of *Ariadne*, the coal depot ship at Alexandria, was informed that he would be supplied with a forge, engineers' stores and tools for making temporary repairs to steam machinery. In 1851 the schooner HMS *Spider* was equipped with basic tools for making and repairing articles for the Devonport Steam Reserve. A forge was ordered to be fitted in it the following March, and in October 1852 it was proposed to install a punching machine. The Master Shipwright, William Edye, opposed this, stating that the work could easily be done in the Yard; he clearly had no conception of such a ship being used for a strategic purpose, and was perhaps protecting his own turf as well. However, the Admiralty ordered the puncher to be supplied.

The experiences with *Spider* must have been encouraging, for in March 1854, with the imminent outbreak of hostilities with Russia likely, Sir Baldwin Walker directed the Portsmouth Yard officers to fit out another sailing ship, the training brig *Rolla*, in a similar fashion 'for making good any defects in machinery of Steam Ships...composing the Baltic Fleet'. Murray replied that two forges, a lathe, vice bench and tools could be fitted in eight days, and suggested that the paddler HMS *Harpy* was an alternative possibility. The advantages of a steam repair ship accompanying a steam fleet were obvious, and Walker acted on this suggestion, fixing on the third-class paddle steamer HMS *Volcano*, designed by Symonds in 1836, 733 tons Builder's Measure, and lying in Woolwich Basin (Figure 99).[1]

On 30 March Walker sent a drawing to that Yard showing the proposed internal arrangements and asking for a report on the feasibility of the scheme, which would involve extra accommodation for some 40 men, about 100 tons of machinery and tools, 15 tons for the foundations of the machinery, and 70 tons of pig iron and other materials. The hull was surveyed and declared to be sound, and it was possible to provide extra accommodation with a poop and forecastle. Nasmyth's was

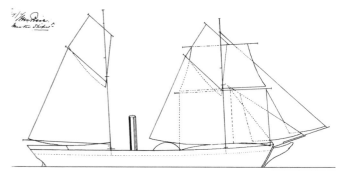

99 A sail plan of *Volcano* prepared while she was fitting out. *(TNA ADM 87/48)*

selected to be the principal supplier and installer of the machinery, and they returned a drawing and estimates within three days of being notified.[2]

The machinery to be fitted comprised one 8hp steam engine, a cupola of 30cwt capacity and ladles, four portable smithy hearths, various hammers, tongs and other tools, bellows and blast distribution pipes, grindstones, a 7cwt steam hammer, two portable punching and shearing machines, a self-acting planing machine, a machine for screwing bolts and tapping nuts, a drilling machine to bore holes up to 8in diameter, four independent drilling machines, a 15ft bed lathe, a slotting and paring machine, and the requisite shafting (Figure 100). Woolwich Yard would supply coppersmith's tools and vices. All of the machinery was to be manufactured by Nasmyth except the screw-cutting lathe, which was supplied by Whitworth.[3]

Volcano in the Baltic

On 29 April (the day before war was declared) the armament of one 32-pounder 56cwt pivot gun and two 32-pounder carronades was ordered, and a fortnight later Walker urged that only absolutely necessary work be carried out, to hasten completion. By 2 June the shipwrights had completed the structural alterations and the ship was ready for the machinery to be fixed (Nasmyth's sent down a supervisor for this purpose), and in a month the machinery was ready for testing. Drawings were prepared at Woolwich showing the internal arrangements. The storage was found to be inadequate, and it was suggested that she should be supplied with a tender to carry foundry sand, coal, coke, pig and wrought iron. In the event the ship was loaded with approximately 88cwt of iron, 10cwt of iron plates including 19 coal box plates, and 20cwt of steel of various types, and an enormous list of tools was suggested to be forwarded, with 350cwt of various grades of iron, and about 50cwt of steel.[4]

On 19 July *Volcano* was ready for trial down the river. The staffing of the workshop was to be done by volunteers from the Steam Factories, who would get an extra allowance of 2s per day and rations, be paid seven days a week to work as required, and get their positions back at the Factories on return. The establishment was decided as

		per day
1	Smith	6s 4d
1	Smith	6s
2	Hammermen	4s
2	Turners	6s and 5s 8d
1	Coppersmith	6s
2	Boilermakers	5s and 4s 4d
1	Cupola trimmer	4s
1	Leading man	9s 1d
1	Moulder	7s 7d

These rates do not include the 2s bonus. The men were to be supplied with a hammock, bed and two blankets each, and were to be on the same footing as the ships' company as regards advance of pay, monthly allowance, clothing and so on. Just before departure it was decided that some of the men could be used in the engine room when necessary, so that extra engineers need not be carried. Engineers from the Fleet were to be made available to assist in the Factory when executing repairs, so the complement could be kept low.[5]

She left Woolwich on 28 July 1854, commanded by Second Master James Ryan, sailed through the Sound on 7 August, and anchored in Led Sund, Åland Islands, on 14 August. She had displayed heavy rolling characteristics caused by the weight of the additional machinery: the mess-traps had been smashed as there were no fittings and locks to retain them. Because of the weight she was also a much more sluggish performer under both sail and steam than before. The next month her engineers made good the defects of *Zephyr*. She towed the hospital ship *Belleisle* off and on during the rest of the campaign of that year, and arrived back at Woolwich on 12 October, carrying the driving shaft of *Ajax*.

Not surprisingly for a first attempt, some of the arrangements could have been improved upon. The zinc roofing fitted between the paddleboxes had been found to be useless, and the Inspector of Machinery Afloat with the Baltic Fleet, John Ward, recommended leading the flues from the forges and the auxiliary boiler into the funnel. Atherton thought this unnecessary, but suggested that portable lengths of funnel tube might be provided. The mechanics were returned to the Woolwich and Portsmouth Factories, and the ship was checked over; 40 to 50 additional stays were required in the boilers, and many rivets needed renewing.

100 *Volcano* being equipped with workshop machinery, as interpreted by an *Illustrated London News* artist *(From* Illustrated London News, *5 August, 1854)*

The machinery had done more than degrade the performance of the ship; the quality of life in the gun room had been adversely affected by the irruption of the men from the Steam Factories. Ryan wrote in complaint:

Great inconvenience had been experienced from Engineer & leading Factory man sleeping in Gun room, their habits & manners, being totally different, from what we have been accustomed to in the Service, and the Engineer being only an Assistant & not entitled to the Gun Room Mess.

He accompanied this letter with a sketch (which, incredibly, was acted upon) showing suggested alterations to the partitions that would segregate the uncouth mechanics and their displeasing table manners (Figure 101).

The Factory men were not only socially undesirable but expensive as well. New manning arrangements were adopted for the Baltic campaign of 1855, Walker writing:

With a view of obviating the necessity of hiring at considerable expense Mechanics for the purpose of effecting any repairs which may be required to the machinery of the Ships of the Fleet I submit the following directions be sent to the C in C. All supernumary Engineers to be borne on the Flag Ship's books and Victualled on board *Volcano* for service in the Fleet. 20 men to be selected by the Inspector of Machinery Afloat from Leading Stokers and Stokers in the Fleet, and entered on the books of the *Volcano* as Stokers to be employed in effecting the repairs of that Ship, and to receive the allowance of ⅓d per diem when so employed, and that whenever the machinery of any Ship may require repair, the Chief Engineer of that Ship is to superintend the work in conjunction with the Inspector of Machinery Afloat.[6]

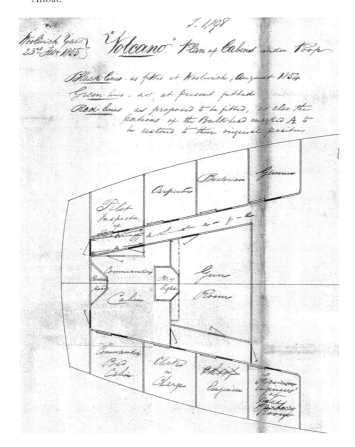

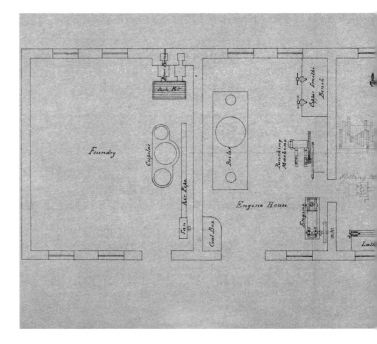

Volcano's performance was clearly seen as successful, as more ships dedicated to logistic purposes were procured. Two iron screw steamers, *Robert Stephenson* and *Alfred*, were purchased, renamed *Bruiser* and *Abundance*, and fitted out by William Fairbairn & Sons as a floating mill and bakery respectively (Figure 88). The installations were completed in three months, and proved very satisfactory. The mill, powered by a drive taken off the ship's 80hp engine, was able to grind 1120lb of flour per hour while the ship was steaming at 7½ knots. The vessels were stationed in the Black Sea to supply the troops around Sebastopol, and produced 1,284,747lb of bread during the first three months of 1856. Temporary land-based workshops, under the Inspector of Machinery of the Black Sea Fleet, were established at Kazatch Creek, which were capable of performing heavy repairs.

Chasseur in the Black Sea

On 28 May 1855 Walker ordered the purchase of the iron screw ship *Chasseur*, 543 tons and 70hp, to be fitted out as a second floating factory for the Black Sea. She cost £12,500. Unlike *Volcano*, she was not used for the repair of marine engines, as the Inspector of Machinery had hoped, but rather to attend to the *matériel* of the Army in the Crimea. The Ordnance Department were therefore responsible for specifying the machinery and installation, a committee from Woolwich Arsenal drew up the details, and the War Department bore the cost of purchase and equipping the vessel.

The Woolwich officers reported to the Treasury on the multiplicity of functions that the ship could perform. For general Army purposes, it could cut up timber and supply planed wood and iron components for huts, hospitals, stables, ovens, pumps, and other equipment. For the Artillery, it would repair gun carriages and guns, while for the Engineers it would prepare timbers for mining, gun platforms, magazines, wharves, tram roads, and repair pontoons and boats. Some of the machinery would be driven from the ship's engine, but some would be portable to take into the field. The builders, Messrs

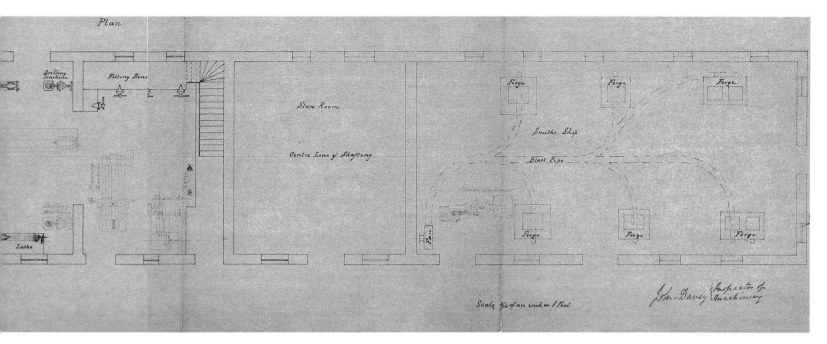

102 This plan of part of the Hong Kong Steam Factory shows the machinery taken out of *Volcano*. (TNA ADM 87/69)

Smith of Newcastle on Tyne, were responsible for the fitting out, which was under way by the end of June.

The manning was arranged quite differently from that of *Volcano*: the foremen and the 32 men were selected from Tyneside firms, with Woolwich supplying four gun fitters and armourers. A factory manager was appointed at £20 per month, the same as the Captain, and ten sailors were hired to work the ship itself. After the war the local industrialist who had picked the staff stated that 'no portion of the army had served more efficiently than that factory and the men belonging to it', admittedly not a hard task.[7]

Volcano left Sheerness for the Baltic again on 15 May 1855, towing a pair of gunboats, but got into difficulties and had to return. However, by 21 May she was off Norway, towing HMS *Badger*, and on 1 June anchored off Nargen Island. Under the new manning arrangements the factory work was done by engineers and stokers of the Fleet; John Ward considered the men were more manageable than those drawn from the Factories, who were also liable to sea-sickness. He wrote from *Volcano* on 8 July that he had examined the machinery of the blockships *Hastings*, *Hawke*, *Russell* and *Cornwallis*, and that the thrust bearings of *Hawke* and *Russell* were so worn that they had been replaced by spares and new sets cast on *Volcano*. Later she attended to *Cossack's* screw and *Amphion's* screw shaft, other heavy repairs involving broken pistons and slides. She sailed for home on 1 November.

Walker assigned her to Portsmouth, as most of her crew had been drawn from ships allotted to that Yard, so that she could attend to their mechanical defects on their return. The War Department were most unlikely to wish to retain the services of *Chasseur*, and the Commodore Superintendent at Woolwich was asked to report whether she could be fitted up 'as an efficient Floating Workshop like the *Volcano*, to be stationed at one of the Dockyards to assist in keeping in repair the machinery of Vessels in the Steam Reserve, or to attend a Fleet'. Following this report Walker submitted that she might be transferred to the Admiralty, to be employed at Sheerness or elsewhere, and it was at Sheerness that *Chasseur* was to see her time out as a floating factory.[8]

Supporting the Steam Navy at Hong Kong

HMS *Volcano's* campaigning was far from done, however: she was selected in March 1857, in preference to *Chasseur*, to support the steamers during the Second China War. Some measure of land-based logistical back-up had preceded her, to which she may in fact have contributed, for John Davey, who was to be Inspector of Machinery Afloat for the China Squadron, had been ordered in that month to select, either from *Volcano* or from Portsmouth Factory, the materials for two large forges, anvils and forge tools, a portable drilling machine and a portable punching machine for dispatch to China, almost certainly for the new factory at Hong Kong. The Naval Yard there was originally planned by Major Aldrich RE in 1845; as designed, it consisted mostly of storehouses, but a small smithery was provided.

Prior to sailing for the East *Volcano* was docked and bilge pieces were fitted in an attempt to mitigate her rolling propensities. Her 21-year-old copper boilers were condemned, and leaks in the workshop caused by deficient caulking were attended to. It had apparently been originally intended to employ Engineer Officers from the Yards in key positions, for Walker wrote that they were demanding unreasonable pay and allowances:

> …and there being no absolute necessity for the services of these men, as mechanics can doubtless be found in the Fleet who though not so well skilled as Smiths &c are sufficiently so, to do all the work that will be required from them, I submit that the Superintendents of Portsmouth and Woolwich be informed that the terms named by the Engineer Officers are considered unreasonable and will not be allowed.

Volcano anchored at Hong Kong on 10 November, and her engineers fixed the factory gear in working positions. The following month she steamed up the Canton River, condensing water to supply the other ships in the expedition, and played a part in the capture of Canton by sending three officers and 16 men ashore to take charge of Macao Fort. The crew were not included in the subsequent share-out of prize money, but the ship's Master protested, and they got their cut.[9]

In February 1858 the factory machinery was struck down and *Volcano* sailed for Whampoa, where major repairs were made to the screw shaft of *Assistance*, and by April a demand was sent home for a fresh supply of engineer stores. The summer had made working conditions in the factory below deck intolerable, and in August the ship returned to Hong Kong, where John Davey proposed abandoning its use as a floating factory. He sent home a plan of the Hong Kong Steam Factory, showing how he would propose to place machinery removed from *Volcano*. The Factory was already equipped with three cupolas, forges, and a boiler and engine which drove four lathes and a punching and drilling machine. *Volcano* was to give up its steam hammer, planing, slotting, and drilling machines, and two pieces of kit not part of its Baltic equipment, a large boring lathe and a Steam Arm, the pet name of a small shaping machine originally devised by Nasmyth in 1836 (Figure 102).

The Factory [would be established] with a staff of 1 Blacksmith 1 Boilermaker 1 Moulder and such mechanics as are generally found in a Squadron with a few supernumary Engineers from the Fleet. The whole under the Superintendence of a resident Engineer would then be able to make good the repairs of a larger

Fleet than has been on this Station — any number of Chinese as Blacksmiths and Coppersmiths being always available at from 3 to 4/- per day…Should this meet with their Lordships approbation, there would be no necessity for the *Volcano* remaining. Though available during the Winter months, yet from the extreme heat of the Summer the Workmen are laid prostrate especially in the After Factory, which would have been rendered useless had I not removed the Factory Engine and Boiler with the Stoke Hole, even this has not been sufficient as the summer heat increased, the effect of the high temperature has been, that out of twenty-two Mechanics there have frequently been only four fit for duty. Indeed during the part of July and August the after Factory was obliged to be discontinued working. The men I would propose to retain for service in the Factory on shore are John Boggust, Blacksmith and James Rumble, moulder, most excellent workmen in the *Volcano*. These men are willing to remain for a Year or two and to instruct Chinese if required, provided they are allowed about £6-12 per month, with accommodation and rations — their time also to count as if serving afloat. The Boilermaker, Wm Smith is at present under a 3 year agreement at £16 per month with accommodation & rations, only a few months of which has as yet expired.

The Commander in Chief there was at once convinced of the practicality of this plan, and ordered *Volcano* home once the machinery and necessary stores had been landed, which was completed by the end of the year. The ship finally anchored at Spithead on 13 May 1859.[10]

Despite the limited value of the ship during the summer months, the concept of a mobile facility for heavy repairs afloat was plainly vindicated, and as *Volcano* was approaching Portsmouth the Second Secretary at the Admiralty, W. G. Romaine, wrote to Walker to ask him to report on what three or four ships he would propose to be adapted as floating factories to accompany squadrons in the event of war. The Admiralty wanted plans for an ideal internal layout submitted as soon as possible, and Walker requested designs to be submitted from the Yards. Sheerness sent two drawings, showing *Chasseur* as fitted and a proposed layout for a ship of similar size, while Miller supplied from Portsmouth a drawing of machinery arranged for an *Odin* class paddler (Figure 103).

Miller proposed a formidable array of machinery: two screw-cutting lathes, two bolt- and nut-screwing machines, two shaping machines, a planing machine, a slotting machine, a circular saw, three lathes (one for wood turning), two drilling machines, a pipe-bending machine, a coppersmith's forge and two smiths' forges, a 7½cwt steam hammer, two punching and shearing machines for plates, a plate roller, a levelling block, a plate furnace, pot furnaces for brass, a large cupola to cast one ton and a small one to cast 5cwt.

The Sheerness drawings show that a screw ship like *Chasseur* had the advantage of an uninterrupted workshop space along the hull, and the power from the machinery, as in the floating mill, was derived from the ship's own engine. The principal differences of equipment, in her Black Sea configuration, from that of *Volcano* lay in the absence of cupolas and the steam hammer, as the Army did not require the fabrication of heavy components. The drawings produced for a revised *Chasseur* are little different: the principal alterations were a different arrangement of forges and boiler, and the addition of a cupola

103 Proposed plans for ideal Floating Factories, as prepared by the Engineering staff at Sheerness. *(TNA ADM 87/72)*

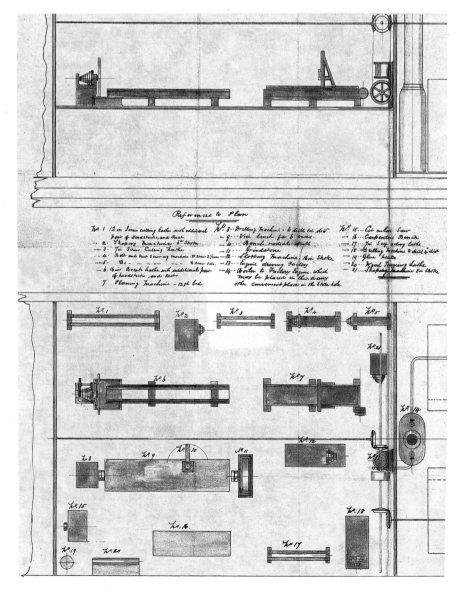

104 Engineering
afloat on HMS
Vulcan in the 1890s.
(From The Navy and
Army Illustrated,
5 August 1896)

of 1 ton capacity and a portable brass furnace. No steam hammer was proposed; presumably experience had shown that its presence was not justified.[11]

In the event the paddler *Rosamond* was altered, at Portsmouth, along the lines of *Volcano*; tenders for the machinery were accepted in September 1861. Metallurgical equipment was also required on ships to cater for a new weapon, Martin's shells, which were filled with molten iron. In order to test the practicality of this unpleasant-sounding device the steam liner *Colossus*, the Portland Coastguard ship, was equipped in April 1860 with a cupola and its necessary fittings, at a cost of £768. An assistant moulder from Portsmouth Dockyard was sent to assist in determining the potentiality and requirements of the cupola, and Admiral Sir Spencer Robinson (now the Controller) considered, reasonably enough, that instructions should be supplied to the officers who might have charge of them. They were to be informed about the practices adopted in the Foundry of the Factory in working small cupolas (capable of melting half a ton of metal per hour), the ordinary sources of danger, and those arising from the

operation's being carried on in the stokehole or other parts of a ship, with the precautions to be taken, and the best way of coping with any accident 'as might happen from want of care and judgment or from any other cause'.

Volcano was repaired, with a light topgallant forecastle for additional accommodation, and tenders sought to replace the machinery that had been removed at Hong Kong. By March 1861 she was fitted to serve the Steam Ordinary at Portsmouth, where she spent the rest of the decade, though in a sudden agitation in December 1861 she was ordered to be commissioned with all dispatch. Her remaining 24 years were spent in Reserve and Harbour Service.[12]

It was decided that subsequent floating factories were to be built of iron, but none followed. The remarkable efforts of the Admiralty during the late 1850s in developing mobile logistical support to the Steam Navy were not maintained. The next significant successor to *Volcano*, though her purpose was rather different, was the torpedo-depot ship HMS *Hecla*, purchased in 1878 while building as a merchant ship. She was converted to carry and maintain torpedo boats, and had a very successful career, though not as a Fleet repair ship. Her successor, HMS *Vulcan* of 1889, far from being an adaptation of an existing vessel, was a highly specialised design intended to carry six second-class torpedo boats and maintain them and their weapons (Figure 104). Metal-bashing on a large scale, such as Nasmyth had equipped *Volcano* for, was not envisaged: a 2cwt steam hammer, contrasting with the 7cwt one of *Volcano*, was proposed, but was probably not installed in 1896, when the workshop was photographed. Compared with the equipment Blaxland and Miller had proposed the outfit seems rather sparse for a considerably larger ship: five lathes, two drilling machines, planing, slotting, shaping, punching and shearing machines, and a hot air furnace capable of melting 2cwt of iron or brass.

Rather than supplying a specialist ship to accompany a fleet, ships were provided with their own workshops, whose capacity naturally varied with the size of the ship; battleships of the 1890s were formidably equipped. The revival of a true floating base like *Volcano*, which, as has been seen, counted towing a hospital ship among her functions, had to wait until the next century.

—ⱳ—

Notes:

1   ADM 1/3492, ADM 84/5, ADM 85/10, ADM 87/47.
2   ADM 87/48, ADM 93/11.
3   ADM 85/16.
4   ADM 87/48, ADM 85/18, NMM NPC/4940, 4942.
5   ADM 84/12, ADM 93/11.
6   ADM 135/501, ADM 87/52, ADM 53/6266, ADM 84/13, ADM 87/52, ADM 93/13.
7   ADM 87/52, ADM 92/17, ADM 87/54, William Fairbairn, 'Description of a floating steam corn mill and bakery' *Proceedings of the Institution of Mechanical Engineers*, 1858, pp.155-159, 3 plates; T 1/5949A/15307; *Minutes of Evidence before the Committee of Inquiry on the Economy of Her Majesty's Dockyards*, 1859, p.214.
8   ADM 135/501, *Minutes of Evidence before the Committee of Inquiry on the Economy of Her Majesty's Dockyards*, 1859, pp.126-127; ADM 85/27, ADM 92/18, ADM 93/16.
9   ADM 93/16, ADM 1/5590, ADM 93/17, ADM 53/6267, ADM 1/5708.
10 ADM 53/6267, ADM 87/69, ADM 53/6268.
11 ADM 87/71, ADM 87/72.
12 NMM POR/R/34, POR/R/35, POR/P/64, POR/P/65, POR/R/36.

CHAPTER 10

Integrating the Factories

KEYHAM FACTORY was coherently organised internally, but geographically separated from the South Yard. Initially this was no handicap, as the maintenance of steam engines could be seen as something apart from general dockyard duties, but with the prospect of the phasing out of all sail-only ships the two sites needed to be physically integrated. Portsmouth was a single site, but the limitations of the Factory meant that extra facilities needed to be provided on a large scale. The new works here and at Chatham and Sheerness were to be the occasion for a fresh batch of innovative designs.

Keyham Tunnel

Keyham and Devonport yards were separated on the shore line by the Ordnance Board's Morice Yard, and inland by the built-up areas of Devonport and Keyham and the old Plymouth Dock fortifications, on rocky land elevated above the yards. It was obviously an inconvenience for the two facilities to be so completely separated, especially as Keyham was not intended to be a completely independent yard, but to be under the Admiral Superintendent at Devonport, though having its own Chief Engineer. A tunnel was the obvious solution, but it posed problems of its own quite unrelated to any geographical or geological difficulties. These were caused by the presence of the eighteenth-century Plymouth Dock lines. Ten years later, with the complete rethinking of the landward fortifications of the dockyards, these obsolete defences would not have been considered of any importance, but in the early 1850s they must still have seemed to have some value.

Accordingly, on 28 April 1852 the Admiralty sent the first proposal for a tunnel to the Board of Ordnance. No serious objections were raised, and the idea was approved on 14 May. The tunnel was intended for the transit of horse-drawn traffic and pedestrians. Greene immediately prepared a section showing the means for forming the tunnel floor and a plan of the gateway area at Keyham. The Ordnance had agreed in principle, so now it was the turn of the local inhabitants who lived over the route of the tunnel: they would have to be notified (and doubtless compensated in some way), especially as some land would have to be permanently appropriated for use as ventilating tunnels.[1]

By September 1853 Greene was asked to prepare an accurate working plan and sections, and further liaison took place with the Ordnance, who were asked to make their own survey of the ground. The problem to be overcome was 'the evil of an opening through the works', though there were ways in which the ingenuity of the Royal Engineers could get around this. The main essential was that the parts of the tunnel that were open to the air should be completely exposed to the flanking fire of the garrison.[2] The Commanding Royal Engineer suggested that the most secure arrangement would be to have no open sections of the tunnel at all, and barriers with a ditch in front

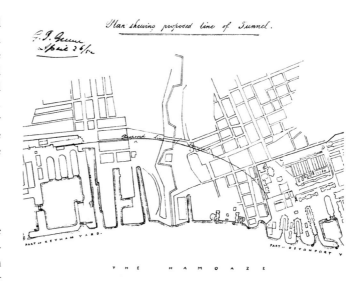

105 Devonport and Keyham linked, as first sketched by Greene in 1852. *(TNA WO 44/314)*

placed at intervals in the tunnels, defended by musketry casemates in the side of the tunnel.[3]

On 2 June 1854 the Act of Parliament enabling the construction of the tunnel was passed. Mr Scamp laid a line of flags indicating the route. The Keyham end of the tunnel under Moon Street was to be done by cut and cover, and the rest by tunnelling. As many openings to the surface were to be left as the Board of Ordnance would permit. Early in 1855 Greene prepared a plan showing the general strategy for removing the spoil from the site, the quays from which it was to be shipped, and the dumping ground. This was to be on the southern side of Millbrook Creek, on the other side of the Hamoaze. By February 1855 Greene had produced a set of drawings, and the portion of the tunnel within Keyham Yard had been executed. Only a small amount of work had been done by this time, for the winning tender for the tunnel (Messrs Smith of Woolwich) was not accepted until 17 March (Figure 105).[4]

Some rethinking clearly took place at this stage, for in June the ground was resurveyed and a new plan was prepared. Further design studies for the Keyham end, where the tunnel had to pass through some coal vaults, were made in August, and on 17 October it was decided that work could proceed. James Macdonnell was the supervising engineer at this stage, and from December 1855 drawings signed by him survive. The drains and sewers existing at the Keyham end had to be accommodated, and the air shafts had to be determined and designed. Greene recommended that a modified version of the subterranean defences be built; no drawings have been found to show what form these were to take. By March 1856 there had been progress at the Keyham end, working through the coal vaults, and while it was proposed strengthen the brickwork under the escarp of the fortifications, Macdonnell had designed the

necessary to support the roof of the tunnel which is cut out of solid slate, by three feet of brick arching. No Railway Engineer would ever have dreamed of this…You must please to consider this as a private communication as I should be eaten alive if known to have betrayed the secrets of the prison Home — You may have the official information as regards our Line at any time if you will write to me for it…

Iron grilles for the tunnel shafts were designed at the end of 1856, and in July 1857 plans were drawn up for tram rails for the horse-drawn tram carts. In the same month tenders were accepted for paving the Keyham entrance with pitched stones, and in September, a little late, it was realised that a self-acting metal valve was required to keep the tide out of the drain to the Tunnel. In December Greene signed a plan of the Keyham entrance. In February 1858 the matter of joining Keyham to the main line and communicating directly through the tunnel to Devonport was raised. Greene was to report as soon as possible 'after communicating with Mr Brunel' as to the best point of junction with the Cornwall Railroad, and to propose the name of a railway engineer for the job of preparing railway lines for Keyham, and a direct line through the tunnel to Devonport. It was to be a long time before anything came of this suggestion.

A drawback of the tunnel soon became evident. This was the added scope it gave for the traditional means by which the workers compensated for low pay: pilfering from the Yard. It became unhappily apparent that it was necessary to establish a police beat in the tunnel to prevent stores from being thrown into the ditch of the fortification in the open sections.[6]

In 1862 a branch of the tramway was made up through an open cutting from Morice Yard to the portion of the line in the ditch of the fortifications. This, appropriately, was designed by the Commanding Royal Engineer at Devonport. The line was flanked by a Carnot wall, the only drawing of fortifications connected with the tunnel to have been found. In March 1865, after the tunnel had been in use for some seven or eight years, it was belatedly decided that gas lighting should be laid on, as, not surprisingly, accidents had happened. In September of that year the Cornwall Railway offered to construct a branch line into Keyham and complete the system within the yard; nothing was proposed about sending it through the tunnel. In May 1876 a standard-gauge line was opened in Devonport Yard, and in January 1879 a plan was finally drawn up to bring the railway through the tunnel, which involved running the line through the North Smithery (Figures 106, 107). Additional gaslights were fitted in 1892, and corrugated iron dripshields were fitted after 1894.[7]

entrance into South Yard. On 21 May a tender for the asphalt floor of the tunnel was accepted. In December plans were drawn up for carrying a Keyham sewer over the open section of the tunnel, within an arch, and the plans of some of the tops of the tunnel shafts were drawn up.[5]

It had apparently not been part of the original concept that a railway line should be put through the tunnel. This was an uncharacteristic lapse on the part of Greene and Scamp. Some approach must have been made to the projected Cornwall Railway Company, as their chairman wrote in a confidential letter to the First Lord (enclosing sections of the tunnel with profiles of locomotives and rolling stock showing that they would not get through, and incidentally providing a glimpse of how the Yard was viewed from outside):

As nothing would be easier than to make a junction with the intended Cornwall line about a quarter of a mile from Keyham works, it does appear to me to have been a great oversight…Scandal says that the Engineer has thought it

Greene at Portsmouth

The principal want at Portsmouth had been an adequate smithery. A plan drawn up by James in 1849 shows a large square building with a chimney at each corner behind the south end of the Factory: the same plan and apparent dimensions as those of the smithery that was in fact to be built. Only three drawings survive from this project, of cast iron girders and columns, all probably from November 1849, one anonymous and the other two signed by the draughtsman James Murray (it is not known if he was related to the Chief Engineer).

Colonel Greene now drew up plans for the great Smithery.

It is not known how much Greene drew on James's original design, which was presumably in external visual conformity with his other buildings, but he seems to have taken over the floor plan. He pulled something very different out of the hat, with a massive iron-framed structure clad in corrugated iron: it was functional and impressively massed in a way that James's temporary smithery had no ambitions to be. A chimney at each corner of the building carried the smoke away (Figures 108A, B and C).

By June 1851 he reported to the Board in detail on his proposals, recommending the adoption of the original scheme, with slight modifications. A grand central chimney was shown on a drawing of that month, but annotated 'It is not intended to construct this except it be considered by the Officers to be absolutely necessary'. The old Metal Mills were finally done away with, and a tender for their demolition was accepted in August. On 20 September 1851 Fox, Henderson's tender of £7,136 to construct the New Smithery was accepted, and at the end of the month Greene sent them tracings of the foundations. User reaction to the plans was provided by the Master Smith at Woolwich. A plan signed by Greene survives from this month, showing the building being constructed round

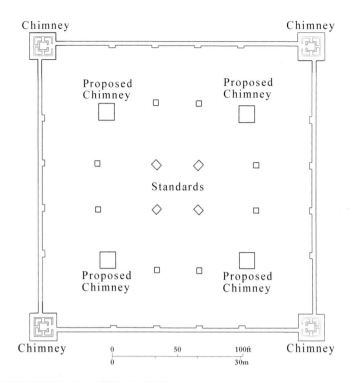

108A and **B**
A monument of the new industrial design, the outline of Greene's Smithery at Portsmouth may still be discerned, though the loss of its chimneys has reduced its impact. (Left: Plan redrawn from English Heritage A940995 Below: © Crown Copyright. NMR BB 96/10708)

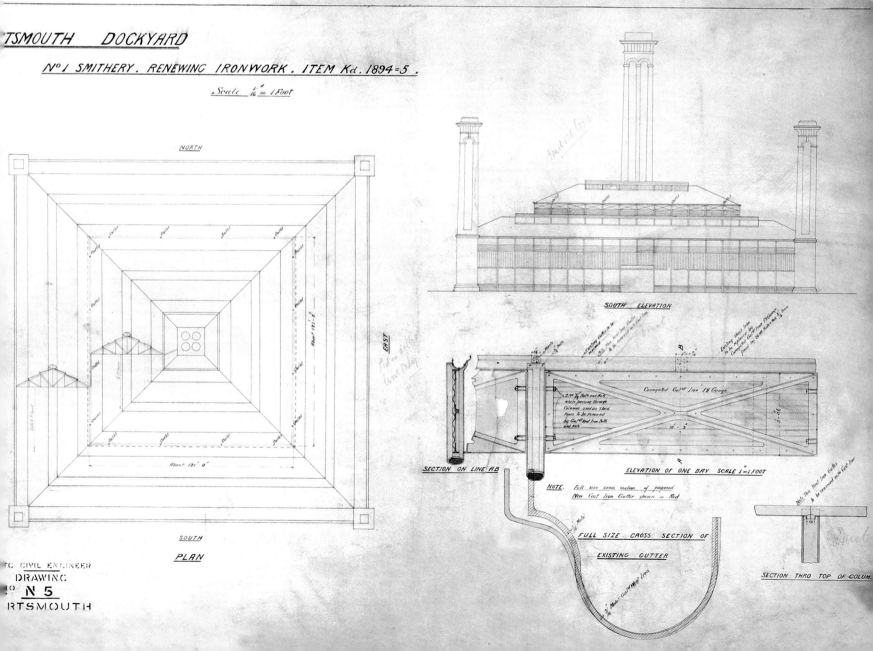

108C The stacks of the Portsmouth Smithery can be discerned to the rear of this 1902 photograph of the battleship *Vengeance*. The covered slips include a Baker design to the left. *(NMM neg. no. G10125)*

one of James's smitheries, which was clearly being worked until the last minute, and was the probable cause of reported delays.[8]

Work began on the foundations of the north-west chimney in January 1852, and by March Greene and Murray had produced detail drawings for exterior features (including the lettering VR, 1852, which still survives on the bases of the corner chimneys), details of the exterior windows and a zinc sash and frame, as well as plans and sections of the windows. Fox, Henderson were clearly thought well of by Greene, and in May he suggested that they be asked to tender for fitting the forges and air flues, which they did successfully. In June they tendered for strengthening the middle row of columns, so evidently Greene got the design of that wrong first time, but there is no evidence to suggest that the firm had been called in to advise on the alterations.

By October the concrete foundations for the central chimney were in varying degrees of progress: a drawing annotated by Greene indicates the state of each part at the time. In December the old smithery that had occupied part of the site was finally abandoned, and at the beginning of 1853 Murray was preparing drawings for the masonry under the smithery cranes. In June convicts began dismantling the shell of the old

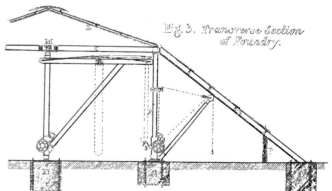

109 Comparable with Greene's Smithery was James Downie's foundry at North Woodside, though designed to stand up to different stresses and strains. The upper roof was entirely independent of the rest of the framework of the foundry, and was not subjected to any strain. The shape of the building was quite different from that of Greene's: the sloping struts that carried the main thrust were used to form side lean-to roofs, and the plan was L-shaped. An underground smoke tunnel carried the combustion products of two cupolas into a chimney 210ft high. This gave an uninterrupted floor space of 84ft total width between the dwarf side walls. *(From J. Downie, 'Description of an Iron Construction of Foundry' in* Proceedings of the Institution of Mechanical Engineers, *1856)*

smithery, and during the summer Greene was preparing drawings for the central chimney. This was fed by smoke tunnels, like the Woolwich chimney. Greene clearly did not share Lloyd's doubts about the effectiveness of this as a means of smoke removal, as he was to introduce the same system at Keyham. By September 1855 the building was in use, although Greene delayed the installation of a 5 ton Nasmyth hammer and its ancillary equipment on account of Nasmyth not taking proper account of the foundations.[9]

This remarkable building, which formed a model for Greene's South Smithery at Devonport (see pp.134-137), still survives in its essentials, though much ironwork has been renewed, and it has long been shorn of its five chimneys. It is not until one enters the building that the surviving remnants of the great display of metal framing and roofing can be seen, above and around the storage racking that now occupies the interior. Greene was to design a related building for the South Smithery at Devonport, as will be seen later.[10]

The great exemplar for such a building was of course Paxton's Crystal Palace, also constructed by Fox, Henderson, and by the end of the century a myth had grown up that the Smithery was put together from spare parts left over from that project.[11] At least one analogous building, long destroyed, was a contemporary foundry at the North Woodside Iron Works, and an interesting comparison (Figure 109). This was another all-iron construction, with the exception of horizontal timber framing for the tops of the cranes. The point of this design, unlike the Smithery, was to resist the great lateral strains caused by heavy lifting cranes: the thrust of the cranes was carried down to the ground by a series of sloping struts at the sides and ends of the foundry. After the foundry had been in operation for several years, the designer, J. Downie, stated that the structure offered an effective resistance to all the strains occasioned by the work of the foundry without any injury or distortion to the framework of the building. Downie made no mention of Portsmouth Smithery in the account of his own building, which was apparently equally successful. No apparent weaknesses had revealed themselves in the first years of its use, although it had been subjected occasionally to strains of between 45 and 50 tons on the cranes.[12]

Among the new works authorised at a Board Visitation of September 1855 was a new Iron Foundry, on the south side of the South Inlet dock, as originally intended in Denison's plan. The portion of the Brass Foundry fitted up as an Iron Foundry

110 The Foundry, Portsmouth.
(© Crown Copyright. NMR, AA 045930)

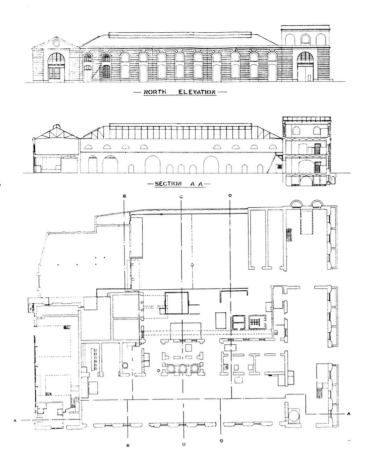

111 A contrast in construction to his Smithery, Greene's Foundry at Portsmouth was designed to a rigid plan not readily capable of being altered, nor has it. Greene and Scamp seem to have anticipated future needs as accurately, but with a different conclusion, as at Keyham. *(Adapted from Fiches 332256, 332979, held by Unicorn Consultancy, Portsmouth)*

— NORTH ELEVATION —

— SECTION A A —

112 Fairbairn's plan of the Foundry is one of the most detailed to survive of any Dockyard building. *(NMM neg. no. D8571)*

was now quite inadequate to meet the demands for castings, but progress with the new building (originally estimated at £30,000) was slow, and in January 1857 Greene was urged to make as much haste as possible. He had designed a massive fireproof construction, featuring the boxing-in of the head of the main staircase with an elegant iron enclosure simulating wood, and with external features echoing James's buildings, with a water tank on the roof. Unlike James's earlier Foundry, rail access was provided for, and the areas for the various processes and functions were physically segregated (Figures 110 and 111).

A contract for the Foundry was made with Edmund Smith on 24 February 1857, being assigned to his brother George the next year. Six foundry cranes were delivered in March, and the four 20 ton cranes originally intended for Keyham Foundry were also sent. Later in the year it was proposed to remove the engines from the gunboat HMS *Blazer* and adapt them for use in the Foundry, and by November drawings had been prepared of the metal roof over the Foundry, together with details of the roof of the drying stores for the moulds behind the Foundry, and the roof tank with its massive support girders. In August the next year James Murray prepared drawings of the chimney shaft, and the 1859/60 Navy estimates now gave its cost, with the roof tank, as £35,000. A plan, cross-section and elevation were made in August 1860, and a tracing was supplied to Fairbairns, who were to provide most of the machinery. Shafting and the essential basic equipment, cupolas, blowing fans and cranes are shown in the drawing, one of the most

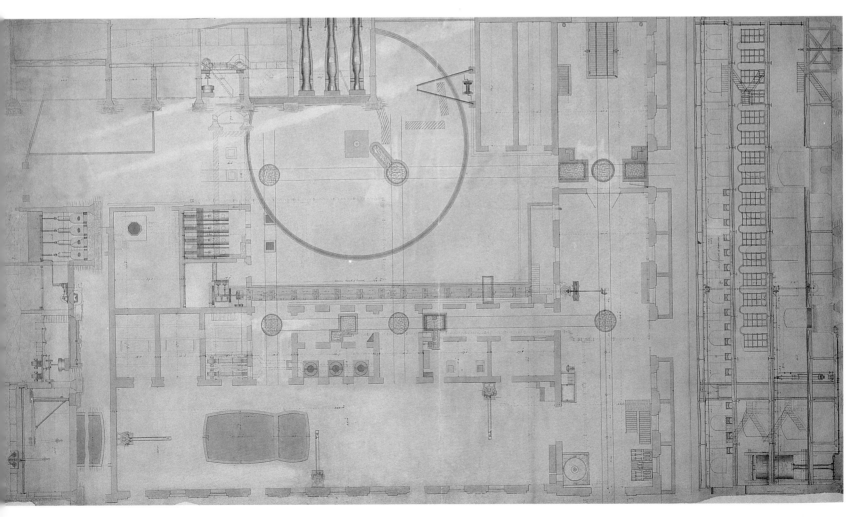

detailed and informative to have survived and a fine example of Victorian draughtsmanship (Figure 112).[13]

The Foundry was clearly then preparing for tooling up. By 14 September 1860 Smith, then also engaged on enlarging three docks, had been paid £3,330, and at the end of the year railway lines connecting the building with the Factory and Stores were approved. Hydraulic appliances were extensively used in this building, Armstrong's supplying the equipment for £3,854 (see Table 10). The railway system, which connected this building to other parts of the dockyard, was not completed until the next year; a tender for rails and turntable was accepted in February 1861. That year Greene, in evidence before the Commissioners on the Control and Management of the Naval Yards, stated that the foundry was just finished and commencing operations, although it could not have been fully operational until late 1861 at the least.[14] The cupolas in James's Foundry, as has been seen, were designed by Murray. That design was not going to be repeated, in view of the proven superiority of Ireland's patent cupolas (Figure 113).[15]

Key to the integration of all the different elements of the Portsmouth Steam Yard into a functional whole, without wholesale demolition and replanning, was the roofing-over of open spaces. This underpinned Scamp's improvements at Sheerness, although the first suggested use of this structural device on a large scale in a Yard may possibly have been at Chatham, when during a Board Visitation of 1851 it was submitted that the Smithery Yard be glazed over, though nothing was done about this until July 1865, when the tender of the Regent Canal Ironwork Company was accepted (Figure 101). At Woolwich the spaces between the Fitting and Erecting shops, the Smithery and the lathe shop and Coppersmiths' shop had all been glazed over by 1858, to give cover for the tram roads between the buildings. The programme of new works at Portsmouth for 1860/61 included the insertion of an additional floor into James's Punching and Shearing shop (as he had envisaged), and the roofing over of a space between the new Smithery and its Engine house, again as a covered passageway, for £1,366 (Figure 114).

In the 1861/2 works the Iron store by the Portsmouth

Table 10 **Hydraulic appliances supplied by Armstrong's for the Portsmouth Foundry** (only major items listed)

	£
Hydraulic machinery for lifting and lowering wagons	700
Hydraulic hoist to lift 2 tons 10½ feet	230
hydraulic hoist to lift 1½ tons 46 feet	320
2 hydraulic capstans	640
1 accumulator	575
2 sets force pumps to be fixed in vicinity of accumulator, pressure pipes, bends, valves, cocks etc.	750

Smithery was roofed over, and in 1864 the remainder of the space was enclosed for £1,980 and standards for a travelling crane were inserted, the area becoming the Smithery Erecting shop. The iron roofing of the Smithery was removed, and replaced by glass and slating, at a cost of £2,393. A traveller road was inserted next to James's Brass Foundry. The space between the Factory and the Smithery now remained, and this was roofed over in 1866, openings were made in the Factory wall,

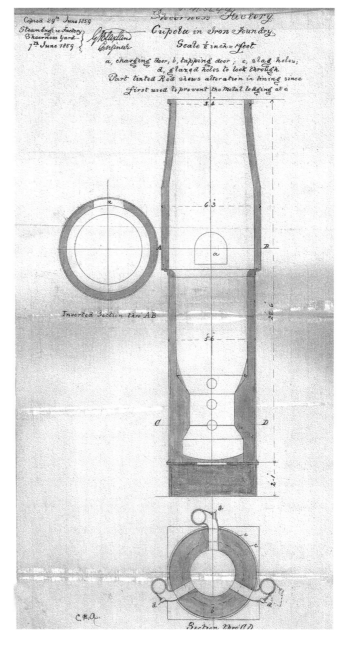

113 Sectional drawing of Ireland's cupola as modified at Sheerness to allow the metal to run more freely. *(TNA ADM 85/54)*

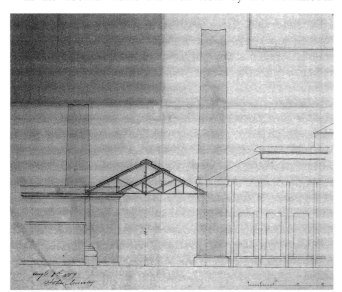

114 The infilling of areas by the insertion of metal roof trusses was a cheap way of creating workshop space. Here are some drawings of the rehandling of the Iron Store by Greene's Portsmouth Smithery. *(TNA ADM 1/5715)*

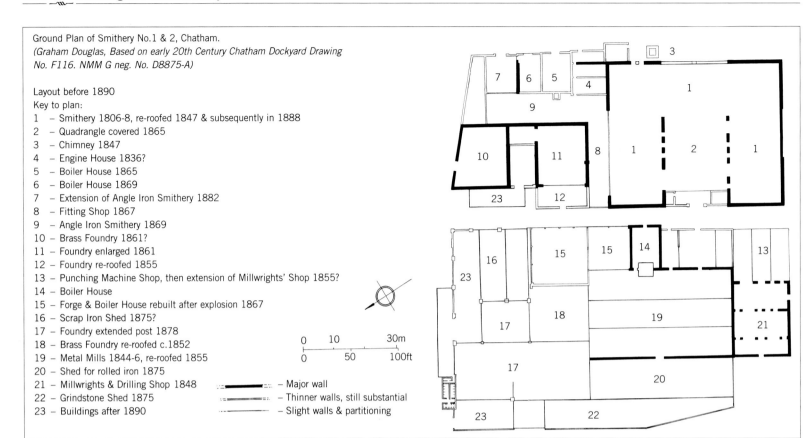

Ground Plan of Smithery No.1 & 2, Chatham.
(Graham Douglas, Based on early 20th Century Chatham Dockyard Drawing No. F116. NMM G neg. No. D8875-A)

Layout before 1890
Key to plan:
1 – Smithery 1806-8, re-roofed 1847 & subsequently in 1888
2 – Quadrangle covered 1865
3 – Chimney 1847
4 – Engine House 1836?
5 – Boiler House 1865
6 – Boiler House 1869
7 – Extension of Angle Iron Smithery 1882
8 – Fitting Shop 1867
9 – Angle Iron Smithery 1869
10 – Brass Foundry 1861?
11 – Foundry enlarged 1861
12 – Foundry re-roofed 1855
13 – Punching Machine Shop, then extension of Millwrights' Shop 1855?
14 – Boiler House
15 – Forge & Boiler House rebuilt after explosion 1867
16 – Scrap Iron Shed 1875?
17 – Foundry extended post 1878
18 – Brass Foundry re-roofed c.1852
19 – Metal Mills 1844-6, re-roofed 1855
20 – Shed for rolled iron 1875
21 – Millwrights & Drilling Shop 1848
22 – Grindstone Shed 1875
23 – Buildings after 1890

0   10   30m
0   50   100ft

━━━━━ – Major wall
┅┅┅┅┅ – Thinner walls, still substantial
┄┄┄┄┄ – Slight walls & partitioning

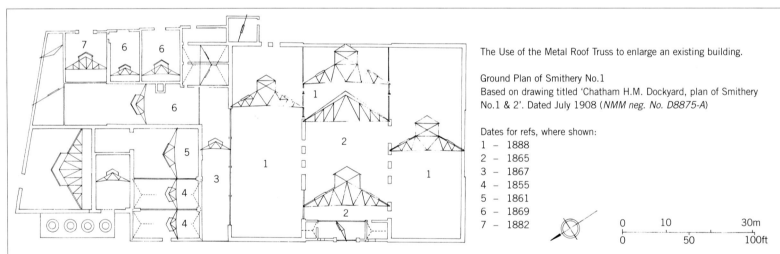

The Use of the Metal Roof Truss to enlarge an existing building.

Ground Plan of Smithery No.1
Based on drawing titled 'Chatham H.M. Dockyard, plan of Smithery No.1 & 2'. Dated July 1908 (*NMM neg. No. D8875-A*)

Dates for refs, where shown:
1 – 1888
2 – 1865
3 – 1867
4 – 1855
5 – 1861
6 – 1869
7 – 1882

0   10   30m
0   50   100ft

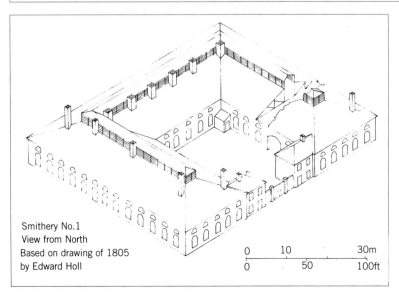

Smithery No.1
View from North
Based on drawing of 1805
by Edward Holl

0   10   30m
0   50   100ft

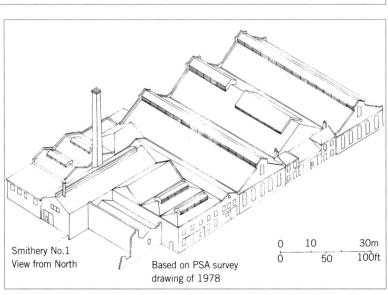

Smithery No.1
View from North

Based on PSA survey
drawing of 1978

0   10   30m
0   50   100ft

and this space became an Erecting shop, an arrangement similar to that made at Keyham a few years before.

In 1865 drawings were prepared for another expansion: the building of an additional shop to the west of the Factory, which again had its wall opened to allow mutual access. The winning tender for this came from Bramble, for £7,100. This all-metal building, known originally as the additional Factory Smithery, was initially free-standing, but a sectional drawing of July 1867 shows, faintly sketched in, the glass roof that soon joined it to the Factory (Figure 116).

After the building of an armour plate shop (which will be discussed later) to the north of this building it became the Boiler Smithery, as foreseen by James. The original Steam Factory now presented its original appearance only when seen from the Basin. It had been transformed into a complex of buildings leading into each other, linked together by iron roofs. Since that time the additional Smithery has been destroyed, and most of the openings in the Factory walls have been closed up again, restoring much of its original appearance, but the larger part of the great sequence of 1860s iron roofs remains intact, presenting together with the Smithery a remarkable display of structural ironwork.[16]

Slip No. 7 at Chatham

The original purpose of the covered slips had been to enable shipbuilding to be carried on throughout the year, and it has been seen that the Pembroke roofs were a transposition of the wooden roofs into the new medium of iron. Within a few years

115A, B, C The Chatham Smithery. The lower photograph shows the front of the original smithery by Holl, and the drawings its successive alterations. *(G. Douglas / M. Williams)*

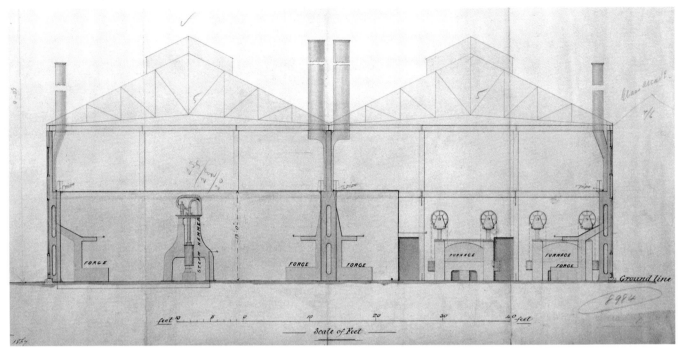

the slip was to be transformed from a simple cover to part of the mechanism of construction of the ship itself.

The strength of the iron slip roofs had not been calculated to support any loads, but there was an obvious temptation to lash hoists to them for lifting ships' timbers into position, which had been yielded to. In response to this practice, an Admiralty Circular of June 1846 stated that the framework of the iron roofs over slips and buildings was constructed only for the support of the covering material, with an allowance for wind, snow and certain contingencies, and therefore the suspension of weights from them would be risky, and was prohibited. New

floors for storehouses had been intended to be constructed to carry a safe load of from 2cwt to 4cwt per square foot; but it was suspected that in the construction of storehouse floors generally this precaution had not been strictly adhered to, and, worse, that the floors were usually loaded without regard to construction. It was laid down that instructions with reference to the roofs be printed on a board, which was to be displayed conspicuously on each roof. The safe loading of floors was to be ascertained, and notices were to be placed in storehouses as well.

The shipwrights got around the circular of 1846 by attaching

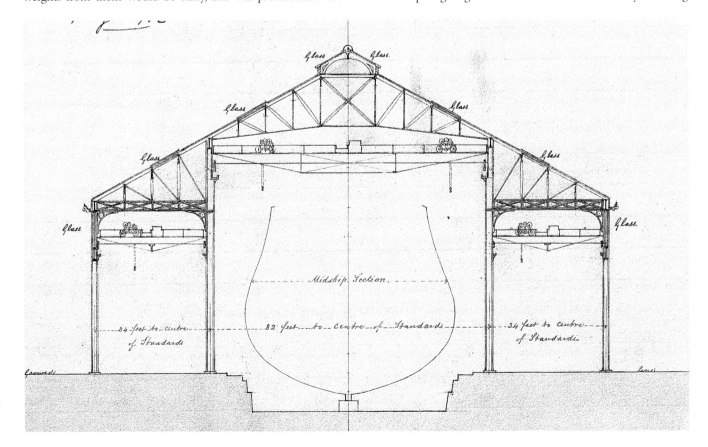

fixings for their own convenience to other parts of the iron slips, and among the works authorised at a Board visitation at Portsmouth that year was a movable derrick for the standards of slips 3, 4 and 5 to facilitate erection of staging round ships and prevent misuse of the iron roofs. In 1851 the Chatham officers initiated the design of a new type of slip roof, no longer just affording protection from the weather (which became largely irrelevant with the advent of iron and steel shipbuilding) but one that was stressed for and provided with travelling cranes over all three aisles. The slip was now essentially a factory space with a central nave, whose primary function was the manoeuvring of heavy components into place. This design was to cope with all future types of ship, box-battery ironclad, turret ship, pre-Dreadnought and submarine, staying in use till the last boat to be constructed at Chatham had been built under it. They put the plan up to Greene, who approved. It has been seen that Rivers, the Clerk of Works, was asked to prepare drawings for the previous slips; he may possibly be considered the originator of the concept.[17]

On 30 July 1851 Greene wrote to Walker that the Board had agreed to the suggested general arrangement and section of the new slip, and that the idea of incorporating a travelling crane had been generally approved. The distance between the standards, because of the extra weight, would have to be reduced as much as possible, consistent with the efficient working of the slip as a shipbuilding mechanism, and the Surveyor was asked to provide the dimensions. The Master Shipwrights Laire and Fincham were consulted; they stated that the main standards should not be less than 80ft apart, and the side berths not less than 36ft wide. The new slip was to be built in front of the South Mast Pond, and a tunnel connecting this with the Medway had to be part of the package.[18]

The troubles with slips 4, 5 and 6 were not over. Greene had borings made beneath them, in anticipation of further difficulties, and on 8 May 1852 it was reported that the standards and coping of No. 6 were deviating, and it appeared as if the new works would be needed to prop the whole thing up. The works were therefore to be pushed on as quickly as

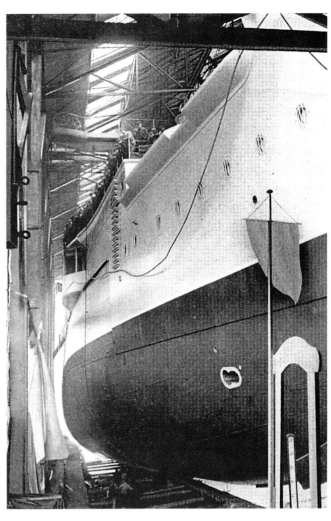

118 The battleship *Goliath* under construction in No.7 slip awaiting launch in 1898. *(From* The Navy and Army Illustrated, *April 16 1898)*

possible. Despite the need for hurry, Baker's were delayed in completing the south side of No. 7 slip and the adjoining sea wall for want of instructions for forming the pit for the hydraulic crane that was to be placed on the sea wall. Next month Greene (it is not known whether he was referring to the recurring trouble or some new revelation) censured the

120 Proposed roof for No.2 dock at Chatham, with cranes and travellers for armour plating. (See also Figure 123) *(NMM P/32)*

119 The contemporary slip roofs at St. Peter's Dockyard, Newcastle, also introduced travelling cranes, but the design is far less advanced. *(Practical Mechanics Journal, vol.IV, 1851)*

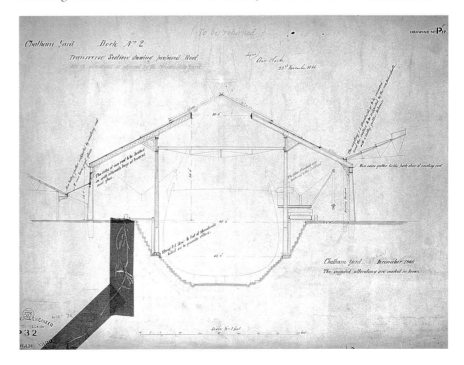

workmen and superintending officers for taking insufficient care. He finalised drawings of the mast tunnel and other works connected with the new slip, and the foundations for the outer standards, and was able to start the design of the roof on being informed that the load on the travellers would not exceed 5 or 6 tons. A batch of drawings for the roof, signed by Greene, are dated 16 July 1852.

Perhaps unsurprisingly, Baker's did not get the contract for this job; on 21 September 1852 Henry Grissell & Co.'s tender of £13,050 was accepted. The central traveller was not contracted for until next spring, when the same firm signed a contract to supply and fix a traveller and two crabs, chains and tackles, to be tested to 25 tons in the centre, for £1,579. In March 1853 Greene, sorely tried by what must have been a catalogue of errors, pronounced himself very dissatisfied with the works at Chatham, and brought the general management to the notice of the Board, to what effect is unknown. The unhappy tale continued, and in June a fracture was discovered in one of the standards of the roof over Slip 6. This was mended in the same way that a previous one had been. The standards of the North Extension were to be relieved from the masonry, and

121 No. 7 Slip today. (Mike Williams)

the part of the roof and trestling that was likely to sustain damage was to be shored up. The three roofs were to be very carefully examined, and relieved at such parts as were liable to injury by strain. Greene must have considered that some of the blame might have been attributable to Baker's use of flawed castings, for in a departure from past practice Grissell's were now told not to paint any castings for the roof of No 7. (Previously it had been specified that they be painted with three coats of good oil colour, which may have covered up any small flaw lines.) Unfit castings were to be rejected; it seems barely credible that this should have had to be stated. The progress of the works still failed to give satisfaction, with wasteful expenditure of granite, and in October it was recorded that Greene proposed a 'snub to the Clerk of Works'.[19]

There was also uncertainty over the stress imposed by the travellers, and the need to keep pace with ever-expanding ship size. The travellers were tested at the beginning of 1855, and Grissell's were asked to supply additional ones. Something was probably expected to go wrong with the roof, and in May Rivers was ordered to inspect it; as a consequence Grissell's supplied another iron truss. In November the travellers were

tested to 25 tons, originally to be suspended for 12 hours, but this was thought an excessive demand, and was rescinded. The slip was now considered to be too short, and Greene prepared drawings for its extension; Grissell's tender for this work, £2,700, was accepted on 27 August 1856. This involved taking down all the galvanised iron and a portion of the standards from the extension of No. 6, shoring the roof, and piledriving for the iron standards. By the end of the year half the ironwork had been delivered. In the meantime, to get the slip functioning, the coffer dam that had shut the works off from the Medway had been removed, probably at the beginning of 1856, tenders for its removal having been asked for in December 1855. Some trouble was experienced with the travellers: in January 1856 a wheel broke, and in May the traveller beam deflected, causing another fracture. Rivers suggested using wrought iron wheels, and considered that the speed of the side travellers could be doubled, though reinforcement would be needed if this were to be done. The space between slips 6 and 7 was covered over to provide an extensive covered working space, and it appears that this work was entrusted to Rivers, while the wooden slip No. 2 was covered with galvanised iron for £1,388 by local contractors Foord & Sons of Rochester.[20]

The story of the Chatham roofs may be taken down to the end of the century. A traveller was added to the work space between Slips 6 and 7 in 1861, supplied by Aveling's, who supplied an additional traveller and crab for No. 7 slip for £145. These cranes proved so useful that brackets and girders were added for travellers in between Slips 4, 5, and 6 in 1863, and gas lighting was introduced in No. 7 the following year.

An interesting project of 1866 shows a proposed roof over No. 2 dock, by then the principal dock used for building ironclad warships, and the roof was specially designed for this function. Turret ships required considerable quantities of components to be lowered into the middle of the ship (Figures 120 and 123). In 1868 the roof, which was to be used first over *Sultan* (not a turret ship), laid down that year, was costed at £2,800, a significantly lower sum than the cost of No. 7. It had been the intent to make this roof permanent, but that idea was abandoned, and a temporary roof was built. This was removed after 1903. More travellers were placed between Slips 5 and 6 in 1872, in which year No. 7 was re-equipped with powerful new cranes with wrought iron girders. The cost was estimated at about £3,200, or a quarter of the original roof and travellers:

> This work being wholly unforeseen, and arising from the adoption of a new design for ships of war, it is hoped that the expense may be met from the vote for contingencies…When the *Superb* [to be launched as *Alexandra*] is ready for launching a small portion of the masonry at the stem of the slip will have to be removed.[21]

The innovation in HMS *Alexandra*, requiring the slip roof to be re-equipped, was the first protective steel deck above the waterline as a protection against plunging fire. The specification stated that these girders in No. 7 slip roof were to sustain a proof load of 80 tons in the centre of each. The greatest load to be lifted by the traveller would not be much more than 20 tons (nearly four times that borne by the original), so that the strength of the girders would have to be reduced as much as

122 The ironclad *Sultan*, built at Chatham between 1868-71. Like a number of other ironclads of the era, she was quickly outdated, but her robust construction resulted in a long life as a hulk. She was not finally broken up until 1947, after over 40 years of harbour service. *(Chrysalis Picture Library)*

possible so as not to place an excessive strain on the cast iron standards. The traveller itself would weigh 30 tons; when carrying a load of 20 tons the weight at one end would be about 36 tons, so a proof test of 60 tons was suggested, as had already been applied to the roof between Slips 6 and 7 and in the workshop beside No. 7. It is not known how the roof withstood all this, but something gave way in November 1897, when a plan and elevation were made to show a broken standard.

Slip 7 had many years of useful life left, though the increasing dimensions of battleships meant that the whole hull was no longer under cover, but the days of the others as building slips were over (Figures 119, 122 and 125). In April 1901 a sketch was made for a dam to close No. 3 slip, and the Annual Estimates of 1904/5 allowed for the conversion of Nos. 3 and 4 into boat

123 A drawing by Captain Coles illustrating his turret. *(PRO ADM 87/74)*

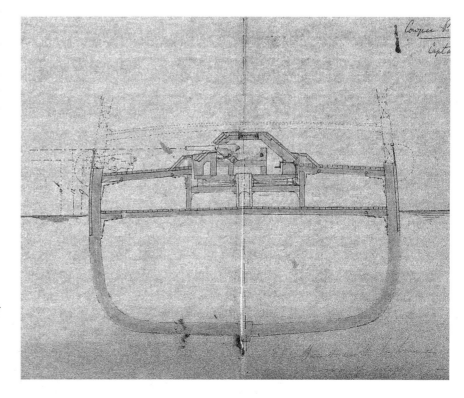

stores; 5 and 6 were to follow.[22] The Canadian submarine *Okanagan*, the final vessel to be built at Chatham, launched in 1966, was fittingly built under No. 7 slip, which had proved, like Keyham Factory, to be adaptable for all subsequent purposes.

The Sheerness Boat Store

The free-standing, rigidly framed structure of no. 7 slip was a great step on the way to Greene's most celebrated design, the Sheerness Boat Store, probably the most significant early multi-storey iron-framed building to survive. The contractors were those responsible for the roof of slip no. 7 at Chatham, Henry Grissell & Co. The building had an immediate predecessor at Sheerness: in June 1856 Greene produced a design rehandling Holl's Boat House, removing alternate standards on the ground floor to give five bays instead of ten, adding new girders to support the floor, new columns on the first floor, and a traveller in front of the building to handle the boats over the slipway (Figure 125). The roof was to be raised. Another drawing shows the end elevation of the building refenestrated, and the waterfront completely rehandled with sliding doors on the first floor. Fox, Henderson tendered to provide an additional storey,

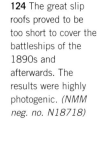

124 The great slip roofs proved to be too short to cover the battleships of the 1890s and afterwards. The results were highly photogenic. *(NMM neg. no. N18718)*

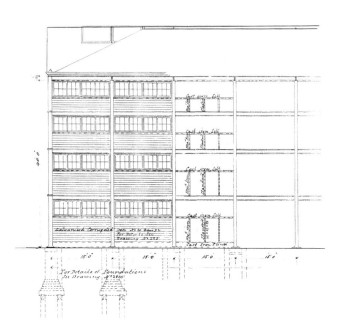

125 One of Greene's drawings for the Boat Store. The interior and exterior. *(TNA ADM 140/1332)*

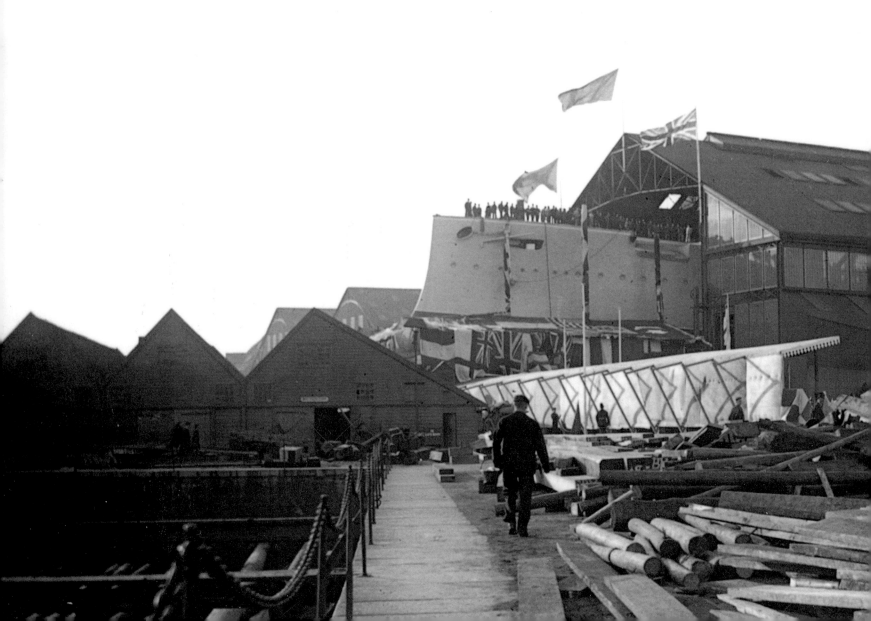

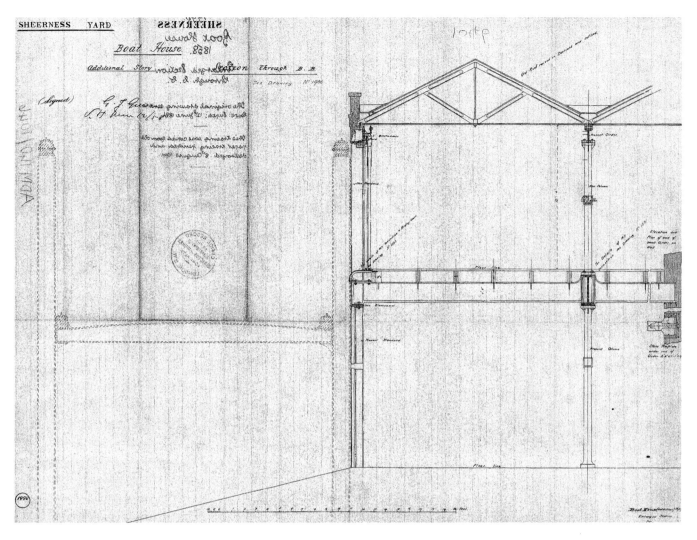

and the building was authorised at the Board visitation of July 1856. This building does not survive.

Next year in July two designs were produced for a completely new Boat Store, apparently versions with and without an external traveller; in October Walker had no objection to the first design, but thought it should be made 'a little broader than is necessary for the present longest Boats namely 42 feet'. In January 1858 he was bothered by the cost:

£25,000 appears to be a large and extravagant sum…I therefore submit whether this Estimate might be reduced by adopting the arrangement described by design No. 2…without the Travelling Cranes as proposed…By so doing more space will be left between the Boat House and No. 4 Dock…

The external travellers were abandoned. Unlike Greene's Smitheries, the Boat Store was a four-storey building, consisting of three aisles, each 45ft wide, as Walker had suggested. The central aisle was for the purpose of shifting the boats around, with a travelling crane at each level (Figures 126A, B and 127). This was a handling system much in advance of those available in other warehouses, either in the dockyards or outside.

Grissell's were supposed to have finished by 1 May 1859, but the penalties were not enforced by July, as the firm had made 'great exertions at great expense'. In that month it was decided to floor the Boat Store with old iron ballast, and the contractors were to finish the building with berthing at the west end,

cradles to take boats into the store, and the travellers. Treasury sanction for the final payment was given on 1 August 1860. The lessons of Beatson's Boat Store at Portsmouth were learnt. That had turned out to have a very limited value, because of a considerably narrower space, which did not run the whole length of the building, for handling the boats. Subsequent boat stores at Portsmouth reverted to earlier models, those built in 1875 and 1882 being weatherboarded single-storey timber buildings which would have fitted without notice into an eighteenth-century dockyard. (Figure 128).

There was nothing backward-looking in Greene's building, which has become a classic example of early iron-framed construction. The substantial exterior masonry walls of Beatson's building were discarded as unnecessary, as were the trussed beams. The construction was of repetitive units of cast iron standards and cross-beams and rivetted wrought iron longitudinal girders, with rigid bolted connections at the ends. The standards were of H section, enabling a more efficient mechanical connection to be made with the horizontal beams than if standards of circular section had been used, as had been the case in all earlier metal-frame structures except Greene's Slip No. 7 at Chatham. The use of standards of circular section was, like the Fox, Henderson slip roofs at Pembroke Dock, an example of transference of design directly from one constructional medium to another, without making full use of the properties of the new material. Greene's innovations in this respect do not appear to have attracted any notice in the

126B and **127**
The Boat Store. The interior and exterior. *(© Crown Copyright. NMR AA 98/0407, AA 98/04613)*

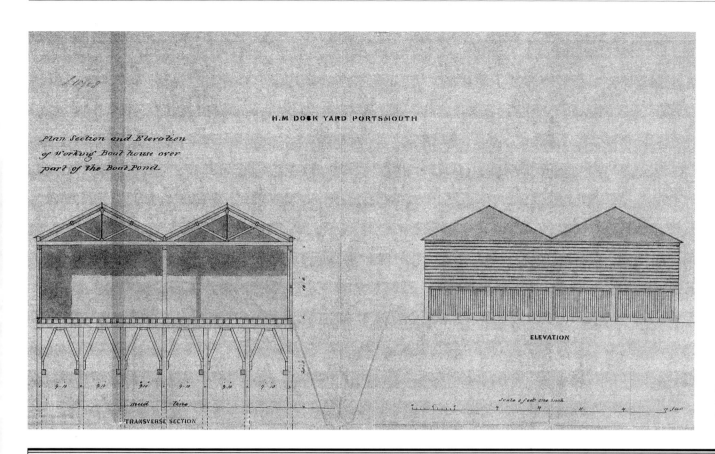

H.M DOCK YARD PORTSMOUTH

Plan Section and Elevation
of Working Boat house over
part of the Boat Pond.

ELEVATION

TRANSVERSE SECTION

128 The 1880s boat stores at Portsmouth, original drawings for which still survive. *(TNA ADM 1/5715)*

NEW MATERIALS

The upper floors of the Boat Store were wooden, fireproof construction not being aimed at here, but the outside of the building was clad in corrugated iron. By this time Admiralty architects had considerable experience with this material. In June 1850 the Patent Galvanised Iron Works, Millwall and Birmingham, wrote to the Admiralty soliciting for a certificate as to the durability of their products, they had supplied all the Yards. This was used as an occasion to obtain reports, which showed a very mixed state of affairs.

At Deptford the roofs over the Timber Shed had been covered in 1844, and a great number of sheets were already decaying, the galvanised coating was disappearing and rusting had begun. Painting was needed. The roof of No. 1 Slip of August 1845 was in a much better state. Humphrys reported that the Woolwich roofs were in excellent condition.

At Chatham, Lang (the Master Shipwright), Lawrie and Rivers were not very enthusiastic. The galvanised iron used there had been of two kinds, that of Messrs Morewood & Rogers, used plain on the roofs of Dock No. 2 and Slip No. 3, and the corrugated type manufactured by Messrs Malins & Rawlinson and used on the new roofs to Slips 4, 5 and 6. The former was placed in 1847, and a few of these sheets were decidedly rusty, with portions

of the iron surface corroded, while the zinc in other parts was decomposing in large patches, and in a short time the iron would be unprotected. The corrugated galvanised iron had been placed on the new slip roofs in 1848, and much rusting had subsequently occurred, deterioration being worst in the channels. Lawrie and Rivers forecast a short life for the covering, and expected heavy repairs to be required in 8 to 10 years:

> This seems to us so great a drawback, as to neutralise any advantage it might have on the score of cheapness in the first cost, or of lightness in the case of the corrugated Iron from its being used without a lining — How this latter may answer in heavy gales, we have not yet had sufficient experience to form a judgement.

At Portsmouth, Fincham and Mould had a much better experience, though the results had not been uniform: in one case a galvanised iron door of the new Chain Cable Store showed defects after only 10 months, and a coating of paint was applied to remedy the matter. On the other hand the galvanised iron used in 1847 for roofing HMS *Nelson*, which had since that date been lying in ordinary, still continued to be in very good condition, as did the iron on the

roofs over Slips 3, 4 and 5 erected in 1846. They could not offer a definite opinion after such a short time, but noted that the galvanising process had been very much improved.

From Devonport Captain Williams wrote that the new Steam Hammer Shop (erected in 1848-49 by Fox, Henderson), roofed with the corrugated material, was generally sound, but here and there defects were perceptible, apparently caused by blisters in the original manufacture. Two new houses on the Officers' Terrace, also erected in 1848-49, had been covered, remarkably for polite buildings, with Morewood & Rogers' plain galvanised tinned iron, laid with wooden rolls on boarding. He had nothing good to say about this material.

Master Shipwright Abethell wrote from Pembroke Dock that although some of the material had been in place for nearly four years, no deterioration was observable.

Greene clearly thought the cheapness of the material, together with the possibility of increased durability in future, made its use well worth while on the Boat Store. The manufacturers were confident too: exhibit no. 3 of Henry Vavasseur & Co., Sumner St, Southwark, at the International Exhibition of 1862 was a specimen of galvanised iron used on No. 1 slip, Portsmouth.[23]

contemporary technical press, any more than Scamp's in factory planning. This was probably because the world of the Royal Yards was perceived as self-contained, in spite of the extensive background of the senior engineering staff in private industry. This contemporary neglect has been made up for in recent times, with Greene being recognised by architectural and structural historians as a pioneer of functional design and a harbinger of the Modern Movement.

—⁓—

Notes:

1 A set of undated lithographed plans, showing the route of the tunnel at the Devonport end in relation to the properties above, was clearly prepared for this purpose.

2 WO 44/314, ADM 12/556, MFQ 218/6, UD 004972D, NMR PLM/113-124.

3 No drawings showing the musketry arrangements have been located, but it does not sound very conducive to the easy passage of traffic. In the 1854/5 estimates £35,000 was allowed for the tunnel. An undated album of lithographs was published at Plymouth showing plans and sections, 1853-54, with an alternative route marked. This shows that, as an alternative to having the line completely underground with subterranean defences, the opposite solution (plainly more practical given the purpose of the tunnel) had been adopted, namely exposing the area falling within the defence lines to the full, so as to lay it open to the maximum degree of fire.

4 ADM 12/572, WO 44/502, NMR PLM/126-7, ADM 1/5632, UD 004992/B, UD 004993/B, UD 004994/B, UD 005007/B, UD 005008/B, UD 005010/B, UD 005011/B, UD 005012/B, ADM 12/604.

5 ADM 12/604, NMR PLM/128-131, UD 004975/D, UD 004976/X, NMR PLM/132, NMR PLM/135, UD 004977/X, UD 004982/X, UD 004983/B, ADM 12/619, UD 004998/B, UD 004974/D, UD 004973/D, UD 004986/X.

6 BL Ms. Add. 495193, UD 004987/B, UD 005000/B, ADM 12/636, ADM 85/58, UD 005009/B, ADM 12/652, ADM 1/5697.

7 UD 004988/B, ADM 1/5929, ADM 1/5939, UD 11598/B, DRO(P) 1404, UD 004970/B, UD 005005/B; the later developments of the railway in the Yard are covered in P Burkhalter, *Devonport Dockyard Railway*, (Truro, 1996).

8 At the end of the year Mould reported a delay in the proceedings, and Fox, Henderson gave an explanation that has not been preserved; it may well have related to difficulties caused by this intrusive building. UP 333626, NMR PTM/1245, UP 333622, KH, ADM 12/540, ADM 85/6, NMR PTM/1244, NMM ADM/Y/P/140.

9 The underground flues and the furnaces had been designed by Nasmyth; the furnaces were highly thought of, but there had been frequent collapses of the firebricks in the crowns of the flues, and some alterations were suggested. Greene suspended work on the foundations as Nasmyth's plan 'did not take sufficient account of the soil, & so near such lofty chimnies & iron columns all built on concrete foundations & without piling'. This had been ordered together with a patent hydraulic crane capable of lifting 50 tons, traversing on an overhead railway, one end of which was supported by the steam hammer, the other on four cast iron columns. It was operated by a hydraulic reservoir supplied by two pumps that acted as a 'magazine of power'. Nasmyth was to resubmit the drawings with calculations for determining the adequacy of the foundations. By the summer of 1857 Murray was making drawings of the part of the roof around the central chimney that was to be covered with corrugated iron, and Greene was still at work on details of the central chimney in October.

10 ADM 12/556, UP 333467, 333515, 333516, 333519, 333520, 333522, 333523, 333524, 333535, 333624, 333629, 333631, 333632, 333633, 333638, KH, ADM 12/572, ADM 85/19, ADM 85/28, ADM 85/31, ADM 85/33, ADM 93/15, Nasmyth Order Book no. 1, ADM 12/640.

11 A reasonable number of detail drawings survive: most are signed by Greene or Murray, and none by the Fox, Henderson office. A count shows 14 by Greene, six by Murray, and two unattributed.

12 J Downie, 'Description of an Iron Construction of Foundry, and an improved process of moulding pipes and hollow cast ware', in *Proceedings of the Institution of Mechanical Engineers*, 1856, pp.164-172.

13 By September the Foundry had run to an excess of £3,173 5s 9d over the estimate, and the opinions of Officers were asked for on the number of gas fittings needed. Murray was still working on details of the internal arrangement of the base of the chimney shaft in 1862: probably it was another instance of a chimney failing to come up to expectations.

14 ADM 87/56, ADM 84/17, ADM 12/636, POR/R/35, ADM 93/16, ADM 93/17, NMR PTM/1244, NMR PTM/1180-3, NMM ADM/Y/P/136, POR/R/34, CHA/H/107, ADM 12/700, ADM 87/76, NMR PTM/1185.

15 In October 1854 the Admiralty bought the rights for the past, present and future use of Ireland's patent cupola for £150, and were supplied with instructions and drawings. They were immediately installed at Woolwich, where the consumption of coke was reduced from 3.5-4cwt per ton of iron melted to 2.3-3cwt per ton. In preparing the new Foundry, user reaction to Ireland's design was canvassed; the Superintendent of the Royal Laboratory, Woolwich, reported a great improvement effected in the quantity melted for less coke burnt. The performance in the other Yards was even better than that of Woolwich; at Keyham Factory it was 1.5cwt per ton and at Sheerness during 1857/8 it had been 1.5cwt per ton, during 1858/9 2cwt per ton. Murray's cupolas were performing at the rate of 4cwt per ton, so the adoption of Ireland's design for the new Foundry was certain. ADM 85/20, ADM 84/13, ADM 85/54, ADM 85/52, WORK 41/418-20, ADM 12/619, ADM 12/636.

16 CHA/H/83, ADM 12/764, ADM 12/652, ADM 140/115/3, ADM 1/5715, POR/R/34, KH, ADM 12/732, UP 333628, UP 333636, UP 333514, UP 333518, UP 333547, UP 333540, UP 333619, UP 333623, UP 333625, ADM 12/748, UP 333513, UP 333543, UP 333918, UP 333527, UP 333544, UP 333525, ADM 12/748, UP 333630, ADM 1/5930, UP 333637, UP 335526, UP 333511, UP 333541, UP 333620, UP 333542, UP 333539, UP 333536, KH, NMR PTM/1238.

17 CHA/H/62, ADM 12/540.

18 Baker & Son again got the contract for excavating and constructing the masonry slip and its related tunnel, and by the end of September Greene had prepared drawings for the piling for the floor of the slip and the wharf wall. Baker's at once found that the plans presented some difficulties, and, with their recent fiasco at Chatham in mind (see p.49), wrote at once to Greene. Rivers was ordered by Greene to report back. He stated that it would make the job easier if the piling system was slightly altered. In the event this did not serve, and piling with whole timbers instead of half timbers was employed. By the following February the pits for the outer standards were about to be started. These originally were to have counterforts between them, but it was decided that these could be dispensed with and the spaces very carefully filled with suitable material, well rammed. The Estimates for 1852/3 included £20,000 for the slip and the mast tunnel, £10,000 for the roof and the travellers, and £500 for oak block paving between Slips 3, 4, 5 and 6. CHA/H/83, NMM S/90, NMM S/114, CHA/H/84, CHA/H/85.

19 CHA/H/85, CHA/H/86, NMM S/82, NMM S/92, NMM S/93, CHA/H/86, ADM 140/66/1-8, CHA/H/87, CHA/H/88, CHA/H/89, ADM 12/572.

20 CHA/C/2, ADM 87/56, NMM S/126, NMM J/42, NMM S/89, CHA/H/92.

21 CHA/H/146.

22 CHA/H/107, NMM J/44, NMM S/50, CHA/H/119, NMM P/32, NMM P/29, ADM 12/812, CHA/H/148, CHA/H/146; Sir William Laird Clowes, *The Royal Navy*, vol. 7, p.24, (London, 1903), gives the thickness of the armour as 2in, and appears to be the principal source for stating that this was the first armoured deck to be built into a ship; the section of the *Endicott Report on Fortifications*, Washington, D.C., 1886, which deals with characteristics of principal foreign warships, gives the deck armour as $1/1^{1}/_{2}$in (pp.108-109); NMM S/118, NMM S/66, NMM P/33, NMM S/67.

23 A full account of the design and historical significance of the Boat Store is A W Skempton, 'The Boat Store, Sheerness (1858-60) and its place in structural history', in *Transactions of the Newcomen Society*, 1960, pp.57-78. ADM 140/1044-6, ADM 140/1328-1332, ADM 85/45, ADM 12/619, ADM 12/668, ADM 12/684, ADM 92/19, ADM 83/63, *Illustrated Catalogue of International Exhibition of 1862*, (London, 1862), part 6, p.25.

CHAPTER 11

Mechanisation Supreme

The mechanisation of the Sawmills

A large proportion of woodworking shops in the eighteenth century were ephemeral buildings, clustered around building slips, and which have left no traces. Others were located in non-specific buildings that have since been used for other purposes, again leaving no trace. For example, the semi-quadrangular storehouses at Portsmouth of 1786 included workspaces for shipwrights, wheelwrights, carpenters and joiners. As has been seen, Brunel's steam-powered sawmills at Chatham came into operation in 1814, but timber continued to be converted into planks by hand into the second half of the nineteenth century. Logs were cut over sawpits by pairs of sawyers using double-handed saws. Protection from the weather was given by open timber sheds; again, none of these have survived. However, the surviving North Saw Pits of 1825 at Sheerness were covered by one of the earliest free-standing iron frame buildings (later infilled with brick). In the same year a second iron-framed fireproof woodworking shop was added behind the three main dry docks. This was an integrated carpentry shop containing three sets of sawpits separated by timber seasoning sheds, with carpenters' shops, timber stores and mould loft on the first floor, and additional storage space in the attic. These buildings may well have been designed by Holl and constructed after his death.

In England, the development of woodworking machinery had lagged behind that of machine tools, with the exception of the blockmaking machinery, which remained unique for some 40 years. In 1845 Captain Beatson installed a sawing machine at the Portsmouth sawmills which was pneumatically powered, but the system proved a failure. The next piece of sophisticated woodworking equipment appears to have been Cochrane's sawing machine, delivered at Woolwich in September 1847. This was a most elaborate device, capable of cutting curved ships' timbers, and its performance in the Yard was favourably commented on by the contemporary technical press; it clearly needed a highly skilled operator to run and maintain it. More user-friendly and less expensive equipment was needed, and in the Great Exhibition it was the simple and cheap American machinery that attracted attention.

In 1848 Captain James drew up plans, in association with Engineer Thomas Miller, for a new sawmill at Portsmouth. This was a conservative design of massive appearance, which drew its power from the adjacent 80hp factory engine (Figure 60). The six reciprocating saws 'could get through eight to ten logs daily, doing the work of sixteen pairs of sawyers'.

Though the sawmills at Chatham and Portsmouth were efficient, other wood processing shops were backward when compared with private trade. Captain Milne identified the woodworking shops in particular as ill-equipped and archaic, with no machinery at all in use in some of the joiners' shops. In the summer of 1853 he visited the Yards in company with Baldwin Walker and Greene. At Sheerness he ordered that no work should be done by hand in the sawpits that could be done in the Mills; the investment in the machinery was to be recouped as much as possible, even if this meant laying off sawyers. The Devonport Sawmills, which had been supplied with Burnett's planing and moulding machine as recently as 1850, were particularly unsatisfactory: this was one of the places where the joiners performed every operation by hand. There were only two sawing frames, one bench circular saw and two others for minor purposes; this had seemed an adequate number to Lloyd in 1838, but no longer fitted the bill. All the timber had to be moved in and out through a single door, with the attendant inconveniences. It will be remembered that the location of this building had been determined by the proximity of steam power in the Millwrights' Shop, but Lloyd must have miscalculated on this point as well, for when the engine was fully at work driving the machinery of the Shop there was not enough power to drive the saws properly as well. The planing machine was to be driven by the same engine; in the circumstances this was obviously a useless arrangement. The Sawmills were also badly placed, away from the timber stacks. The modernisation of the Sawmills in all the Yards accordingly became, under Admiralty initiative, a priority project for the 1850s.

At the same time as the Admiralty party were inspecting the Yards the Master Shipwright at Chatham, Francis Laire, and the Chief Engineer, Alexander Lawrie, were dispatched to tour the country looking at the latest equipment. At Portsmouth they were impressed by the sight of Burnett's large planing machine at work. This had been installed in 1850, and planed both sides, and both edges, at the same time. It processed common boarding at the rate of 80ft per minute, and deck planks at the rate of 50ft per minute. It also cut mouldings, as well as rebates and grooves, of every size and form very well. However, like Cochrane's sawing machine, it was rather complicated, and great care was required in working it. They considered that an active and intelligent workman ought to be selected and sent from Chatham to be instructed in its use, so that a similar machine being sent from Devonport could go to work at once. At the Joiners' Shop they saw the new tenoning and power mortising machines being set to work for the first time: the first performed to their satisfaction, but not the second.

They continued to Liverpool to look over Furness's workshops and inspect his widely publicised range of tools (Figure 129). The planing machine was very compact, though providing only the degree of levelling attainable with an adze. It made a very smooth job, however, but not good enough to be painted without further preparation. It would nevertheless be very useful, as only a little cleaning up was required afterwards; indeed, its work would be adequate for most purposes. It planed only one side and the edges in the first operation, but then the other side could be passed through the machine and planed without injury to the finished side. Its great

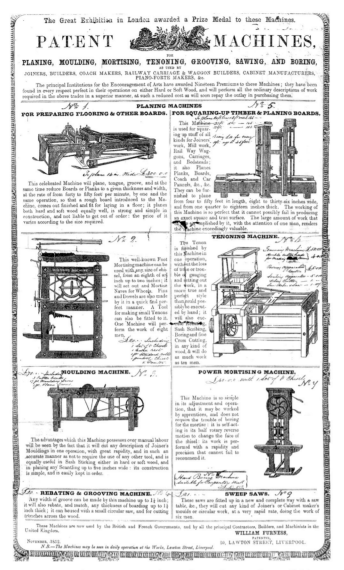

virtues were that it was simple, easily understood, not liable to break or get out of repair, and as the cost was only £300 it would be a very good and useful machine in a sawmill where it was not necessary to have one so elaborate as Burnett's. The machine would also tongue, groove, rebate, and plane the edges to a bevel, and also strike mouldings up to a very large size. A piece of moulding 8in deep could be very smoothly worked. The only drawback was in the size of the workpiece it would take: only up to 3in thickness, whereas deals used in the Yards were mostly 4in and sometimes 5in thick. To handle these the machine would need some modifications, but these would present no difficulty, though the price would be increased a little.

The foot mortising machine was thought a more useful instrument than the power mortising machine; it was in constant use at Laird's shipbuilding yard in Birkenhead, and highly thought of by the operators. The moulding machine was compact, and would be very useful in a joiners' shop. It was simple and easily changed from one pattern to another, and in addition to striking them, it planed the flat and edges of the moulding.

Laire and Lawrie were most impressed with the tenoning machine. It made plugs in a very convenient manner, greatly superior to the machine in use at Portsmouth, which required the pieces to be previously cut and sawn to the size, while the Furness machine cut the plug at once from a piece of board whose thickness corresponded to the length of plug required. It was also a multi-purpose tool, functioning as a boring machine, and a circular saw could be attached for cross-cutting small pieces. It would only cut short pieces off, of 6 or 7in, but they thought that with a bit of tweaking it would cross-cut rails of any length. A cutter attachment was also available for making gratings. A specimen turned out by the machine was well made, and came truly together. Lawrie and Laire took it away as a sample. Altogether the tenoning machine was an impressive piece of woodworking technology. The sweep saw appeared to be ingenious and likely to be very useful.

The visit was not solely for the purpose of seeing woodworking machinery; they also visited the Albert and Queen Docks to see Armstrong's hydraulic cranes and hoist in operation, and were impressed with their performance. At the Mersey Iron Company (Messrs Horsfall and Company) they saw demonstrated a patent system of rolling tapered iron for ships' knees and other components, and considered that this could be usefully incorporated at the Chatham Metal Mills. Although it did not perform all the processes for making knees, it would be useful for many other pieces of shipwright's ironwork, such as crutches.

They recommended the purchase of the planing machine for Yards that had not been supplied with one, and the acquisition of a set of foot mortising machines, tenoning machines and sweep saws by every joiners' shop; these would effect a great deal of labour-saving. A single moulding machine should go to every Yard. In addition, they were very pleased with the performance of the hydraulic machinery, and were confirmed in the opinion that the pair of hydraulic cranes being constructed for Chatham Wharf wall would be extremely valuable pieces of equipment.[1]

In June 1854 a serious fire partially destroyed Brunel's Chatham Sawmills, and Greene decided after an inspection to rebuild on the same site. Lawrie went to Woolwich to see what new machinery was available. Improvements had taken place there: one of the saw frames had been altered to make it available for cutting curved work. For the rebuilt Chatham Mills Lawrie designed an oar-making machine, which was built for £135, and was ready for work in September 1856. This became one of the sights of the place, being described by Dickens as:

…set with knives and saws and planes, which cut smooth and straight here, and slantwise there, and now cut such a depth, and now miss cutting altogether, according to the predestined requirements of the pieces of wood that are pushed on below them…[a] wonderful sight.[2]

In October 1854 McDowall & Sons of Johnstone were ordered to supply three sawing frames for £2,275, with wrought iron moving frames, two powered by independent steam engines; Woolwich Factory constructed a high-pressure boiler for the machinery. The need for modernisation was pressing, and in April 1855 Greene noted that it was urgently necessary that Pembroke Dock Sawmills be completed within the year. To simplify the preliminary arrangements the Woolwich and Chatham Mills, which were considered to be the most up to date, were to be taken as standards for the arrangement of

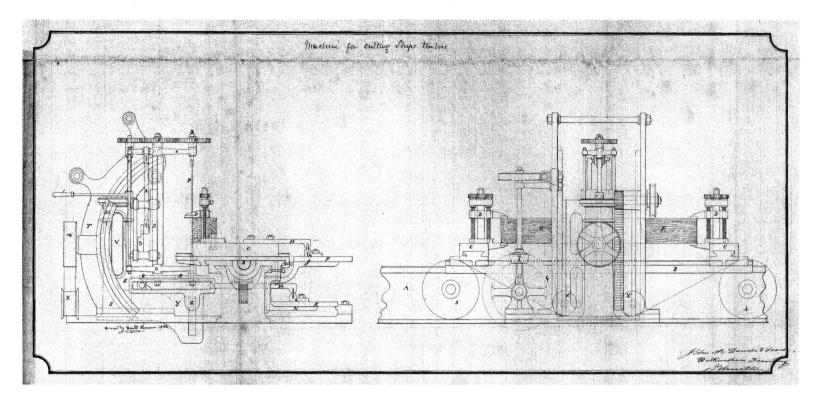

Machine for cutting Ships timbers

machinery. In July 1856 the Joiners' shop at Chatham was equipped only with a hand mortising machine, a steam tenoning machine, and a circular saw, but more formidable equipment was on order for the Sawmills. McDowall's had a curvilinear sawing machine in hand, for cutting ships' timbers according to templates; it unfortunately proved to have insurmountable teething problems (Figure 130).

Other, less ambitious equipment made by them proved to be

more satisfactory, and their mortising and tenoning machines were ordered after having been seen at work at Woolwich Arsenal. A satisfactory curvilinear saw frame had been developed by the end of the decade by James Horn of London, and a building to house it was included in the 1859/60 estimates. The machine cost £925, and was finally delivered by the end of February 1861.[3]

The new Sawmills built at all the Yards in the late 1850s, of which those at Sheerness and Devonport remain today, all had the same general design, dictated by the nature of the woodworking machinery (Figure 132). James's massive and costly Portsmouth Sawmills, rather than the cheap building at Devonport, was taken by Greene as the model. The fire at Chatham was responsible for this, ensuring that fireproof construction was stipulated. They were rectangular buildings

130 McDowall's curvilinear sawing machine was another over-ambitious piece of equipment. *(TNA ADM 85/39)*

131 The cast-iron framework to the sawmill at Sheerness Dockyard, showing the shrink rings applied to the lugs cast at the floor joints. *(© Crown Copyright. NMR BB 94/20844)*

WOODWORKING MACHINES

At Woolwich, where all the woodworking facilities were contained in a single building, the following machines were introduced between 1854 and 1857:

two cross-cut saws;
a turning lathe;
a planing machine;
a rotating planing machine;
a foot mortising machine;
a tenoning machine;
a joiners moulding machine;
a power mortising machine;
machines for rabbeting and grooving, cutting plugs, and cutting grooves in jalousie frames;
a Nasmyth's planing machine (not an Admiralty order, but seized as a Russian prize);
two 1 ton cranes, a portable steam engine and pumps, an elevator, a 6hp high-pressure engine and boiler;
hand mortising and wood turning machines;
a boring machine;
a sawing machine with curvilinear gear;
an open-sided sawing machine;
a small sawing machine;
a machine for preparing rough timber.

132 The Sawmill at Devonport. By contrast with the variety of designs for other building types in the Yards, sawmills were relatively standardised. *(Ministry of Defence)*

(brick at Sheerness, ashlar at Devonport) with internal iron frames of large round tapering columns with shrink rings holding the floor joists (Figure 131). The roofs were of composite construction with wrought-iron trusses and cast-iron struts. Engine and boiler houses lay to one side; the saw frames were placed centrally along the building (Figure 133). A basement, open to the air at both ends of the building, housed the foundations for the machines, which in the case of curvilinear saw frames were of considerable size, and had to be deeply set to withstand the continuous severe vibration. It also housed the shafting and belt drives. Water collected in these pits, and so pumping apparatus had to be provided. Easton & Amos supplied the vertical saw frames and circular saws, James Horn the curvilinear ones, and McDowall's the planing machines. In dedicated sawmills such as these there was no other equipment; all other operations were performed in the Joiners' shops, which were located on the first floors of these buildings.

The Sheerness Sawmills were contracted for by Rigby's (exclusive of the ironwork) and Fox, Henderson, who were ready to fix the basement columns and first floor girders in November 1856. Sawdust was moved on an endless web from the sawpits to the furnaces to be used as fuel: this was an idea that had impressed Lawrie when he saw it in action at Liverpool. In November 1854 plans and estimates were ordered to be prepared for the new Devonport Sawmills, and the contract for the metalwork (together with that of the South Smithery) was secured by Fox, Henderson in November 1855. The Mills were ready for service in December 1858. Despite the precautions, a fire in February 1865 involved repairs to the tune of £814.[4]

By the end of the decade Milne's programme of modernisation in the Sawmills and Joiners' Shops had been carried out. The woodworking facilities of all the Yards were now mechanised and supplied with up-to-date machinery. The metalworking shops also now needed to be brought up to a uniform standard, and in particular the discrepancy between the brand new Keyham Factory and the facilities available in the South Yard at Devonport needed to be addressed.

The Devonport Smitheries

The Smitheries at Devonport had been overtaken by the technology of Keyham, and the South Smithery, which dated back to 1776, needed an effective rebuilding. In December 1854 Mr Hopper, the Clerk of Works, put forward his suggestions. He noted that in the present Smitheries there were four first-class or Anchor fires, 15 double and 62 single fires, making a total of 81 fires in the two shops, 11 of which were almost useless because of their confined position. The proposed New Smithery would occupy the whole area of the present South Smithery, Drill and Fire Hearth Shop, Steam Engine and Fan Rooms, Iron Store and Chain Cable Cleaning machine. It would contain four first-class or Anchor fires, 15 double and 68 single, together with a blast furnace, making a total of 88 fires. Three steam hammers were to be placed so as to be handy for any of the fires. However, Edye and Trickett objected to these arrangements as being inconvenient. They did not consider that a blast furnace should be fitted, and thought that two steam hammers would suffice, though the Master Smith held the blast furnace to be necessary.

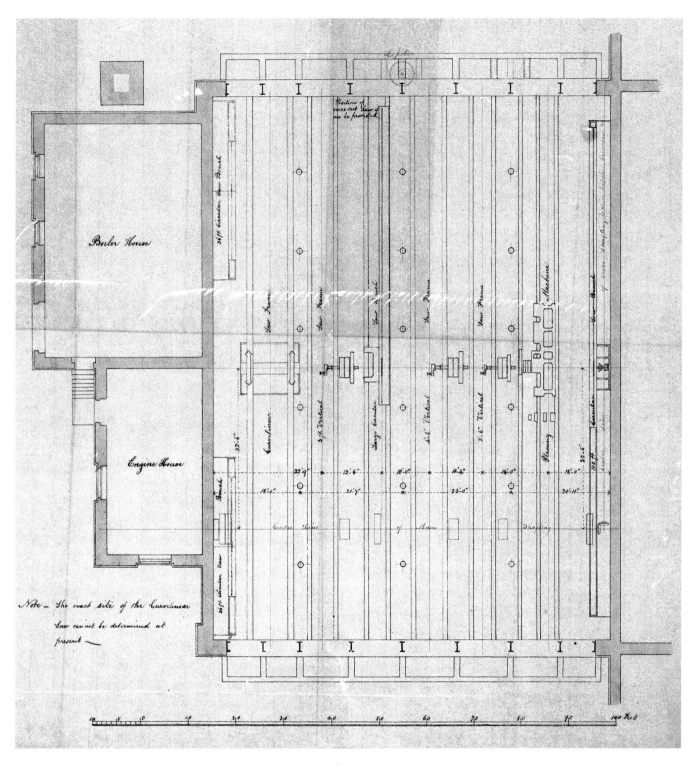

133 A plan of the Sheerness Sawmill, dated April 1856. *(TNA ADM 95/97)*

By 20 January 1855 two plans had been drawn up, which differed in many respects (the difference is unknown), and Greene's plan was selected. A revision of this allowed for a provision of 66 forges, two small steam hammers, and a large drill shop with a vice and fitting shop over. The design, another impressive demonstration of Fox, Henderson's structural ironwork, resembled a smaller version of Greene's Portsmouth Smithery, having an inner square of H-section standards, connected at the top to rectangular open lattice girders, as used by Greene on the No. 7 slip roof. The corner chimneys of the Portsmouth building were repeated but the great central stack was omitted (Figures 134A, B and 135).

By September 1856 Hopper could report that:

The new Smithery is progressing very favourably; the 4 Chimneys will be finished in about 3 weeks one half the lower roof is fixed & will be in a very forward state by the time the Chimneys are completed and the scaffolding removed, there will then only remain the slating, skylights & windows to complete the present contract…the slates for the whole of the Building are on the ground.

The presence of the old Smithery caused difficulties, as the main access to it was through the centre of the new works, and it had to remain operating. Next month Scamp wrote to Hopper that the construction of the part adjacent to the old building could no longer be deferred, and that he should if

134A and **B**
Interior and exterior
of the Devonport
Smithery. *(© Crown
Copyright. NMR BB
96/038545)*

possible make arrangements for constructing the standards and the roof. The brickwork between the standards could be deferred. However, Trickett and Edye replied that the putting-up of the walls or even the standards to take the roof over the Drilling Shop would be a complete barrier to carrying on the works at the Smithery. They added that a high-pressure boiler would need to be installed to drive the Nasmyth hammers, as the boilers in the adjacent Sawmills were low pressure and could not be used for this purpose. The new structure would not permit the use of some of the archaic machinery that was still working in the old Smithery.

> The rude way in which the Anchors are now forged…with the Hercules or Ring Monkey…requires the whole force of the Shop to work it, frequently amounting to 60 men…this is usually performed in large private establishments by a Steam Hercules…the present Hercules is worked by Ropes over a pulley fixed in the roof, which could not be done in the New Building.

Hopper suggested that the Hercules be operated by steam from the steam hammer boilers.

Ancient machinery also survived at Portsmouth, where there were two more hand-operated Hercules. The high roofs of Greene's two Smitheries were conceived for equipment that was a qualitative leap from these old devices and did not have to be suspended from massive trusses or wall brackets; in 1860 a 30 ton steam hammer was to be called for at Portsmouth. By March 1857 £7,828 had been spent on the new Smithery. Other manufacturers besides Nasmyth were now producing steam hammers, and a Condie's patent steam hammer was delivered to Sheerness (Figure 136). Two Hercules were still present in the original Smithery there, doubtless replaced by this machine. A new Yard Smithery, another metal-framed

structure, had been built up against the old one at Sheerness, and a difference of opinion arose between the Master Shipwright and the Chief Engineer, Mr Blaxland, over some of the internal arrangements. In the event Blaxland's plan was approved; he had used on a small scale the methods of the Quadrangle, taking 'advantage…of the present Iron Standards and walls…for carrying the shafting.'[5]

The Factories and Smitheries in production

Control over all these buildings was divided between the Chief Engineer and the Master Shipwright of each Yard. This division was not effected wholly logically: the Shipwrights were determined to retain as much territory as possible in the new era of naval architecture. All the machinery, in both departments, was under the chief engineer, but he had no control over, or hand in the selection of, the men who worked it, in the trades belonging to the Master Shipwright. The men in the Sawmills and Block Mills at Portsmouth had in fact been selected by Murray between 1846 and 1849, with a resulting increase in production, and the Smithery at Devonport was under Miller, the Chief Engineer there, during the same period, but the Master Shipwrights had fought a rearguard action and regained this authority. In fact Lloyd thought the arrangement at Devonport did not work well.

By 1858 the determination of the Shipwrights to hold as much turf as possible had produced a crop of, as seen by the Chief Engineers, anomalies. The Shipwrights' Department at Portsmouth controlled the Brass and Iron Foundries (which the Engineers admitted worked smoothly), the Millwrights' Shop, which made bolts, hinges, screws, yokes and steering wheel fittings, but no engine parts, and also the condenser shop.

These arrangements seem to have varied from yard to yard. At Chatham the Millwrights' Shop, together with the sawyers

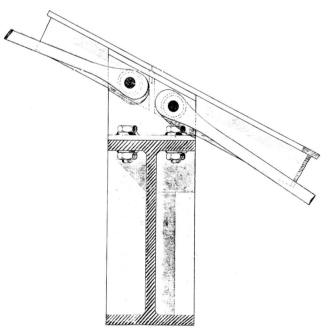

135 Detail of a joint, from the roof of the Devonport Smithery, showing the symmetrical I-section beams that represented a considerable structural advance from earlier types that were strengthened by parabolic bottom flanges. These were utilised in the rigid frames developed at the Quadrangle and the Sheerness Boat Store. *(Adapted from Fiche 333622, Devonport Management Ltd.)*

136 Condie's steam hammer, as supplied to Sheerness Dockyard. *(Derived from TNA ADM 85/40)*

137 Here are some of the typical iron components required for wooden ships, in this case HMS *Renown*. The introduction of steam machinery into wooden hulls led to an increase in their number. *(TNA ADM 87/66)*

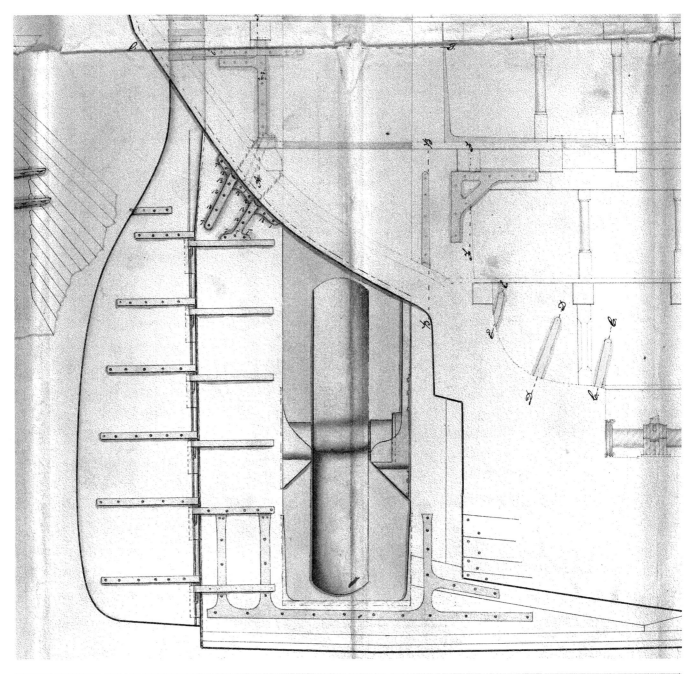

138 Metal components on HMS *Princess Royal* in 1854 included water tanks and structural ties including these trussed beams. *(TNA ADM 87/47)*

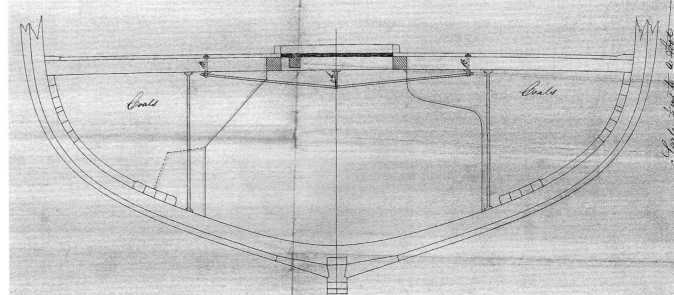

and the operators of the oar-making machine (but not the joiner who worked the planing machine), were under the Chief Engineer. At Devonport the division between the two departments appeared more plausible because of the physical separation of the Factory at Keyham from the South Yard, and Trickett had no objection to the Millwrights' Shop remaining under the Master Shipwright, as long as the cost was no greater than it would be at the Factory. He did think, though, that more work would be got through if he had the supervising of it. The division also extended to fitting out steamers. Those being completed by contractors had the boilers and machinery put in by Yard labourers under the Master Attendant; those being completed by the Factory had them installed by Factory men. When iron ships came into the Yards the Master Shipwright and Chief Engineer made a joint report, and hull repairs were done by the boilermakers.

Atherton considered that the Shipwrights' Department should be capable of performing all the processes required to build a ship, with the exception of foundry work, though he doubted whether the current Master Shipwrights had the experience to supervise metalworking. There did not seem to be the same eagerness to replace manual labour by machinery as was the case in the Factory. The Ryder's forge at Woolwich Yard Smithery, introduced at the request of the master smith, had not done a week's work in the three years that had elapsed since its installation, while two similar machines in the Factory Smithery were constantly in use.[6]

What were these buildings actually producing? The Yard Smitheries under the Master Shipwrights made metal components for wooden ships; as yet no iron ship had been built in a Royal Yard. Knees, crutches, anchors, capstan spindles, pillars and other items such as strengthening pieces required in the conversion of sailing line-of-battle ships to steam were made with Nasmyth hammers, whose introduction had almost everywhere been the cause of great economies.

In March 1852 a survey was made of the performance of the hammers. Before their introduction at Woolwich in the years 1846 and 1847, 145½ tons of ironwork were forged in the Yard Smithery by the Hercules and tilt hammers, at an average cost for labour of £6 16s 3d per ton. In 1850 and 1851 165¼ tons were made by the 30cwt Nasmyth at a cost of £4 4s 9d per ton. Furthermore, the work done by the Nasmyths was generally of a more elaborate nature, and if the work had been similar the difference in cost would have been much greater. Twenty by two inch eyes for stopper ring bolts were made in one day for the *Agamemnon* by the Nasmyths at a labour cost of £1 3s 7d; had they been forged by hand they would have taken two men 10 days at a cost of £4 2s 6d. If the hammers were removed at least 50 hands would have to be taken on, and the work would not be as well done. Chatham estimated that the saving of manual labour at the fires might be taken at 50 per cent on heavy work. Nearly everybody in the shop was now familiar with the working of the 12cwt hammer, and it was not necessary to detail a man to work it.

The same story was repeated by the other Yards, with the exception of Devonport, where three hammers had been installed in the South Smithery in 1848, and had never been used since being tried, though that in the North Smithery was worked profitably. Walker put this down to lack of information and experience, and suggested that the Master Smith be sent to

Woolwich for training, though this cannot have had much effect, as the hammers were still not in use in 1855, when it was suggested that they be transferred to Keyham.

Tanks for storing fresh water on board were more metal fittings that needed fabrication and repair. These were nothing new, however, having been invented by Richard Trevithick in 1808. Characteristically, he failed to profit from this, but the tanks were well established on ships by 1833 when a purpose-built facility for their storage and maintenance at the Royal Clarence Victualling Yard was designed by Taylor. The structural use of trussed beams has been noted in several buildings, and this technique was transferred to naval architecture to support hatchways, as seen in the beams fitted to *Princess Royal* at Portsmouth in 1854, another example of shipwrights' ironwork.[7]

On 26 December 1854 Admiralty Circular 177 was issued, which when acted upon was indirectly a contributory cause of another new type of shipwrights' work, this time in wood:

> The Steam Ships of Her Majesty's Navy being frequently at the present time employed on urgent services, and on voyages of considerable length, where Coals are expensive and difficult to be obtained, it becomes a matter of great…importance that Commanding Officers should give their best attention to the subject of employing, on all proper occasions…the power of Sail in conjunction with Steam…it is obvious that Steam should never be used when the service can equally well be performed without it — that Sail should never be dispensed with when it can be usefully employed to assist the Steam — and that *full* Steam Power should not be employed when reduced power would answer equally well. It is by a judicious combination of Sail and Steam that an Officer will best display his judgment…Instances have occurred in which Ships have been improperly forced head to wind by the full power of Steam, and have expended all their store of fuel before the end of the voyage…

This was reinforced in 1856 by Circular 263, which directed that steam power should be used only when the service of the ship could not be performed without it. As a consequence, when the screw was not kept in regular work, considerable difficulty was experienced in the bearings of the shafts of propellers, which had stood still for several hours or even days. An attempt was made in wooden ships with copper sheathing to protect the wrought iron screw shaft by a brass casing, wherever exposed to the action of the sea water; however, the electrolytic reaction with the copper caused serious and rapid corrosion of the iron shaft, and its bearings soon became injured. A similar, though less serious, reaction also took place in iron vessels, and the shaft was consequently cased throughout with a brass tube. However, the friction and wear of the bearings were very great, sometimes amounting to as much as an inch in the course of a few months.

John Penn, the marine engineer and manufacturer, conducted a series of experiments on bearing materials, and found lignum vitae to be the most satisfactory material. The *Himalaya*, which had experienced very serious wear, was fitted by P&O with the bearings almost immediately after Penn's discovery of the remedy. The ship, then purchased by the Admiralty as a troopship, steamed 20,000 miles in her first 10

139 *Himalaya* demonstrated the practical efficacy of the lignum vitae bearings. In this contemporary picture, which misrepresents her proportions, she is also advertising patent wire ropes. *(TNA ADM 87/54)*

139 *Himalaya* demonstrated the practical efficacy of the lignum vitae bearings. In this contemporary picture, which misrepresents her proportions, she is also advertising patent wire ropes. *(TNA ADM 87/54)*

months' service with no signs of wear. In January 1855 drawings showing the fitting of screw propeller bearings with lignum vitae were sent to all the Yards, and in March the Surveyor submitted that the material be used in all cases if the construction permitted. New work was thereby created for the Joiners' Shops. Iron ships still had many significant wooden components, such as the engine bearers of HMS *Greenock*, which were of African teak 2ft 1in deep (Figure 140), and so the Sawmills still had plenty of work to do.[8]

Variations in design of shipwrights' work from Yard to Yard had developed over the years In an attempt to rationalise this, in June 1854 a set of drawings of fittings manufactured from iron, brass and wood was prepared at Portsmouth, and the

processes were broken down to show the relative costs of manufacture. Considerable savings could be effected if cast iron was used (Figure 141). For example, a gun-training eyebolt and socket, all of wrought iron, cost 11s 11¼d; with the eyebolt of wrought iron and the socket of cast iron, it cost 8s 6d.

A seaman could tell at which Yard a Navy ship had been fitted out by looking at major pieces of equipment and tackle, and in October 1860 a survey of these practices was carried out. Devonport and Portsmouth, for instance, had their own variants on the Admiralty pattern anchor, and quite different arrangements for catting and fishing them, which meant that men transferred from one smithery to another had to learn a new set of practices (Figure 142).

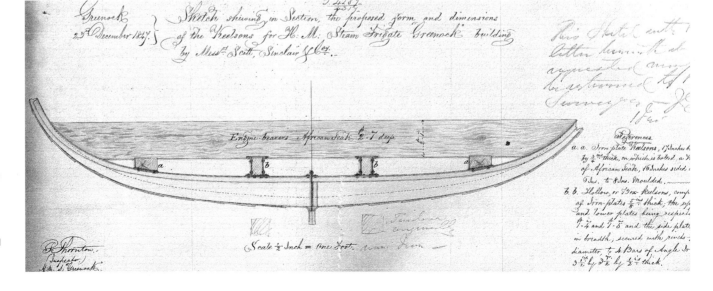

140 The teak engine bearers of HMS *Greenock*, typical of some of the massive pieces of timber needed to be worked into an iron ship. *(TNA ADM 83/48)*

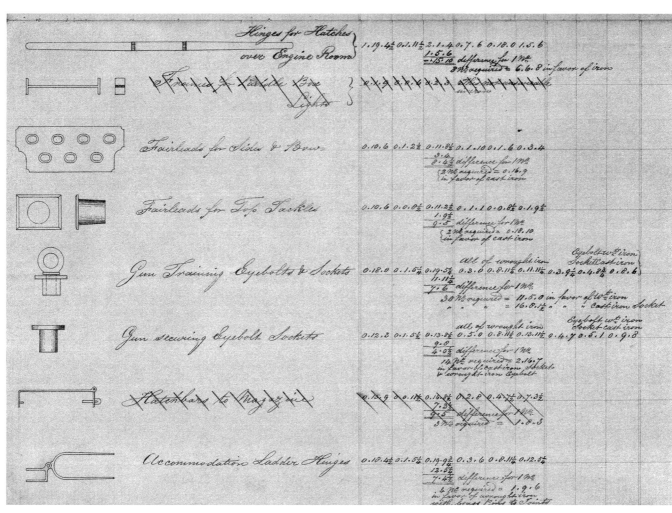

141 This shows
standard
components, made
in different ways at
each Yard, with the
relative costings.
(TNA ADM 87/48)

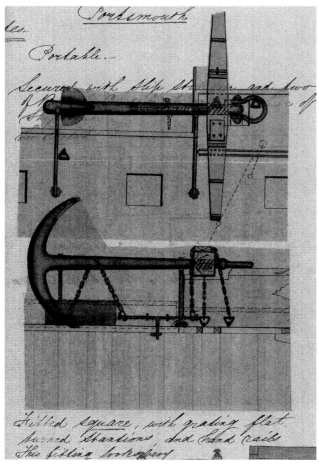

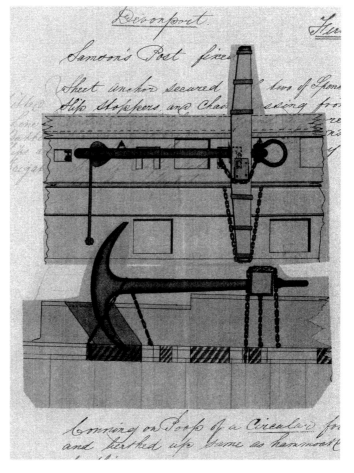

142 This shows the
differing ways in
which anchors were
catted and fished at
Portsmouth and
Devonport, and the
difference in the iron
components.
(TNA ADM 87/76)

It is not known how seriously attempts were made to bring about uniformity in this respect. The carving of figureheads remained the preserve of a few family firms, and the practice continued well into the age of steam: Hellyer & Son carved an up-to-date *Rifleman* with trousers, shako and rifle for £7 10s in 1845, and later produced a fine portrait for *Royal Albert* (Figure 143).[9]

The principal products of the Factories were new and repaired boilers, both for marine engines and for land engines. The design of boilers developed, and the Factories had to cope with the whole range of types, varying from the archaic leaky boilers of the unlucky *James Watt*, which, Murray wrote in January 1855, would have to be taken out 'on account of the objectionable arrangement as well as insufficient mode in

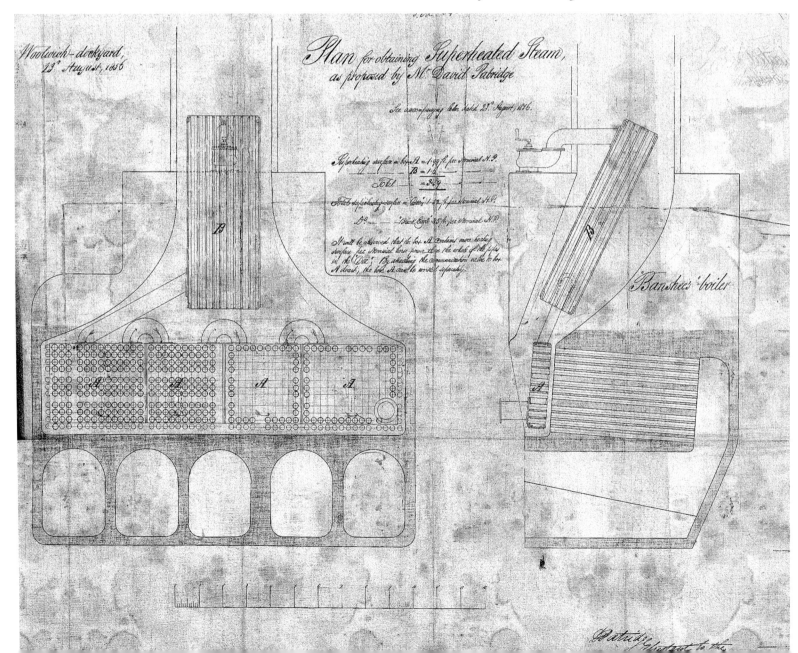

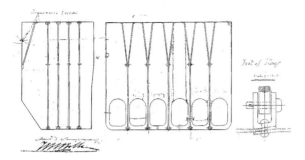

145 Arrangements of stays in the boilers of *James Watt (From TNA ADM 85/22)*

which the stays are attached to the bottom', to the sophisticated superheated steam boiler designed at Woolwich in August 1856 by Atherton's senior assistant, David Patridge, for testing in the fast packet boat *Banshee* (Figures 144, 145).

Two widely differing types of boiler for powering workshop machinery were the high-pressure single-flue boiler supplied by Fox, Henderson to drive the fan engines at Pembroke Dock Smithery in 1846, worn out by 1859, incorporating internal structural ironwork that might have been components of one of their buildings, and the cylindrical twin-flue boiler with a dome for Chatham Sawmills in 1859 (Figure 146).

Industrial machinery, as previously noted, was often made in the Factories, which helped each other: tools for the trenail

mooting machine at Woolwich were supplied by Portsmouth, and Woolwich constructed machinery similar to that in use at Portsmouth for bending copper pipes for Devonport. Travelling cranes were made at Woolwich for use there and for Portsmouth Factory. Sometimes private firms were given a hand as well. In January 1848 boilers for the *Fairy* were held up by a strike of the boiler plate makers, and Penn's were supplied with a set from Woolwich, on the condition that they replaced them later. The face plate made at Woolwich for the large Whitworth lathe was used to face the screw of the *Agamemnon*. The screw had also been cast and bored there, but this was an exceptional circumstance: 'on the clear understanding that all risk and responsibility will rest with Messrs Penn — that they defray all expenses of materials & workmanship and 10% on the expense incurred.'

The Factory Smithery could be called on to repair and forge massive components, such as the intermediate shaft of *Sans Pareil*, which was found (at Devonport in August 1852) to have developed a fracture at the air pump crank. These jobs required a great deal more accuracy than Yard Smithery work such as anchors, and the steam hammermen, at Portsmouth at least, did not have the requisite skills. Murray's chief assistant testified that several crankshafts forged there had failed, including one made since the 5 ton Nasmyth hammer had been put into service. He put this down to the fact that the rates of pay, though adequate

146 Boilers for Yard machinery also varied greatly in their construction. *(TNA ADM 85/56)*

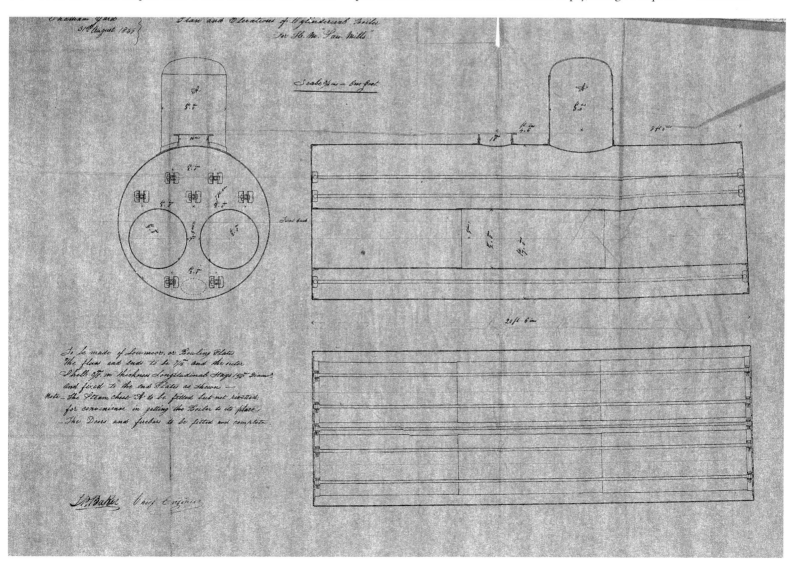

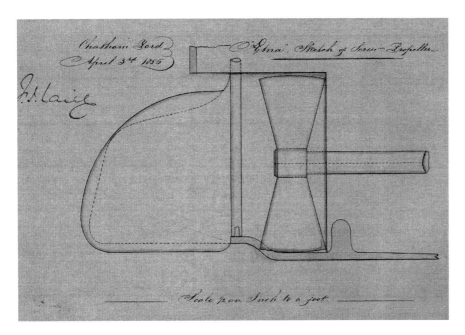

147 The unfortunate error in design of HMS *Aetna's* screw is evident from this drawing. *(TNA ADM 87/59)*

launched at Chatham it was found that the screw fouled the iron heel on which the rudder was stepped, and some hasty alterations had to be made (Figure 147). In December 1853 all the parts made at Portsmouth Factory for *Duke of Wellington* broke down.[10]

The light turning and fitting shops and brass foundries produced more delicate components for engines and their ancillary equipment. The Kingston valve was one of these. The manufacture and maintenance of these valves, now used for injection as well as for ejection of boiler water, suddenly became a matter of importance in 1853, when it was found that Portsmouth Factory had only one set of the valves, with the ships of the line *Caesar, Majestic, Hannibal, Algiers, Royal Albert,* and *Exmouth* converting to steam and all requiring to be equipped. The launching of a swarm of steam-powered gunboats during the Russian War created the need for a regular supply of the valves, and drawings were sent from Portsmouth to Woolwich for guidance (Figure 148).

During the 1850s, besides this installation of an unprecedented number of Kingston valves over a short period, a lot of factory time was taken up by the introduction of surface condensers on a large scale. In this device the steam was condensed to form a vacuum by contact with a system of water-filled pipes, instead of having an injection of cold water sprayed into the condensing chamber. It had been tried with success by Edward Humphrys' brother in the 1830s, and when Humphrys was Chief Engineer at Woolwich he had been most impressed by the performance of Hall's surface condenser on the gunboat *Grappler*.

Shortly after Humphrys left Woolwich to return to private industry (replaced by Atherton), Grant's condensers were installed in several of the big screw ships. Trouble was experienced in 1855 with those on *Nile, St Jean d'Acre, Caesar,* and *Exmouth* at Devonport: the Master Shipwright, Edye, found on no less than seven occasions that the pipe leading the condensate away had snapped. In his opinion this was caused by the great expansion (about 2¼ in) of the shell of the condenser when heated by the steam. He proposed, as a curative, packing the joint where the pipe left the condenser, to allow for expansion, but his opposite number at Portsmouth, Abethell, thought that the weight of water round the tubes together with the rolling of the ship had been the cause, and that stays between the condenser and the shell would solve the matter (Figure 149). Such stays were being fitted to all new condensers; the modification of the old ones was another Factory job.

for the less skilled men, were not good enough to attract good steam hammermen. Woolwich had the services of a very fine operative, hired at 7s 8d a day for a seven-day week, who had made crankshafts up to 10 tons in weight, with only one failure. Were the man to leave, Atherton thought a competent replacement would be very difficult to find at that rate of pay, and rather than use a man with inferior abilities, he would let the hammer stand idle.

Some of the repairs that had to be done at short notice were more embarrassing than others. In April 1856, when the floating battery *Aetna* (an unlucky name: its predecessor had been burned on the stocks a year before) was about to be

Jockeying between the Shipwrights' and Engineers' Departments led to a demarcation of labour, imposed in this case by the management rather than, as in private Yards, by trade unions protecting the jobs of their members. Condensers, Kingston valves and their pipes were fitted on board by the shipwrights, connected with the boilers by the Chief Engineers' department, and on completion placed under the chief engineer of the ship.

Demand for this equipment was heavy, and in February 1856 Walker directed that the Woolwich Factory should report on the number of condensers for gunboats that could be made by 1 April, ordering 50 to be made. Atherton replied that the Coppersmiths' Shop was short-handed, but if the body of the condenser was cast in brass the work could be divided between the Coppersmiths' Shop and the Brass Foundry. Cocks and

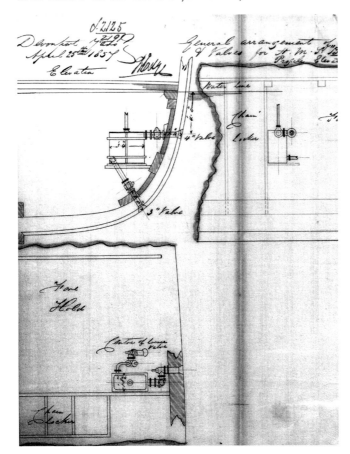

148 Working Drawings for Kingston valves sent to the Steam Factories in preparation for their in-house manufacture. Gunboats such as this were produced in large numbers for the proposed assault on Kronstadt; the size and placing of Kingston valves is evident from the sectional view. *(TNA ADM 87/64)*

connecting pipes were to be supplied by contract; the firm involved was Tyler & Sons, Warwick Lane, Newgate St, London. Eight per week could be made, or 12 if priority was given to the job. Keyham was also involved in the production of condensers for gunboats. By an Admiralty order of 20 April 1857 paddlers, except those for home service, were also to be fitted with condensers. The cost of condensers and cocks for various classes of ship was:

	£
Royal Sovereign (liner)	841
Agamemnon (liner)	800
Shannon (screw frigate)	678
Challenger (screw corvette)	561
Conflict (screw steamship)	377
Flying Fish (gunboat)	250
Lapwing (gunboat)	203

It was still proving difficult to attract key staff, and this sometimes prevented important jobs from being done in the Yards. Abethell found that in December 1855 a competent foreman could not be obtained from private trade for the wages paid at the yard, and asked whether the furnaceman of the steam hammer could be sent to the forge of Fulton & Nielson to be trained in forging large crankshafts and other heavy articles. (In the event James Bartholomew went to the Mersey Iron Company to superintend manufacture of plate for a floating battery; after this he was to be sent elsewhere to gain further experience.) Portsmouth had been in similar straits. The crankshaft for *Simoom* had not been forged, as Murray was unable to find a competent man to work the steam hammer, and asked to borrow the forgeman from Woolwich, who had made a similar shaft for *Termagant*. He could not be spared, and there was no alternative to hiring one from a private establishment. Murray tried, but none was to be had. In the end the drawings were sent to Woolwich, and the shaft was forged there.[11]

More engineers afloat were urgently required for war service, and the small number of those who had come from the

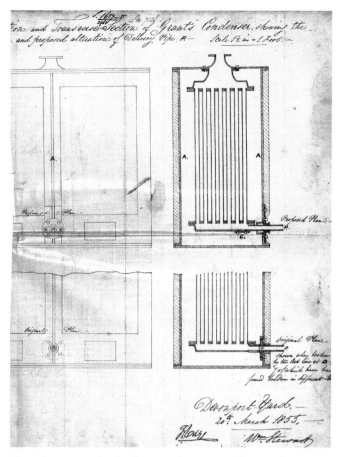

149 The damaged condenser and Edye's proposal to remedy matters. *(TNA ADM 87/52)*

Factories was quite inadequate. Anyone with experience was considered, even the unpromising Scotsman who wrote:

Lords & Gentlemen I do not know well how to adress you But in short I feel inclined to go into the navie if my services be required and I prove cappable of shuch in the mean time I may inform you that I have not been at sea I have been ingineer in some of the river Clyde Boats I came to London 5 weaks ago and have been working in messrs Rennies Hollan st Blackfriers ever sinse and if a Character be required they can say nothing about

150 A typical gunboat, this is *Skipjack*. *(TNA ADM 87/55)*

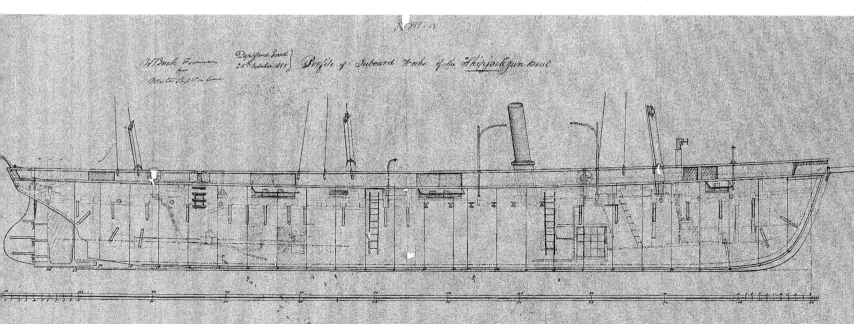

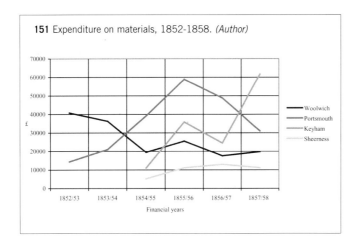

151 Expenditure on materials, 1852-1858. *(Author)*

152 Labour costs at the factories, 1852-1858. *(Author)*

me being so short a time thare but by riting to Messr Blackwood & Gordon Engineers & ship Builders you may have my Character for I was thare 14 months their place is Abercorn foundry Paisley Scotland. I do not know that this may be required but if it may please your lordships to give me directions I shall be happie to proseed. [signed] James Conbra

He was not turned down straight away, but instead was asked to produce his certificates. Experience was more important than social graces. The incumbent of St Dunstan's, Canterbury, recommended a virtuous engine driver on the Canterbury & Whitstable line who 'bears a most excellent character and never touches intoxicating drinks', but he was turned down because of lack of practical experience as an engine fitter. Inducements of up-front payment were introduced.

The Russian War brought about an increased demand for skilled men. In October 1854 the Admiralty approved of Walker's suggestion that Acting Assistant Engineers, as well as those who might be subsequently entered, should be appointed supernumaries to the steam vessels on the Home and Baltic Stations, for familiarisation with marine engines under working conditions, and be granted 3 months' advance pay. The contract was for temporary service at sea for a period of not less than 6 months. The following month 13 engine fitters from Woolwich Factory volunteered to become Assistant Engineers. Volunteers had to report to Woolwich at their own expense to be examined, and Atherton found himself bombarded with applications from afar. He offered to draw up a suitable form so that he could have a fair idea of their practical experience and educational acquirements before inviting people from distant parts of the country to make their way to Woolwich. Not all accepted proved to be suitable: six Engineers in Sheerness Steam Reserve were ordered to be discharged from the Navy and to refund the amount they had been advanced, and they were not permitted to re-enter Her Majesty's Service in any capacity whatever. It is not known what their failings had been.

The new gunboats (Figure 150) were equipped with high-pressure engines with locomotive-type boilers, a type largely unfamiliar in British marine engineering. Men with suitable experience had to be recruited; railway managers informed Walker that such people could be had for £4 a week. He submitted that this be done, and 12 men were soon recruited for *Cornwallis, Hawke, Russell, Starling, Thistle, Snap, Pelter, Ruby, Pincher, Gleaner, Snapper,* and *Badger.* The first three vessels were blockships intended for harbour defence, the others

gunboats acting as tenders to line-of-battle ships. The men were appointed to the blockships before they were allotted their gunboat tenders. A very large number of passing certificates were issued for assistant engineers in the summer and autumn of 1855; their mechanical experience had mostly been gained in private industry. The more experienced men had spent periods training in the Factories. A typical example was Henry Tonkins, certified by Murray as Assistant Engineer 2nd Class. He was 28 years old, and had served in 12 different ships. His shortest period of service had been for 17 days, and the longest, on *Sampson,* for 2 years 8 months, with a total sea time of 5 years, 7 months and 8 days. His harbour time had been 1 year, 8 months and 4 days, with 118 days spent at Woolwich Factory.

Walker clearly wanted the Factories to be a regular source of skilled men afloat, and in December 1855 the Board approved his submission for the entry of Factory boys with a view to their becoming Naval Engineers after about 5 years' service. Fourteen boys at Woolwich, nine at Portsmouth and five at Devonport were examined. However, the general standard of education of the Factory boys was not high; by the end of the decade many of the rivet boys at Keyham were unable to read.[12]

In 1847 Lloyd had estimated that one fourth of the engines of the Navy would need to be repaired every year. Years later he thought that his reckoning had been accurate at the time; but then the machinery was all to drive paddle-wheelers, and always at work. The introduction of the screw, as has been seen, led to the ships in commission performing their services mostly under sail, and the maintenance of the majority of the steamers in Ordinary meant that Portsmouth Factory, two years after

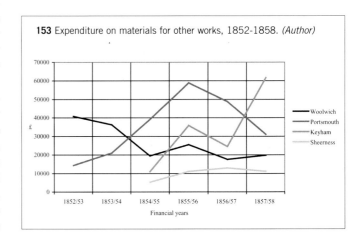

153 Expenditure on materials for other works, 1852-1858. *(Author)*

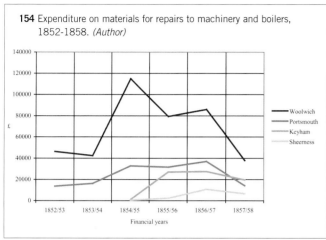

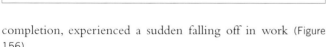

154 Expenditure on materials for repairs to machinery and boilers, 1852-1858. *(Author)*

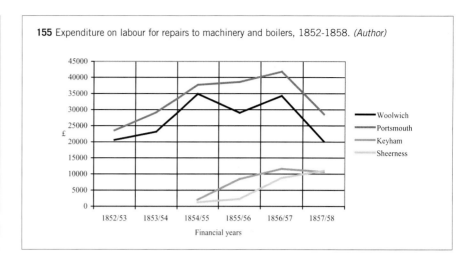

155 Expenditure on labour for repairs to machinery and boilers, 1852-1858. *(Author)*

completion, experienced a sudden falling off in work (Figure 156).

The figures for 1851/2 only go up to the end of 1851. With the outbreak of war, and Sheerness and Keyham coming into operation, expenditure rose dramatically (Figure 151). Labour costs at the Factories during the same period were as shown in Figure 152. After the Portsmouth Factory had been established for two years, an examination of the figures revealed that the average cost of articles produced differed from that of those produced at Woolwich. There was no consistent pattern to the divergences. The officers were asked for an explanation, and to check whether any deviations had been made in the bookkeeping. A notable difference in the financial performance of the Factories persisted (Figure 154). Labour costs, represented in the same way, were as shown in Figure 155.

The two older Factories roughly correspond with each other, as do the two newer Factories. The costs of materials on other works performed at the Factories show a different picture, with Portsmouth expending more than Woolwich, and Keyham rapidly establishing itself (Figure 153). The labour costs also show a different picture (Figure 156). Woolwich labour costs were higher for these works than those at Portsmouth, and Keyham and Sheerness show a parallel increase. Much of the difference in the performances of Woolwich and Portsmouth may be the consequence of the former Factory largely dealing with the older paddle warships, while the big new screw line-of-battle ships, too large to be dealt with there, were sent to Portsmouth. Portsmouth, also, was a fitting-out yard for ships built at Pembroke Dock. Ships returning from the Baltic in

October 1855 were assigned to specified ports for refits and repairs: 14 to Sheerness, 20 to Portsmouth and 14 to Devonport. The liners among them were distributed three for Sheerness, five for Devonport, and six (plus five blockships) for Portsmouth. None of these ships was sent to Woolwich, which according to Atherton was never at full stretch throughout the war. It was largely occupied in making boilers for supply to the other Yards, which resulted in a high value of materials consumed, while the labour costs were proportionally low for such work.

Since the establishment of Woolwich, the composition of the work force in the Yards, comprising established men, hired men and Factory staff, had varied as shown in Figure 157. The steady growth of Factory personnel roughly paralleled that of the established staff. The 1850s were notable as a decade during which hired men played a relatively small part of the workforce, and the sudden increase in Yard staff at the end of the decade was possible only because of the existence of the pool of hired labour. The next decade was to see new technology, and an arms race with the French, increase the capacity of the yards still further.[13]

156 Labour costs for other works, 1852-1858. *(Author)*

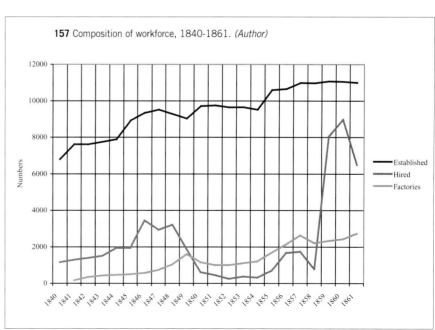

157 Composition of workforce, 1840-1861. *(Author)*

158 HMS *Warrior* at Devonport during her first commission, 1861-64. The Quadrangle is shown on the left, and Scamp's clock tower to the right. *(Chrysalis Picture Library)*

Notes:

1 POR/R/11, POR/R/12B, NMR PTM/1191; Field, 1994, p.5 ADM 12/476; Cochrane's sawing machine is described in all its complexities in *Mechanics' Magazine*, vol. 50, 1849, pp. 313-319 (3 plates) and pp.344-349 (1 plate); many subsequent types of woodworking machinery are illustrated in T Robinson, 'On woodworking machinery', in *Proceedings of the Institution of Mechanical Engineers*, 1875, pp.248-267, 7 plates; MLN/155/1, ADM 87/50, ADM 95/97, CHA/C/1.

2 'Chatham Dockyard' in *The Uncommercial Traveller*.

3 ADM 12/588, ADM 95/97, CHA/H/88, ADM 84/13, ADM 85/25, CHA/H/94, ADM 85/39, ADM 85/40, ADM 85/44, CHA/H/100, CHA/H/104.

4 ADM 85/51, ADM 85/36, ADM 85/45, ADM 95/97, NMR PLM/95, ADM 85/38, ADM 12/619, ADM 12/652, ADM 12/604, ADM 12/764.

5 ADM 85/51, ADM 12/588, ADM 95/97, ADM 93/12, ADM 85/40, ADM 85/42, ADM 87/76, ADM 85/41.

6 *Minutes of Evidence before Committee of Inquiry on the Economy of Her Majesty's Dockyards*, 1858, *passim*.

7 ADM 95/97, ADM 87/47.

8 ADM 84/14, ADM 84/17, John Penn, 'On wood bearings for screw propeller shafts', in *Proceedings of the Institution of Mechanical Engineers*, 1856, pp.24-34; ADM 93/12, ADM 83/48.

9 ADM 87/48, ADM 87/76, ADM 87/15, ADM 87/44.

10 ADM 85/22, ADM 85/37, ADM 85/57, ADM 85/56, ADM 84/3, ADM 84/10, ADM 2/1388, ADM 84/6, ADM 84/5, ADM 87/59, ADM 85/13.

11 Science Museum Library, GOOD A/1442, 'Blow-off pipe for marine steam boilers', *Transactions of the Society of Arts*, vol. 51, 1837, pp.30-34; ADM 87/46, ADM 87/50, ADM 87/64, Edward Humphrys, 'On surface condensation in marine engines', *Proceedings of the Institution of Mechanical Engineers*, 1862, pp.99-124; ADM 87/52, ADM 87/58, ADM 87/64, ADM 93/13, ADM 89/1, ADM 85/26.

12 ADM 85/18, ADM 85/29, ADM 84/13, ADM 85/20, ADM 84/14, ADM 93/12, ADM 84/16, ADM 84/15, ADM 84/17, ADM 85/52.

13 *Minutes of the Select Committee on Chatham Dockyard Extension*; ADM 85/7, ADM 85/51, ADM 89/4, ADM 87/55.

CHAPTER 12

The First Iron Warships

THE TECHNOLOGY OF BUILDING SHIPS in iron was developed by private firms, and there was no disposition on the part of the Admiralty to supplement, let alone replace, its established facilities for building wooden ships. It was the development of the iron-hulled armoured warship and its emergence in the 1860s as the essential component of a battle fleet that finally decided that some of these vessels, and following them other types, would be built in the Yards. By the time that this new shipbuilding policy had been determined on by the Admiralty the technique of iron shipbuilding had made great progress. The obvious approach to building a ship in iron was to translate the wooden structure as directly as possible into iron, the vessel being built up by

transverse frames. The section of the *China* in Figure 159 shows the keel construction replicating that of a wooden ship.

During the 1840s a new method was in the air. Longitudinal framing is usually associated with the naval architect John Scott Russell, but as with so many innovations several men were toying with the concept at the same time. This involved longitudinal iron beams taking the majority of the structural load; the structure was lighter and resisted hogging and sagging (the arching or drooping of the hull in the middle caused by the action of the sea) by about 25 per cent, as calculated by contemporaries. Brunel was to use the system in forming the keel of the *Great Britain* in 1840, and it formed the basis of the internal framing of *Warrior* and other warships (Figure 160). It offered greater ease and speed of construction in many ways, though greater accuracy and skill were required. In particular, as a Chief Constructor of the Navy was to write:

> In framing the bow of a long fine ship on the vertical system, it is found that the work is extremely difficult to execute, and that it is so circumstanced as to allow only a few men to be employed

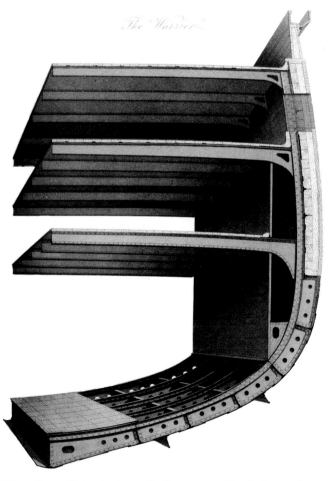

159 Transverse section through the mail steamer *China*, showing transverse framing. *(From E. J. Reed*, Shipbuilding in Iron and Steel, *London 1869)*

160 Section of *Warrior*, showing a mix of transverse and longitudinal framing. *(From E. J. Reed*, Shipbuilding in Iron and Steel, *London 1869)*

upon it, and those men work at the greatest disadvantage, and consequently cannot build quickly. This is a very important point, because if it were required to build an iron navy rapidly, no amount of pecuniary compensation could enable the builders to frame the bows of such ships quickly.

But that event was to lie in the future; the French steam fleet that gave rise to such apprehensions from the late 1840s on was, like the Royal Navy, composed of wooden vessels.[1]

Armour plates

Alarm at the threat of the modernised French fleet, with its superior basin, slip and docking capacity, was never far away and was often rampant. Rear-Admiral Sir Charles Napier, commanding the Channel squadron, admittedly not one to underrate the French menace and here using the last generation of paddle frigates as an example, was mightily impressed when he came into contact with the hardware in 1849:

A great deal has been said to disparage these Vessels but after examining the *Cacique* I am of opinion that we have a great deal to apprehend from them in the event of war. We have only four Steamers afloat carrying Main deck guns, *Terrible*, *Sidon*, *Odin* and *Penelope* — and the *Leopard* building. *Terrible* is a fast vessel but that is her only qualification — she carries little Coals and is too crowded with machinery and coal Bunkers on deck to carry men. *Odin* carries 360 tons of Coal only — is cramped for room — too low and cannot carry many men. *Sidon* from having a clear Main deck is capable of carrying a Battalion with ease and heavier Guns. *Leopard* is between *Sidon* and *Odin* and I fear will not have room enough. As for all our other misnamed Frigates what could they do against a Fleet of 27 Steam Frigates? Our Screws may be good in their way but they are only auxiliaries. Whether it is their Lordships intention to construct more Steam Vessels at present, I do not know but if it is I do most strongly recommend that we should construct real Frigates…

Captain Chads, commanding the gunnery school ship HMS *Excellent*, carried out experiments at Shoeburyness to show that Cherbourg Arsenal could be bombarded from without the breakwater by night, using small steamers. The purpose of these experiments was, not unreasonably, to be kept

confidential, for Chads credited the French with almost superhuman powers of engineering:

Should it be known in France means might be adopted to remedy the evil…by raising an outer battery 800 or 1,000 yards from the Breakwater…a most serious undertaking but not beyond the talent & energy that have perfected that Breakwater.

Access to what would now be regarded as highly sensitive sites was taken as a matter of course a century and a half ago, but in November 1852 some restrictions were imposed on foreign visitors to the Yards: they were not to witness any experiment, were to be restricted as much as possible from entering buildings, and were not to make notes or sketches or enter into conversation with workmen. At Devonport the police regulations further stated that they were not to go on board ships in dock, or into Engine Houses, Sawmills, Smitheries, the Hammer Shop or Mould Loft. (In 1859 many Chief Engineers thought these rules unnecessarily restrictive. Keeping foreigners from access to design or new construction was reasonable, but the tools in use in the shops were no different from, and in many cases the identical models to, those to be found in foreign Yards.)[2]

The Russian war cast the two navies together as allies, in a campaign in which French innovation in the form of armoured floating batteries proved highly successful. The idea of protecting warships by iron plates was of course far from new, experiments had been performed in many countries, but it took a long time before any gratifying results could be seen. In 1842 tests by HMS *Excellent* showed that plates of wrought iron, ⅜in thick, riveted together to the thickness of 6in and fixed over the planking of a ship's side, gave no protection against 8in 65cwt guns and 32 pounders of 56cwt, fired with their distant charges of 10lb at 400 yards. Nonetheless, the idea was not dismissed, and in March 1844 Fincham sent the Surveyor sections of a proposed 12-gun iron steamship with protective iron bulwarks. In 1846 an old and flimsy steamer, the *Ruby*, was used as a target. The ship was in a very bad state, which made the gunners' task easier, and the effects on such a weak target were decisive. Shots left a neat hole where they struck, but there was severe damage to the opposite side of the vessel. The idea of using iron ships in action was dropped after this test and the iron frigates on order were converted to troopships.

In 1850 further experimental firings took place against an iron target similar to a section of *Simoom*, one of the converted frigates, which showed in an alarming manner how it would have stood up in action. This time the results were reversed. Most damage was caused to the front of the plate, and was so severe that it was thought that two or three shots could endanger the ship. An unexpected effect of the greater resistance of the target was the disintegration of the shot into a multitude of flying fragments, which would search the interior of the ship with devastating effect. The inescapable conclusion was that 'iron is not a material calculated for ships of war'. Backing the metal with wood did not much mend matters. However, research into armour was considered worth pursuing, and in May 1851 two iron targets designed by Captain Chads were ordered to be made at Portsmouth (Figure 161).[3]

These targets were of ⅜ and ½in iron, backed with wood, and clearly were not intended to be tested by a warship's main

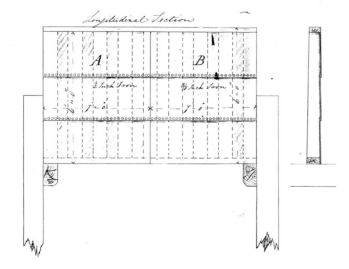

161 This iron target for testing armour plate was designed by the Captain of HMS *Excellent* in 1851. *(TNA ADM 87/37)*

armament. Experience with these targets probably resulted in the designing of detachable screen plates to protect gunboats' crews against small arms fire in March 1855, when William Rice, the Master Shipwright at Woolwich, produced a drawing showing the method of attaching them. Eighteen plates were to be provided for each vessel, to be placed according to the direction the vessel was engaged. The plates were to be 2ft 6in by 1ft 9in by ⅜in thick, and must have proved successful, as in November gunboats returning from sea to Devonport to be refitted were ordered to be equipped with screen plates running the whole length of one side of the vessel (Figure 162). This was small potatoes compared with the 10cm wrought iron armour of the French floating batteries, but it was the first application of armour to a Royal Navy ship.

Floating batteries were ordered for the Navy to join with the French ones in the Crimea, and the opportunity was taken to train key personnel in the new material. In January 1856 Mr James, the furnaceman of the steam hammer at Portsmouth, was sent to the Mersey Iron Company Works at Liverpool to superintend the manufacture of plates for a floating battery. This supervisory duty would effectively be in-service training in heavy forging work, and when the plates were completed he could, if necessary, go to other works to further increase his knowledge. It was clearly the intent to have key personnel trained in the technology of armour plate, against the day when its problems would have been resolved acceptably.

By 1858 metallurgists felt that they had the matter cracked. The newly invented homogeneous metal (combining the properties of wrought iron and cast steel) made by Shortridge, Howell & Jessop, which was claimed to be double the strength of iron and capable of being made exceedingly tough, was to be tested by HMS *Excellent*. Robert Hughes, Lloyd's assistant, was sent on a tour of ironworks to see at first hand what their capacities were and, incidentally, to find out whether the French had made any approaches to buy armour plate.[4]

At Liverpool, for example, visiting the Mersey Iron & Steel works (Figure 163), Hughes saw puddled steel made by Clay's process, and got some hot information. He was shown large heavy plates made for Westwood, Baillie & Campbell, shipbuilders on the Isle of Dogs, at £56 per ton; they did not know the ultimate destination of these plates. They had also been asked to tender for 800 tons of plates by Taylor of Marseilles and several other agents of French firms in London, and had been told that Krupp had been invited to tender but his price was £100 per ton.

He summed up his investigations:

It appears numerous enquiries have been made of several of the principal manufacturing houses, and in one case, a specification has been received, from Parties in London and France, for plates evidently intended for sheathing or Battery purposes, yet, as far as I could learn, no contract has been entered into nor orders received for making any.

The Military Attaché at Paris, Lt-Col. Claremont, had some rather more disquieting news in a confidential report:

I did not exaggerate when I talked to you of the success of their experiments, firing at iron plates to cover the side of a ship; they blazed away at twenty metres, 50-pounders, first, with hollow

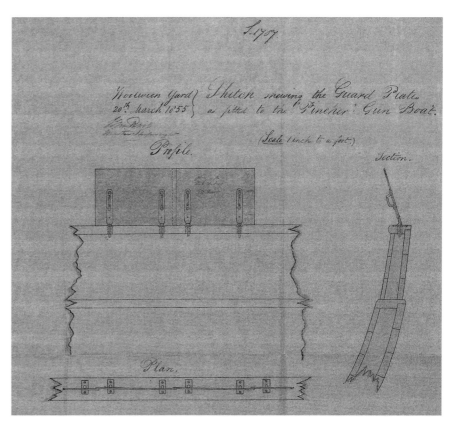

shot, which went off into dust; then with solid shot, which was also smashed; and, finally, with cast-steel shot, which was split, but also split the plates, without, however, penetrating.[5]

On 20 August 1858 Captain Hewlett of HMS *Excellent* reported on the test of a Joseph's coat of plates of different composition from different manufacturers fitted to *Alfred* (Figure 164). French and English ironmasters had tied in producing a satisfactory armour; Hewlett had no doubt as to the great superiority of the common 4in wrought iron plates over anything else of the same thickness that had yet been tried. Sixty-eight-pounder guns were used. Four-inch steel offered much less resistance, and homogeneous metal was about the same. A bizarre *vertical* sandwich of homogeneous metal and

162 The first application of armour was not intended to stand up to the attack of great guns. This system of armour was to protect the crews of gunboats from small arms fire. *(TNA ADM 87/52)*

163 The rolling mill at the Mersey Works in the early 1860s. *(NMM neg. no. 5260)*

African oak, not surprisingly, offered very little resistance. Two inches of homogeneous metal covered with 3in of African oak did little better: shot penetrated, and threw a shower of splinters inboard to a considerable distance. Vulcanised India rubber offered no resistance at all. Hits near the edges of the plates did the most damage, strikes in the centre the least. The larger the plates were made, therefore, the more efficient the protection would be. No shots striking wrought iron plates actually penetrated, even at 100 yards, and the wood behind showed little injury. That behind steel plates was much driven in. At 400 yards the heaviest description of wrought iron shot penetrated only a little more than 2in, red-hot shot and shell only 1in. At 200 yards the penetration was much greater, but still the plates resisted. At 100 yards fire was much more effective: iron was driven completely back into the wood, shaking the framework very much, but none actually penetrated, though this was very nearly achieved.

The Captain had the plates photographed before and after the test, hiring:

> …a man from the Town for this purpose, and placed him under the direction of Mr May, the Chymist of this Yard, who has taken a great deal of trouble and devoted much of his time and attention to this, in order that we might obtain good specimens, and preserve them from publicity.[6]

Gauging the French Threat

This was timely. In 1856 Walker had sent two of his staff to France to find out what they could of the state of the engineering facilities in the Yards. Messrs Sweny and Barnes reported that Cherbourg was still unfinished and partially equipped. Brest was the most important French yard with regard to steam machinery. Its factory was very large, well built, and capable of erecting a number of marine engines; the tools were in good condition, but there was scarcely any work being done. They were informed that it was not the Government's intention to construct many engines in the Imperial establishments, but that the object was to be prepared to manufacture them, independently of the trade, in case of emergencies. At Lorient the factory establishments were well built and large, but not so well equipped; the factory buildings at Rochefort were cramped and some inadequate, but the smithery, boiler, and erecting shops, all under one roof, were well supplied with good tools. Toulon would not be up to much until the new shops at Castigneau were opened, but Indret impressed: 'a very fine establishment, with shops well adapted for first-rate work'. Across the Channel some were not so struck by the place; a French Parliamentary Commission noted that the Loire was not 10ft deep at Indret, so no large vessels could be fitted out there, and recommended its suppression. (It survived.) Among the private firms, at Taylor's Works, Marseilles, the tools were good, but none novel, though at Mazeline's, Le Havre, the fitting shop was supplied 'with superior tools…There is a superior vertical planing machine, invented by one of M. Mazeline's workmen'.

All this did not sound like a dreadful menace. However, the potential was there, for in any building contest the French would have the advantage of 78 slips to 43, and in England only Keyham could dock *Himalaya*, *Niagara*, and *Orlando*, though when the planned lengthening of docks had occurred, Chatham, Portsmouth and Pembroke would be able to as well. In 1858, however, the balance of the fleets, as perceived at the Admiralty, was very close (Table 11).

164 *Alfred* after the test firing. Note the varied effects of the impacts. *(TNA ADM 87/69)*

In June 1858 Lt Colonel Claremont reported again. The Creuzot Works had the capacity to make marine engines with a total of 4,000 or perhaps 5,000hp, and the firm had recently delivered three engines of 800hp each, six of 250hp, and five of 200hp; but Claremont could not find out the names of all the vessels they were intended for and did not press for the information. Orders for five engines of 600hp each had recently been placed. There had been no attempt to conceal the facts about these engines, though usually Government orders were supposed to be secret, nor was there any sign of hurry to get the job done. The Forges et Chantiers de la Mediterranée, near Marseilles, a firm that made nothing but marine steam engines, had been at the last gasp, having run out of work, but had just received a life-saving order for one 900hp engine for an iron-sided frigate, three of 600hp and two of 150hp. The most they could turn out in a year would be 4,000hp.

The Chief Engineer there was Arthur Taylor, the son of the person who first established the works (a part of the diaspora of British engineers over the Continent during the first part of the century). Claremont thought it might be useful for the new Consul at Marseilles to cultivate his acquaintance. The Consul did indeed do a bit of fishing, for the not inconsiderable consideration of £200 a year, but as the Admiralty thought his information was very low-grade, not including information on private yards, he does not seem to have profited by M. Taylor's acquaintance. The real meat of the report followed:

[At Toulon]…they were…laying down the first timbers of an iron-sided frigate…to be called the *Gloire*; and these timbers appeared to me quite as large and heavy as those of a three-decker. There are to be two of these frigates built here…but four others are to be built in the other ports. They are to have thirty-six heavy guns, most of them rifled 50-pounders, which will throw an 80 lbs hollow percussion shot. Their engines will be of 800 or 900 horsepower, and they will be cased with wrought iron; there is, also, some question of their being fitted with a submarine spur. Altogether they will be most powerful machines of destruction; and so convinced do naval men in this country seem to be of their irresistible qualities that they do not mean to lay down another line-of-battle ship, as they say that, in ten years' time, they will have become quite obsolete…

There was no unusual degree of activity, except at the new steam-yard of Castigneau, which covered an immense area of ground, and would be a formidable establishment when complete. The intention was to make engines of the largest size.[7]

At Le Havre, Mazeline's works claimed to have turned out 6,000hp of engines in one year, and now had a Government order for two 700hp engines; they claimed that they did not know for what ships they were intended, but Claremont was in no doubt that they were for the iron-sided frigates. 'One thing I cannot too strongly call attention to is, their determination about iron-sided frigates, which really seem as if they would bring about a complete revolution in naval matters.'

Another source brought more disquieting news about the level of technical back-up for the French Steam Navy. Since 1854 the steam-machinery establishments and the metal workshops had been greatly enlarged and improved, being provided with the best tools and machinery, both French and

Table 11 The balance of the fleets, 1858

In screw ships the estimate drawn up by Captain Milne was:

	England	France
Liners	35	32
Blockships	9	
Frigates	21	6 + 15 converting
Mortar frigates	3	
Floating batteries	8	5
Corvettes and sloops	51	17 Corvettes
Gun vessels	27	80 Sloops and gun vessels
Gunboats	151	28
Mortar vessels		5

The position for paddle vessels was

	England	France
Frigates	16	20
Others	44	9

The Russian Navy was also a major factor in the equation. Milne reckoned this as comprising

Baltic Fleet:		Mediterranean Fleet:	
Screw liners	8	Screw liners	1
Screw frigates	6	Screw frigates	3
Paddle frigates	9	Screw corvettes	5
Screw corvettes	4	Small steamers	2
Transports	1		
Gunboats	75	Pacific Fleet:	
Small steamers	18	Screw frigates	1
		Screw corvettes	3
Black Sea Fleet:		Gun vessels	5
Screw corvettes	7	Small steamers	6
Small steamers	8	Transports	2

foreign. Furthermore, a new generation of skilled workers was being trained, with a great increase in the number of apprentices for metalwork, who were being well educated, and would form 'a class of steady, clever, and well-informed workmen'.

The visit of Queen Victoria and Prince Albert to Cherbourg afforded an opportunity to have a good look at the menace across the Channel, and an artist and two photographers were included in one of the ship's companies; sadly, their efforts do not appear to have survived. More open was the action of Count Platen, the Swedish and Norwegian Minister at the Court of St James's, who simply asked to be supplied with drawings of the Marine Hospital at Woolwich, the New Smithery at Devonport, the Flour Mill and Bakery at Deptford, and the ropery machinery at Portsmouth and Chatham. News of French advances in gunnery as well as armour were conveyed in October 1859 by reports from different quarters of France of activities in the various Yards in rifling cannon by machinery.[8]

A fortnight after Colonel Claremont sent his confidential report from Paris, Baldwin Walker, who had frequently said no major change in building policy should be made until forced, wrote the often quoted words:

This time has arrived. France has now commenced to build Frigates of great speed with their sides protected by thick Metal Plates…[estimated dimensions of projected ship, 280 ft long, 6,096 tons, coals for 7 days]…the attention of my Department has been directed to the preparation of Designs & the mode of construction of Vessels of this Novel Character & the Design forwarded…was prepared some months ago…

He reckoned the relative position of England and France with screw liners as 30 to 28; in 1854 the figures had been 11 to 7. Furthermore, the French ships were on the average more highly powered.

Worse, the engines ordered but not yet afloat amounted to 5,300hp in England, and 11,150hp for France, which included the power for the four iron-plated frigates. The First Secretary of the Admiralty, Henry Lowry Corry, had been waiting for the result of the *Alfred* experiments before making any statement about building armoured ships, but had noted prophetically (not that any great degree of clairvoyance was needed):

If we are actually the most wealthy and most prosperous nation of the world; if our naval resources, our mechanical skill, and our means of producing the material elements of a Steam Navy, are unequalled, surely we ought not to allow ourselves to be outstripped by a Power immeasurably our inferior in all these respects…if the steam-engine, as applied to the Navy, has added greatly to the national expenditure, it has also added…immeasurably more to the national wealth.[9]

—⁂—

165 *Warrior's* sister ship, *Black Prince*, again pictured at Devonport. Note Quadrangle stacks in the background. (Chrysalis Picture Library)

Notes:

[1] J Scott Russell, *The Modern System of Naval Architecture*, 3 vols., (London, 1864-5); E J Reed, *Shipbuilding in Iron and Steel*, (London, 1869), p.94 ; E Corlett, *The Iron Ship*, rev.ed. (1990), p.45.

[2] ADM 1/5598, ADM 13/185; the Navy's aggressive plans against the threat of Cherbourg are outlined by Lambert, (1991), p.11; ADM 1/5715.

[3] Early projects for armouring ships are described in J P Baxter, *The Introduction of the Ironclad Warship*, (Cambridge, MA, 1933); *Reports of Experiments tried as to the effects of Shot on Iron*, 1850; ADM 87/14, ADM 87/37; a detailed account of the early tests against iron ships is given by D K Brown, *Before the Ironclad*, (London, 1990), Chapter 8.

[4] At Newcastle upon Tyne, Morrison's works had three steam hammers fit for forging heavy plates, and he had been asked to tender for 500 tons. He quoted £24 per ton, but was turned down, and was told that another party had undercut him. At Gateshead, Hawks, Crawshay & Sons had an extensive rolling mill, and their largest steam hammer was of 4 tons, capable of making the heaviest forging for battery plates or other purposes. At Sunderland, J & E Lumsden and Thomas Panton & Co. could forge plates, while at Middlesborough Messrs Bolc & Vaughan had rolling mills as well as three large steam hammers capable of making large forgings. Sheffield was disappointing. At the homogeneous metalworks of Shortridge, Howell & Jessop he found that their process was not adapted to making large pieces. They had not received any enquiries about plates. Tarton & Sons could not make plates larger than 3-5cwt. Finally, at Glasgow, the Parkhead Forge could make 60 tons of battery plates per week, if given 10 days' notice, at about £30-35 per ton. The owner, who could see which way the wind was blowing, had just had a new long-stroke hammer put in specially for battery plates 'as he rather believes in them', but had not had any communication with France on the matter. The firm had made the plates for the floating battery built by Napier & Sons, Glasgow.

[5] ADM 87/52, ADM 87/56, ADM 89/1, ADM 93/17, ADM 85/51, ADM 116/1.

[6] ADM 87/68, ADM 87/69.

[7] At Indret the engines of the *Massena* and *Castiglione* were ready, those of *Ville de Bordeaux* and *Ville de Lyon* very nearly so. These were all of 800hp; the maximum annual capability was 3,000hp, and they had on order two 900hp engines, one for an iron-sided frigate, and two of 400hp.

[8] ADM 116/2, BL Ms. Add. 4951, MLN/142/2, MLN/142/3, Review of *Enquête Parliamentaire sur la Situation et l'Organisation des Services de la Marine Maritime ordonné par la Loi du 31 Octobre, 1849*, in *Edinburgh Review*, 1853, p.250; ADM 13/7, ADM 84/19.

[9] ADM 92/20,

	England	France
800hp and upwards	4	4
600hp and upwards	12	18

Minutes of Evidence before Committee of Inquiry on the Economy of Her Majesty's Dockyards, 1858, p.215.

CHAPTER 13

HMS *Achilles*

GLOIRE, THE VESSEL THAT FORCED Baldwin Walker to his decision, was trumped by two far superior ships, *Warrior* and *Black Prince*, built respectively by the firms of Mare and Napier, on the Thames and Clyde. Unlike *Gloire*, which had a wooden hull to which the iron armour was bolted, these were iron-hulled. *Gloire's* fabric soon rotted, while the durability of *Warrior's* hull needs no comment, as she still lies, restored, in Portsmouth harbour. Her designer, Isaac Watts, combined the transverse and longitudinal systems of framing in the hull, and this method of construction was to be retained for the first iron warship to be built in a Dockyard.

Although no iron ships had been built in a Royal Dockyard, the Admiralty had been acquiring a body of in-house expertise on the matter since October 1845, when instructions were issued for Inspectors for supervising the building of iron steam vessels ordered by the Navy. They were to familiarise themselves with the details of materials and construction, and to be able to prepare descriptive sketches. The background of one of these men is known, and if all had a similar CV quite a pool of experience was available. In January 1856 Isaac Cockell, Modeller at Chatham, offered himself as a candidate for overseer of iron ships building under contract. He had been in iron shipbuilding for two years before entering the Yard in 1843, and during the next 13 years he had spent four years at the ship's side, nine as draughtsman and modeller, and had passed the Inspector's examination. He was accepted. When, therefore, the decision was made to build ironclads in the Yards, a body of highly competent supervisory staff already existed.[1]

In order to match or surpass the ambitious French programme this was a necessary decision, and it was logically the next step in the mechanisation of the Yards. The first two ironclads were very long ships, and though the following four were shorter, they were not the kind of thing Walker had in mind, being forced on him through political pressure. The next batch were to return to the dimensions of *Warrior*. In September 1860 Walker (whose title had now been changed to Controller of the Navy) requested all the Yards to send him 1⁄16in scale drawings showing the longest ship that could be built on their slips, and built and repaired in the docks. These drawings showed what alterations to slip roofs and other features would be needed for the longer ships in prospect.

Preparing the ground at Chatham

Chatham was selected to be the pioneer in iron construction because of its proximity to the skilled workforce of the Thames. It was not equipped as a steam yard, and it had no facilities for dealing with, and consequently no experience of, marine steam engineering. It also lacked a basin. Greene had been notified on 3 October to prepare a plan and estimate of the building works that would be required. On 15 October Walker submitted that three 'Iron cased Frigates of the *Warrior* Class' be built, the Admiralty approving the construction of one at Chatham and the others by contract. A week later Walker decided after correspondence with the Chatham officers that the best place for the erection of sheds 'for Forges, Furnaces &c for the purpose of building an Iron Ship' in No. 2 Dock (the longest building space available at Chatham) would be between 1 and 2 docks. This area was to be transformed into the first iron shipbuilding shop in a Naval Yard, a new class of building. This time there were to be no mistakes in creating an inflexible masonry design.[2]

On 25 October 1860 the original design drawings were sent to Chatham and, as a first step, a half-block model of the port side was to be made and sent to Walker. At the end of the month two firms, Sanderson's Park Gate Works and the Bowling Iron Company, contracted to supply the armour plates for the 'Iron Cased Ship', as it was referred to before being named. Some of the altars at the head of No. 2 dock would need to be cut away to accommodate the ship. The dock was closed by an old caisson. Oliver Lang, the Master Shipwright, sent a drawing showing that the replacement of the caisson 'which can even now be scarcely considered safe' by a dam would give a little more room (making alterations to the masonry of the dock unnecessary), give more working space for staging at the bow and stern, and enable the ship to be placed on 2ft 6in instead of 4ft blocks, requiring 18in less water for undocking (Figure 166).[1] In the event the caisson was retained and used as a dam. The old wooden roof of No. 1 dock was to be removed, partially to begin with, as a precaution against fire from the dockside furnaces that would have to be installed. Many of the forged components of the ship were to be supplied by contract, and machinery for the Yard needed to be supplied, Portsmouth lending some. Another major ironworks, the Butterley Iron Company, contracted to supply beams for £8,500.

Treasury sanction had been given for £3,000 for the building work, and at the end of November Grissell's were given the contract for the working sheds, valued at £2,170. The work was to proceed forthwith and completed as soon as possible, and three days later Greene sent drawings to the Clerk of Works. The first stage in constructing the building was the removal of part of the roof over No. 1 dock, using the materials to form a floor over the dock to provide a working surface. By December the keel plate bending machinery, levelling slabs and furnaces (two plate furnaces and two angle iron furnaces) were being planned. Three hydraulic rams and their pumps were prepared at Woolwich for the armour plate bending machinery (a

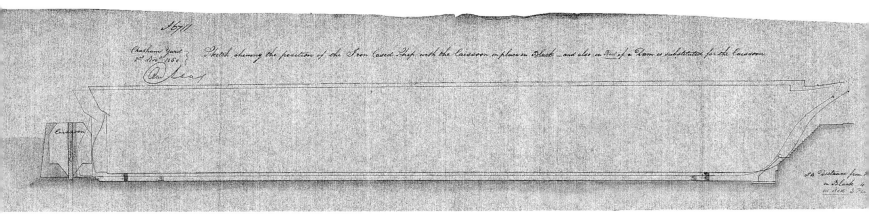

completely new piece of equipment), and in January 1861 Simpson & Co.'s offer for the shafting was accepted. The Controller forwarded drawings showing the proposed arrangement of machine tools and furnaces and plans of the foundations. Foord's of Rochester were to prepare the foundations, at an estimated £980. The dock was to be equipped with staging on each side to carry travelling cranes to assemble the ship, and Taylor's tender of £1,981 for two cranes was accepted.[3]

At the beginning of February the Board directed that Factory rates of pay were to be adopted for men employed on the ship, and rates of pay for classes of workmen not contained in the Factory list were approved. Leading men were to be paid,

for the present, the rates allowed at Steam Factories. An addition to the pay of two or three of the principal leading men would be taken into consideration on the special application of the officers.

As originally designed, the ship was to have had a knee at the bows giving a similar profile to *Warrior*, but at the beginning of March the Controller (now Admiral Sir Robert Spencer Robinson) wrote that the stem was to be altered. By the end of April the new design of the stern was approved and forwarded to the Thames Ironworks and Shipbuilding Company, who were the contractors for that massive forging. Comparing it with the original specification on which they had begun the stem, the firm stated that there would be a considerable increase

166 Lang's drawing showing *Achilles* in No. 2 Dock, Chatham. *(TNA ADM 87/77)*

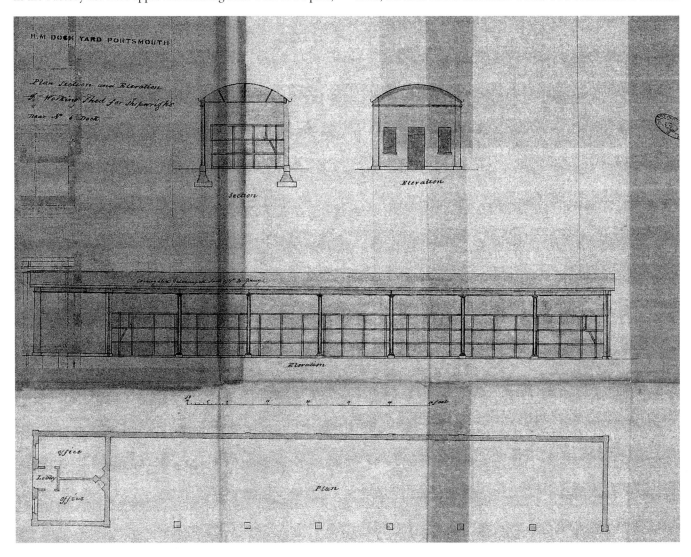

167 A shipwrights' working shed of 1859. *(TNA ADM 1/5715)*

in the weight of forging and of planing work, increasing the cost. On 12 March the Yard was informed that the 'Iron Cased Ship' was to be called *Achilles*.

Large slotting machines had never been required at Chatham before, and three tenders and sketches for slotting machines were sent by Smith, Beacock & Tannett, Collier & Co., and Fairbairn. Smith, Beacock & Tannett's appeared much the best from the sketches and specifications, but it was £300 more expensive, and Collier's tender was accepted. They also contracted for punching and shearing machines, a plate-bending machine and a planing machine. Whitworth's were to make an angle iron shearing and punching machine, and Messrs Galloway's a double vertical riveting machine. Some difficulties appear to have arisen with the heavy plant. By June Woolwich had sent one double angle iron furnace to Chatham, and one plate furnace was about to go, but work had not begun on the second one, as it seemed to be too small to work the longest plates used for *Warrior*. Furthermore, the hydraulic presses and pumps of the armour plate bending machine were nearly completed, but the frames were delayed for want of materials.

A second, wooden-hulled, ironclad, *Royal Oak,* was to be armour plated at Chatham, and another plate-bending machine would be required. Robinson sent a sketch of the hydraulic press used for bending armour plates for *Resistance* (one of the smaller ironclads that followed *Warrior* and *Black Prince*), which was being built by Westwood & Baillie at Millwall, and that firm

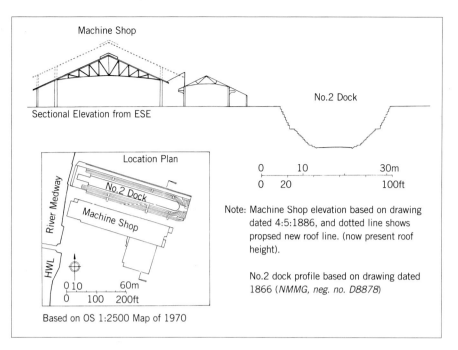

Machine Shop

Sectional Elevation from ESE

No.2 Dock

Location Plan

River Medway

No.2 Dock

Machine Shop

HWL

0 10   60m
0   100   200ft

Based on OS 1:2500 Map of 1970

0   10   30m
0   20   100ft

Note: Machine Shop elevation based on drawing dated 4:5:1886, and dotted line shows propsed new roof line. (now present roof height).

No.2 dock profile based on drawing dated 1866 (NMMG, neg. no. D8878)

sent a tracing and specification. Their offer of a machine, which bent the plates when cold, for £960 was accepted on 29 August. The plates it was to bend were 4½in thick and 5-6ft wide, and this machine was now intended to plate *Achilles*, the machinery being forwarded at the end of 1861. Further

168 This iron-framed working shed, which still stands next to No. 2 dock at Chatham, was the first building to be designed for the construction of an iron ship. (English Heritage)

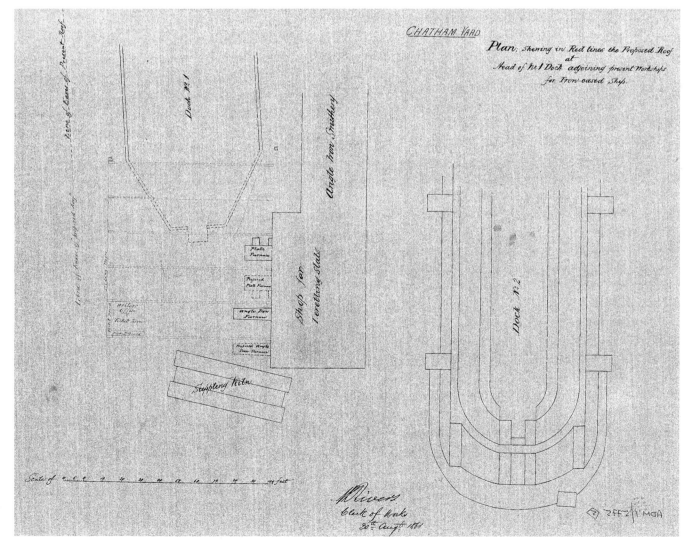

169 A drawing by Rivers, the Clerk of Works, showing the planned roof over the head of No. 1 Dock. (TNA MRH 11/88)

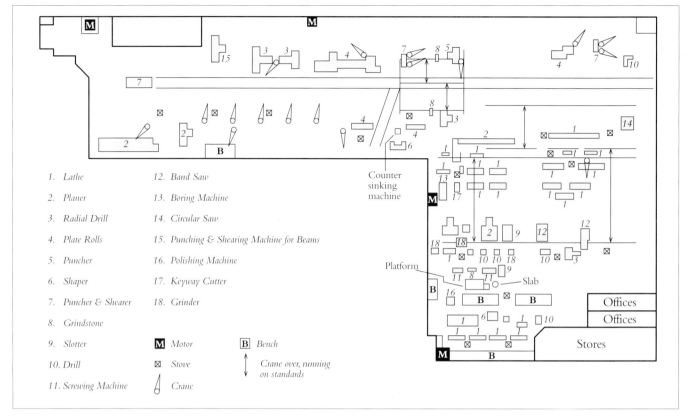

1. Lathe	12. Band Saw
2. Planer	13. Boring Machine
3. Radial Drill	14. Circular Saw
4. Plate Rolls	15. Punching & Shearing Machine for Beams
5. Puncher	16. Polishing Machine
6. Shaper	17. Keyway Cutter
7. Puncher & Shearer	18. Grinder
8. Grindstone	
9. Slotter	**M** Motor **B** Bench
10. Drill	⊠ Stove ↕ Crane over, running on standards
11. Screwing Machine	⏾ Crane

arrangements were made for the supply of iron, Mare & Co. of Millwall supplying plates and angle iron, Galloway's sending rivets, and it was laid down that all iron was to be tested with a tensile strain of 22 tons/inch lengthways and 19 tons/inch crossways.[4]

The plans for the working shed were now drawn up. Recent shipwrights' dockside working sheds, such as that designed in 1859 for No. 6 dock at Portsmouth, had been long, narrow, open-fronted buildings with a curved corrugated iron roof (Figure 167). By contrast, this was to be a major building, the widest long-span roof so far built in a Yard, though as there was no need for great height it was not so spectacular as the slip roofs (Figure 168). It was also short, just over 90ft over the head of No. 1 dock, covering working space, an office, and the angle iron and plate furnaces, though it was later extended to cover the whole length of the dock. Sheds for an angle iron smithery and the levelling slabs, replacing the old working shed between the two docks, abutted the roof, and were later structurally integrated. This building was designed by Rivers; the first surviving drawings are dated 30 August 1861. Most of the machinery must have been in place by 8 October, when

Robinson asked for a probable launch date for *Achilles*, and construction of the long span roof probably commenced in November, when a plan of the standards was made. A further building was required for the plate-bending machinery for *Royal Oak*, which was to occupy the adjoining No. 3 dock. This new plating shop was built next to No. 7 slip, and was a modest affair: Foord's constructed the iron roof for £131 and the building, clad in corrugated iron, for £254.[5]

Work begins

Construction of the ship had begun on 1 August 1861, the sophistication of the dockside machinery at once marking it out from its foreign adversaries (Figures 171, 172 and 174). Major components were made by contract, as the smithery at Chatham was not up to the job. Messrs Rigby & Beardmore were making the stern frame, but the design was changed, as it was decided not to fit a lifting screw, and work was halted, new drawings being sent in March 1862. Because of the alterations the job came to £6,000 instead of £4,000. The Thames Iron Shipbuilding Company completed the stem and knee piece in

172 *Achilles* taking on a more familiar appearance, with *Bombay*, 84 guns (1828), under repair, at Chatham, 1863. *(NMM, neg. no. C5531-18)*

February, but it proved imperfect, and Isaac Watts (*Achilles'* designer) had the expense of straightening it charged to them. A model of the ship showing the method of construction was ordered to be made for the International Exhibition held in London that year, but was not sent; the Admiralty was criticised for not preparing any models specially for the exhibition. The Westwood & Baillie plate-bending machine was set up in the spring, a larger machine with rolls 16ft long was requested (and not provided as no funds were available), and specifications were issued for 28 ton travelling cranes to plate the ship. Tracings of the machinery were forwarded to Devonport and Pembroke Dock, as all the Yards would now need to have this facility.

The brief era of the steam-powered wooden battle fleet was now over. Robinson issued a circular on 3 April ordering men to be taken off from all shipbuilding works, or conversions of frames, 'except for the Iron Cased frigates', until further orders. The men taken off were to be employed on the most urgent repairs, or on preparing ships ordered to be got ready for commissioning or the First Division of the Reserve, and no further fittings were to be proceeded with in any other of the line-of-battle ships or frigates. The first sign of trouble with the iron suppliers came in April, when Mare & Co., Moser & Sons and the Bowling Green Iron Company were asked to hasten the delivery of their orders.

Public or private?

Although no iron ship had been built in-house before by the Navy, it was confidently expected that the Yard would make a good job of it. Lloyd, who had now received his final appointment as the first Engineer-in-Chief of the Navy, had little doubt on the matter. He was positive that wooden ships were not built so well by contract as they were in the dockyards, and that an iron ship built in a Royal Yard would be more reliable than an iron ship built elsewhere. Engines could be safely bought by contract, for any faults soon came to light and the reputation of the firm suffered immediately, but it took time for a ship's defects to reveal themselves. Admiralty inspectors could only partially remedy the situation, for if the builder was determined to get the work done very cheaply, it was impossible for any number of officers to ensure everything was well done. 'I have seen enough to know the difference between the quality of work in the dockyards and in private yards; there is no comparison between the two.'

Achilles was about to be commenced when Lloyd made these statements, which were to be vindicated by her builders. Working on *Achilles* was considered, by the Yard officers at least, as conferring status. An ex-Royal Marine Sergeant with upwards of 20 years' service, now a labourer at Chatham, who in November 1861 had caught and lost the top joints of two fingers in machinery, petitioned for remuneration or a superior

173 Two views of the dock today. *(Mike Williams / English Heritage)*

174 This photograph of the French warship *Magenta* fitting out shows the contrast between the mechanised dockside at Chatham and the complete absence of travelling cranes at Brest. *(From Henri le Masson, De La Gloire au Richelieu, Paris 1946)*

in arrears. Most of them refused to return to work at the Captain Superintendent's ultimatum, and were sacked on the spot. Not surprisingly, the Captain was told:

> My Lords have approved of your having discharged Eighty one hired men employed on the *Achilles*, on account of their refusing to return to their duty. The names of these Men are to be forthwith sent by you to the other Dockyards, in order that they may not be re-entered.

In all, 89 men were finally blacklisted. Shipwrights, hastily retrained, were to complete the ship. This procedure enabled vocal representatives of private shipbuilders to criticise the Admiralty: not, of course, for sacking the men.

Myths of extraordinary persistence were generated at this time. The reader is in a position to judge the validity of such charges as 'The Admiralty are chiefly to be found among the lees and dregs of scientific progress…Portsmouth [is a dockyard] of the knee-breeches and shoe-buckle period.' The same source may, however, be accurate in saying that:

> For some time before the iron *Achilles* was fairly taken in hand by the wooden shipwrights, gangs of them…were sent for a week's, a fortnight's, or a month's instruction in the Thames Iron Shipbuilding Works, Orchard-street, Blackwall. This short apprenticeship in an extremely new branch of trade finished the training of the dockyard iron shipwrights, who are and were the instructors of their less favoured fellow-workmen…By such hands has *Achilles* been put together.

The consequence was of course that private yards ought to have the work in preference to dockyard workers, who were not only ill trained but improvident to boot:

> Why should improper persons be encouraged in wrong courses by the reflection that Government will provide for them in their age? Why should dockyard workmen, like other workmen, not be required to form habits of providence and self-dependence? Why, in a word, should Government offer the bounty of superannuating, to its own and the public loss, and to the positive detriment of those whom it is designed to serve?

This cast of mind seems curiously familiar. The author was not, however, to find many future followers of his unlucky assertion that 'What shipbuilding really stands in need of is complete and perpetual emancipation from mathematics', though innumerate browsers in volumes of the *Transactions of the Institution of Naval Architects* may sympathise.[6]

The Controller was very far from sharing this rosy picture of the virtues of private workmanship. Fighting his corner, opposing any significant reduction in naval expenditure, he wrote:

> The total abandonment of Ship building in our Dockyards would be a dangerous measure to adopt in the present transition state of our Military Navy — Nothing is yet decided as to the material and Form which it will be necessary to give to Ships of War. The relative advantages of Iron & Wood as material are nearly balanced one day, and the next a new discovery of the power of Artillery disturbs all foregone conclusions…Every

job. He had served as hired labourer from 5 June to 29 August 1861, when from good conduct and abilities he was transferred to work on *Achilles*, where he continued to give satisfaction. The Captain Superintendent submitted that having been transferred to *Achilles* he held the best appointment available. Boilermakers were hired in numbers to bring their skills to the job; when it was decided that no vacancies of any kind among the workmen were to be filled without previous sanction, men for *Achilles* were exempted.

On 14 June a party from the National Association for Promotion of Social Science toured the Yard. There was indeed an interesting situation for them to observe: shipwrights were learning the skills of metalworking under the reluctant instruction of the hired men. The Admiralty were doubtless meditating this step on 28 April when the Captain Superintendent was asked to report whether any cases had occurred of boys apprenticed to one trade transferring to another, and if so under what circumstances, whether a fresh indenture was required, and whether full time had to be served in the new trade. On 3 July the hired men downed tools in protest at working with and training shipwrights and being paid

maritime power, according to its means, has considered it indispensable to clothe its Military Navy in Iron Armour, and the chief Naval Power, after ourselves in Europe, has perfected and prepared a large number of Ships which can only be met on equal terms by a similar disposition of Force…All our experience of Contract built Ships is unfavourable. The work is slow, very expensive, requires an immense amount of inspection as to workmanship and materials and in no case has such a ship been perfected without large expenditure of time and money in the Dockyards. Should it be found by experience that Iron is the best material for our Ships of War, our past experience teaches us that no reliance whatever can be placed on private Shipbuilders keeping any engagements they may enter into with the Admiralty. Apart however from all considerations of Ship building it is clear that our present large force afloat, and the reliefs that it requires, are insuperable objections to any considerable reductions in the expenditure of Wages in our Dockyards.

The necessity to update the design of ships while on the stocks was the kind of unwanted measure that could cut into (or destroy) the profits of the builder. *Achilles* was a good example: Robinson's proposals to alter her to carry the 4½in armour plating right round the ship about 3ft below the water line aft and 2ft 6in forwards, tapering to 3in thickness at the stern and the backing to 6in, and reducing the armament from 50 to 30 guns, and the complement to 550, were accepted in May 1862. In August, Lang's proposal to carry the belt up to the beams of the main deck was agreed to.

Furthermore, things were liable to go wrong with ambitious projects, further endangering profits. The Thames Iron Co. undertook to forge and deliver rough from the hammer the after piece of keel required for £228, in 12 days from the receipt of the order. Lang thought the price reasonable, but stipulated that if in planing it any defects were found they should supply a replacement as soon as possible, free. Some plate-bending rolls broke, and Collier's were requested to supply new ones at their own cost. The Master Smith, Cotsell, was sent to Rigby & Beardmore's to examine and report on the stern frame that had been planed. He found a defect, and remained to supervise its being made good. As there was no means at Chatham to weld the sternpost, the firm got that job as well; the weld turned out to be defective, and had to be scarphed (a form of jointing).[7]

The suppliers of armour plate proved to be no more reliable than the shipbuilders. In May 1860 trials of 4½in plates from the Thames Ironworks at Portsmouth were unsatisfactory, doubtless just as the makers' exculpatory statement was found: 'We only hold ourselves responsible for faithfully manufacturing the plates according to the instructions given to us and not for any trial by shot'. Much better were the plates supplied by Westwood, Baillie & Co. and Palmer & Co., whose merits were about equal: 'they resist sufficiently to stand a considerable hammering at a short distance from the heaviest description of Shot, indeed much more than they are ever likely to get in any action'.

As at the shipyards, Admiralty inspectors kept an eye on things. Jacob Crane, Forgeman at Woolwich, was at Park Gate Works, Rotherham, supervising the making of plates for *Defence* and *Resistance*, and stayed there to superintend the manufacture of plates for *Achilles*. Men were rotated to spread the experience among the Yards; Crane was replaced by a smith from Portsmouth. A sample of the Park Gate armour was tested at Portsmouth in June, part not being backed by wood: this area was penetrated by a single shot. For the first time the plates were taken off after the firing to examine the effects of the shot upon the rear part of them, and Captain Hewlett, in charge of the gunnery training ship HMS *Excellent*, noted: 'I have been very much struck with the injury they invariably received in that part even from the first blow, and when backed by wood. In some cases the fracture being greater than that exhibited by the blow in front' (Figure 175).

The armour plates for *Achilles*, which unlike those of *Warrior* were not to be tongued and grooved to fit together, had to be appropriated from elsewhere: 100 tons of armour plate lying at Thames Ironworks originally meant for *Warrior* were forwarded to Chatham.[8]

In May 1862 Robinson, sorely tried by the failures of the ironmasters, wrote:

> The supply of Armour Plates is in an unsatisfactory state, and I beg leave to call their Lordships' attention to the difficulty experienced in procuring them. 9 firms at the beginning of this year were after survey of their Premises considered to be capable of supplying Armour Plates of 4½ inches thickness, viz. Mr Sanderson, Parkgate Works, Rotherham; Lancefield Forge Company, Glasgow; Mersey Company, Liverpool; Messrs. Hill & Smith, Brierley Hill, Staffs.; Mr I. Walton, 10 Lawrence Pountney Lane, E.C.; Messrs. T. Brown & Co., Atlas Works, Sheffield; Messrs. Rigby & Beardmore, Parkhead Forge, Glasgow and the Butterley Co., West Alfreton, Derbyshire.

Tenders had been accepted for the supply of armour plate from five of these firms for six ships: *Achilles*, Sanderson★; *Royal Oak*, Thames★; *Royal Alfred*, Brown★; *Ocean*, Butterley; *Prince Consort*, Sanderson; and *Caledonia*, Lancefield. Only four firms (those

175 A sample of *Achilles'* armour after testing by HMS *Excellent*. (TNA ADM 1/5756)

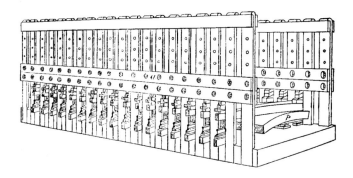

176 Armour plate being bent to shape in a cradle using the wedge and tup method. *(From E. J. Reed,* Shipbuilding in Iron and Steel, *London 1869)*

asterisked, plus Hill & Smith) had succeeded in making plates capable of passing the test. In November 1861 a tender had been accepted for armour plate for *Caledonia* from Lancefield; the order was to be delivered within six months. No plate had stood the test after five months. In January 1862 Butterley's tender for *Ocean* was accepted, the plates again to be delivered within six months. By that time no plate had been completed, let alone tested. After this fiasco in June the Thames Iron Company agreed to supply 200 tons of 4½in armour plate for *Ocean*, and 108 tons were delivered, but all subsequent batches were rejected after test. In November 1862 they agreed to supply 453 tons by 31 March 1863. By then none had been delivered, and the sample plates had all failed. By April 1863 108 tons had been accepted and 272 tons rejected; the order was cancelled.

When plates for the *Royal Sovereign* were required, in view of the poor showing made by several of the tenderers Robinson submitted that the offer made by Brown's be accepted forthwith: 'there is no doubt of [their] capability…or of the excellence of the work they turn out'. But Brown's were to let him down as well. The firm developed its technique, rolling a 12in armour plate in the presence of the Admiralty (though the Board declined to purchase it for testing for £660), and followed this up by producing a 4½in armour plate 40ft long, from which a plate 35ft by 3ft 6in could be rolled.

However, pieces of freak dimensions were not what was required, which was 217 tons of tapered armour for the topsides of *Achilles*, to be delivered by 15 March 1863. By the end of July Robinson was 'obliged to call their Lordships attention to the manner in which Messrs Brown & Co. have failed to comply with their engagements for the supply of Armour Plates. It will be seen…how very far short of their promises have been their performances'. By 22 July only 153 tons had been delivered. The order was finally completed seven months in arrears.[9]

New workshops

However unsatisfactory the supply of armour plate might be, there was no doubt that it was here to stay, and armour-plating shops had to be provided in all the Yards. The technique of bending it cold was soon abandoned, the process at Chatham being described by a French observer:

> Near the dock where the *Achilles* was under construction a special workshop was set up to bend and fit the armour plates. It consists of a furnace in which the plates are reheated for several hours at a low fire, only being brought to a dull red for sharper bends. A crane takes them out of the furnace and brings them to a hydraulic press made by Westwood & Baylie [sic]; it is equipped with a firmly set up casting table on which are placed steel formers which the plate overlays and is bent to shape by the pressure of a hydraulic piston which…produces a thrust of 1,300 tons, driven by pumps positioned at the sides. To facilitate the operation, the piston can be moved towards one side or other of the workpiece by a screw and carriage mechanism as on a tool holder, sliding on a cast iron platform which is joined to the one below by four enormous screws which are adjusted to suit the workpiece…The method is slow and requires much trial and error, but it achieves the remarkable result of rendering the surface of an armour plate as even as sheet metal: it is guaranteed not to alter the quality of the iron at all…there are sheds with several planing machines which plane the surfaces of either side of the plates and enable them to fit with a high degree of accuracy.

The planes and cutters were expensive. Those supplied by Smith, Beacock & Tannett to Keyham cost £1,840 and £600 respectively, and were bought instead of punching and shearing machinery for Devonport Smithery and tools for Keyham. After much discussion, the armour plate shop was located in the Quadrangle, a use that could not have been foreseen when the building was designed. The smoke tunnels and shafting were to hand, and by using Quadrangle space it was estimated that five months and £2,000 would be saved. The go-ahead was given in May 1862.

At Portsmouth a new building had to be built, which abutted the north end of the new Smithery: a cast and wrought iron structure, built by Bramble in the same year for £2,156, it was demolished in the 1890s. The equipment installed was so successful that drawings were sent to Keyham to enable their furnace to be altered. The plate bending was done using a different system from that used at Chatham, that of 'wedge and tup', in which the heated plate was placed in an iron cradle on packing bars. A further set of bars was placed on top of the

177 *Royal Oak* being plated at Chatham. *(NMM, neg. no. C5531-N)*

plate, and wedges were hammered under these bars to force the plate to the desired shape (Figure 176). This method of bending was quicker, and better suited to plates requiring a high degree of curvature, but some subsequent adjustment by a hydraulic press was invariably required.

The days of Woolwich were now numbered (the question of leasing the Yard was raised in 1865), but Grissell's built an armour plate shop there, the machinery of which was driven by an engine taken out of the gunboat *Mastiff*. It had to be extended in 1863, when the foundations for another plating shop at Pembroke Dock, connected with the head of the dock by a railway, were taken in hand.[10]

By February 1863 *Achilles* was nearly half completed, with 1,000 hired artificers working on it (including men for taking down the frame). The essential nucleus of this workforce was 160 shipwrights, 200 iron ship men, and 70 rivet boys, occupied in putting the frames and bulkheads together, and plating the bottom of the ship. The average proportion of hired men to established men employed was 621 to 340. Some of these had been recruited from seaman and marine pensioners; after the difficulty with the boilermakers, the Admiralty took the view that it was desirable to encourage the entry of men accustomed to obeying orders.

The travelling cranes on the staging were so busy that it had not been possible to alter the rails for the armour-plating cranes that had been fitted to the dock next door to plate *Royal Oak* (Figure 177). By the end of March Danzig fir was urgently required for the upper deck, and in April boilers and heavy parts of the machinery were to be brought to Chatham by barge. Penn's were informed that the whole of the machinery was to be delivered by early July. Overtime was to be worked during the summer. The lower masts were to be of iron, made by Finch & Heath at Chepstow, superintended by the leading man of shipwrights, and were sent by rail, unlike the other heavy components, which were sent by sea. *Rhadamanthus*, the first Royal Navy steamer to cross the Atlantic, by a happy coincidence brought the sternpost of the Navy's first Yard-built iron ship from Glasgow. Woolwich constructed a cupola for the ship, to supply molten iron for Martin's shells. It discharged its combustion products into the fore-funnel, but this was ordered to be removed by August.

A final difficulty with a contractor arose: during the turning of the upper piece of the rudder at Westwood & Baillie's, the Admiralty inspector discovered a flaw. Westwood & Baillie did not think it bad enough to condemn it, and the inspector thought it might be made good. A Shipwright Officer and the Master Smith went to report. A new caisson was made for the dock, to be fitted as soon as *Achilles* was floated out. That took place on 23 December 1864, at 2300 hours, but *Achilles* immediately grounded on a sandbank that had accumulated at the entrance to the dock. She was pulled off by the combined efforts of *Monkey*, *Bustler*, *Locust* and *Sheerness* and several hundred men on the capstans of a sheer-hulk.[11]

A new role for the Yards?

Despite the prophecies of disaster, *Achilles* proved a well-built ship, and had a long and successful career. Iron shipbuilding was firmly established in the Yards, and new buildings were required. Shipbuilding machinery had to be procured. The expense would be worth it, for Robinson thought that at least £20,000 would be saved per ship by building in the Dockyards, and the experiences with the first ironclads had not been encouraging:

> All our Contractors have complained that we require work of exceptionally good character, such as some of them say is quite unusual in the trade: others again, compare it to engine-making rather than Ship-building work and have made it the subject of claim for extra payment; but, if after all this very extra good work, which is so superior to ordinary work, (in their estimation) we find watertight compartments leaking in water faster than pumps can clear it, false bottoms leaking, sluice doors & valves not acting, [all these faults had been found in *Warrior*, *Black Prince*, *Resistance* and *Defence*] what other term than slovenly can be given to work confessedly inferior to the very superior workmanship which has yet produced such results as these?

However, *Achilles* had been expensive, and this had to be explained. No direct comparison was possible, as there was no ship of a similar design, but taking *Minotaur* as reasonably similar, it appeared that she would cost £350,623 (in the event £349,322), and take 43½ months to build, a cost of nearly £50 per ton. *Achilles* cost £388,219 and was built in 40½ months, a cost of £57.73 per ton. The discrepancy was partly due to the fact that it was the first of its kind, and partly because of the greater speed of construction, but mostly because she had to be fitted out in the stream, 3 miles from the Yard (Figure 178). The Chatham officers reckoned the extra cost of this to be £50,000. As soon as *Achilles* had been floated out, the keel of *Bellerophon* was laid down in No. 2 dock, and a century of shipbuilding in iron and steel at Chatham had begun. More heavy shipbuilding plant was needed, mostly for armour plating.[12]

However, the Yard still had a great disadvantage in the lack of any basin, and the fitting-out of the big ships had to be done in Gillingham Reach at a great increase of time and trouble; weather conditions had to be just right for heavy loads to be placed in the ships without danger and the risk of damage. The

178 *Achilles* fitting out in Gillingham Reach. *(Royal Engineers Library)*

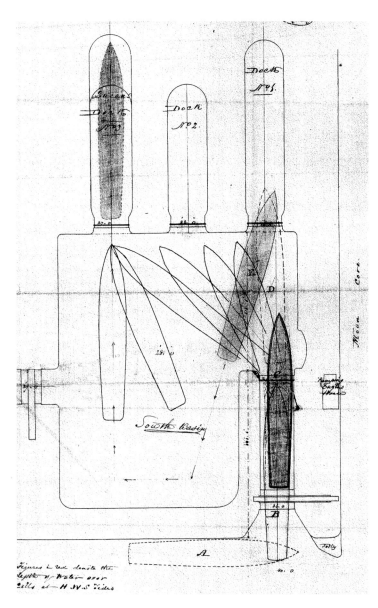

Table 12 **Work done by the Steam Factories, 1 April to 31 December 1863**

	Work done on	Percentage of factory staff employed	Percentage of wages
Woolwich	Building and converting ships	9	11 ¼
	Ships in commission	32	32 ¼
	Ships in reserve	11	11
	Dockyard services	25	22
	Manufacturing	23	23
Sheerness	Building and converting ships	1	¼
	Ships in commission	27	27 ¼
	Ships in reserve	28 ½	27 ¾
	Hulks, taking vessels to pieces	8	9 ½
	Dockyard services	12 ½	12 ¼
	Manufacturing	22 ½	22 ¼
Portsmouth	Building and converting ships	11	11
	Ships in commission	9 ¼	9 ¼
	Ships in reserve	24 ¾	24 ¾
	Hulks, taking vessels to pieces	4	4
	Dockyard services	31	30 ¼
	Manufacturing	17 ¾	18 ½
Keyham	Building and converting ships	2 ¾	2 ¾
	Ships in commission	11 ½	11 ¾
	Ships in reserve	31 ¼	32
	Hulks, taking vessels to pieces	1 ¼	1 ¼
	Dockyard services	32 ½	30 ½
	Manufacturing	20	21

179 The manoeuvres required to dock *Warrior* in Queen's Dock, Keyham. *(TNA ADM 1/5838)*

180 *Minotaur's* profile drawn onto Queen's Dock *(TNA ADM 1/5838)*

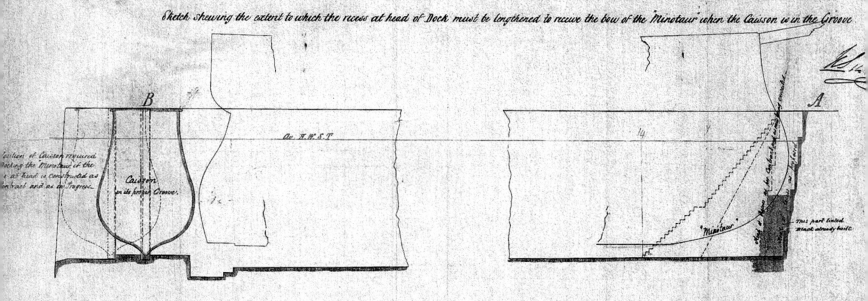

creation of an extension to adapt the base for the foreseeable needs of the Steam Navy would obviously involve civil engineering projects on a momentous scale, and for years to come Chatham-built ironclads would receive their machinery and masts from the sheer hulks while moored in the Medway.

The Steam Factories played little part in the construction of new ships; if they had been essential for this purpose Chatham would never have been selected as a building yard for ironclads. Figures for the period between 1 April and 31 December 1863 show their place in the scheme of things (Table 12). The Factories, as these figures show, were primarily for maintenance of the ships and the infrastructure of the Yards.

The new ships were of unprecedented dimensions. In autumn of 1861 difficulties were foreseen in docking *Warrior* in Keyham, as it could only be managed at high water of spring tides. Greene suggested that the most economical method would be to lengthen Queen's Dock and provide additional pumping engines to raise the level of water in the basin rapidly. These would also serve as reserve engines in case of the ordinary pumps breaking down. But how could it be got into Queen's Dock? Townshend, the Superintendent Civil

Engineer, drew up a plan to demonstrate the possible evolutions with a scale cut-out of *Warrior* (Figure 179). The Master Attendant proposed to shunt the ship into No. 1 Dock, reverse it out into the basin and then into Queen's Dock. But this could not be done as things stood, as No. 1 dock had cills 23ft deep while the ship drew 25ft. In turn, the Master Attendant criticised Townshend's suggested evolution of edging the ship round gently: 'The pivotting of the *Warrior* on paper is one thing and her gyrations on the water is another'. Damage would be done to the sides of the ship and the masonry in attempting it. The work of deepening No. 1 dock was begun in January 1863. Queen's Dock itself was not long enough for the new ironclads of the *Minotaur* class, and further adjustments would be needed there (Figure 180). At Devonport the jetties would have to be extended into deeper water to enable her to lie alongside. The ever-increasing length of major warships, particularly in the latter years of the nineteenth century, was to be responsible for a programme of dock extension (Figure 181). Indeed, the inadequate number of dry docks, and their shortness and lack of breadth, were problems never solved in the Yards. The supply of docks capable of

181 Work under way in 1880 on the reconstruction of the eighteenth-century No. 3 dock at Devonport. Note the Millwrights' Shop and the North Smithery to the rear. *(TNA ADM 195/60)*

182 (Opposite, top) The four central battery ironclads of the *Audacious* class were smaller than their immediate predecessors, and were designed for service primarily on foreign stations. One of them is pictured here in Plymouth Sound. *(Chrysalis Picture Library)*

183 Another early iron built warship, the screw corvette *Active* (1869), entering Portsmouth harbour. *(Chrysalis Picture Library)*

handling capital ships of ever-increasing dimensions needed a massive programme of investment, which was never undertaken on the scale required. Other problems, in their way just as pressing, had to be addressed at once: the steamers needed coaling facilities.[13]

—⚍—

Notes:

[1] ADM 83/37, ADM 89/1.

[2] POR/R/34, ADM 135/2, NMM ADM/Y/C/49-63, NMM ADM/Y/PE/1-5, ADM 12/684, ADM 135/2.

[3] ADM 87/77, ADM 92/21, POR/R/35, CHA/H/104.

[4] CHA/H/105, CHA/H/106, CHA/H/107, CHA/H/109.

[5] ADM 1/5715, MP 11/88, NMM J/12, NMM J/13, CHA/H/107, NMM F/16, NMM J/18, NMMJ/31.

[6] *Minutes of the Select Committee on Chatham Dockyard Extension; Record of the International Exhibition, 1862*, (Glasgow, n.d.) p.183 (the section on Naval Architecture was contributed by no less than E J Reed and N Barnaby); CHA/H/109, CHA/H/110, CHA/H/111, M Waters, 'Changes in the Chatham Dockyard Workforce, 1860-90, part 1', *Mariner's Mirror*, vol. 69 no. 1, 1983, pp.55-63; P Barry, *Dockyard Economy and Naval Power*, (London, 1863), pp.67, 77, 134; P Barry, *The Dockyards, Shipyards, and Marine of France*, (London, 1864), p.37.

[7] ADM 1/5802, CHA/H/110, CHA/H/111, CHA/H/112.

[8] The plates were to be attached by bolts made by Tupper & Co., Limehouse, who galvanised them, but this was a waste of time and money, as Chatham reported that the galvanised nuts and bolts were roughly coated, partly filling the thread, so the nuts had to be recut to fit.

[9] ADM 87/75, ADM 1/5732, CHA/H/105, CHA/H/106, POR/P/64, ADM 1/5756, CHA/H/107, CHA/H/114, ADM 1/5802, CHA/H/110, CHA/H/111, CHA/H/112, ADM 1/5840, ADM 1/5841, CHA/H/116.

[10] M. le Contre-Amiral Paris, *L'Art Naval A L'Exposition Universelle De Londres De 1862*. (Paris, n.d.) pp.30-31; ADM 1/5802, ADM 1/5803, ADM 12/716, ADM 12/732, E J Reed, *Shipbuilding in Iron and Steel*, (London, 1868), pp.470-473; ADM 12/748, ADM 12/764.

[11] CHA/H/113, *Labour Charts for Dockyards and Steam Factories 1862-3 and for Nine Months to 31st December 1863*, (London, 1864); ADM 1/5941, CHA/H/111, CHA/H/112, CHA/H/116, CHA/H/117, CHA/H/119, NMM NPA 4585, R G Hobbes, *Reminiscences and Notes of Seventy Years*, (London, 1895), vol. 2, p.308.

[12] The machinery ordered for 1866/7 comprised:

	£
2 shaping and planing machines for armour plate	900
1 plate shearing machine	900
2 drilling machines	490
2 smaller drilling machines	200
2 punching and shearing machines	1,200
Traveller for lifting 9in armour plate	500
Crane for plate furnaces	170

[13] ADM 1/5840, ADM 1/5941, ADM 1/5942, ADM 1/5838, MP 11/88.

184 (Opposite, bottom) The small central battery ironclad *Research*, converted from wooden sloop *Trent* while under construction. Built at Pembroke between 1861 and 1864, her slightly unusual name was a reflection of her somewhat experimental nature. She was placed in reserve in 1878, and sold for scrapping in 1887. *(Chrysalis Picture Library)*

CHAPTER 14

Coaling the Navy

Early schemes

The advent of the new motive power necessitated the storage of large quantities of coal, not only at the Dockyards but also at strategic locations determined by the bases of a likely enemy and the limited range of the steamship when using its engines alone. Portland was well placed for these purposes: it was opposite Cherbourg and roughly midway between Devonport and Portsmouth. The significance of its location was realised by a Royal Engineer officer in 1835, when he put forward suggestions for fortifying the anchorage:

> …in the event of the Construction of a Breakwater…a very secure Naval Establishment might be formed there at a small expence. As this may be a subject of importance at a future period, especially on the further introduction of Steam Vessels, I consider that the rights of the Crown over this part [of Portland] should be rigidly preserved.

At that time the Weymouth packet boats were the principal steamers seen in the area, and no special arrangements were provided for them. The first ship to be used as a floating coal depot may have been *Pallas*, a fifth rate converted for the purpose in 1836 for service at Devonport; but the initial arrangements proved most unsatisfactory, and in 1838 the Admiral Superintendent suggested several alterations to increase its capacity and facilitate trans-shipment. A depot was established at Alexandria early on.

At Woolwich, the first large-scale home of the Steam Navy, where large quantities of coal needed to be stored and transferred to ships, a remarkably far-sighted suggestion was made by the Captain Superintendent in September 1844. Captain Sir Francis Collier proposed that a large dumb barge, built of iron, be built as an additional depot, and he sent a crude illustration (Figure 185).[1] However, nothing came of this at the time, although the Captain's concept was to reappear again, wonderfully transformed.[2]

Many old ships were turned into coal hulks: line-of-battle ships had a good capacity, and were useful where there were deep-water anchorages. Shore-to-ship coaling was also considered; Denison was asked to report on the techniques of coaling in use at South Shields and the other ports in the area. When James replaced him at Portsmouth one of his tasks was to find a suitable location for a coaling depot. The site should be sheltered from prevailing winds, have space for a depot to contain 10,000 to 20,000 tons of coal, and be protected by existing defence works or be able to be defended by new ones. James prepared a mock-up of a steamer's deck prepared with openings (the Surveyor had this layout adopted for steamers fitting out), and he considered that with a proper supply a steamer should be coaled in a day. First of all he settled on Rat Island at Gosport, which could be placed in charge of the officers of Clarence Yard (the Victualling Yard close to the island), and have three sides deepened to receive steamers, the fourth prepared for colliers to unload. However, he finally settled on Calshot Castle, still very much in use as a coast defence battery. The Board of Ordnance did not object, asking only that the depot wall form an integrated defence network with the Castle. Nothing came of this scheme.

Another far-sighted plan, this time for containerised transport of coal to the Yards, was submitted in December 1846 by the solicitors to the Bristol & Poole Harbour Railway, who proposed having a floating dock at their Bristol terminus:

> …by which means their Iron Barges containing the Boxes with Welch Steam Coals…will be placed on the Line and conveyed without shifting, or break of Gauge direct to Her Majesty's Stores either at Gosport or Portsmouth or by means of a Pier alongside of which a Steam Ship may lie and the Coals be placed at once on board — affording thereby a continuous supply of Best Steam Coals in first-rate condition…

They had submitted a scheme to supply 21,000 tons annually to Mr Russell, contractor for supply of coals at Southampton for the South Western Steam Navigation Company, the P & O Steam Navigation Company, and the Royal West India Mail Company, and to the Engineer in Chief of the last, and they had promised to support the plan. There would be a small increase in price, but this would be more than compensated for by the excellent condition of the coal. This offer was not taken up. Neither was a plan devised at the same time by Captain W H Hall:

> At all the great naval ports there should be a large Depôt for coals, capable of receiving several thousand tons, — a 12 month's consumption, for the supply of Steamers employed, or likely to be employed. Each Depôt should be so situated as to be independent of the Dockyard and other permanent establishments — They ought to have Jetties running into deep water; so that two, or more, of the largest Steamers, may go alongside and be coaled at the same time. The coals should be brought down in Waggons similar to those used in loading

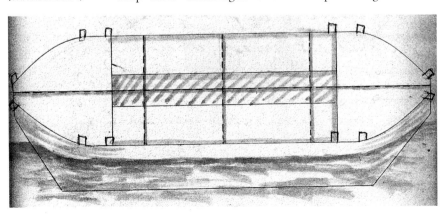

185 The proposed floating coal depot of 1844.
(TNA ADM 83/34)

Colliers in the Tyne, with Shoots, &c, complete. Each Depôt ought to have a branch to a main Railway, in case of the communication by sea being interrupted by contrary winds, Gales, Strikes of Seamen for wages, or any other cause. The coals should be kept under cover, and in separate compartments of 50, 100, 200, 300 and 500 Tons, the more readily to stop ignition and to facilitate the issue, without being premeasured…

In addition to these dockside facilities at the major bases he proposed a network of jury-rigged coaling vessels around the coasts of the British Isles. These were to store, in addition to coal, water and provisions, gunner's, carpenter's and engineer's stores, and ammunition, for issue in emergency. The ships should be armed with two or more large shell-firing guns aft, with an all-round command. Additional armament could be fitted, making each depot available as a blockship in emergency, and able to be taken to any other port or station at home or abroad. All coals for immediate use were to be kept in the main or upper covered deck, in measured quantities. Coal wagons ran along the bottom of the hold, and were filled by gravity. They were raised to the deck by steam-powered derricks and discharged through shoots into steamers' bunkers. The steam engine would also be used for unloading colliers, weighing the anchor, warping the ship ahead, and other purposes. There was no end of uses for such a vessel: they could be given a fender all round and show two coloured lights at night as a navigational marker, and act as a training ship for boys and new recruits (Figure 186).[3]

The hulks that were fitted out as coaling depots were more modestly equipped with just a steam boiler and derricks to load and unload coal. Messrs Blyth of Limehouse were the first suppliers of this machinery, sending a 20hp engine and machinery for *Malabar*, the Portsmouth coaling depot, in 1848, for £1,450 and £300 fixing charge. They were also asked to recommend a competent man to be in charge of the machinery, and one was engaged at 6s a day. Ellice was pleased by the performance of this equipment after six months' trial in which no improvements had suggested themselves, and recommended that Blyth's supply and fix four additional sets of hoisting apparatus for £1,080. The five sets would then be capable of delivering 75 tons of coal per hour. By 1850 most of the Yards had been equipped with coal hulks and in June an Admiralty Minute was sent asking for information on the number of steam vessels that could be coaled at the various ports in the space of 24 hours. The replies showed a variety of capabilities (Table 13). The performance of Chatham was by far the worst, not surprisingly, for this was the last of the Yards to be equipped with facilities for the Steam Navy.[4]

Woolwich could coal six ships, but only if all other work was dropped. Sheerness officers noted that *Fortitude* was moored in Salt Pan Reach, two miles from the Yard, and was capable of holding 1,600 tons. Two small steamers could be coaled in the Camber, and 'in <u>very fine</u> weather & smooth water two alongside the Dock Yard, but the present Coal Store being so far detached…would unavoidably cause a proportionate loss of time, and Labour'. Portsmouth, with *Malabar*, could do much better: she could deliver 30 tons per hour using three of her derricks, and *Maidstone* 11 tons per hour, though it was thought unlikely that the coal trimmers on the steamers would be able to keep pace with such a speed of delivery. Devonport had two

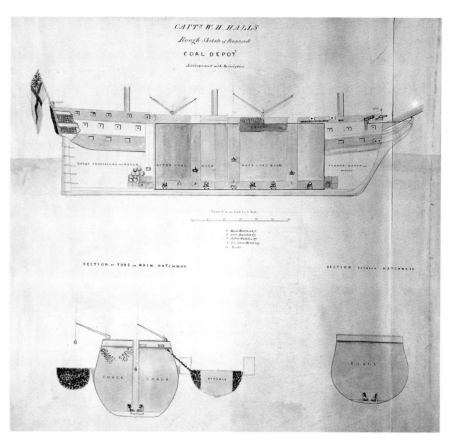

186 Captain Hall's proposal for a floating coal depot. This was not a hulk, but had limited seagoing functions. *(Admiralty Library, Whitehall)*

Table 13 **Coaling capabilities of the various ports, June 1850**

Number that could be coaled at the same time:

Woolwich	6 of any description
Chatham	1
Sheerness	2 of the largest class from hulk *Fortitude*
Portsmouth	2 of any kind from dockyard jetties
	2 of any kind from hulk *Malabar*
	2 small frigates from hulk *Maidstone*
Devonport	4 of any description
Cork	2 first class

Coals that could be put on each vessel in 24 hours:

Woolwich	105 tons each
Chatham	200-250 tons
Sheerness	240 tons each
Portsmouth	336 tons from dockyard jetties
	720 tons from *Malabar*
	480 tons from *Malabar*
	131 tons each from *Maidstone* if bags previously filled. 72 if bags not filled
Devonport	150 tons each in 2-5 hours if bags filled
	300 tons each to the other two in 24 hours
Cork	220 tons to one or 150 tons each to two

Number of men required:

Woolwich	30 per vessel who must be relieved by relays
Chatham	70 + horses relieved by the same number
Sheerness	52 to be relieved
Portsmouth	108 men and 12 horses at the dockyard jetties
	48 on each of the hulks to be relieved by the same number
Devonport	120 for 5 hours or 80 men for 24 hours
Cork	60 for 24 hours

187 This
atmospheric
photograph shows
Pitt and
Camperdown with
other coal hulks in
Portsmouth Harbour.
*(TNA ADM 195/79/
28285)*

floating coal depots: *Pallas*, with 150 tons in bags and 650 tons in the holds, and *Jupiter*, with 150 tons in bags and 950 tons in holds. This was not a satisfactory situation with a steam battle fleet about to be brought into commission.[5]

More ships were converted to act as coal depots; *Malabar* was taken as a model and made available for inspection by potential tenderers. *Pitt* and *Camperdown*, fitted out at Portsmouth in 1856, had to be able to raise coal from one collier on each side at a time, each hoist having two coal buckets, to hold not less than 10cwt (Figure 187). Each hoist was to raise one of these buckets at not less than 120ft/min. The Government would provide timber sleepers and foundations for machinery and engines, and the assistance of shipwrights would be given free.

Taylor & Co. were the contractors for these ships for £1,580. Apart from fitting the machinery, the conversion work needed for a ship with a capacity of 1,800 tons could be done in 20 days by 20 shipwrights, with other trades and labourers in proportion.[6]

These hulks also fulfilled a strategic role. The average steamship stowed enough coal for about 12 days and at full steam would average about 190 miles a day: her coal would therefore carry her about 2,280 miles. The distance from England to Madeira was 1,250 miles and from England to Cape Verde 2,300 miles, but from Cape Verde to the Cape of Good Hope was 4,900 miles. In November 1859 it was decided to plug this gap by establishing a floating coal depot at Fernando Po. *Vindictive* was selected, the cost being hull with fenders £5,043, without £4,502, and the machinery £1,585 (Figure 188).

In early 1858 Captain Milne, while serving on the Board, prepared a paper showing the quantity and cost of fuel required for the Navy. He calculated the total horsepower of home-based ships at 69,400, and as a rule of thumb the expenditure of coal was reckoned to be about one tenth of the horsepower: that is, 6,940 tons per day. Assuming that the ships would average two days' steaming a week, this amounted to 666,240 tons in a year, and with coal at £1 a ton the cost would be £666,240. Abroad, 900,480 tons would be consumed in a year, but the cost was much higher, £2 5s per ton, which put the cost up to £2,200,000. By May 1860 the coal hulks listed in Table 14 were attached to Depots. It will be seen that Chatham ships still had to go to Sheerness to coal.

Coal hulks were to serve the Steam Navy for at least another 35 years, but more sophisticated methods were envisaged by some of the foremost engineers of the day.[7]

Plans for mechanised coaling with specialist buildings

In 1851 Milne had put forward a suggestion that mechanical coal-handling methods be applied, with steam power (where installed at the base) being used to run a mechanism employing a shaft or endless chain, or where steam power was not available, an adapted hydraulic crane powered by an elevated reservoir. He was particularly impressed with the devices developed by Blyth's, who in addition to developing derrick systems for coal hulks had proposed a covered coal store divided into compartments, each equipped with a shoot for coaling a vessel lying alongside. The compartments were loaded by a single crane at wall-plate level. This transferred the coal to a trolley with a hatch in the bottom, which ran along a railway running under the apex of the roof (Figure 189).

Table 14 **Coal hulks attached to depots by May 1860**

Depot	Ship	Tonnage
Woolwich	Aigle	990
	Messenger	733
Chatham	Enterprise	471 – to go to Nore
Sheerness	Ocean	2,291
	Fortitude	1,760
	Columbine	492
	Benbow	1,773
Portsmouth	Camperdown	2,404
	Malabar	1,715
	Pitt	1,751
	Maidstone	947
	Helena	549
	Lily	432
	Orestes	460
	Griffon	231
Devonport	Jupiter	1,173
	Bacchus	1,084
	Lavinia	1,172
	Pallas	951
	Fly	485
	Favorite	432
	Harlequin	433
	Nimrod	502
	Racehorse	438

The next year John Coode, the Resident Engineer at the Portland Breakwater works, probably aware of the Admiralty's interest in such an installation, drew up a specification for a mechanised coaling base at Portland:

The present slope at the foot of the Hill to the Westward of the Engineers Office will have to be excavated so as to admit of the erection of a Store capable of containing about 5000 tons of Coal, with Railways leading to and from the same — an Engine and Boiler House, Stack and other adjunct works — The Character of work in these buildings will be similar to that of the Workshops already erected at the Depot…Between the rails on the Turn out Road laid upon the Jetty, there must be fixed a wrought iron hopper made of Boiler plate to receive the Coals when tipped from the Railway Waggons. The Coaling Apparatus will consist of a trough and endshoot formed of best Staffordshire Boiler plate…The trough will be carried at the inner end upon a shaft working on bearings in a cast iron saddle piece, fixed to a Block or Pier of Masonry. Inside the Harbour Wall there will be a proper wrought iron Pontoon, working in a tide well, formed in the Masonry. A cast iron Cylinder will be fixed upon this Pontoon, in which there will be a plunger, to act as a support to the outer end of the Coaling Trough, by means of hydrostatic pressure; to these there will be attached proper racks and palls to form a locking apparatus; at each end of the trough before described there will be tumblers fixed on proper wrought iron shafts, working in brass bearings — through the Coaling trough there will be a double line of endless chains working over the tumblers, and carrying scrapers or bed plates for the purpose of conveying the Coal — To this apparatus there must be fitted all gear works, brackets and shafting, necessary for connecting the same with the Engine from which the power will be derived. Coal store to be powered by a condensing steam engine & a high pressure steam engine.

This specification does not deal with the internal workings of the coal store, which Coode must have worked out at a later

188 (Left) The coaling arrangements as fitted to *Vindictive*. (TNA ADM 1/5744)

189 (Right) Messrs Blyth's proposal for a covered coal store. (TNA ADM 7/617)

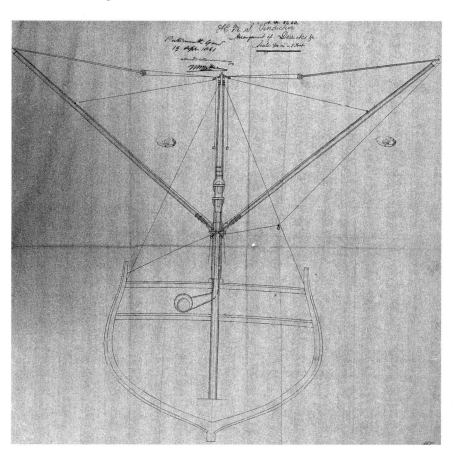

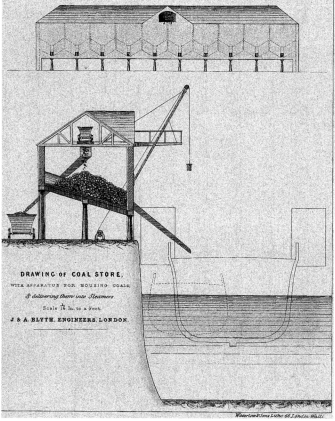

DRAWING OF COAL STORE, WITH APPARATUS FOR HOUSING COALS, & delivering them into Steamers. Scale 16 In. to a Foot. J & A. BLYTH, ENGINEERS, LONDON.

190 The coaling device on the inner arm of Portland Breakwater. *(Author's collection)*

Table 15 Coode's projected costs of conveying coal from South Wales to the principal Yards, August 1857

To	By vessel	By rail	By vessel and rail
Portsmouth	10s	12s 6d	9s 9d
Devonport	9s	14s	10s
Portland	9s	6d 11s	8s

Table 16 Forecast labour and working charges (pence)

	Receiving	Issuing	Total
Portsmouth	6⅝	6¾	13⅜
Devonport	12¼	12¼	24½
Portland (estimated)	3	2½	5½

date. He never patented this coaling device, nor any other of his ingenious devices (neither did Isambard Kingdom Brunel), but H. Mackworth in May 1857 patented an analogous endless band apparatus 'which not only carries the material up into the ship…but drops it gently into place by means of a downwardly inclined part'.

Coode's project could go no further forward until the Breakwater had reached a suitable state, and nothing further was done until 1856 when he succeeded James Rendel as Chief Engineer at Portland. In that year the coaling jetty on the inner breakwater was ordered to be proceeded with. £20,000 was allowed for the coal store and its jetty. The breakwater was to be used as a depot, equipped with the latest machinery, for unloading, storing and transferring coal as well as a sea defence. The coal store was to have a capacity of 4,000 tons; in 1860 HMS *Warrior* had a record coal capacity of 853 tons. The coaling shed was, however, designed with the wooden battle fleet of the 1850s still in mind. HMS *Agamemnon*, a typical example, when first coaled on 29 January 1853 took on 485 tons, and expended 44 tons in steaming from the Nore to Spithead. Its bunkers of coal could easily be expended in a week.

The coal store would hold enough to refuel some six or seven steam liners, and its capacity was probably designed with a view to keeping the Channel Squadron at sea. The fuel was to be unloaded from colliers by cranes placed at wall-plate height on the northern end of the building (unlike Blyth's design, which loaded at the side), which would unload into wagons running on four lines for the length of the building. (Considerable lengths of these lines survive in the roof space today.) These would discharge into the main body of the store. In the absence of any contemporary drawings it is not known whether there was any subdivision of the coal in the mode proposed by Captain Hall for his modified hulk.

Below the main body of the building were three tunnels: a central one with two railway tracks, and one single track one on each side. Shoots led through the floor of the main body to load wagons in the central tunnel. There was apparently no such arrangement for the side tunnels, which were probably used to hold made-up trains of loaded wagons in readiness. It is not known how the coal was trimmed down into the shoots, probably just as coal trimmers would have worked within a ship. The trains would then be drawn out along a railway running the length of the Breakwater to discharge over Coode's loading device, being shunted back into the central tunnel to be reloaded while a second locomotive pulled the next train out, making the operation virtually continuous. The size of the wagons used is not known, but basing them on contemporary GWR practice a train the length of the coaling shed would be some 15 wagons with a total capacity of about 120 tons. Four trainloads, the contents of the tunnels, would therefore suffice to coal a line-of-battle ship, and by the time this had happened two trains would be reloaded and ready to go again (Figure 190).[8]

This system was designed to handle waterborne traffic. There was the possibility, which eventually came to pass, of a rail connection between Portland and the coalfields, and on 8 August 1857 Coode sent a memorandum to Walker on the relative projected transport costs. The cost of conveyance per ton from South Wales to the principal yards was estimated as shown in Table 15. The forecasts for labour and working charges were all in favour of Portland (Table 16).

This showed that great savings could be effected at Portland, assuming that the new techniques delivered what Coode promised. He stated: 'The indirect saving effected by detaining the vessel only one half the time is at <u>least</u> as important as the direct saving and such as in many cases would be of the utmost importance.' He gave the following estimates as to how much could be unloaded from colliers in a 10-hour day:

Portsmouth	80-100 tons
Devonport	200-290 tons
Portland (estimated)	500-600 tons

At Portland, in addition, the vessels would receive their water directly from pipes on the jetty while lying alongside taking in coals. Milne, established as the Board's specialist in coaling matters, was keen to expedite mechanical coaling. Four days were allowed at each coaling base to fuel ships on passage to the East, and this could mean that there was very little difference in passage time between steam and sail. He visualised coal being brought to Portsmouth by rail via Brighton from the Thames, with coal depots at the Steam Basin, by the sheerlegs, worked by steam; at Watering Island; and at a wharf run out from Royal Clarence Victualling Yard. During the 1850s Welsh coal, which produced much less smoke than North Country coal, overhauled it as the most widely used fuel. The Russian War had shown the great operational disadvantages of clouds of black smoke and accelerated the change (Figure 191). The figures for 1854 and 1855 are not given. The marked preference for Welsh coal for service abroad is evident.

In an Admiralty visit to Portland in 1856 the development of

Portland as a complete naval base to counterpose the French menace had been discussed, and Rendel was asked to prepare a scheme. His death prevented his completing a design, but Coode took over the task, and on the Admiralty visit to Portland in August 1858 he showed his plans to the party. In January 1859 he wrote a long letter to the Admiralty describing his Yard, the first to be specifically designed for the Steam Navy. This would be a state-of-the-art undertaking, with three building slips, an outer basin and two inner basins, three dry docks and two coaling jetties (Figure 192). The whole dockyard was protected by a breakwater of its own. The latest technology, hydraulic machinery, was now incorporated in the coaling equipment. Armstrong, in an account of his innovations, referred to the use of his machinery at Portland:

> The object…is to provide power for working hydraulic cranes and hauling machines, and more particularly for giving motion to machinery arranged by Mr Coode…for putting coal into war steamers. A reservoir on the adjoining height affords an available head of upwards of 300 feet; but in order to diminish the size of the pipes, cylinders, and valves connected with the hydraulic machinery, a hydraulic pumping engine and accumulator are

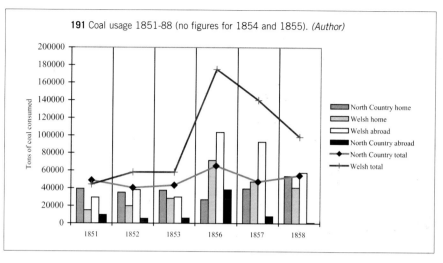

191 Coal usage 1851-88 (no figures for 1854 and 1855). (Author)

interposed, for the purpose of intensifying the pressure and diminishing the volume of water acting as the medium of transmission.

All that materialised out of these grandiose plans were the mechanised coaling system and the great coal store. On 19 April

192 Coode's plan for a self-contained steam yard at Portland. (TNA ADM 1/5730)

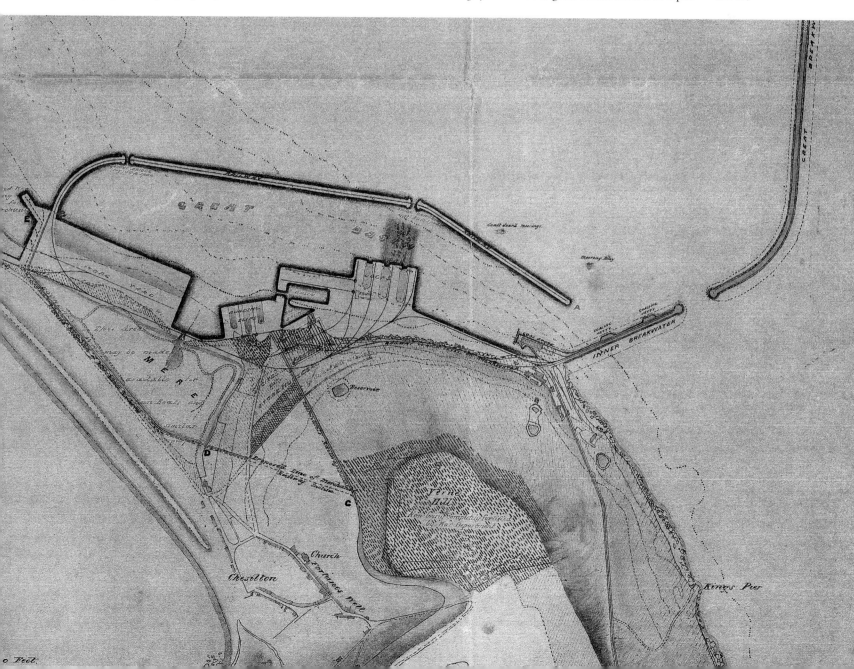

1858 Coode received five tracings from Armstrong's of the hydraulic cranes and steam machinery for the coaling shed. In December further drawings of the hydraulic cranes were sent. Next February stone was set aside ready for the construction of the coaling wharf, and in the meantime a coal hulk was required. *Pitt* was sent from Portsmouth for this purpose. She did not prove entirely satisfactory, the Captain of HMS *Colossus* writing on 14 September 1860:

> The coal depot ship *Pitt*, having on board nearly 1100 tons, expects a collier with 400 tons more. On former occasions when *Pitt* was so loaded a party of men had to continually pump until several hundred tons were coaled by the Channel Fleet.[9]

The coaling jetty was completed by the end of 1859, and tests with such equipment as was in place had given disappointing results. An undated account, probably from 1859, sheds further light on the intended workings of the system at the point of delivery:

> Wagons will fetch the coal [from the Store] and convey it along a railway on the superstructure, and will discharge it at one side of the jetty upon a wrought iron trough from which it will slide down. This trough about 52 feet in length varies its inclination according to the level of the sea and the height of the port-hole of the ship which is to take in coals, and the wall…has a groove cut in it for this purpose, to the height midway between high & low water. It was evident that for the most part the inclination of the trough would not be great enough to allow…the coals to slide down by the force of gravity, and sometimes even the inclination is in a reverse way from the ship. To remedy this they are obliged to make the coal pass along by an endless chain, which has scrapers attached to it, & which is set in motion by a machine, thus moving along the inclined trough. The apparatus

193 John Wood's proposed design for a coal store and distributive system at Portsmouth. *(TNA ADM 1/5838)*

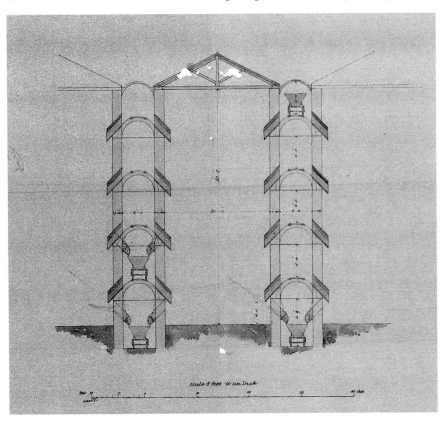

Scale 8 feet to an Inch

in the year 1858 was still in the workshops. The stone-work which was to support it was not completed; but it had been tried: and besides its complication, an objection was made that it broke up the coal and made much dust.

During 1860 the Coal Store was ready, apart from a small portion of the slating of the roof, and the internal arrangements were nearly completed. During the second quarter of 1861 the hydraulic apparatus was complete, with the exception of the hauling gear, which Armstrong's were engaged in altering. By the end of September all was ready for use as soon as moorings for the colliers had been completed. *The Times* optimistically announced: 'The only limit to the rapidity with which the coals can be sent aboard by these means, is the rate at which they can be trimmed away in the bunkers by the men. A ton a minute can, it is said, be safely counted on.' However, in June 1863 the Admiral of the Channel Squadron reported that there was no coaling depot at Portland. The system in fact had proved to be an utter failure.

It appears to have been unusable from the start, for no big ship attempted to use it until 1866. On 12 July of that year Rear-Admiral Admiral Yelverton, in command of the Channel Squadron, was informed that 1,000 tons of coal would be sent to Portland for his use. The new ironclad HMS *Lord Clyde*, which had a coal capacity of 600 tons, came alongside the coaling jetty at 8.15 a.m. on Thursday 9 August. Coaling commenced at 8.25 a.m., and by noon only 61 tons had been taken on board. When coaling stopped for the day at 5 p.m. 146 tons had been loaded. The next day the operation ran from 6.35 a.m. to 2 p.m., when it was completed with 400 tons loaded in total. (By comparison, on 20 August, taking on coal in the conventional way from a hulk in Plymouth Sound, 490 tons was taken on between 10.40 a.m. and 4 p.m.)

The Captain, Roderick Dew, wrote to Yelverton about 'the present inconvenient system of coaling at Portland', and the Admiral directed his Chief Engineer, assisted by the Chief Engineers of *Pallas* and *Liverpool*, to make a report and suggest means of improving things. On 17 August the Chief Engineer submitted plans for the modification of the system. On 23 August the *Dorset County Chronicle* noted the visit of the Naval Lords to Portland, where, among other things, they viewed the coaling arrangements. Next May the same source, reporting the next Admiralty visit, stated that 'their Lordships are about to carry out some very desirable improvements both at the coaling jetty and elsewhere'. But the matter was past mending. Another hydraulic device, equally unsuccessful, was installed at Moon Cove, Keyham, but nothing is known about its design, and Coode had been asked to communicate with Bernays at Woolwich, sending him drawings of his device, but the Yard officers there declined to adopt it.[10]

The failure of the Portland coaling system did not deter other attempts at a covered coal store with an internal distributive mechanism. On 4 July 1863 John Wood, the Assistant Civil Engineer at Portsmouth, forwarded the latest plans for a proposed coaling depot at Watering Island, next to the chain cable store (Figure 193). Scamp appraised this project and summarised its history, implying in passing that a satisfactory system had not been developed.[11]

The surviving drawings leave unanswered some questions about the working of the building. The building is divided into eight cells for coal storage, separated by passages that hold five superimposed railway tracks carried on arches. Shoots lead from either side of the tracks into the coal spaces, and the lowest tracks have the shoots reversed to feed a wagon. Elevators on the jetty side of each side of each of the tracks lift the wagons to the desired level for unloading. This bizarre system was clearly devised to prevent breakage of coal through falling excessive distances while being dumped, for the distance between the bottom of the lowest shoot and the storehouse floor is only 4ft. The method of working was, presumably, for trucks to be lifted to the first-floor track and unloaded, and when the store was filled up to the level of the shoots, lifted to the next level, and so on until the space was completely filled. The short fall of coal would apply only from the first stage; after that the drop would be some 10ft. Coal would then be drawn from the store on the lowest two levels and sent out to the ships. There is no suggestion of any loading device such as Coode's. It is not known whether the system was tried experimentally on a small scale; possibly the failure of Portland militated against its construction.[12]

The final solutions

Means for getting the coal from the deck into a ship's bunkers and out of them into the stoke-holes were easier to contrive. Walker suggested providing leather shoots between the decks, and some were made at Devonport, but they proved to be too stiff to be easily stowable, and the Master Shipwright at Devonport, William Edye, prepared a drawing in February 1858 of a portable iron shoot, which split in two along the diameter to be suspended between the beams when not in use (Figure 194). The following year Lloyd ordered tramways to be fitted to the coal bunkers of *Galatea*; Thomas Baker, the Chief Engineer at Chatham, sent drawings to show the arrangements that were already being installed on *Ariadne*, and these were approved.

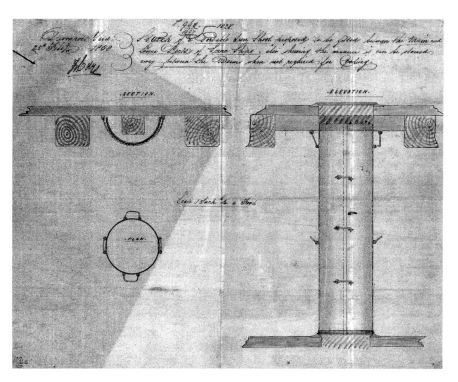

Coal buckets, pulled by hand, were suspended from overhead rails, which connected the bunkers to the furnaces.

Unsophisticated techniques had perforce to be applied at Portland, which was too useful a location for the great covered store to be abandoned. In November 1866 it was suggested that 12 mortar vessels be converted to coaling lighters. The Controller proposed in September 1867 that *Vernon* be converted to a floating jetty for coaling, and this was ready to be towed out by January 1868. During August four mortar vessels were ordered to be fitted out as additional coaling lighters. The Coal Store was accordingly modified in the early months of 1869 by adding three coaling stages on the north-

194 Edye's portable iron shoot for coaling. *(TNA ADM 87/67)*

THE WAY FORWARD FOR COALING THE NAVY

In 1885 a Committee on Coaling Facilities reported on the state of affairs. Their principal recommendations were:

1. That coal hulks be abolished.
2. That present haulabouts be replaced by properly constructed lighters of 150 tons capacity.
3. That a proportion of lighters, one in five, have steam propelling power.
4. That ships shall not enter harbour solely for the purpose of coaling.
5. That as a rule heavy ships shall coal from lighters from coal in bulk.
6. That coal be handed on board in small baskets of about 50 lbs, over temporary stages on ship's side rigged for the occasion.
7. That a proportion of the shovels used in coaling, be light steel pointed, scooped, for working on heaped coal or coal in bulk.
8. That a proportion of short coal bags… to hand in coal similar to the basket system be supplied.
9. That labour for putting coal on board be paid at a price per ton, and that men be encouraged to earn as much as possible, also that outside labour be utilised as much as possible.
10. That the yearly coaling allowance of 9s be abolished, and that seamen when coaling be paid according to quantity of coal shipped, at the rate of 1s 4d per ton for all coal put on board over and above a

quarter of a ton per man per hour for the number of men employed coaling and trimming in bunkers.
11. Facilities in construction for receiving coal on board the new class of ship of war recommended to the attention of the constructor's department for possible improvement.
12. That any store of land-borne coal required in time of war beyond the ordinary accommodation of the respective depots be kept in trucks on railway companies sidings, within an hour's run of the depots.
13. That all coal depots be placed in connexion with railway system.

Not all these prescriptions were implemented quickly; some coal hulks still had years of service left. Numerous recommendations were made for individual depots, the most important of which was the use of travelling hydraulic cranes to load ships or lighters from shore-based coal dumps, where covered space was to be provided. The characteristic outline of these cranes was to be a feature of naval bases for many years. Not surprisingly, they recommended that the hydraulic equipment at Portland and Keyham (which must have been rusted solid by this time) be demolished, together with the great coaling shed. The building was too good to lose, though, and remains the principal feature of Portland Port today.[13]

Table 17 **Tonnages of coal held by the major depots**				
Year	1867	1868	1869	1870
Portland	1,568	2,187	842	1,430
Portsmouth	7,299	3,627	6,717	8,901
Devonport	5,517	4,256	3,040	2,856
Haulbowline	1,702	668	743	619

195 The Coal Store in 1908, with the Channel Fleet in the background. *(Author's collection)*

196 The Coal Store today. *(English Heritage)*

east side of the building, from which coal would be trans-shipped to lighters, which would carry it out to the ships (Figure 195). This necessitated bagging the coal up in the shed first, so losing the advantages of bulk handling that Coode had envisaged. These arrangements were all working satisfactorily by the beginning of 1870. The major depots had held tonnages of coal on 31 January of each year as listed in Table 17.

With Portland breakwater due to be finished in 1872, the Admiralty decided to take steps to enable coal to be brought in by train (in June 1867 the Traffic Manager of the Great Western Railway had submitted a plan of transit for Welsh coal to Portland), and the Estimates for 1871 included a sum of £800 for interest on the outlay for a branch line connecting with the Weymouth and Portland Railway (which had opened in 1865). The line was completed in 1876.[14]

Work began on the construction of a new coaling jetty in 1890, one consequence of the report published by the Committee on Coaling Facilities in 1885.[15] This was to operate on completely different principles from Coode's original plan. Gone was any idea of storing coal under cover. It was dumped in an enormous hole in the centre of a purpose-built pier and handled by travelling hydraulic cranes. Ships either moored alongside or had the fuel brought out to them by colliers. By 1892 the sinking of the cylinders for hydraulic machinery and the formation of the pier and coaling camber were completed. New coaling lighters were approved, and the use of hulks was finally to be discontinued. On 24 October 1893 the coal tip was tested, and measures were taken in hand to increase its efficiency: these included the fitting of a turntable, hydraulic capstans, removing the automatic controlling gear of the pumping engine, and increasing the load on the hydraulic accumulator rams. Completion of the superstructure, with six cranes, boiler house, engine house, fitters' shop, shelter,

weighbridge and railway system, was delayed until 1896, partly because of bad weather (Figure 197).

The new coaling arrangements at first proved to be a great disappointment. Testing the coaling facilities was one of the purposes of the summer manoeuvres of 1901. The officer in charge at Portland, Captain Jerram of HMS *Boscawen*, wrote a critical report. Not only were the physical arrangements quite inadequate, but the organisation was defective:

> The present Plant with the present Staff does little more than ensure sufficient for the Destroyers; and that at a slow rate. Only eight Destroyers can coal at a time, as there are only eight billets, at four of which the appliances are very antiquated and slow. Three of these billets, and possibly a fourth could not be used by Destroyers with a strong Northerly wind.

Furthermore, there were only eight men trained to work the hydraulic cranes, who could not work continuously day and night, and although the weather was fine, with clear moonlit nights, great inconvenience and delay was caused by there being no lighting arrangements of any kind, or telephone communication.

Things were finally got right, some 40 years late: plans for a great extension of the coaling jetty were drawn up in 1902, and

197 (Above) The new coaling depot at Portland as completed. Note travelling hydraulic cranes and the Temperley transporter, also the gunnery target at lower left. *(Author's collection)*

198 (Below) Portland coaling jetty in its final form, photographed in March 1906, showing the Temperley transporter. *(TNA ADM 195/78)*

contracts were made in 1903. It was finished by March 1906 (Figure 198). In that year, as the coaling arrangements at Portland took their final shape, plans were drawn up to introduce the new fuel of the century with an oil jetty and two oil tanks. With minor alterations (most notably the covering-over or filling-in

199 (Opposite) The armoured cruiser *Essex* at Portsmouth coaling point. *(NMM, neg. no. G10338)*

of the two great coal tanks) the coaling camber retains its shape to this day. In spite of Coode's and Armstrong's ingenuities 50 years previously, it was ironic that coaling at Portland was satisfactorily performed, in so far as coaling ships was ever to be an efficient evolution, only when it was on the point of being superseded.[16]

The story of the development of coaling facilities came full circle when Captain Sir Francis Collier's idea of 1844 was revived in spades. On 26 August 1902 tenders were asked for a floating coal depot to hold 12,000 tons (11,000 tons in hoppers, the rest in sacks), to be built in conjunction with the Temperley Transporter Company, who were to provide the distributive machinery. The minimum rate of output was to be 500 tons per hour for 6 hours in any condition of coaling. She was launched on 27 January 1904 by Swan, Hunter & Co., and on trials the delivery rate averaged about 440 tons per hour: the deficiency was put down to minor breakdowns of electrical machinery and the inexperience of the drivers, as the appliances were being worked simultaneously for the first time. In the circumstances it was considered that the depot should be accepted without penalty.[17]

This marvellous device, known as C1, was one of the sights of Portsmouth for many years, but it would have been overshadowed by its proposed successor. This suggestion came, in 1907, from the Director of Works, who was proposing to dismantle the coaling point soon to create the enormous entrance locks. It was to contain 20,000 tons of coal distributed over not less than 10 or more than 20 holds of approximately equal capacity at a probable cost of £200,000. Arrangements were to be made for mooring the vessel when two battleships were lashed alongside, and not less than 10 grabs were to be able to be operated simultaneously. It was never built.[18]

The provision of coaling facilities was an obvious necessity for the Steam Navy, and the mass provision of hulks had solved the matter in a rough and ready way in the 1850s. The want of basin accommodation was now the principal matter to be remedied, and Chatham, established as the principal yard for building ironclads but with nowhere to fit them out and no purpose-built Steam Factory, was the obvious first candidate for extension.

—⁂—

Notes:

[1] The Surveyor was asked whether an old vessel was available instead, but there was no vessel that would take 1,000-2,000 tons of coal without drawing too much water. However, a barge of about 180ft by 45ft, 18ft deep, drawing 14ft with 2,000 tons of coal, might be built for the sum of £14,500 in four months, as estimated by Messrs Ditchburn & Mare. Materials from an old line-of-battle ship might be used in its construction, reducing the cost by £1,700.

[2] The order was made before Henry Lowry Corry became First Secretary to the Admiralty, and the first he knew of it was when he saw the rough draft of the 1845/6 Estimates:
'The vote…for that year was unusually large (chiefly in consequence of the policy of the last Government to organise a Steam Navy, on a scale of sufficient magnitude for the defence of the Country with the utmost despatch) and as an additional floating Coal Depot for Woolwich did not appear to me to be a work of urgent necessity, and as, although the tender of Ditchburn & Mare had been accepted, they had not, to my knowledge, received either the necessary authority or information for the actual commencement of the work'.

Corry suspended the construction. Compensation was to be made for loss of profit, and the firm could use the iron on other ships, but they claimed that the sizes of iron had not been suitable for any vessels since constructed, and £7,000 worth of materials remained on their hands. As they shortly received orders for five steamers the Surveyor did not think they had a real grouse. WO 55/807, ADM 1/3429, ADM 83/34.

[3] POR/P/26, POR/R/12B, ADM 92/12, POR/P/30, POR/P/31, MOD (Admiralty) Library, Portfolio K3.

[4] The report from there showed that it was in practice useless for this purpose: 'Since the removal of the *Fortitude* coal depot to Sheerness in August 1848, not any preparations exist at this Yard for Coaling Steamers, nor is there a Store of Coals kept at this Yard; and in the event of its being required of us, to use our best efforts to Coal one in haste, our present available means consists only of seven Barges, each capable of containing from 35 to 50 Tons.- These, (the Tide permitting) might be loaded from the Wharf twice in 24 hours, supposing that Horses and Men could be employed in the Yard in sufficient numbers to load them all at one time; but this, under the present arrangement of the Coal Stores for Yard Engines (and supposing the Coals therein to be made available for the Emergency) could not be done, as a very limited number of Carts only, could be loaded at the same time…Should the usual preparation be adopted of keeping filled Sacks in readiness, it must be observed that no place for their deposit is provided, and that their exposure to the weather for any length of time would cause the destruction of the Sacks, and consequently their usefulness in time of need.'

[5] ADM 2/1387, ADM 2/1388, ADM 93/3, ADM 93/4, ADM 93/5, ADM 83/62.

[6] They involved the following points:
topside amidships cut down;
coaling points cut;
hatchways enlarged;
derricks fitted;
most main deck cabins removed;
orlop deck and sail and storerooms removed;
bulkheads in hold removed;
platform to be laid.

[7] ADM 84/17, ADM 84/18, ADM 94/21, MLN 154, MLN/142/2, ADM 1/5774.

[8] ADM 7/617, Coode Blizard archives; ADM 53/5121, UP 31824, 31783, ADM 1/6518.

[9] NMM WWL/11, ADM 1/5730, MLN /154, *British Naval Documents 1204-1960*, ed. Hattendorf, Knight, Pearsall, Rodger, and Till, (London, 1993), p.661; W G Armstrong, 'Water pressure machinery, *Proceedings of the Institution of Mechanical Engineers*, 1874, pp.119-144; ADM 1/5706, Tyne & Wear Archives 1027/7363 594-5, ADM 12/672, ADM 87/76.

[10] Coode Blizard archives; ADM 1/5753, *Quarterly Accounts for Harbours of Refuge… 1861*, ADM 12/736, ADM 93/17, ADM 53/9162, ADM 50/331, ADM 12/652.

[11] The original estimate of £9,000 was based on a building with 9,520ft² of storage space, and about 10ft in height, equal to about 2,100 tons. It was now proposed to provide 13,540ft² of storage space, 42ft 6in in height, equal to about 12,000 tons. Scamp thought the site was suited only for casual services, and that the main depot should be at the basins of the extension of the Yard, whose design was then being argued over. Nevertheless, he thought the project worth a try. The Coal Store was to be on the exact spot occupied by the old Junk Store (for old ropes and blocks).

[12] ADM 1/5838.

[13] ADM 1/6775.

[14] ADM 87/67, ADM 87/57, ADM 12/785, ADM 12/801, ADM 12/818, Quarterly Accounts for Harbours of Refuge, 1869-70, ADM 1/6195.

[15] The Committee recommended that a new coaling depot at Portland should be built on a camber. The Estimates for 1888/9 held out the prospect of improved facilities, the First Lord announcing:
'We hope during the year to be able to make some progress with works at Portland for unloading sea-borne and railway-carried coal, but until the plans have been more carefully investigated and accurate estimates produced, I did not consider it advisable to sanction any premature expenditure'.
Tracings of the coaling arrangements and the machinery were forwarded in February 1889.

[16] *Brassey's Naval Annual*, (1888-9), p.72; ADM 12/109, ADM 12/1234, ADM 12/1274, ADM 12/1382, ADM 1/7497, ADM 195/78.

[17] The total costs were £152, 150.

[18] ADM 138/217, ADM 138/216.

CHAPTER 15

The Great Extensions

ONE OF THE FOREMOST PUBLICISTS who pointed out the weak state of the Royal Navy *vis-à-vis* that of France was Hans Busk, who logically complemented his fear of a consequent invasion by being one of the foremost activists of the rifle volunteer movement. In 1859, as part of his campaign, he published *The Navies of the World*, in which he summarised the strengths of the European Navies. Writers like Busk had pointed out the enormous investments the French had made in providing basin accommodation and building slips. Their dockyards were far more extensive, covering some 200 acres more than their English counterparts, and there were 76 French building slips available compared with 44, and of these 44 only 9 were suitable for modern first rates. The Royal Navy did, however, have an advantage in possessing 34 docks (two of these under construction at Portsmouth) compared with 24 across the Channel, but of these 28 were too small to receive the largest classes of ship.

The capabilities of the French yards may have been overestimated in these polemics, and the significance of Keyham Factory totally unrealised, but there could be no doubt that a considerable investment in the three major Dockyards was imperative, and work was in progress only at Keyham. By the 1850s many large civilian dockyard schemes had been completed or were in progress. Jesse Hartley's development of Liverpool docks, for instance, was a far greater undertaking than the Portsmouth Steam Basin, and at London, after nearly 30 years without significant expansion, the Royal Victoria Dock (some 3000 by 1000 feet) was opened in 1855. Incidentally, one of the developers of this project was Samuel Morton Peto, who has previously figured in this story as Henry Grissell's partner.

The civil engineering techniques for dock construction were thus thoroughly established when the Admiralty decided on a massive programme of extension of Chatham Dockyard. This was not going to be an *ad hoc* project such as the Portsmouth Steam Basin or the redevelopment of Woolwich, which had

both proved to be inadequate to handle the rapidly increasing steam fleet within an alarmingly short time. Instead it was a carefully worked out scheme that, like Keyham Factory, would be adequate to meet the needs of future generations of ships. Greene and Scamp were to transfer their acquired expertise at factory planning to the layout of docks. Naval dockyards performed quite different functions from civilian ones, and, apart from constructional skills, there were few lessons to be learned from men like Hartley.[1]

Chatham Extension

Ambitious plans to expand Chatham had been made before. In 1821 John Rennie, at the request of the Admiralty, had produced a most grandiose design, involving diverting the course of the Medway and cutting off its original channel to form a basin 240 acres in extent in front of the Dockyard (Figure 200). The basin would have access to the Medway by a canal joining it at Gillingham Reach. This project lay dormant for many years, until on 16 April 1847 the younger Rennie wrote to Auckland, the First Lord, attempting to revive interest.[2]

This project vanished so completely into thin air that Greene (in 1850) knew very little about it, but Scamp preserved a drawing of it, contrasting it with an alternative that he put forward in May 1849. He was concerned about the deterioration that took place to ships laid up in ordinary (on 1 October 1847 this numbered 201 ships),[3] and Scamp proposed that the ships would enter a camber, where the masts might be removed and the vessels unrigged; the water would be pumped out, and the ship would then be raised and transported on a system of cradles to a berth where it would be shored up. The idea of hauling up ships on slips when in ordinary was one that Scamp kept returning to, and after the Russian war gunboats were stored in this way at Haslar in Gosport, though it never happened with bigger ships.

Greene thought there would be no practical difficulties, and on his representations Scamp was allowed £50 for a working model of his project to be built. The model must have looked good, for in August 1851 the Board thought that the plan was 'well calculated to afford great facilities for examining and thoroughly seasoning Vessels of all classes — as well as to supply all the requirement of Slips for building purposes', and might be cheaper and preferable to that put forward in 1846. The Master Shipwrights, however, were sure that the weight of the machinery would adversely affect the structure of large ships when hauled up, and the whole thing was dropped, though Scamp exhibited his model at the Great Exhibition.

In 1857 the expansion of Chatham, shelved during the Russian War,[4] was again mooted, and it was agreed that a basin about 1200ft long by 700ft wide, a Mast House of large dimensions, four additional building slips, a Steam Factory equivalent to that at Portsmouth, and at least two docks were

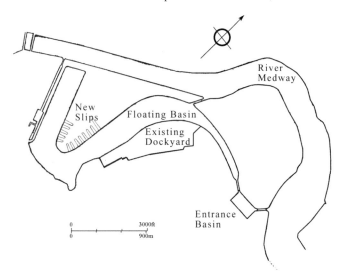

200 Rennie the elder's grand scheme for rehandling the Medway. *(Redrawn from dyeline copy held by Chatham Historic Dockyard)*

required. As things were, the Yard was most inconveniently arranged, and Scamp, who had prepared a batch of alternative designs, was the man to make sure that the new works were rationally planned.[5]

Scamp stressed the importance of fixing a satisfactory layout at the very beginning.[6] The most important question to be decided on was the appropriation of St Mary's Creek and St Mary's Island, which was the basis of Scamp's two preferred solutions. The creek was constantly depositing mud in front of the Yard, which needed constant dredging. If basins were created on the line of the creek easy access would be given to St Mary's Island, which could then be developed and a new establishment planned around the basin complex. Doing away with St Mary's Creek would also put an end to the perpetual silting-up, and economical construction was promised by using inexpensive materials (clay for brickmaking was on the site) and convict labour (directions for a prison holding 1,000 convicts to be employed on Naval Works had been issued in November

1853), which gave an opportunity to provide 'ample Basin space, useful at all times, but essentially necessary to meet the demands of a great War'.

Scamp proposed two large basins lying between the old Yard and St Mary's Island, soon joined by another. Two alternative designs were drawn up for the Factory. One was very similar to the plan of the Keyham Factory, a great covered quadrangle, but the other, preferred by Scamp, incorporated the improvements he had recently introduced at Sheerness, with the advantage that existing buildings would not have to be incorporated.[7] Coal stores were located on either side of a lock joining the two basins, so that, if necessary, hydraulic cranes could work on both sides of the ship at the same time. In the revised plan the coal stores projected over the sides of the central basin.

Greene forwarded to the Admiralty a variant of Scamp's plan, with two basins, and fresh thoughts about entering and coaling (Figure 201). Scamp, mindful of the need to ensure that the proposed works could cope with future demand, accompanied

201 Greene's 1857 plan. *(TNA ADM 1/5703)*

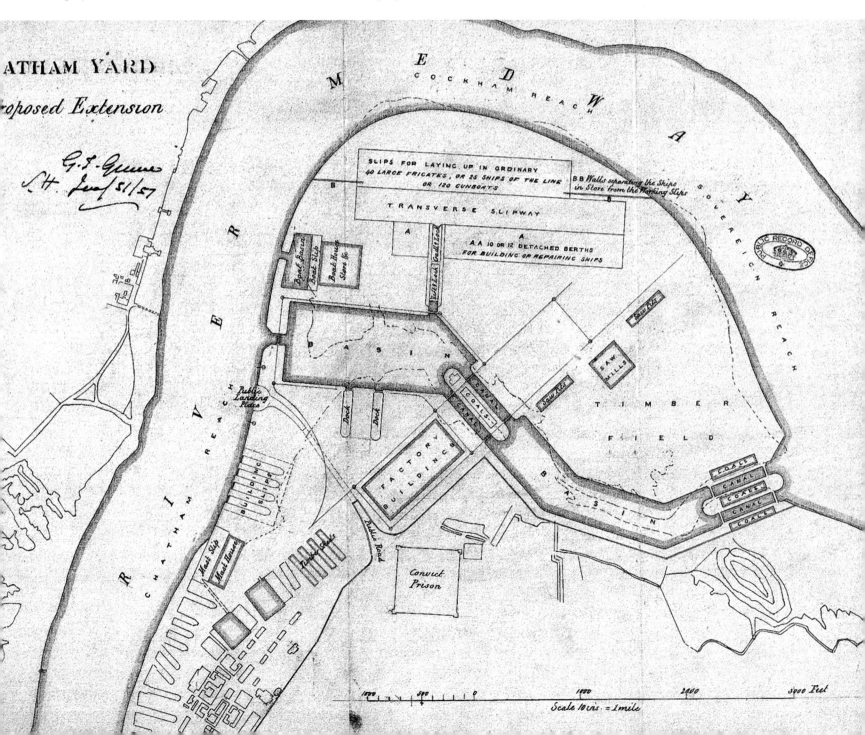

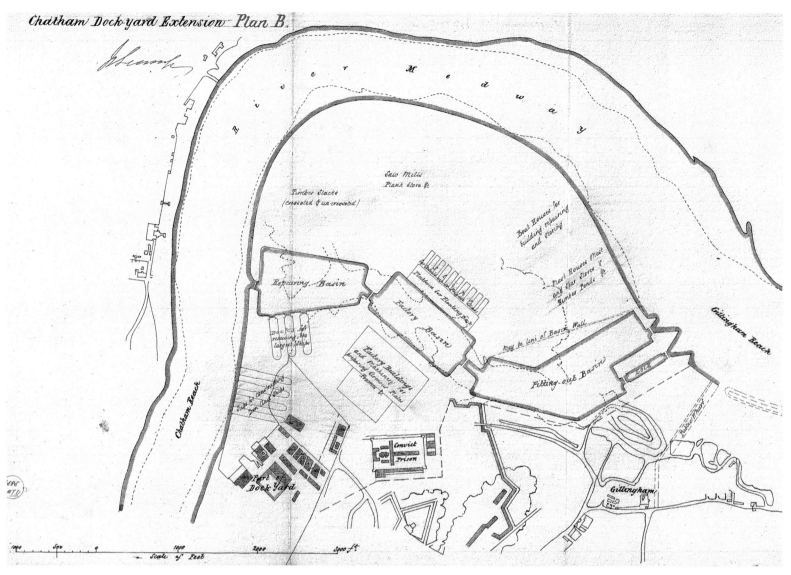

Chatham Dock-yard Extension~ Plan B.

202 One of Greene's proposals for the extension to the Chatham yard. *(TNA ADM 1/5838)*

it with a considered statement of the mistakes that had previously been made in providing shore facilities for the Steam Navy. His proposed scheme was

> …the result of nearly 20 Years' experience in Dock Yard practice, with a view of shewing errors which have been committed by carrying on great works in the large Establishments without a well considered General Plan, and the benefits which have resulted, or might have resulted, in the few instance in which great Schemes have been timely brought to the notice of the Board.[8]

The plans were continually revised by Scamp and Greene, the shapes and capacities of the basins being altered as work proceeded on the embankment of St Mary's Island. In May 1861 the total basin area projected was 60 acres; by comparison Sheerness had 6, Portsmouth 11, Devonport 1½, and Keyham 18. The 60 acres were disposed as a repairing basin of 22 acres, a factory basin of 7 acres, and a fitting-out basin of 30½ acres.

Scamp realised that the geographical potential of the Chatham site enabled the basins to be arranged in sequence as part of the production line. A vessel launched from the slips would be taken into the repairing basin for completing any work necessary before moving to the factory basin, where the machinery and boilers would be placed, and the ship would then

be returned to the repairing basin for the completion of all work connected with the hull. Finally the ship would go to the fitting-out basin to be rigged and have the guns mounted, be coaled and supplied with stores. The concept of a sequence of basins planned as part of a process of operations ranks, along with the flexible layout of Keyham, as Scamp's greatest achievement.[9]

In July a Select Committee on Chatham Dockyard Extension had the necessity for the works spelled out to it. Robinson stressed the great French superiority in basin area, some 221 acres, not including Brest, of which Cherbourg had 51 acres and Toulon 87 acres. A new Steam Factory would be required. The timescale for the repair of machinery meant that for the first six or seven years engines and boilers needed little attention, but then heavy repairs were needed. That period had elapsed since 1855, when the horsepower of the Navy was about 60,000 and the existing Factories were occupied with its repair; it was now about 130,000, and in five or six years all of this would need to be fixed. Should hostilities break out the workload would be enormously increased.

Lloyd considered that the importance of Chatham as a building Yard made the presence of a Factory indispensable, despite the fact that Keyham was not being worked to capacity, for ships and their machinery generally wore out together, and it would be a great economy to have the Shipwrights' and Engineers' Departments together in the same Yard. Greene reckoned that the Factory would cost some £150,000 as against the £400,000 of Keyham, there being no intention now to provide any architectural statements, the technological rhetoric of *Warrior* and *Black Prince* being more potent than Barry's facades. The plan was, however, a doublet of Keyham, though the fitting and erecting and boiler shops were wider, drawing on the lessons of that Factory, where the fitting and erecting shop, as has been seen, had to be widened (Figure 202).

The Factory basin in this design was much too small, and a plan of February 1862 increased the dimensions to 26, 24 and 39 acres respectively, with the site on St Mary's Island opposite the Factory being earmarked for new Metal Mills, Brass Foundry, and Rolling Mills. Sites on the island were also selected for Sawmills, Boat Houses, Mast Houses and Sail Loft, everything but the building slips being effectively transferred to the extension. The increase in the dimensions of the Factory Basin involved the realignment of the Factory.

In June 1863 Greene noted that if the current plans were carried out, the Factory building, Factory basin and the Repairing basin would be finished long before the Fitting-out basin and the entrance locks at the Gillingham end were ready. The only entry would be by the caisson opposite Upnor, which would never be satisfactory as a regular practice. Consequently he prepared a new variant, which made the Fitting-out basin tidal, entry to the Factory basin being through a pair of locks. Scamp agreed that this would speed up construction and reduce the cost, but thought that it would be even cheaper to have the entrance to the repairing basin by a single lock and a caisson, eliminating one lock. The number of docks opening off the repairing basin had not been settled, nor the possible provision of new building slips. Coaling arrangements do not figure in this new batch of drawings.[10] Plans were not finalised, despite consultation over the factory layout from July 1863,[11] and no work had begun when Greene retired in 1864, being replaced by Colonel Sir Andrew Clarke (who at an early stage of his career had been Denison's private secretary in Van Diemen's Land).[12]

Work began in earnest around the end of November, when a clerk and a timekeeper for the Extension were appointed. By March 1865 about half the embankment and 2,000ft of river wall on the west side had been completed, the walls of the repairing basin begun and the foundations for part of the factory buildings were in place. A sectional view of the Extension as currently envisaged was published in April, which gives the only illustration of the intended appearance of the Factory; it appears as a metal-framed structure some 100ft high with masonry offices and main entrance and corner blocks containing staircases. Scamp's slips for hauling up ships remain a feature (Figure 203).

By February 1867 the arrangements of the Factory had been

worked out, and were published in *Engineering*. The buildings, grouped in a neat quadrangle, were to occupy an area of 1000ft by 540ft, or considerably over 12 acres,[13] and did not have a vast overall roof as at Keyham. The intention now was to get everything right first time, but whether Scamp's final thoughts on factory planning would have turned out as well in the long run as Keyham did will never be known. He retired in December 1867 on his full salary of £1,000, which he thoroughly deserved. His partnership with Greene had kept the Admiralty in the forefront of industrial design and planning, and after their retirement no more innovative buildings were to be built in the Yards. He died in January 1872.

In 1869 Admiral Robinson initiated an important organisational change. The machinery used by engineers and shipwrights was by now, with the introduction of iron shipbuilding in the Yards on a large scale, little different. The duplication of Smithery facilities was wasteful, and the posts of Chief Engineer and Master Shipwright were merged at Chatham and Portsmouth. The Millwrights, as the Chief Engineers hoped, had been transferred from the Master Shipwrights' Department to that of the Chief Engineer in 1864.

By May 1871 nothing had been done about the Factory, with the exception of some of the foundations, but over £1,148,000 had been spent on the excavations of the basins and docks. As the work of excavating the basins continued, it was becoming increasingly clear that the employment of convicts on public works rarely provided the savings that their advocates maintained would be provided; this was certainly the case at Portland. At Chatham the experience was at first not much more favourable, and the excavations by a combination of hired and convict labour had made so little progress by 1865 that it was then decided to put the construction of the Repairing and Factory basins, the two western docks and the entrances to the two others (occupied by part of the brick-field) and the pumping Engine House out to tender (Figures 204 and 205). Convicts had completed much of the 550ft of the south-east angle of the Repairing basin wall, the only part to be finished. The prisoners had done much better in filling in, levelling and draining 21⅓ acres of wet marsh, converting it into a complete brick-field in less than nine months, the first brick being made in March 1866. It was expected that the annual production would exceed 15,000,000. In July Mr Gabrielli's tender of £568,890 was accepted, but a change was made in the contract in 1869.

The convicts were scheduled to have completed embanking St Mary's Island in that year, and to have been transferred to begin the Fitting-out basin, but because of geological difficulties in the construction of Gillingham Quay, which had to be completed before this work could start, there would be nothing for them to do. It was therefore decided to construct

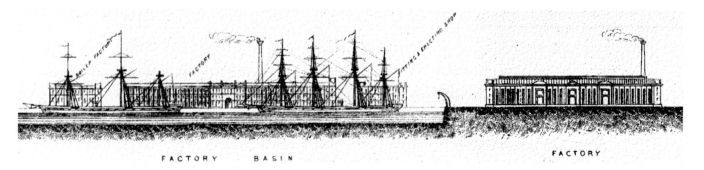

FACTORY   BASIN

FACTORY

203 The extension as visualised, showing the Steam factory. *(Adapted from TNA ADM 1/5939)*

204 One of the temporary pumping houses along the Medway. *(Royal Engineers Library)*

205 Pile-driving in progress along the Medway. *(Royal Engineers Library)*

the Factory basin by hired and convict labour and it was finished on 13 December 1871, the Repairing Basin having been finished on 8 May (Figure 206). Bernays, the supervising Civil Engineer, was pleased with the work of the prisoners, thinking it stood comparison even in terms of external finish, and certainly as regards solidity, with that done by contract. There was no great haste to complete the Fitting-out basin, which was completed by contract and convict labour. The four docks in the Repairing basin were finished as follows: No. 5 in July 1870, No. 6 in April 1871, No. 8 in October 1872, and No. 7 in January 1873 (Figure 208).

Nothing was to come of Scamp's Factory design, any more than his successor Clarke's; a quick-fix solution was on hand and seized upon. With the ever-increasing sizes of ships it was clear that Woolwich no longer had a useful part to play. It was not the shortcomings of the layout of the Steam Factory that determined its fate, but the size of the basin, which was quite incapable of taking an ironclad of the *Minotaur* class. In October 1869 it was announced that the Yard would be disposed of. It was surveyed in April 1870, but it was not until 21 May 1872 that the east end was sold, all lots realising £14,940, about 22½ per cent above the minimum expected. In September the remainder of the site was handed over to the War Department, who retained nearly all the Steam Factory buildings for the use of Woolwich Arsenal.

The great building slips and some other structures were not involved in this sale, having been dismantled and moved to Chatham to serve as the workshop buildings for the new extension, so giving them another century of working life. These slip roofs were particularly amenable for reuse as Factory buildings as they had been reinforced and equipped with travelling cranes. Butchard, the contractor, had prepared special tackle for the purpose of dismantling the Woolwich roofs. As its use would decrease the cost of re-erection, and as Pasley doubted whether this was a job that the convicts could be trusted to perform, he was given the job. In March 1872 Butchard claimed £3,707 1s 1d for taking down and removing the Woolwich roofs; great difficulty had been experienced in removing the glass from slips 4 and 5, a large proportion of which had been set with white lead, and many of the wooden frames were so rotten that they did not hold together.

The saving made by the reuse of these buildings, and an indication of the relative cost of dock and building construction, is shown by the 1872/3 estimates allowing £174,000 for the Extension, £3,000 for tramways, and £6,000 for removal and re-erection of the Woolwich sheds. £9,838 was set aside for machinery for the repair of iron ships, which was installed in Woolwich No. 5, beside Dock No. 8. The roofs from 4 and 6 slips were erected at the heads of docks 5–8 as a boiler shop and an engineering machinery shop, all the factory capacity thus being concentrated around the Repairing Basin, the first to be completed (Figure 210). The site by the Factory Basin remained virtually clear. The decision not to go ahead with the Factory but to make use of the fortuitously available covered slips is best viewed in the light of the shift of emphasis from the built fabric of the Yard (which was probably now seen as essentially transitory and better not perpetuated in such an inflexible and monumental building as Portsmouth Factory, or even the matrix of buildings surrounding Keyham Quadrangle) to the provision of docks and basins, the area in which the French superiority was most evident.[14]

206 Chatham Repairing Basin in May 1874. One of the Woolwich slip roofs (centre) has been brought into use. The ships are, from left to right, the just-completed iron frigate *Raleigh*, the ironclad *Audacious* being re-fitted under the massive sheerlegs and, just visible in front of the Upnor end pumping station, the ironclad ram *Rupert*, in the last stages of completion. *(TNA ADM 195/7)*

207 The battleship *Dreadnought* in dry dock. Built between 1872 and 1879 at Pembroke, she was an improved version of the *Devastation*. *(Chrysalis Picture Library)*

208 Dock No. 8
under construction.
(TNA ADM 195/7)

209 Slip No. 4 being
transformed into a
new Boilermakers'
Shop. *(TNA ADM
195/7)*

210 The Woolwich roofs get a second life at Chatham. The new Machine Shop is seen here behind a new *Majestic* class battleship, *The Empress of India*. (*From* The Navy and Army Illustrated, *March 20, 1896*)

Portsmouth Extension

In 1858 Murray proposed to enlarge the Steam Factory by building on the site originally proposed by Denison on the other side of the basin, but Walker thought that this was just fiddling with the situation, which would remain quite inadequate. The basin had been formed with paddle vessels in mind, and would have been found inadequate even if screw propulsion had not been introduced. As it was, the necessity for expansion was urgent, as there was wharf space for only six large frigates or line-of-battle ships, and the access for these was inconvenient. He proposed creating a new Basin with a Factory, adding barracks for seamen and shore-based coaling facilities to do away with the hulks that were clogging up the anchorage: all works, in his view, that would have to be done sooner or later. However, it was not until after Walker's resignation that Mr Scamp, in 1862, prepared the first design for an extension.

No subsequent scheme was to be conceived on such a scale as this ambitious plan, which involved creating 103½ acres of deep water and 244 acres of reclaimed land. There were to be three basins, a tidal one of 19 acres with three docks capable of accommodating the largest ships at any time, a second basin of 22½ acres with 30ft clearance at high water neaps, with four docks, and a third of 62 acres, 30ft deep at high water springs. This final basin had docks and building slips, and incorporated Scamp's favourite project of slips for ships in ordinary, behind which a large area of reclaimed land served as a timber ground, while a boat house and mast houses surrounded a mast and boat pond, accessible both from the basin and from the harbour. A bastioned trace with a musketry wall surrounded

the whole thing (Figure 211).

Unlike the contemporary Chatham scheme, the basins were originally differentiated according to their depth at tide conditions rather than according to function: the Factory buildings, in three large blocks, were next to the tidal basin and its docks. When Scamp prepared an estimate for the first two

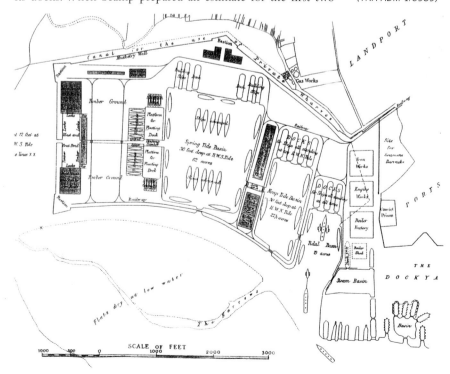

211 Scamp's proposal to extend Portsmouth Yard was far more ambitious than any others. (*TNA ADM 1/5939*)

SCALE OF FEET

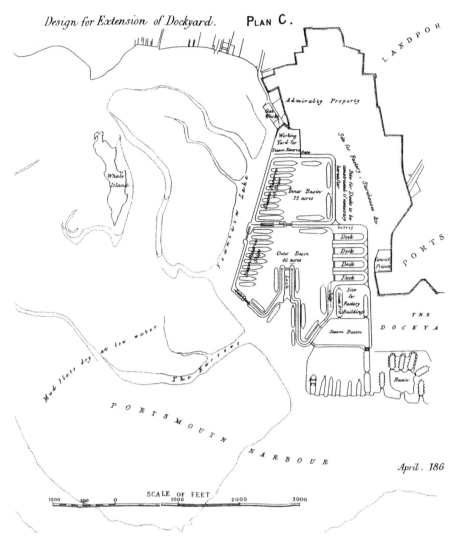

Design for Extension of Dockyard.   **PLAN C.**

April. 186

its maintenance. The entrance lock was recessed to provide a space protected from the action of the tides large enough for the biggest warships. The chief drawbacks of this design were that no use could be made of any part of it before the whole scheme was completed, and that part of it had to be constructed on very difficult ground.

Corry's scheme was rehandled by the Admiral Superintendent and local officers at Portsmouth in June. This persisted with building on the difficult ground near the entrance to the Steam basin, and incorporated two graving docks about as cut off from access to the Factory buildings as possible. Admiral Martin offered a plan of his own, but this, it was thought, would be too intricate in practice. Sadly, the plan concocted by one James Robinson and described by the Hydrographer of the Navy as 'the wildest scheme ever proposed' does not seem to have been preserved.

The three new plans prepared by Greene's office were all variants of each other, balancing basin area against wharfage, and all bearing Scamp's mark in the form of a separate basin with laying-up slips to accommodate ships in reserve. In all these three plans the Steam Factory is shown functioning solely as a Boiler Factory, with a new Engine Factory placed between the old yard and the new Extension. The selected variant had the three basins denominated by function: a Repairing basin of 22 acres, with four docks opening off it, a Rigging basin of 17 acres, and a Fitting-out basin of 14 acres (Figures 213 & 214). The work, not including the basin for the Reserve, which was never to be built, was estimated at £2,250,000 if performed by contract or £1,500,000 if partly done by prison labour, not including any additions to the Workshops or Factories.[15]

The new Factory building to the south of the Deep Dock was never built, though a plan of 1873 shows it would have been an open-plan building constructed around a grid of iron standards. This allowed for alteration and modification, just as Scamp had devised at Keyham and his successor Colonel Clarke had proposed at Chatham. Significantly, mechanical innovations had occurred that meant that some important principles of factory planning were no longer valid. In 1864 it was noted that the direct application of steam power to individual machines, especially punching, shearing and bar-cutting machines, each equipped with its own small steam engine supplied with steam through pipes from a central boiler, made it unnecessary to run a large engine and a great deal of shafting to operate just one or two machines, as might often happen in the Yards, where the nature of the work meant that continuous production lines were rarely required. The design of a workshop was consequently no longer governed by the shafting arrangements, and the man-hours required for maintaining the system were much reduced. The rationale behind a close-grouped and interlocking set of shops such as governed Scamp's latest thinking no longer existed.[16]

212 Noteworthy for being the work of an unqualified civilian with the political clout to get it considered, this scheme was put forward by Henry Lowry Corry. *(TNA ADM 1/5939)*

213 Two elevations of Scamp's proposed Factory for Plan E, shown in relation to the Foundry shown on the right. *(TNA ADM 1/5939)*

basins in February 1863 the neap tide basin, in line with his thinking at Chatham, had been renamed the Repairing basin, and no location was shown for the buildings. This mighty reclamation scheme was made largely unnecessary by the transfer of War Department land of the fortifications to the east of Portsea and the Yard, together with the Pest House Fields, which meant that the design could begin on a fresh basis. In 1864 a Bill made provision for a public wharf with access to Fountain Lake, and as a consequence new plans were prepared by the Works Department.

It was not normal practice, to say the least, for civilian former members of the Board in opposition to get directly involved with technical matters, but Henry Lowry Corry had many years of experience with the doings of the Steam Navy, and he submitted his own plan in April 1864 while the Works Department alternatives were being hatched (Figure 212). This had an outer basin of 46 acres with four docks and an inner basin of 25 acres for the Steam Reserve, with a working Yard for

PROPOSED FACTORY

The Portsmouth Factory remained as a project for many years, plans of 1878 showing its proposed situation. A workshop for repairing iron ships, one façade of which remains, was built between the heads of No. 8 and No. 11 docks, tenders for the ironwork being accepted in June and July 1867, on a site previously occupied by saw pits. Its iron structure was sandwiched between two imposing facades, in a brief return to the tradition that buildings at the principal dockyard should look good, and working sheds were soon extended from it to fill in the space between the two docks (Figure 215).

New power and transport systems

By the time that the Extension was designed the wartime function of Portsmouth was thought to be the repair of a fleet after an action, which would probably have taken place between Portland and Cherbourg, while Chatham, secure from attack up the Medway, specialised as a building yard. The layout of the basins at Chatham paralleled the industrial processes, but the geography of Portsmouth made such a neat arrangement impossible, and each basin had to be successively further from the industrial buildings, making an extensive internal transportation system a vital part of the plan.[17]

James had planned quite a complex standard-gauge railway network for Portsmouth, connected with the main line, but this did not materialise, a simplified rail system around the Steam Basin being begun by Bramble in 1851, and internal communications may be said to have been the most neglected aspect of the Yards. As long as ships remained wooden there seems to have been no feeling that anything drastic needed to be done. It was not determined until the early 1850s to introduce stone tramroad systems in the Yards, and by 1857 this had been done to some extent at Woolwich, Chatham, Portsmouth and Devonport, and to a small extent at Deptford and Sheerness, £25,000 being expended in all.

By 1857 it was clear that granite tramways used for traction engines and heavy moving work were totally unsuitable for sustaining the weights now being regularly placed on them, and, as has been seen, Scamp planned the introduction of railways into Keyham and Devonport, in the latter Yard fitting iron rails to the stone tramways. In November of that year there were over 3 miles of railway line at Portsmouth, and a

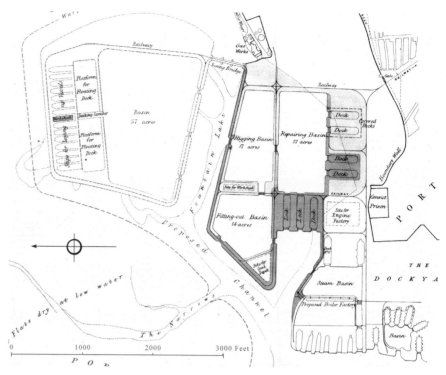

214 Plan E for Portsmouth Extension. *(TNA ADM 1/5939)*

supervisor was appointed. In September 1860 the future expansion of railway facilities was decided upon. One of the reasons for the slow introduction of the railway was the necessity of executing 90° turns in a dockyard, which meant that a large number of turntables had to be inserted and that the full tractive effort of a locomotive could rarely be used in pulling a train of wagons, wasting the potential of the machine. At Portsmouth larger turntables were soon required to allow wagons laden with heavy goods to pass into the Factory at both ends, along in front of the present Factory, along the north wall and round the Steam Basin; lines of railway were to be completed to bring the Factory into connection with all its own branches, with the various wharves, both sides of the Ship Basin, the Camber (where iron was chiefly unloaded) and the various storehouses. The new Foundry was to be rail connected.

Things took a different turn at Chatham, when around 1867 the constant movement of iron plates involved in shipbuilding work was fast wearing out the old tramways, and communications needed to be established between the old Yard

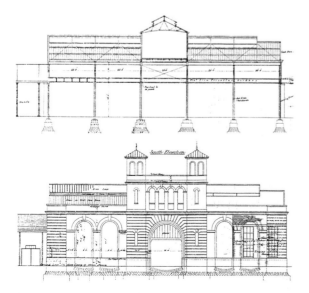

215 The Workshop for repairing Iron Ships, No. 1 Shipbuilding Shop, the first to be built in a Yard. Part of the building, shown here, has survived. *(Adapted from fiche no. 332342 in the possession of Unicorn Consultancy, Portsmouth Dockyard. Photo by English Heritage)*

216 Tramplates as installed at Chatham. The 18 inch gauge was later to be adopted in Admiralty magazines. *(From Engineering, 1 January 1875)*

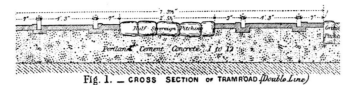

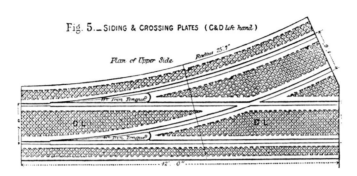

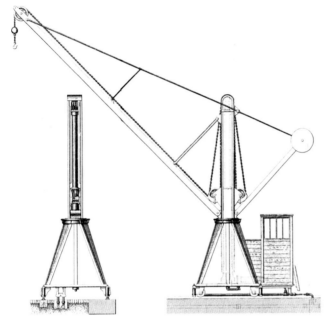

216 Tramplates as installed at Chatham. The 18 inch gauge was later to be adopted in Admiralty magazines. *(From Engineering, 1 January 1875)*

217 An early Armstrong hydraulic crane. *(Adapted from Proceedings of the Institute of Civil Engineers, 1877)*

218 A later Tannet Walker hydraulic travelling crane. *(TNA ADM 1/6775)*

and the extension site. Pasley reported on the potential usefulness of a railway in December 1867, dividing the Yard traffic into three classes.[18]

He concluded that a standard-gauge railway would not be an economical solution. The conveyance of stores would become excessively costly if powerful locomotive engines were to be uneconomically employed in pulling light loads, while the progress of work would be seriously delayed if nothing was dispatched until a trainload had been made up. The trucks would be too heavy to be manhandled, and if horses were employed tracks for them would need to be added, increasing the cost of construction.

He was attracted, instead, by the example of the narrow-gauge railway that served Crewe Railway Works, and which had begun operating on a limited scale in May 1862. The gauge was 18 inches, which allowed extremely tight curves to be negotiated. As adopted at Chatham, cast iron tramplates, with grooves for an 18 in track, would serve to allow horses to be used as well as steam locomotives, and in 1868 a short trial length of grooved plates was laid down on one of the main roads, where the traffic was heaviest. It proved so successful that when the first new docks were opened in 1870 they were connected to the workshops in the new manner (Figure 216). By

the beginning of 1873 nearly a mile of double line and over a mile of single line were operational, and most of the heavy transits in the Yard had been performed by it. Very heavy loads were moved by horse teams or traction engines, and steam locomotives handled the medium loads, such as armour plate, with great success. Special rolling stock was designed for the line: these wagons were so light as to be easily manhandled with small loads, almost bringing to an end the use of horses and carts at Chatham.[19]

Cranes were, of course, another key feature of efficient dockside operations. Not all were up to the tasks required of them. The Fox, Henderson patent derrick crane that was used to erect the Crystal Palace and became a much admired exhibit during the Great Exhibition was, as a consequence, asked for by Woolwich, but within six months was found to be inefficient, and the firm was not paid for it. Steam hoists, moreover, offered more flexibility in use than cranes for handling smaller loads. The acquisition of two Armstrong hydraulic cranes for the wharf by No. 7 slip at Chatham was being contemplated as early as 1852. Lawrie and Laire thought the price was high, £1,100 for two 5 ton cranes 'and if it were an article of competition we should advise rejection', but as such things could not be obtained elsewhere, and the pits for the cranes had been built, they were duly installed. The Armstrong system had been developed as a commercial product with great speed since William Armstrong had lectured on his hydraulic crane and demonstrated a model to the Newcastle upon Tyne Literary and Philosophical Society in December 1845, particularly following the introduction in 1850 of the hydraulic accumulator. This was a cast-iron cylinder, with a heavily loaded plunger, which, inserted into the system, greatly increased the pressure to the

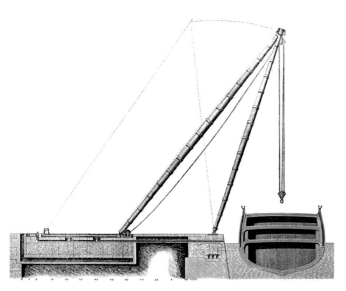

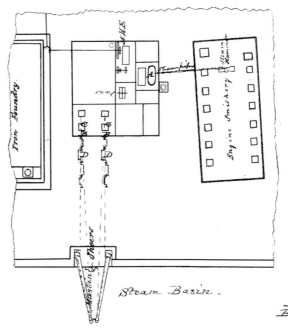

220 An 1856 drawing of the Crab Shed at Portsmouth, placed between James's temporary Smithery and his Foundry. As well as powering the sheerlegs of the Steam Basin, its steam engine also drives a steam hammer in the Smithery and other equipment. *(TNA ADM 85/33)*

219 Powered sheerlegs as installed at Chatham Dockyard, illustrated in 1872. *(Adapted from* Engineering, *23 August 1872)*

water pumped into the hydraulic circuit. A pressure of $600lb/in^2$ was now available instead of $90lb/in^2$, enabling the size of the pipes and machines to be reduced (Figures 217 & 218).

Hydraulic cranes and hoists, however, were never adopted to the exclusion of any other system. Steam, particularly when applied to massive lifting machinery, such as sheerlegs, had much to favour it, and in September 1855 a tender was accepted for a Crab Shed at Portsmouth (Figures 219 and 220). Trickett also improved the Fairbairn tubular cranes at Keyham by driving them by steam: he placed a boiler and water tank in the tail of the crane, which replaced some of the ballast normally carried there.

However, by 1859 it appeared as if hydraulic power might become the predominant system in the Yards, with cranes and hoists being installed throughout the completed Keyham storehouses, and plans being drawn up at Portsmouth for the

use of hydraulic power for various Yard services. This machinery was to be centred on the Camber, where most of the materials for use in the Factory and workshops were unloaded, and a new type of Yard building, the Hydraulic Engine and Boiler House, made its appearance. Drawings, by John Murray, were produced in January and February 1861, and the building, which was enlarged in the early years of the next century when a new hydraulic engine was installed, still remains.

The function of the building (as in all of its kind) is expressed in the short tower housing a pair of hydraulic accumulators, initially powering two 6 ton cranes and a 1 ton capstan, which Armstrong's contracted in September to supply for £1,559 (Figure 221). The building is externally in the house style to which most of the Portsmouth buildings conformed, deriving from James's original Foundry, and by 1892 it was running eight cranes, with lifting powers varying from 1½ to 10 tons, nine

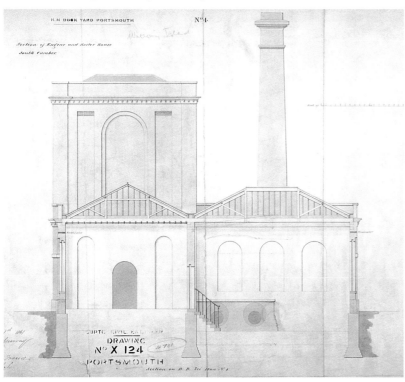

221 The Hydraulic Power House which still stands at the Portsmouth Camber. Drawing signed by Murray, 1861. Photograph of exterior. *(English Heritage Plans Room, A940959 Photo English Heritage)*

capstans, and nine lifts. The lifts were in the new Return Store (the last of the major fireproof buildings to be constructed for the Admiralty, the design now an anachronism rather than a sign of modernity), and clearly planned as part of the programme for making the Camber and Watering Island an enclave of hydraulic power. The engines also supplied pressure for working the nearby chain-cable testing machines, as well as for testing boiler and other tubes.[20]

The new Extensions and their docks also required new pumping stations: for obvious reasons a well-preserved class of building. The first one at Portsmouth, with an 80hp engine, was designed to work with the Steam Basin and Docks 11 and 8, and was at the head of Dock 11. This probably predated the extension works, and was supplemented once they had begun by one at the head of No. 8 dock, drawings for which (by Greene) date from June 1865. This operated a 90hp engine; the boiler house portion has been destroyed but the original metal roof of the engine house remains, though concealed from external view by modern brickwork. It was not in use by January 1866, when a plan shows only the 80hp engine circuit. A hydraulic engine was later added to its equipment. A mixture

of hydraulic and steam-powered dockside machinery was adopted at Chatham: hydraulic power was used for the sliding caissons at the entrance locks at the Fitting-out basin and the capstans, while the cranes and sheerlegs were steam powered. The pumping station, by the Upnor entrance, was completed early in 1874, with machinery designed by the Rennie brothers, who had submitted their original plans in 1869. This was a striking polychromatic building. It, and its eventual partner at the Fitting-out basin end, were to be the only buildings at the Chatham extension that cut the same kind of architectural dash as Keyham. The works were finally completed on 26 September 1885.[21]

Something much more powerful was needed for the three great basins of the Portsmouth Extension, and a main pumping station was built south of the Deep Dock on part of the site that had been reserved for the Factory. This magnificent building (probably designed by Colonel Charles Pasley, who had succeeded Clarke as Director of Works, signing drawings for the great stack in July 1874) expressed a striking visual contrast between the low Boiler House, with a central chimney, set against the monumental Engine House (Figure 222). This was to

222 (Main picture) The Pumping Station created to serve Portsmouth Extension. As well as its eponymous function, it also produced compressed air as a source of power for Yard equipment.
223 (Insert) The pumping stations were the only buildings at the Chatham Extension to deal in established architectural values. This is the one at the Upnor end. *(TNA ADM 195/7)*

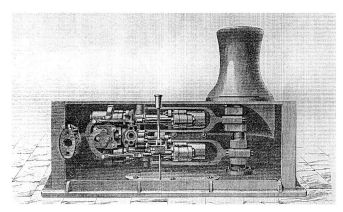

224 A Tannet Walker hydraulic capstan, supplied to Chatham in 1885. *(TNA ADM 1/6775)*

be the most ornate building on the site of the extension: a temple of power, housing not only the main dry-dock pumping machinery of 1,000hp, and two pairs of 120hp engines for general fire and dock-drainage purposes, but also air-compressing machinery. Clarke, after careful consideration, had decided not to use hydraulic power in the Portsmouth extension, but to make compressed air the principal source of power. The air was compressed to 60lb/in^2 pressure into eight wrought-iron receivers, which had a total capacity of 18,000ft3; the larger set of air-compressing pumps could fill the receivers to 60lb pressure in 1 hour.

It soon proved its efficiency. By 1892 no case of a receiver bursting had happened, no pipes had been replaced during the last two years, and the joints had been found to give less trouble than those in steam and hydraulic systems. Clarke reported that the relative efficiency of compressed air machines over hydraulic ones was as 13 to 10, the great advantage being its untroubled operation in the coldest weather, where the hydraulic equipment would have been frozen. (In fact, in the established hydraulic system, concentrated round the Camber and the Foundry, the total length of pressure pipes was about 10,000ft, or nearly 2 miles, placed entirely underground. All that was apparently found necessary during frosty weather was to light small gas-jets in the various engine-boxes at the cranes and capstans.) The proportions of the system were as impressive as the building that operated it. The air pipes had a total length of 14,000ft, or about 2⅔ miles, varied from 3 to 12in diameter, extended round the large basins, and were connected to forty 7 ton capstans, five 20 ton cranes, and to the machinery for working seven caissons and numerous penstocks, besides driving a small workshop engine.

The air system was also used for shipbuilding work, and by the 1890s was sometimes connected with the auxiliary steam-pipes of some of the larger battleships, so that steam need not be got up in the ship's boilers just to work the hydraulic pumping engines on board the ships for gun-drill, and for driving the electric generators. The air-compressing machinery took up slightly more than half the area of the Engine House, there being no structurally expressed division between the pumping and compressing machinery. Six massive cast iron columns supported a central span of girders carrying a water tank, the flanking spans having metal trusses. The grand design gives a taste of how Clarke had visualised the new Factory would look, for a surviving drawing shows it as a continuation of the Engine House facade.[22]

Keyham extension

By 1890 the battle fleet was on the edge of a vast numerical expansion; the Naval Defence Act of 1889 had launched an enormous construction programme that would build 52 battleships in two decades, and the lack of space at Keyham was already serious. There were seven dry docks at Devonport and Keyham, and of these only No. 3 at Devonport was big enough to take the largest type of ship under construction. Under peacetime conditions, when the Channel Squadron and the ships of the Reserve came for their annual refit, the largest had to be docked by turns. In a case of emergency the situation would be disastrous. At least three additional docks and an increase of basin area were wanted, and would 'be an absolute necessity when the large fleet of Ships now constructing are completed'.

The great Keyham extension of the 1890s was to be the last major constructional project driven by a perceived necessity to maintain superiority over the French fleet. French naval policies had fluctuated; during the 1880s the ideas of the *Jeune Ecole* had been influential. These were the key roles of commerce destruction and coastal defence in any war against England. In this scenario the battleship no longer played an important role; the most important naval weapon in any such war would be the torpedo boat, and the construction of four battleships was suspended in order to concentrate on the production of these craft. These small and speedy vessels were to prove incapable of keeping the seas in any kind of weather, but their equivalents were built for the Royal Navy and defence against them became a major concern. The quick-firing gun owed its rapid introduction through being seen as an antidote to them, and the defences of the anchorage and coaling station of Portland,

225 The 'Admiral' class battleship *Collingwood*, photographed after the fitting of anti-torpedo nets in 1890. These ships introduced a number of new features in British battleships, the most important being having their main armament mounted in barbettes. *(Chrysalis Picture Library)*

226 As had been the case at Portsmouth, interested parties offered plans for the extension at Keyham. Here is the Chief Constructor's plan of 1890. (TNA ADM 116/464)

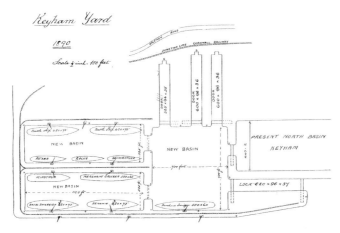

227 A turn of the century view of the quarterdeck of the battleship *Royal Sovereign*. This view was taken at Portsmouth, where she had been built between 1889 and 1891. In the distance to the left is the hulk HMS *Vernon*. (Chrysalis Picture Library)

directly opposite to Cherbourg and its swarm of torpedo boats, were reinforced during the 1890s by the provision of an additional fortified breakwater. By this time the French had restarted a programme of battleship construction, though violent controversies about the role and composition of the fleet continued to rage, and maintained their position in the British view as the only likely enemy.

Popular concern, fuelled by sections of the press, made the enormous costs generally acceptable, and a massive programme of naval construction was given the essential logistical backing, at least as far as dockyard facilities were concerned. Provision for the greatly increased stores of ammunition required, however, lagged behind, but that is another story. Ironically, as the new works were completed a new competitor in the naval race, with industrial resources far superior to those of France, replaced her as the likely opponent. In 1890 the first sea-going modern

German battleships, the *Brandenburg* class, were laid down. In June 1897 Admiral Tirpitz was appointed Minister of Marine, and the naval bill adopted later in the year fixed the requirement at 19 battleships; not an alarming number in itself, but the implications were disturbing. Should the German fleet become a serious and likely opponent, the logistical situation would be completely upset, for Portsmouth and Devonport were not best placed to confront an enemy operating from across the North Sea. Bases on the east coast of Scotland were required, and were eventually provided in various ways, but that topic is also outside the scope of this book.[23]

Scamp's Factory at Keyham was capable of dealing with demands made on it by a greatly expanded Fleet, but the basin accommodation there was not. It was smaller than Scamp had intended, for an extension to provide a further dock along the north side of the Factory was not proceeded with because of difficulties with the ground. Scamp felt that this curtailment could only be justified if a further tidal basin with docks was provided, and in January 1859 he produced a scheme for such an extension, which would in his view bring the basin and dock accommodation into line with the capacity of the Factory: 'an Establishment possessing capabilities not to be found in any other in existence'. Two coal stores each of 8,000 tons capacity were to be jettied out over the basin for mechanised fuelling, and water from Keyham Lake was to be used for scouring the basin. He estimated the cost as £400,000.[24] The matter, however, was shelved for 25 years, the more pressing needs of Chatham and Portsmouth taking priority, and Scamp was never to see any further work undertaken at Keyham.[25]

In June 1890 the Chief Constructor at Devonport prepared

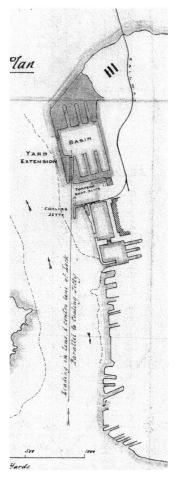

228 The scheme put forward in February 1891. (TNA ADM 116/464)

a plan that gave access through a lock parallel with the North basin to a 12 acre basin with three docks, two 600ft long, the third being an alternative to torpedo boat sheds and slipways (Figure 226). From this basin opened out another two parallel basins of 9 acres each. Each of the 9 acre basins were capable of accommodating four battleships 480ft long (the *Royal Sovereigns*, then under construction, were 380ft long). The afterthought accommodation for torpedo boats in this plan had the great defect of not providing free access to the Hamoaze, and coaling was not taken into consideration.

The Director of Works considered that the subjects of torpedo boat accommodation (a slip to the north of the basin had been built for torpedo boats), coaling facilities and the Extension were intimately bound together, and another plan was produced in February 1891 combining all three. Sheds and slips for torpedo boats and a new coaling jetty separated the new basin from the North Basin. It was accessed by a lock, and three docks were attached to it (Figure 228).

It was decided to call in Sir John Coode (who has figured in an earlier chapter as Chief Engineer at Portland), as a consultant on the scheme. This was to be his last major piece of work, though it is not known how much of the design was due to his office and how much to the Director of Works' Department. He reported in July 1893. By that time torpedo boats had ceased to be matters of moment as far as the Royal Navy was concerned, and the plan did not take their housing into consideration. A tidal basin of 10 acres, in the area proposed by Scamp, was connected by two docks to a closed basin of 35 acres; access to the closed basin, from which a third dock opened off, was normally by an entrance lock. The Controller (Fisher), Hydrographer and Director of Works approved of Coode's plan, with minor alterations, but insisted that the coaling arrangements should be permanently located at the north end of the new Extension. In September 1895 Sir John Jackson gained the contract for the Extension work with a tender of £2,835,455, and the resulting civil engineering work was prodigious and prolonged. The extension was declared open in February 1907 (Figures 229 & 230).

This was to be the final extension to any of the Dockyards. In 1904 the Director of Works, Colonel Raban, prepared a plan for yet another extension at Chatham, excavating St Mary's Island for another basin with additional docks and workshops, but the scheme got no further than on paper.[26]

No new buildings were required at the Devonport or

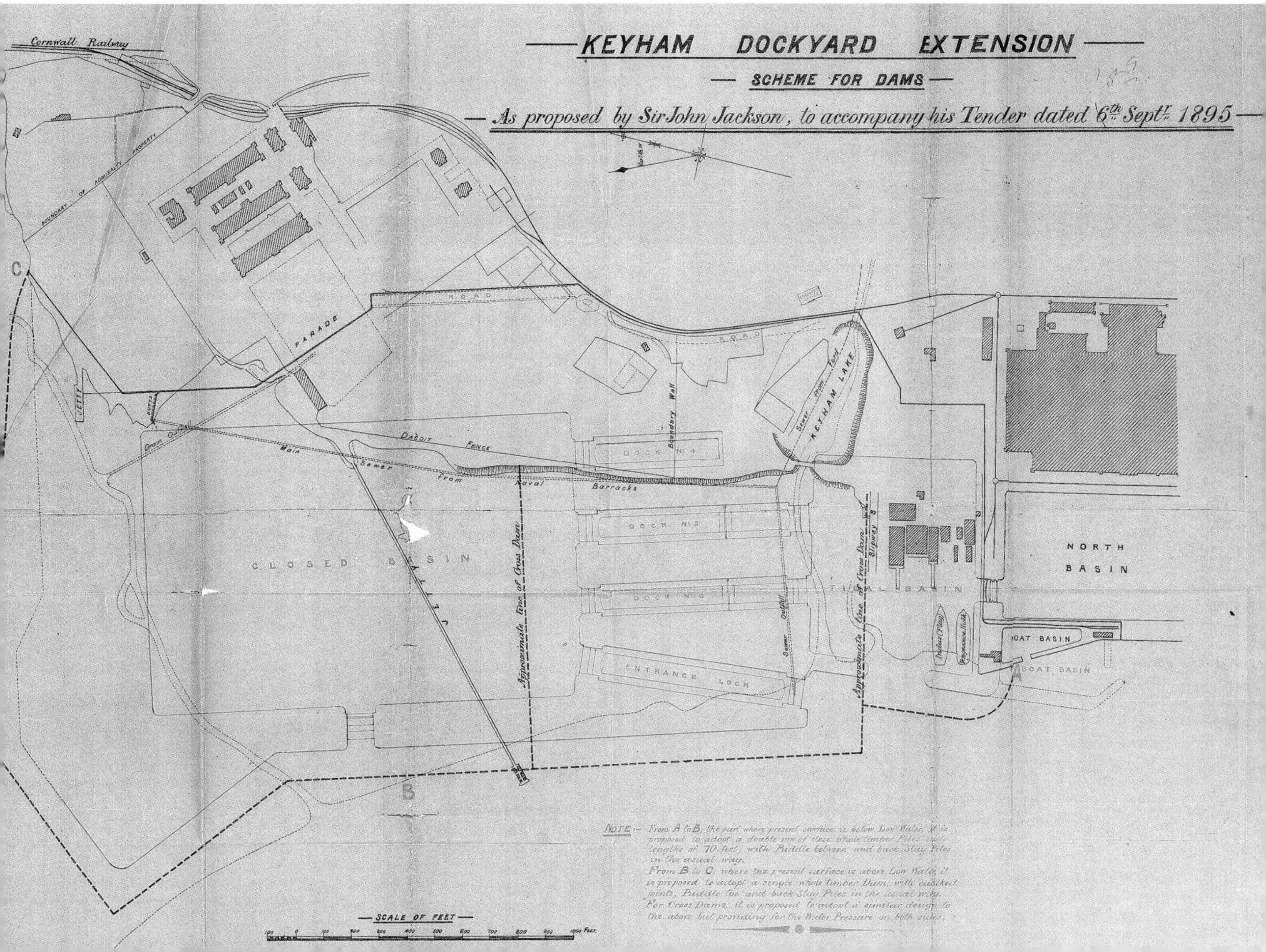

229 The extension as decided on, showing the positions of the cofferdams required for its construction. The naval barracks are shown to top left, and the Quadrangle to the right. *(TNA ADM 116/464)*

KEYHAM DOCKYARD EXTENSION

— SCHEME FOR DAMS —

— *As proposed by Sir John Jackson, to accompany his Tender dated 6th Sept. 1895* —

SCALE OF FEET

230 The job was
highly photogenic.
This photograph,
dated July 1898,
shows the cofferdam
supporting the
railway taking mud
to the barges. A
barge is shown to the
left of the picture.
(TNA ADM 195/464)

Keyham sites. By contrast the 1890s saw a flurry of building activity at Portsmouth, where the building programme of the Naval Defence Act was also causing problems.[27]

Towards the *Dreadnought*

Nearly everything in the Yards had been built too small to cope with future requirements. In 1859 and 1860 the foreparts of slip roofs at Chatham and Portsmouth were raised, and they were lengthened to enable larger ships to be constructed. However, with the nearly universal adoption of metal construction the covered slips became an irrelevance for building purposes, and they were not subjected to further alterations.[28]

Docks, quite otherwise, had to be continuously enlarged and adjusted throughout the century as ships grew inexorably heavier and longer (see pp.167–8); the old Yards were confined sites, and there was little room to spare. A comprehensive account of the extensions of old and construction of new docks in the Yards would be a book of its own, but some account of the building of Docks 14 and 15 at Portsmouth is necessary to finally wrap up the story of the Portsmouth Extension.

These two docks, though in the original plan, had not been built by May 1890, when the Chief Constructor, Henry Deadman, submitted that the work should begin as soon as possible. There were only two docks large enough to take first-class battleships, and one, No. 13, was at present occupied in building *Royal Sovereign*, while the other (the North Lock) was preferably kept open for the passage of the ships to and from the Rigging and Repairing Basins. For slightly smaller ships No. 12

dock, the Deep Dock and the South Lock were available. It would probably be necessary almost immediately to lay down *Centurion* in No. 12, which would tie up that dock for at least 18 months.

In view of the building programme envisaged, the two projected docks, large enough to take any size of battleship contemplated, were urgently needed. In February 1892 Deadman suggested they should be as long as possible without interfering with the railway lines and buildings recently erected, about 500ft. One should be able to be divided for repairing caissons in one part and a ship in the other. They should be at least 90ft wide, this would mean widening the South Lock and its caisson. The Director of Dockyards agreed that they should be wide, pointing out that British docks were narrower than the French.[29]

The breadth of entrance should be 128ft, fully equal to the widest of the Cherbourg docks. The Director of Naval Construction, Sir William White, disagreed, thinking that No. 14 could remain 82ft wide: 'So far as can be seen at present, the tendency will be to increase the length rather than the beam.' The *Inflexible* (1874 design) was as broad as *Royal Sovereign* (1889 design). No. 15 might be 94ft wide. He had recently seen *Victoria* (70ft beam) in such a dock, and 'the impression made upon my mind was that, in the endeavour to provide against possible contingencies, considerable disadvantages have had to be incurred in ordinary working with ships of present dimensions,' as an excessive length of shoring had to be provided, and the volume of water that had to be pumped out was very great.

As White was designing the ships that were to use the docks

231 The big First Class cruiser *Terrible*, pictured early in her career before her funnels were raised. *(Chrysalis Picture Library)*

232 No. 14 Dock, Portsmouth, in June 1896 *(TNA ADM 195/81)*, and hidden craftsmanship in the dock, in 1902. *(TNA ADM 195/81)*

his views carried weight, and Major Pilkington, the Director of Works, considered that the entrances, which had already been constructed, should remain as they were. By April 1893 it was decided that they should be 550ft long, as a consequence of the construction of the new cruisers *Powerful* and *Terrible*, 539ft long (Figure 231), and next summer in a change of heart the width of No. 15 and possibly No. 14 as well was proposed to be increased to 94ft. But in December the alterations were cancelled because of the necessity of having the docks completed before the delivery of *Powerful* and *Terrible*, which had to be docked, examined and have their bottoms coppered before their steam trials, which were of exceptional importance, as they were the first test of a new type of boiler in the Service. Needless to say, they proved too short at 550ft and were later extended. All the Naval docks constructed during the century have magnificent masonry, much of it necessarily concealed (Figure 232).[30]

The proposed Factory building abutting the main power station was never built, but a highly specialised building, a gun-mounting store, was designed in 1885 for that location, and drawings for the shafting arrangements were ready by the next autumn. A new bay was required by 1889, and further additions were designed in 1892. Gun mountings, for both quick-firing and the heavier calibre breech-loading guns, had developed rapidly in the 1880s, and were becoming an ever-increasing proportion of the cost of a warship. Portsmouth was rapidly increasing in importance as a building yard, as No. 5 slip had the potential to be enlarged very considerably. Behind it a Frame Bending Smithery had been built next to the Sawmills, while the roofs of slips 2 and 4 were adapted as shipbuilding workshops. A purpose-built Scrive Board building was designed in 1891; this joined on the north side of the Frame Bending Smithery (Figure 233).

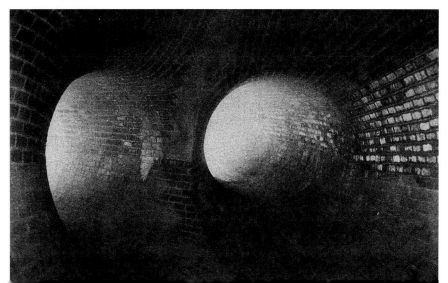

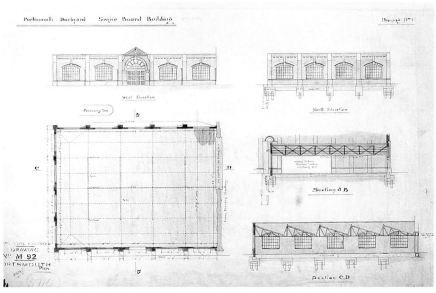

233 This purpose-built Scrive Board Building was to have a very short life, being swept away after a decade. *(English Heritage Plans Room, BB96./10707)*

234 New Boiler Shop, Portsmouth. *(English Heritage Plans Room, BB96./10715)*

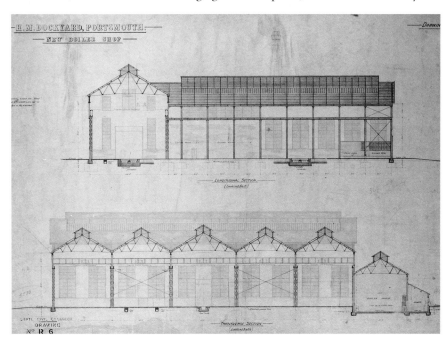

Electrical equipment on board ships was rapidly increasing in quantity and importance, and the Electrical Shop was designed in 1894–95. In 1896 a very large new Boiler Shop was designed, of five parallel aisles 45ft wide (the central one 50ft) each with a travelling crane, with an assembly hall at right angles to these 60ft wide with its traveller running 36ft up. Turntables and railways worked with the cranes to move the plates to and from the furnaces. This great all-metal building was comparable to Greene's Smithery in size, but had a much less impressive chimney; it represented the most powerful architectural statement made in the Yard for many years (Figure 234).

Shipbuilding machinery had now reached massive proportions (Figure 235). The really powerful statements, though, were going to be made on slip No. 5, and to set the scene for this the whole shipbuilding area behind the Factory was drastically rehandled. Everything was swept away behind No. 5; the Sawmills, the Frame Bending Shop, the Boiler Smithery, the Armour Plate Shop, even the brand new Scrive Board. Number 5 lost its roof; 3 and 4 becoming a Shipbuilding Shop and a Laying Out Shop. Dock No. 9 was filled in and became a storage ground for plates, while a new Smithery was

235 The machinery contained within was by now more striking than the buildings. Here, in the works of the Naval Construction and Armaments Company at Barrow-in-Furness, is a wall-planing machine working the stern frame of the cruiser *Niobe*. *(From* The Navy and Army Illustrated, *April 16, 1897)*

designed behind it in 1899, a much more low-key building than the Boiler Shop (Figure 237).

Slip 5 was extended way across the Shipbuilding Road, terminating close to the west wall of James's original Factory building, and here it was that *Dreadnought* was laid down on 2 October 1905, just as the new Factory was being completed to the east of the Extension. Easily the largest building on the site, and red brick externally, it has been left a curiously uninteresting building by war damage and reuse, but when new it presented a fine multi-purpose interior (Figure 238). Travelling cranes by the docksides had grown considerably since the building of *Achilles*, as seen by the one in attendance on *Dreadnought* (Figure 239). In general, at this stage, the heavy industrial plant was more impressive than the buildings.[31]

Dreadnought marked a quantitative leap in warship construction. Her size, all big gun armament, and turbine propulsion (never before employed in a ship of such dimensions) made it spectacularly clear that a new era in naval history had begun. The ship was assembled at Portsmouth and began trials 12 months after being laid down, a remarkable achievement, though stage-managed and never repeated. Of the subsequent variants on her design, before a further leap was made with the introduction of the 13.5 inch gun, three were built at Portsmouth, two at Devonport, and five in commercial yards. Chatham, which had built more pre-*Dreadnought* battleships since 1893 than any other dockyard or civil firm, was prevented by its geography from building ships of such displacement and length, and Sheerness, even more than Chatham, was limited in the size of ship that could be built there. Pembroke Dock suffered from quite different drawbacks: there was plenty of space and a magnificent natural harbour, but its isolation, which had not mattered much in times of relative technological innocence, told against it, and it launched its last battleship in 1897. Of course, these lesser dockyards had plenty of work to do in building and refitting the host of smaller ships that made up the bulk of the Navy.

The belief that the Dockyards were a haunt of obsolete practices and machinery appears to have become established in the mind of engineers in private firms by the 1880s. In the autumn of 1886 the members of the Iron and Steel Institute paid a visit to Chatham Dockyard and were surprised to find instead of the 'antiquated and obsolete' equipment they had expected, 'many modern appliances and methods of working'. The United States Navy Bureau of Construction would not have been caught unawares. The Bureau had, in 1884, despatched one of their naval constructors to tour the principal public and private dockyards of Europe, with a view to reporting on any machinery that ought to be acquired, in order to re-equip the American Naval Yards for the construction of the new Navy, which was to replace the hangovers from the Civil War. He was told 'there will undoubtedly be many things that you will see…which it would be in the best interests of the Bureau to have, or to know where to obtain.' The bulk of his report was devoted to British yards and equipment. He was unimpressed by the mould lofts, but saw many excellent pieces of machinery, particularly a very powerful puncher and shearer made by Craig and Donald of Johnstone, and the hydraulically powered machines in use in the French yards made by the Hydraulic Company of Chester. The hydraulic riveting equipment in almost universal use was excellent, as were the steam cranes. His first visits were naturally made to the Royal Dockyards, and he had no adverse criticisms to make. It is notable, however, that all his praise was reserved for shipbuilding tools. The Iron and Steel Institute had not been so impressed with the Engineering Department at Chatham as they had been

with the Constructor's Department, and the influential trade paper *Engineering* had some pertinent comments to make. As no marine engines were made in the Yards, the Engineering Departments were in fact repairing shops, and the miscellaneous work carried out did not require specialised tools. The power struggles between the shipwrights and the engineers have already been noted, and *Engineering* attributed the superior equipment of the Constructor's Department to its being 'an older and more powerful body than the engineers, and when money is to be spent they can ask with a more powerful voice at head-quarters.' Some of the obsolete practices were due to the Admiralty (like other navies) hanging on to obsolete ships, which were to be used as a last resort in the event of the loss or crippling of their modern successors. As a consequence of this the Institute members noted 'a set of new rectangular boilers for some one of our grand old war vessels. These must have almost made some of the members of the excursion feel that they had renewed their youth.'

236 A turn of the century view of ships of the Mediterranean Fleet, under the command of Admiral Sir John Fisher, at anchor in Aranci Bay, Sardinia. *(Chrysalis Picture Library)*

237 The Smithery of 1899 did not challenge the earlier Smitheries as a building. *(English Heritage Plans Room, BB96./10712)*

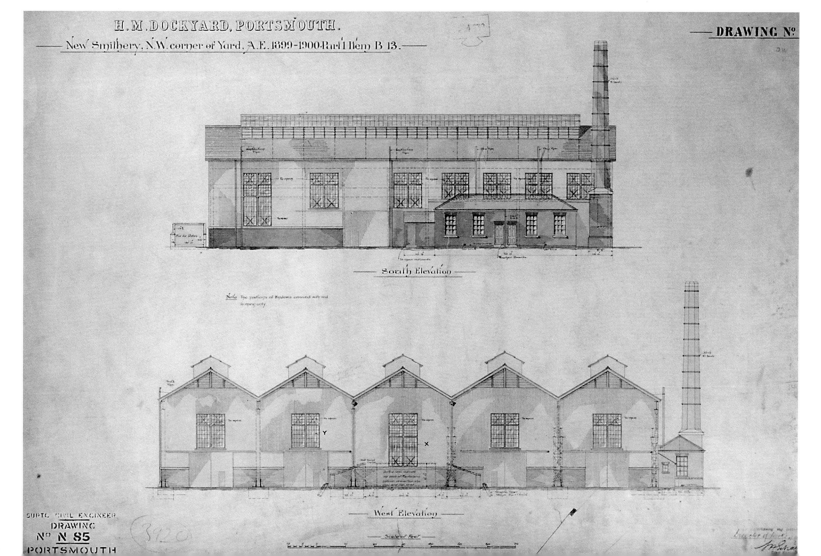

H.M. DOCKYARD, PORTSMOUTH.
New Smithery, N.W. corner of Yard, A.E. 1899-1900 Part 1 Item B 13.

DRAWING Nº

South Elevation

West Elevation

238 The new Factory just finished and awaiting its equipment. *(TNA ADM 195/79)*

by the time *Dreadnought* was launched the infrastructure created to maintain the Steam Navy was still functioning in many ways apart from the physical survival of the buildings. However, the buildings that had been created by the Scamp/Greene partnership contributed nothing to this technical conservatism. The great flexible spaces of Keyham enforced no constraints at all on the equipment that could be arranged and operated within; the constraints were rather those imposed both by the mind-set of many engineers and by the Treasury. The emphasis of this book has been on the industrial buildings created to provide part of the logistical back-up of the Royal Navy before 1870; victualling yards, gun wharves and ordnance yards, together with hospital facilities, provided the rest. All these types of site posed different problems, sometimes requiring answers so specifically tailored to one kind of need as not to be transferable. That did not apply, in the main, to the dockyard buildings where, as has been seen, the greatest navy in the world in its time was supplied with buildings filled with lessons and messages for factory design and constructional innovation that were applicable on a virtually universal scale.

Notes:

1. Hans Busk, *The Navies of the World*, (London, 1859), pp.180–181; for Jesse Hartley and Liverpool see A Jarvis, *The Liverpool Dock Engineers*, (Stroud, 1996).
2. The basin would accommodate 100 ships of the line, and the land opposite the Yard would provide plenty of space for building slips and timber stores and, no part of the original plan, boiler sheds or a Steam Factory. He had been prodded to reactivate his father's plan by proposals in 1847 to allow £7,000 in the estimates for creating an entrance to a new basin at Chatham, part of a large scheme for the improvement of the Yard, which involved the construction of a basin, two dry docks, and 11 building slips. Institution of Civil Engineers Archives, Rennie, Reports, xiv.
3. Of these 132 were unprepared, 29 were prepared in advance, and 40 were prepared for commissioning. Nineteen were roofed entirely, 48 roofed partially, and 134 not roofed. These vessels had cost about £6,200,000 when prepared ready for launching. CHA/H/83.
4. In January 1855 it was decided that the Yard would be developed on the principle of concentration rather than expansion: the works would not extend beyond St Mary's Creek, and would consist of a Basin, two new docks, a mast pond, and a Steam Factory. That summer Scamp visited the place and drew up a scheme that Greene recommended be approved, but still nothing was done. CHA/H/78.
5. These were:
    a basin and docks as proposed by the Yard Officers;
    a basin, docks, a factory which ignored the example of Keyham, slips etc. on the ground exclusive of St Mary's Creek and St Mary's Island;
    two large basins on the line of St Mary's Creek, docks, factory buildings, slips, with St Mary's Island put to various uses; and
    as last, but with Scamp's laying-up slips instead of the ordinary building slips. The old Yard was a nuisance: 'The Metal Mills, and the New Building Slips — and the inconvenient position of the old Slips and Docks — are all obstructions in the way of forming an establishment capable of being worked with the requisite dispatch and economy.' Chatham Historic Dockyard Library, DOC 19.
6. 'I must remark that the great principle which should govern the arrangement of the Naval Establishments, is usually overlooked; as from the manner in which the Establishments have been created, and from time to time extended, the great question of economising labour has been entirely lost sight of. The largest and the most important Establishment [Portsmouth] is the most defective in this respect. The consequence must be an Annual Waste, and what is of much greater importance, the Establishments are not adapted for performing the pressing duties required of them during War with the requisite dispatch.' Chatham Historic Dockyard Library, DOC 19.
7. For boilermaking the punching, shearing, and riveting shops, and facilities for smiths' work and furnaces, were all located together, and for the fitting and erecting shops the space for erecting was placed in the middle of the

Though the major Dockyards were strengthened with the new factory resources during the 1890s, the smaller machine tools that filled them were, if British made, not the cutting-edge technology with which the Steam Factories had been originally equipped. Indeed, some of those machines would still have been in daily use, for they were made to last. The Dockyards were far from unique in this respect. Crewe railway works contained a mix of ancient and modern tools: when a new chief mechanical engineer took over in 1922 he was appalled to find machines he had worked on as an apprentice in the 1880s and which had been far from new then. There was a misguided belief that well-made machinery would last for decades without the need for reinvestment in replacements. This was recognised at the highest level. In 1901 the First Lord, Selborne, was aware that much of the plant in use would have been scrapped by a private firm, and a depreciation account to retool the Yards was the rational solution. But he also noted (correctly):

> It would however be mere waste of time to urge this on the Treasury. Sooner than subscribe to this heresy I think everyone in the [Treasury] building from the Chancellor of the Exchequer down to the charwoman would cheerfully go to the stake.[32]

This, allied to the failure to grasp the need for continual innovation, had led, by the time that Chatham received Scamp's final Steam Factory, to the technological lead in machine tools passing to the United States, with German equipment outperforming English later in the century.[33] As a consequence,

shop, with the fitting shop immediately adjacent. Chatham Historic Dockyard Library, DOC 19.

8 He added:

About 20 Years ago the improvements at Woolwich were commenced without a well considered general Plan, the works were too far advanced when a great mistake was pointed out, suggestions for avoiding other errors by taking too limited a view of the wants of the Service were submitted, and such of them as were submitted to the Board were approved. At Devonport the works in constructing a Basin, etc, were commenced and carried on for some years without a well considered general plan; here the anticipations cannot be considered as having been realised. At Keyham the works were for some Years carried on in the constructing a Basin without a general Plan for Factory Buildings & when the Plan for these Buildings &c was laid down, an alteration to the North Basin was found to be necessary for allowing space for the Factory Buildings… At Portsmouth also the works were commenced & carried on for several years without a General Plan. An extension of the Basin was made before a general Plan was laid down, and, when laid down the reconstruction of Frederick's Battery for an extension was found to be necessary. From the want of a well considered general Plan…Portsmouth must always be a defective Establishment…The improvements at [Chatham] were commenced in 1843 without a general plan, the result is obvious — errors have been

committed and works have been delayed chiefly in consequence of the absence of well considered general plans…the subject though difficult is by no means unmanageable. ADM 1/5703, Chatham Historic Dockyard Library, DOC 19.

9 Between 1857 and 1861 the northern and western sides of St Mary's Island were embanked with stone facings, carried well above the level of the highest spring tides, and £42,000 was spent on these works. The experience of this preparatory work showed that free labour would have to be employed to a much greater extent than originally intended, largely because much work could only be done when tides were favourable. In April 1859 a project to create a new Yard on a virgin site at the Isle of Grain was dropped in favour of the Chatham extension, and the following June Rennie again attempted to revive interest in his father's scheme. ADM 1/5775, ADM 12/668, ADM 12/684.

10 ADM 1/5803, ADM 12/716, ADM 1/5838.

11 In July 1863 Scamp, wishing to settle the layout of the Factory, consulted with Chief Engineers Trickett (now at Woolwich), Blaxland (Sheerness), Miller (Keyham) and Baker (Chatham). The Chatham officers wanted the armour plating and iron shipbuilding workshops distinct and separate from the Factory, which was to contain a smiths' shop, Steam Hammer shop, armour plate bending machinery shop, punching shop, shearing shop, drilling shop and levelling shop, and Baker produced a plan for Greene. Miller supplied him with drawings showing the general arrangement of the

239 *Dreadnought* fitting out at Portsmouth, accompanied by an equally fine travelling crane. *(NMM, neg. no. G10031)*

240 (Opposite)
Dreadnought shortly after completion, early in October 1906. She is carrying water measuring tanks abreast the mainmast, a temporary installation for measuring the loss of feedwater during her steam trials. (*Chrysalis Picture Library*)

boilers, engines, chimney, shafting, and coal stores of the Factory, and by July 1864 the final shape of the Repairing and Factory basins had been determined, the rough outlines of the Factory had been settled, and the first stage of construction planned: this was to be some 1,000ft of the Repairing basin wall. Three docks were now projected for this basin, but the site of one was occupied by the brick kilns. ADM 1/5838, CHA/H/115, CHA/H/118, ADM 1/5888.

12 Obituary of Liet. General Sir Andrew Clarke, *Proceedings of the Institution of Civil Engineers*, 1902, pp.342-345.

13 The range of buildings on the side of the block next the basin were the engine and boiler stores and the offices, the end buildings of the block, as at Keyham, the fitting and erecting shop and the plate-bending and boiler shop respectively. Unlike Keyham, the fitting and erecting shop were to be 478ft long by 128ft wide. The roof consisted of three spans: the portions covered by the side spans were two storeys high, and the central portion one storey high only. The central portion of the shop, equipped with travelling cranes, was the erecting space; the machinery was placed at the sides, and the upper storeys were occupied by lighter machinery. All the staircases for affording communication between the storeys were to be outside the building, so as not to interfere with the clear space within. The boiler shop, also housing the plate-bending and other machines, was to be 479ft by 110ft. The range of buildings furthest from the basin were the coppersmiths' shop, engine-house, iron and brass foundry, and in the centre of the quadrangle were the smitheries and steam hammer shop. The main smithery and steam hammer shop was to be 230ft by 190ft, covered by a roof of three spans, with the springing of the side spans 29ft and that of the central span 41ft above the floor level. This would be provided with travelling cranes, and lit by clerestory windows arranged above the level of the side roofs. Plenty of circulation space would be provided: the roadways on the inner sides of the end buildings would be 60ft wide, with other passages being 25ft. CHA/C/5, ADM 1/5939, Obituary of Major-General Charles Pasley, *Proceedings of the Institution of Civil Engineers*, 1891, pp.389-391; ADM 12/780, ADM 12/812, *Engineering*, 1867, p. 165.

14 They were sent by barge, and by 18 September 1871 one of the roofs had been unloaded there. Butchard claimed £310 for this tricky job, which was so well performed that the breakages were estimated at about £2 15s only. A month later the same firm had moved the armour plate bending shed of 1862-63 (enlarged as late as 1867), not a wholly metal building, of iron standards and a boarded enclosure, a timber-framed roof with board and zinc covering, and three travellers on wrought iron girders, for £390. This had originally been intended to be sold off, and in November there took place a final pre-sale clearance of all machinery not required by the War Department that could be put to use at Chatham. In that month preparations began there of the foundations for re-erecting Woolwich No. 5 slip, using convict labour. ADM 1/6400, ADM 1/6423, ADM 1/6195, CHA/H/139, CHA/H/142, CHA/H/146.

15 ADM 12/652, ADM 92/20, ADM 1/5939.

16 Curiously, Clarke saw himself placed in a similar position to that in which Scamp and Greene had been at Keyham:

'These considerations have led me to devise a plan which will allow of alterations and modifications being made to almost any extent, and at any time, in the arrangements of the factory, without necessitating alterations in the structure of the building. The difficulty however in the adoption of this plan in its entirety is the existence of the foundations above referred to which I am unwilling on grounds of economy wholly to abandon'.

His plan, the details of which are not known, consequently retained some of the buildings, and was submitted to a Committee of Yard Officers with Colonel Pasley, the Superintending Engineer since July 1864, as chairman, who were much in its favour. Acting upon this report, some of the foundations were demolished, and it was decided to proceed. The shops were moved 100ft further back from the factory basin, and a reversion was made to a plan resembling that of Keyham Quadrangle. The shops were all enclosed in one building, about 1000ft in length and 450ft wide. A storehouse occupied each end; the rest of the enclosed area was divided across its breadth by rows of double columns, placed about 60ft apart, dividing the building into 14 bays, each 60ft wide, and covered by a light pitched roof. As at Keyham, partitions would be introduced to form as many compartments as required, and in some of the spaces an intermediate row of double columns would carry girders on which 30ft travelling cranes would run. In the other spaces, travellers, the full span of the roof, would be employed, having a clear run from end to end. ADM 1/6117, *Parliamentary Paper, Navy (Dockyards)*. April 1874; ADM 12/748, James Fletcher, 'On improvements for heavy tools for general engineering and iron shipbuilding work', *Proceedings of the Institution of Mechanical Engineers*, 1864, pp.189-228, 12 plates; *Engineering*, 1871, pp. 372-373.

17 ADM 12/780, ADM 12/795, NMR PTM/447, NMR PTM/1176.

18 1) light stores for which horse-drawn carts and the existing roads were perfectly suitable;
2) intermediate loads, such as castings and forgings not exceeding 14 or 15 tons in weight, these were the most destructive, because most constant, kind of traffic;
3) exceptionally bulky or heavy loads, such as marine boilers and sternposts of large ships, which had to be moved so infrequently as to be unlikely to strain the roads.

19 For the Crewe tramway, see B Reed, *Crewe Locomotive Works and its Men*, (Newton Abbot, 1982), chapter 11; ADM 1/5697, ADM 12/636, ADM 87/76, *Engineering*, 1875, pp. 1-3, 53-54.

20 By January 1859 the following Taylor's steam hoists were in use:

Deptford	1
Woolwich	2
Chatham	1
Sheerness	nil
Portsmouth	2 + two sets of cylinder winch engines
Devonport	1
Keyham	1

ADM 12/540, CHA/H/87, CHA/H/90, ADM 12/604, ADM 85/33, ADM 85/44, ADM 12/556, ADM 12/572, ADM 85/52, ADM 84/20. DDM, POR/R/34, ADM 87/77, KH, POR/P/63, POR/P/65, UP 336543, UP 336541, J T Corner, 'Description of the lifting and hauling appliances in Portsmouth Dockyard', *Proceedings of the Institution of Mechanical Engineers*, 1892, pp.295-312.

21 *Engineering*, 1867, p.165; E A Bernays, *Lectures on Chatham Dockyard Extension Works*, (Chatham, 1879); R G Hobbes, *Reminiscences of Seventy Years' Life, Travel and Adventure*, (London, 1895).

22 KH; Colonel Sir Andrew Clarke, 'Portsmouth Dockyard Extension Works', *Proceedings of the Institution of Civil Engineers*, 1881, pp.226-227; J T Corner, loc. cit.; NMR PTM/447, NMR PTM/1174, UP 336472.

23 T Ropp, *The Development of a Modern Navy. French Naval Policy, 1871-1904*, (Annapolis, 1987), *passim*; A J Marder, *British Naval Policy, 1880-1905*, (London, n.d.[1941]), pp.291-2, and chapter xxiv.

24 In March he produced a revised plan incorporating two boat cambers and showing that a further extension northwards was possible, but the form of that could only be determined after a careful site inspection. This land was available, and he urged that the chance of procuring it should not be lost. The opportunity was taken, and in March 1860 Sir John St Aubyn's solicitors made a formal proposal for sale of the land, all conditions being completed by April 1864.

25 The matter was, of course, one of money. The Controller and Financial Secretary thought the cost of £1,500,000 prohibitive. However, other reasons were contributing to the development of the land owned by the St Aubyn estate. A slipway for torpedo boats had been built to the north of the basin, together with a very large coal store. In the late 1880s a sketch was prepared showing a coaling jetty built out from the northern extremity of the Basin to allow colliers to be discharged into railway wagons serving the store and lighters to be loaded up to take the coal out to the ships, and in October 1888 a more elaborate scheme was hatched with a coaling jetty projecting out over the mud flats in front of the Seamen's Barracks. In this the jetty had been moved much further north so as not to interfere with the extension, shown 'as originally proposed'. That is not; no less than six docks now open off the basin, access to which is gained by a lock. Possibly this drawing preserves Scamp's last thoughts on the subject.

26 ADM 214./4.

27 ADM 1/5560, ADM 116/463, ADM 116/464.

28 POR/R/9, POR/P/15, POR/P/16, POR/P/18, ADM 140/626-7, ADM 140/625/1-3, ADM 140/631, ADM 87/15, POR/P/23, POR/P/22, F W Cumberland, 'Iron Roofs erected over Building Slips, Nos. 3 and 4, in Her Majesty's Dockyard, Portsmouth', in *Papers on Subjects Connected with the Duties of the Corps of Royal Engineers*, IX, 1847, pp.59-65, NMR PTM 1056.

29

Cherbourg	453 x 128	
	461 x 108	
Brest	375 x 111½	
	325 x 111½	
Toulon (2)	375 x 116½	ADM 116/804.

30 ADM 116/804, ADM 116/846.

31 NMR PTM/1360, 1361, 1362, 1366, 1367, 1376, NMR PTM 1381, 1388, NMR PTM/1522, NMR PTM/1169, 1170, 1171, NMR PTM/1221, ADM 195/79, UP 332243, UP 332264, UP 333265, UP 332349.

32 *Engineering*, October 22 1886, November 5 1886; P Hichborn, *Report on European Dock-Yards*, (Washington, D.C., 1886); B Reed, *Crewe Locomotive Works and its Men*, (Newton Abbot, 1982), p.150; ADM 1/7633.

33 See L T C Rolt, *Tools for the Job*, rev. edn, (London, 1986).

Select Bibliography

Secondary sources

Unpublished papers

Weiler J, 'Army Architects, the Royal Engineers and the development of building technology in the nineteenth century', unpublished PhD thesis, 1987, University of York

Books and pamphlets

[Anonymous], *The Ports, Arsenals and Dockyards of France. By A Traveller,* (London, 1841)

[Anonymous], *The Record of the International Exhibition of 1862,* (Glasgow, n.d.)

Atkinson N, *Sir Joseph Whitworth,* (Stroud, 1996)

Barry P, *Dockyard Economy and Naval Power,* (London, 1863)

Barry P, *The Dockyards, Shipyards, and Marine of France,* (London, 1864)

Bartlett C J, *Great Britain and Sea Power 1815-1853,* (London, 1963)

Baxter J P, *The Introduction of the Ironclad Warship,* (Cambridge, Massachusetts, 1933)

Bernays E A, *Lectures on Chatham Dockyard Extension Works,* (Chatham, 1879)

Bradley I, *A History of Machine Tools,* (Hemel Hempstead, 1972)

Brassey's Naval Annual, 1888-9 (Portsmouth, 1889)

Briggs Sir J, *Naval Administrations 1827-1892,* (London, 1897)

Brock P W and Greenhill B, *Steam and Sail in Britain and North America,* (Newton Abbot, 1973)

Brown D K, *Before the Ironclad, 1815-1860,* (London, 1990)

Brown D K, contributions in (ed. Lambert A) *Steam, Steel, and Shellfire,* (London, 1992)

Brown D K, *Warrior to Dreadnought,* (London, 1997)

Burkhalter P, *Devonport Dockyard Railway,* (Truro, 1996)

Busk H, *The Navies of the World,* (London, 1859)

Cantrell J A, *James Nasmyth and the Bridgwater Foundry,* (Manchester, 1984)

Cattell J & Falconer K, *Swindon: the Legacy of a Railway Town,* (London, 1995)

Clowes W L, *The Royal Navy,* vol.5, (London, 1900) and vol.7 (London, 1902)

Coad J G, *Historic Architecture of the Royal Navy, an Introduction,* (London, 1983)

Coad J G, *The Royal Dockyards, 1690-1850,* (Aldershot, 1989)

Corlett E, *The Iron Ship,* rev.ed. (London, 1990)

Dickens C, *The Uncommercial Traveller,* (London, 1861)

Dickinson H W and Jenkins R, *James Watt and the Steam Engine,* 2nd edn, (Southampton, 1981)

Endicott W C, *Report of the Board on Fortifications or other Defenses,* (Washington, D.C., 1886)

Fairbairn W, *On the Application of Cast and Wrought Iron to Building Purposes,* (London, 1856)

Fairbairn W, *Treatise on Mills and Millwork,* 2 vols., (London, 1863)

Fairbairn W, (ed. Pole W) *The Life of Sir William Fairbairn, Bart,* (reprint Newton Abbot, 1970)

French J W, *Machine Tools commonly employed in Modern Engineering Workshops,* 2 vols., (London 1911)

Gilbert K R, *The Portsmouth Blockmaking Machinery,* (London, 1965)

Giles C and Goodall I, *Yorkshire Textile Mills 1770-1930,* RCHME, (London, 1992)

Greenhill B and Giffard A, *Steam, Politics, and Patronage: The transformation of the Royal Navy 1815-54,* (London, 1994)

Hamilton C I, *Anglo-French Naval Rivalry 1840-1870,* (Oxford, 1993)

Hamilton, Sir R Vesey, (ed.) *Journals and Letters of Sir Thomas Byam Martin,* vol. 3, (London, 1902)

(ed. Hattendorf, Knight, Pearsall, Rodger, and Till), *British Naval Documents 1204-1960,* (London, 1993)

Hichborn P, *Report on European Dockyards,* (Washington, D.C., 1886)

Hobbes R G, *Reminiscences and Notes of Seventy Years,* vol. 2, (London, 1895)

Hurst L, 'The age of fireproof flooring', in Skempton A W (ed) *The Iron Revolution, 1780-1880,* (London, 1990)

Jarvis A, *The Liverpool Dock Engineers,* (Stroud, 1996)

King J W, *European Ships of War. Report to the Senate,* (Washington D.C., 1877)

Kirkcaldy D, *Results of an experimental inquiry into the tensile strength and other properties of various kinds of wrought-iron and steel,* (Glasgow, 1862)

Laing E A M, *Steam Wooden Warship Building in Portsmouth Dockyard 1832-52,* (Portsmouth, 1985)

Lake J, *Historic Farm Buildings,* (London, 1989)

Lambert A, *Battleships in Transition: the Creation of the Steam Battle Fleet 1815-1850,* (London, 1984)

Lambert A, 'The Royal Navy and the introduction of the screw propeller, 1837-1847', in (ed. Fisher S) *Innovation in Shipping and Trade,* (Exeter, 1989)

Lambert A, *The Last Sailing Battle Fleet: Maintaining Naval Mastery 1815-1850,* (London 1991)

Lambert A, contributions in (ed. Lambert A) *Steam, Steel, and Shellfire,* (London, 1992)

Marder A J, *British Naval Policy, 1880-1905,* (London, n.d. but 1940)

McDermaid N J, *Shipyard Practice as applied to Warship Construction,* (London, 1911)

McNeil I, *Joseph Bramah,* (Newton Abbot, 1968)

Moorsom W & Jackson G B W, *Drawings, Specification, Quantities &c of the Bromsgrove Engine Factory - Erected for the Birmingham and Gloster Railway Company,* (London, 1840)

Morriss R, *The Royal Dockyards during the Revolutionary and Napoleonic Wars,* (Leicester, 1983)

Morriss R, *Cockburn and the British Navy in Transition,* (Exeter, 1997)

Nasmyth J, (ed. Smiles S) *An Autobiography,* (London, 1883)

Paris, Contre-Amiral, *L'Art Naval A L'Exposition Universelle De Londres De 1862,* (Paris, n.d.)

Peebles H S, *Warshipbuilding on the Clyde,* (Edinburgh, 1987)

(Rankin S, ed.), *Shipbuilding on the Thames and Thames-Built Ships,* (London, 2001)

Rawlinson R, *Factory Furnace and other Tall Chimney Shafts,* (London, 1858)

(ed. Raymond H M), *Modern Shop Practice,* vol.IV, (Chicago,1917)

Reed B, *Crewe Locomotive Works and its Men,* (Newton Abbot, 1982)

Reed E J, *Shipbuilding in Iron and Steel,* London, 1869

Rennie G (ed.), *Illustrations of Mill Work. Atlas to the New Edition of Buchanan's Work,* (London, 1841)

Riley R C, *The Evolution of the Docks and Industrial Buildings in Portsmouth Royal Dockyard 1698-1914,* (Portsmouth, 1985)

Rodger N A M, *The Admiralty,* (Lavenham, 1979)

Rolt L T C, *Tools for the Job,* rev.ed. (London, 1986)

Ropp T, *The Development of a Modern Navy. French Naval Policy, 1871-1904,* (Annapolis, 1987)

Rowlandson T S, *Lecture on the History of the Steam Hammer,* (Eccles, 1864)

Scott Russell J, *The Modern System of Naval Architecture,* 3 vols., (London, 1864-5)

Smiles S, *Industrial Biography,* (London, 1863)

Steeds W, *A History of Machine Tools 1700-1910,* (Oxford, 1969)

Taylor G L, *The Autobiography of an Octogenarian Architect,* (2 vols), (London, 1870-2)

Tinmouth N, *An Inquiry relative to various important points of Seamanship, considered as a branch of practical science,* (London, 1845)

Tomlinson C, *Cyclopaedia of Useful Arts & Manufactures,* (London, 1854)

Tredgold T, *The Steam Engine* (3rd ed.) vol.1, (London, n.d. but 1850)

Tucker G, 'Warehousing' in Carr R J M (ed.) *Docklands,* 2nd.ed. (London, 1987)

Wade Martins S, *The English Model Farm,* (Oxford, 2002)

Weiler J, 'The making of collaborative genius - Royal Engineers and structural iron 1820-1870', in Skempton A W, (ed) *The Iron Revolution, 1780-1880,* (London, 1990)

Parliamentary Papers

Reports of Experiments tried as to the effects of Shot on Iron, (1850)

Minutes of Evidence before Committee of Inquiry on the Economy of Her Majesty's Dockyards, (1858)

Quarterly Accounts for Harbours of Refuge, (1861 and subsequent years)

Labour Charts for Dockyards and Steam Factories 1862-3 and for Nine Months to 31st December 1863, (1864)

Navy (Dockyards), (1874)

Articles

[Anonymous] 'Description of the Large Chimney... in Woolwich Dockyard' in *Papers on Subjects connected with the Duties of the Corps of Royal Engineers,* IX, 1847

[Anonymous] Review of 'Enquête Parliamentaire sur la Situation et l'Organisation des Services de la Marine Maritime ordonné par la Loi du 31 Octobre, 1849', in *Edinburgh Review,* 1853

[Anonymous] 'Four Days at Portsmouth on the Eve of War', in *Rahper's Magazine,* 1854 [issue not known]

Armstrong W G, 'Water pressure machinery', in *Proceedings of the Institution of Mechanical Engineers,* 1874

Armstrong W G, 'The History of the Modern Development of Water-Pressure Machinery', in *Proceedings of the Institution of Civil Engineers,* 1877

[Atherton C], 'Memoir' in *Proceedings of the Institution of Civil Engineers,* 1875

Barlow A, 'The Blockmills at Portsmouth Dockyard in the Eighteenth to Twentieth Century', in *Mariner's Mirror,* vol. 88, 2002

Barrett J, 'On the construction of fire-proof buildings', in *Proceedings of the Institution of Civil Engineers,* vol. XII, 1853

[Brandreth, Captain H R] 'Memoir' in *Proceedings of the Institution of Civil Engineers,* 1849

Buchanan R A and Doughty M W, 'The choice of steam engine manufacturers by the British Admiralty, 1822-1852', in *Mariner's Mirror,* vol. 64, 1978

Cantrell J A, 'James Nasmyth and the Steam Hammer', in *Transactions of the Newcomen Society,* vol. 56, 1986

Clarke, Colonel Sir A, 'Portsmouth Dockyard Extension Works', *Proceedings of the Institution of Civil Engineers,* 1881

[Clarke, Lieut-General Sir A], 'Obituary' in *Proceedings of the Institution of Civil Engineers,* 1902

Coad J G, 'Historic architecture of HM Naval Base, Portsmouth, 1700-1850', in *Mariner's Mirror,* vol. 67, 1981

Coad J G, 'Historic architecture of Chatham Dockyard, 1700-1850', in *Mariner's Mirror,* vol. 68, 1982

Coad J G, 'Historic architecture of HM Naval Base, Devonport, 1689-1850', in *Mariner's Mirror,* vol. 69, 1983

Cooper C C, 'The production line at Portsmouth Block Mill', in *Industrial History Review,* 1982

Cooper C C, 'The Portsmouth system of manufacture', in *Technology and Culture,* vol.25, 1984

Corner J T, 'Description of the lifting and hauling appliances in Portsmouth Dockyard', *Proceedings of the Institution of Mechanical Engineers,* 1892

Cowper E, 'Description of the wrought-iron roof over the Central Railway Station at Birmingham', in *Proceedings of the Institution of Mechanical Engineers,* 1854

Cumberland F W, 'Iron Roofs erected over Building Slips, Nos.3 and 4, in Her Majesty's Dockyard, Portsmouth' in

Papers on Subjects connected with the Duties of the Corps of Royal Engineers, vol. IX, 1847

[Dinnen J], 'Memoir' in *Proceedings of the Institution of Civil Engineers*, 1867

Downie J, 'Description of an Iron Construction of Foundry, and an improved process of moulding pipes and hollow cast ware', in *Proceedings of the Institution of Mechanical Engineers*, 1856

[Ewart P], 'Memoir' in *Proceedings of the Institution of Civil Engineers*, 1843

Fairbairn W, 'Description of a floating steam corn mill and bakery' in *Proceedings of the Institution of Mechanical Engineers*, 1858

Fitzgerald R, 'The Development of the Cast Iron Frame for Textile Mills to 1850', in *Industrial Archaeology Review*, X, 2, 1988

Fitzgerald R, 'The anatomy of a Victorian crane: the Coburg Boiler Shop and its technological context', in *Industrial Archaeology Review*, XII, 2, 1990

Fletcher J, 'On improvements in heavy tools for general engineering and iron shipbuilding work', in *Proceedings of the Institution of Mechanical Engineers*, 1864

Humphrys E, 'On surface condensation in marine engines', in *Proceedings of the Institution of Mechanical Engineers*, 1862

[Humphrys E] 'Memoir' in *Proceedings of the Institution of Civil Engineers*, 1868

[Irvine, Colonel] 'Memoir' in *Proceedings of the Institution of Civil Engineers*, 1851

James, Captain H, 'Description of the Steam Basin, Docks, and Factory, and other works recently executed in Portsmouth Dockyard', in *Professional Papers of the Corps of Royal Engineers*, n.s. vol. III, 1853

Johnson and Skempton, 'William Strutt's Cotton Mills', in *Transactions of the Newcomen Society*, XXX, 1955-56

Kingston J, 'Blow-off pipe for marine steam boilers', in *Transactions of the Society of Arts*, vol. 51, 1837

Knight R J B, 'The Introduction of Copper Sheathing into the Royal Navy, 1779-1786', in *Mariner's Mirror*, vol.59, 1973

[Lloyd T], 'Memoir' in *Proceedings of the Institution of Civil Engineers*, 1875

Morriss R, 'Sir George Cockburn and the Management of the Royal Navy, 1841-6', in (ed. Duffy M), *Parameters of British Naval Power 1650-1850*, (Exeter, 1992)

[Murray A], 'Memoir' in *Proceedings of the Institution of Civil Engineers*, 1873

Pasley, Colonel C W, 'Captain Sandham's Mode of Curing or Improving Smoky Chimneys; with Remarks also on Count Rumford's System, &c.' in *Papers on Subjects connected with the Duties of the Corps of Royal Engineers*, II, 1838

[Pasley, Major-General C], 'Obituary' in *Proceedings of the Institution of Civil Engineers*, 1891

Penn J, 'On wood bearings for screw propeller shafts', in *Proceedings of the Institution of Mechanical Engineers*, 1856

Robinson T, 'On woodworking machinery', in *Proceedings of the Institution of Mechanical Engineers*, 1875

[Scamp W] 'Memoir' in *Proceedings of the Institution of Civil Engineers*, 1873

Skempton A W, 'A history of the Steam Dredger, 1797-1830', in *Transactions of the Newcomen Society*, vol. 47, 1977

Sutherland R J M, 'Shipbuilding and the long span roof', in *Transactions of the Newcomen Society*, vol. 60, 1988-9

Sutherland R J M, 'The right to survive', in *New Builder*, May 17 1990

[Trickett J] 'Memoir' in *Proceedings of the Institution of Civil Engineers*, 1889

Waters M, 'Changes in the Chatham Dockyard Workforce, 1860-90, part 1', in *Mariner's Mirror*, vol. 69, 1983

Williams, Captain M, R.E., 'Description of Wrought Iron Roofs erected over two Building Slips in the Royal Dockyard at Pembroke...' in *Papers on Subjects connected with the Duties of the Corps of Royal Engineers*, vol. IX, 1847

Wood J L, 'The development of the Steam Hammer in Scotland', in *Transactions of the Newcomen Society*, vol. 56, 1986

Index

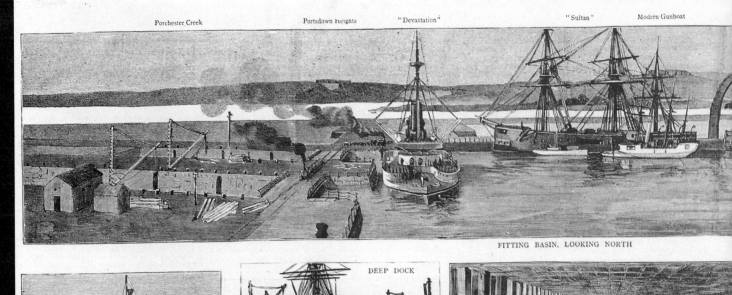

Porchester Creek   Portsdown Heights   "Devastation"   "Sultan"   Modern Gunboat

FITTING BASIN, LOOKING NORTH

THE SEMAPHORE AND ARCHWAY LEADING TO
TROOPERS' JETTY

DEEP DOCK

STEM OF THE "COLLINGWOOD" DOCKED

THE ROPE WALK

MAST HOUSE, TORPEDO BOATS, AND PRINCE OF WALES'S FISHING BOAT

NASMYTH'S HAMMER

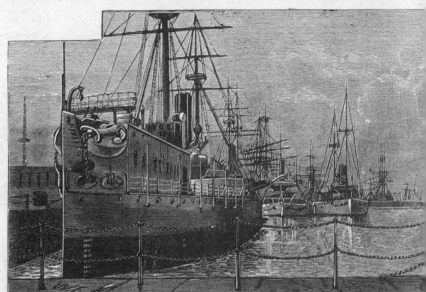

"Colossus"   "Cyclops"   "Rupert"   FITTING BASIN

MOULD LOFT

DOCK GATES, LOOKING OUT